From the Grave:
A Roadside Guide
to Colorado's Pioneer Cemeteries

From the Grave:
A Roadside Guide
to Colorado's Pioneer Cemeteries

Linda Wommack

CAXTON PRESS
Caldwell, Idaho
1998

Library of Congress Cataloging-in-Publication Data

Wommack, Linda, 1958 --
From the Grave : A Roadside Guide to Colorado's Pioneer
Cemeteries / by Linda Wommack ; with a foreword by Dennis
Gallagher.
    p. cm.
Includes bibliographical references (p.   ) and index.
ISBN 0-87004-390-0 (cloth)
ISBN 0-87004-386-2 (paper : alk. paper)
    1. Colorado--Genealogy. 2. Colorado--Guidebooks. 3. Cemeteries-
-Colorado--Guidebooks. 4. Pioneers--Colorado--Biography.
5. Pioneers--Colorado--Genealogy.   6. Inscriptions--Colorado--
Guidebooks. 7. Registers of births, etc.--Colorado.
    I. Title.
F775.W66   1998
929' .5' 09788--DC21   98–36374
                                                                  CIP

Lithographed and bound in the United States of America by
CAXTON PRESS
Caldwell, Idaho
164139

Dedicated to the pioneers responsible
for the growth of Colorado.

In memory of my brother,

Stephen Daniel Wommack
1959–1983

A special pioneer in my lifetime.

Table of Contents

Maps

Illustrations

Foreward

Linda Wommack has put together the first guide to our state's oldest, and often hard-to-find graveyards. The result is a comprehensive guide to Colorado's pioneering cemeteries.

She has selected a good cross section of Colorado pioneers who rest in graves scattered throughout our state's boneyards. This unique guide will serve to entice students of Colorado history into wanting to know more about our state's oldest cemeteries.

Her cheerful style helps us realize that death is a part of life to be accepted, cherished, relished—before "nos habebit humus," "the earth will have us."

Some of my earliest family memories recall visits to Mount Olivet Cemetery to bring flowers and prayers to the graves of relatives and friends. I always enjoyed these visits to Mount Olivet—not a "dies irae"– "a day of wrath," but a place where youngsters chase the cranky swans in the big pool . . . a special holy ground, a place to sing "requiescat in pace," "rest in peace," for aunts, uncles, and grandparents.

I know I will carry her cemetery companion with me as I travel across Colorado, searching out those old resting places of pioneers who, like ourselves, have lived and loved, won and lost along the journey of this special mystery called "life."

I especially like her code of conduct which encourages us to be respectful while visiting these pioneer final resting places. I remember my Grandmother Flaherty warning me, "Never walk across a grave, go around it."

The ghost stories from each area located near these cemeteries remind us that many believe in the "communion of saints," while others were even encouraged to vote for the saints, in the past.

So, dear readers, cast a cold eye on life, on death. Enjoy Ms. Wommack's book . . . while you can.

Former Colorado State Senator Dennis Gallagher

Acknowledgements

As one can imagine, research for such a book is similar to piecing together a jigsaw puzzle. A piece, once found, often leads to another piece. The information before you is the best I could piece together.

The research required for this book was often overwhelming. Without the help of several people and institutions, this book would have been impossible. I would like to thank all the people involved with this work. From the many libraries, genealogy associations, historical societies, to the cemetery archivists, caretakers and local historians. It is hoped this work reflects their input.

I am indebted to many people who gave freely of their time in an effort to make this the best possible work of its kind. A very grateful "thank you" to my husband, Frank who traveled across the state, taking me to many cemeteries, caught my errors, helped map out the entire project, and offered many suggestions, as well as living with this project as I did. To my mother Joyce Wommack, who provided her vast genealogy knowledge, grammatical expertise, endless hours of research and computer help, and kept me from wandering too far from my goal. There would be no book without the help of these two precious souls.

To all of my family who stood beside me and to my friends who understood, and offered their help, I thank you. To friend and fellow historian June Shaputis, who taught me so much, not the least of which was a sense of humor, to Maggie Stephens of Fort Morgan, who offered historical research, grammar advice and great conversation, and to Sue Oswald who gladly traveled with me from cemetery to cemetery, eager to search and learn as I was.

A personal thank you to Senator Dennis Gallagher, who very generously gave his time, thoughts, ideas, and most importantly, his keen knowledge, and to Tom Noel, Professor of History at Denver University, for his support and advice.

The purpose of this book is to pinpoint the location of the burial sites of Colorado pioneers. For the most part, exact locations of grave sites are given. When not available, approximates are given. Cemetery records confirm burials where no marker exists. This is noted in the entry.

The entries are not meant to be complete biographies, yet every effort was made to list correct information with respect to dates of birth and death. Where historical research differs from the epitaph, a note is indicated.

Introduction

A walk through a cemetery is a walk in history. Here will be found those who laid the foundations of the towns and communities we know today.

Colorado's development began with the pioneers. History books tell stories of their struggles and accomplishments. Today their monuments and gravestones mark the silent cemeteries across the state. It was the end of their journey, and they were forgotten. Historians asked no questions about the end of their lives. This book attempts to pay tribute to their memories, to tell their story–from the grave.

A life-long fascination with Colorado history and the people has led me down several historical paths. While it is always interesting to follow the lives of our early pioneers, we are generally left with a visual remembrance, such as a house, a building in town, or a landmark. We read of their contributions to this great state, and marvel at what they did in their day. One question always remained with me. What eventually happened to these people? How did they live out their lives? And what about their final resting places? The final monuments to their lives, come full circle.

I have visited cemeteries across Colorado since I was a child, with my parents. Whether searching for history or genealogy, it was always fascinating to piece together family plots, connecting names and visualizing the pioneer life. My interest has led to the research included in this volume.

This book is neither morbid nor irreverent. The cemeteries I visited across the state are very peaceful. They are places of love and remembrance. They are places of time and a testament to those who have gone before.

Death is a fact of life. Cemeteries are places of finality, yet a historical and emotional semblance of who we are and where we have been. The tombstones in these cemeteries are monuments to those responsible for the growth of our state. Famous or ordinary, each played a role in our present and the future. Other burial sites such as battle memorials are tributes to the struggle of land and people.

The book is organized in five chapters, including a cemetery overview highlighting origin, history and genealogy information. The narrative takes on an east/west directive, as this was the course of the pioneers. The chapters are divided by the state's two major highways:

I–70 and I–25, including metro Denver. The east/west highways are listed first in each chapter, followed by north/south highways.

Each chapter concludes with a complete cemetery listing by county. A general map of each region is provided for quick reference. Depending on your interest and travels, a detailed road map is recommended for your trips. I have done my best to direct you when the route deviates from the interstates and highways. Those cemeteries are generally listed in the "Off The Beaten Path" portion, indicating a side road off the highway. There are many side roads and dirt roads!

History of the individual cemeteries is given, when available. Several cemetery records of origin are simply not available, or cannot be documented. The names listed in each cemetery are in alphabetical order. For simplicity and pioneer time line perspective, only years of birth and date are listed, when available. Many of the tombstones give the month and date. Block and plot numbers are given if the information is available and recorded by the cemetery. When exact locations are unknown, it is noted. But I attempt to give a general location. Many of the cemeteries have a map of the grounds, and it is recommended you visit their offices.

In my research I stumbled across this quotation from the diary of an early pioneer, name unknown:

> *My story is not much, but my life as I cross these*
> *miles is mine. I hope it will be read for who we are*
> *and what we have done.*

I can do no better than bring that story to you the reader, as that writer wished.

Linda Wommack
Memorial Day
May 26, 1997

Of the many epitaphs and obituaries in my research, the following seems to be most appropriate:[1]

The Measure of A Man

Not – "How did he Die?"
But – "How did he live?"
Not – "What did he gain?"
But – "What did he give?"
These are the units
To measure the worth
Of a man, as a man,
regardless of birth.
Not – "What was his station?"
But – "Had he a heart?"
And – "How did he play
His God given part?"
Was he ever ready
With word of good cheer,
To bring back a smile,
To banish a tear?'
Not – "What was his church?"
Nor – "What was his creed?"
But – "Had he befriended
Those really in need?"
Not – "What did the sketch
In the newspaper say?"
But – "How many were sorry
When he passed away!"

---

[1] Used with permission from the Deer Trail Pioneer Historical Society.

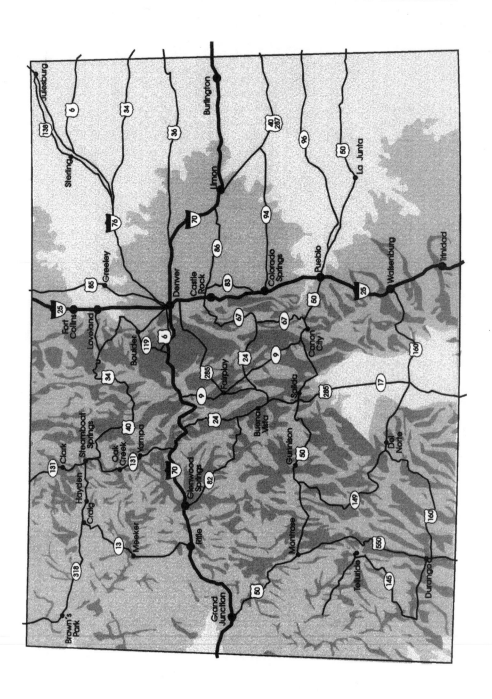

Chapter One

Colorado Cemetery History

In the shadow of the hillsides, in the hot prairie sun, in the cities
and atop the mountains, Colorado's cemeteries provide a testament to the history of this great state. From border-to-border,
cemeteries reveal the lives and deaths of our Colorado pioneers. Their
silent stones hold clues about early Colorado life, tragedy, disaster,
hope and endurance. They also serve as a treasure hold of past community and social structure. Cemeteries seem to be the last resource
for the historian, the curious and the genealogist. For this is indeed
where our history lies.

The traditional cemetery is in doubt as more and more restrictions
are imposed. Green lawns, flowers, and shrubs are being eliminated
to conserve water, destroying the park atmosphere our pioneers strove
to achieve. Meanwhile monuments often are limited to flat markers,
prohibiting artistic memorials. The rules suppress freedom of expression, making it difficult to express the love and tribute to our dearly
departed that has made the American cemetery so unique.

The history of the pioneers buried in our Colorado cemeteries, as
well as the cemeteries themselves, must be documented before they
are lost to decay and neglect.

Death has been marked and memorialized since the beginning of
the human race, reflecting an unwillingness to pass unnoticed into the
unknown. Tombstones and monuments are erected as signs of love
and respect for the departed, yet are also a symbol for the grieving
survivors–an effort to make sure each life will be remembered. The
cemetery allows us to share our grief, proclaim our beliefs, and grant
respect for our dearly departed loved ones. It is an open air museum,
a grand collection of the human spirit captured in stone and memories. It is a place of entombment, yet in symbolism, it is more for the
living than the dead.

Cemeteries of the Eastern United States followed the tradition of
nineteenth century Europe. Graveyards situated next to churches

Trailside burial in northeastern Colorado, probably
on the Overland Trail near Julesburg.

connected faith and the hereafter. The garden cemetery emerged in
the mid-nineteenth century, a product of the Rural Cemetery
Movement. Boston's Mount Auburn Cemetery, opening in 1831, was
the first such cemetery in the United States. Modeled after Per e
Lachaise in France, the cemetery was graced with thick green grass,
flowers, wide curved drives for carriages, and an abundance of trees.
With this natural setting came a resurgence of artistic stone carvings.
Visitors were no longer intimidated, they were greeted with serenity
and solitude, and beauty. The cemetery became a place of repose, and
sculptors showed the difference in their ornate and detailed carvings.
A sense of pride had been reborn in America's cemeteries.

With the western migration of the mid-nineteenth century, the traditional cemetery changed. From the Mississippi River west, the land
was vast, open and overwhelming. Wagon trains crossed this country
via several routes. Yet few knew the human cost of the way west, until
well into the journey. All routes were dotted with burial mounds. With
all the hardship endured, this migration united a nation and
strengthened a frontier. As family members were lost and buried
along the trail, the loss turned to determination as the survivors continued toward their destinations.

As settlements rose across Colorado, so did the cemetery. The
cemetery of the West is as traditional in spirit as in the East, yet more
practical. Throughout the prairies of eastern Colorado, hundreds of
small cemeteries dot the land, recounting in stone and wood, the lives
of these early settlers.

Early Colorado statutes allowed any three individuals the right to
create a cemetery. Family cemeteries on the home ranch were a common practice. Funeral homes and undertakers were not available in
many cases, and weather played an important role at the time of

death. The deceased person was "laid out" in the family home, and a wooden coffin was hastily constructed from available lumber. A grave, usually dug on the family farm or homestead, was the beginning of many pioneer cemeteries.[1] A brief religious ceremony was performed in the home of the deceased, often led by a family member, as there were few clergymen in the early days. Burial records for these rural graves are often nonexistent, as there were no laws requiring death certificates prior to statehood in 1876.

In the larger settlements, and in the mountain camps, cemeteries were laid out away from the city if possible. A growing community needed room to expand; a cemetery in the heart of town was not good for business. Many cemeteries across the state became popular spots for Sunday picnics. The carefully manicured grounds, including shrubs, trees and flowers, gave cemeteries an inviting "park-like" atmosphere the whole family could enjoy. Public transportation was provided by buggy and later by trolley car.

Our pioneers maintained their religious beliefs as they built a new life on a new frontier. The deceased were buried facing east, following the Judeo-Christian fundamental belief of the resurrection rising from that direction. Most Colorado cemeteries follow this tradition when possible, depending on ground layout.

Colorado's cemeteries became a natural setting as our pioneers settled an expanding land and began a new way of life. Social values are prominent in each cemetery and are as diverse in each region as the state itself. Economic status may be reflected in the type and size of tombstone, or monument, or even mausoleum. Family plots may range from a grouping of headstones, to areas with wood or wrought iron fencing, to elaborate stone exedras including a mourner's seat, and intricate carvings. Individual cemeteries typically include county plots, or pauper sections, usually located on the outer edge of the cemetery. Set aside for those who could not afford to purchase burial plots, this section has been historically referred to as the Potter's Field, a biblical reference.

Cemeteries reflect our social history, often indicating particular hardships. The lack of medical care often resulted in mothers dying in childbirth, as well as young children, without proper treatment, dying from disease. Diphtheria, typhoid, and the nationwide Spanish Influenza outbreak of 1917–1918, claimed many pioneers, many of whom were infants. Cemeteries across the state have designated sections for babies and infants, a particularly sad reflection of our pioneer history.

Colorado cemeteries were placed on hills or ground that was attractive in appearance but difficult to farm. Roads were built according to the lay of the land, and generally to save whatever trees were in the area. While Protestant, Catholic, and Jewish citizens shared the same cemetery, they were usually segregated by belief.

Organizations such as the the Elks and Masons, their sister groups, the Eastern Star and Rebekah Lodge, and the Independent Order of Odd Fellows, set aside plots of land for their brethren, in an effort to continue fraternal bonds into eternity.

The International Order of Woodsmen of the World and its sister organization, Women of Woodcraft, were an early day fraternal insurance company. The policy paid fifty to $100 toward the purchase of a tombstone for the policy-holder. Their monuments, in the form of whole or half trees, are common throughout Colorado cemeteries. Their markers gave durable advertising, adding to the motto of the organization, "When silent, he speaks."2

The Grand Army of the Republic, organized in the nineteenth century to honor Union Civil War veterans, was responsible for the creation of Decoration Day, now celebrated as Memorial Day, an honor to all veterans of the armed services.

Beautification of the cemetery took on an added significance on Arbor Day each year. Civic organizations and school children planted trees, shrubs, flowers, and donated their time to keep the burial ground tidy and maintained. Arbor Day was adopted in 1899. Its founder, J. Sterling Morton wrote, "Trees are the monuments I would leave. The cultivation of flowers and trees is the cultivation of the good, the beautiful, and the noble in man."

The graveyards of Colorado contain some of the earliest forms of art and written history in our state. Much can be learned about our state's pioneers from studying these tombstones. Selection of the materials used in these stones indicate what was available in the area, as well as the importance placed on remembering the deceased. In several cases, primarily along the westward trails, travel and the urgency to keep moving did not allow time for stone monuments to be erected in the event of death. Sometimes travelers intentionally concealed graves to protect them from wild animals and looters.

Materials used to create monuments varied with the conditions, locations, and time. Limestone was the most commonly used stone in the time of the pioneers, followed by sandstone, granite, bronze, and marble. As time passed, limestone and sandstone proved to be inadequate, as it did not hold up in Colorado's severe climate. Granite, difficult to quarry in the early days, improved with technology, and known for its durability, eventually became the stone of choice. Several quarries existed in early Colorado, providing access and low cost materials. The marble quarry at Marble, Colorado, famous for such memorials as Lincoln, and Washington monuments, in Washington, D.C., also provided material for countless Colorado tombstones. Mail order catalogs, such as Sears & Roebuck, and Montgomery Ward, offered a variety of tombstones, such as Vermont marble, produced in the eastern United States. Wood could be worked quickly and was often used as a marker in the winter or if death occurred on the trail. Wood was also used when nothing else was available, or when one could not afford a stone memorial. The cost and difficulty in transporting heavy stones overland is evident in the early years in the overwhelming use of local materials.

The quality of the stone craftsmanship is exemplified in the design of the monuments across the state. Simple artwork, often called "folk art," exists side-by-side with elaborate, ornate and complex carvings of accomplished stone sculptors. Several examples are found across the state, from the larger city cemeteries of Denver, to the work of the Fiorini family in Durango's cemetery.

Border motifs carry many symbols, including carnations for love, the cedar tree for the Messiah, clover for Trinity, cloak for compassion, columbine for gentleness, cornucopia for the Resurrection, the fern for sincerity, garland for virtue and the gate for entrance into Paradise. Grain or wheat symbolized Eucharist, grapevine for labor, the hourglass for mortality, ivy for eternal life, the lamb for innocence, the olive branch for peace, rope for eternity and the anchor for hope. The angel stood for the messenger of God, rose for love and beauty, rising sun for dawn of new life, scales for equality, sea shell for hospitality, star for birth of life, sword for justice, thistle for sorrow, thorn for grief, urn for destiny, wings for immortality, and wreaths for strength and peace. These symbols changed both regionally and with the attitudes toward death, giving us a glimpse of the values held by our early pioneers. Within this context, we find a major category of funerary expression, that of triumph over adversity.

Some of the most personal history of our state's pioneers are found in the inscriptions and epitaphs of their tombstones. From the nationally-recognized figures such as Buffalo Bill Cody or Doc Holiday, to the homesteader on the eastern plains, or the miner or prostitute in the mountain mining camps, all lives (and deaths) signify a past experience, a pioneering spirit. A little investigation will also lead us to the tragedies of the common pioneer.

Denver's Fairmount Cemetery, holds the remains of Colonel John Chivington, a Methodist preacher and military man best remembered for his brutal attack on Indians at Sand Creek. A memorial at Kiowa is for pregnant Henrietta Dietemann and her son, murdered by Indians. Monuments at Meeker, Beecher Island and Summit Springs, all reflect human tragedy during the Indian Wars.

Unlike most histories, cemeteries record the commonality of us all. The history of rich and poor, famous and infamous, is recorded on these many tombstones and memorials all across Colorado.

Colorado is nothing without its past, its history, and most of all, the pioneers who struggled and endured to set the foundation for the great state it is today. Our cemeteries are testament to the history and lore of those great people, a place to learn and enjoy our rich past.

— — —

A Word About Gravestone Rubbings

Creating a gravestone image by rubbing chalk, crayon or charcoal on a piece of paper placed over the stone is a way of obtaining cemetery art. The subject of gravestone rubbings can be controversial for those involved with the preservation of the cemetery. When attempting a rubbing, please use care and caution, and if possible, ask the cemetery caretaker for permission. He or she may even have an added tip or two to the ones provided below:

A small tool box or fishing tackle box will hold the materials needed for a rubbing, and is small enough and handy to pack and carry. Items included should be a soft-bristled brush, such as a toothbrush, and a rubber eraser. Do not use a wire brush, as this causes finite scratches in the stone. Masking tape will keep the paper in place, and doesn't leave a residue when removed. Newsprint, or large, thin poster paper are the types of paper best used. They seem to be more durable and add to the effect of the rubbing. For large stones, poster tubes work well for storing the finished rubbing.

Flat chalk, or jumbo crayons work best and are easy to work with. Charcoal is also used, but is messy, leaves smudges, and is only for the practiced stone rubber. Finally, an old pillow or garden kneeling pad provides some comfort, as the process is time consuming.

Once the gravestone is selected, use the brush to remove any dirt and moss or other growth from the surface. Apply the paper, covering the entire surface, and secure with the masking tape. Be sure there are no wrinkles, lumps, or air pockets. With the flat of your palm, press lightly over the surface so the raised places and crevices make imprints. The paper will adhere to the stone's design.

Working from the center outward, lightly establish the design by rubbing the surface with the flat side of a dark crayon. Pressing more firmly, fill in the design by working from the outside edges inward. Raised areas will register the color while the depressed areas will remain white.

Do not remove the paper until you are pleased with the outcome; it will be next to impossible to realign. When you are finished, gently remove the tape and lift the paper. For larger rubbings, rolling the paper onto poster rolls preserves the work nicely.

The rubbing is now suitable for framing.

— — —

Chapter One Notes

[1] Many rural cemeteries still exist. Some will be found in the appendix. If the burial ground is on private land, I have chosen not to include it in the appendix.

[2] The tree image as a monument, meant pain and loss, and do not always indicate a member of the Woodsmen organization.

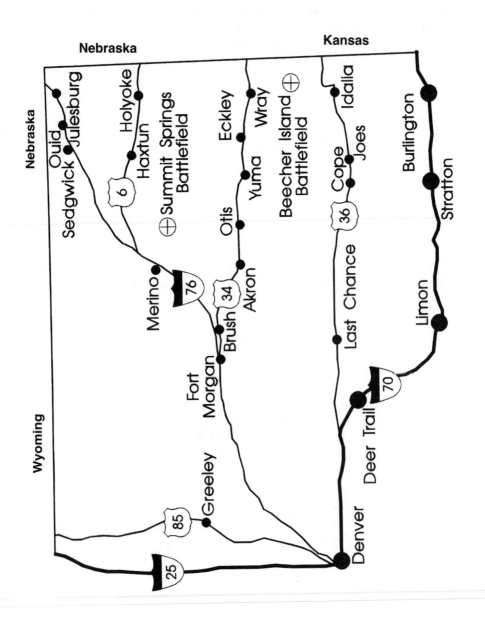

Chapter Two

The High Plains

T he northeastern quarter of Colorado is known as the High Plains, a portion of the Great Plains that cover the entire north-south border of the United States west of the Mississippi River, and from the Rocky Mountains east to the Mississippi River.

This particular region was created by rock deposits and silt carried by the rivers, causing a sediment land foundation due to erosion of an earlier mountain range preceding the Rocky Mountains by several hundred million years. We have archeological evidence of prehistoric man in the area some 13,000 years ago.

The South Platte River was the mainstay on the High Plains. Born atop the Continental Divide in the South Park mountain range, this slow-moving river was the primary route used by the Indians, explorers, trappers, traders, and early pioneers, as a water resource and for navigation.

The Apache Indians roamed this area as early as the sixteenth century. By the 1800s, the Kiowa, Arapaho and Cheyenne had moved into the region. The buffalo were plentiful and the South Platte provided a vital waterway. The Indian nations would fight desperately for their land until the fateful climax in the 1860s.

One of the first recorded expeditions across the High Plains was led by two French brothers, Paul and Pierre Mallot, in 1739. Their party traveled the Mississippi River to the Platte, then moved west across the plains to the Arkansas River.

Colorado was part of the 1803 Louisiana Purchase. Following the War of 1812, exploration of America's newest acquisition began in earnest. Major Stephen H. Long led an expedition to the West in 1819, searching for a route through the South Platte Canyon. While he failed in this endeavor, he did succeed in naming much of the American West, including all of eastern Colorado "The Great American Desert," claiming it unfit to settle. Because of this report, eastern Colorado remained largely unsettled for decades.

In 1840, John C. Fremont, in an effort to shorten the journey to California, led a party of explorers through the region. They followed the South Platte River and parts of the Oregon Trail, which traveled through the extreme northeast portion of the state. Fremont's diary reports he camped near present-day Orchard, Colorado, encountering Indian inhabitants of the area without incident. Other famous roads crisscrossed the High Plains, including the Overland, Chisholm, Smoky Hill, Texas-Montana and Mormon trails.

The South Platte River proved its importance once again, as the West was opened to expansion with a fury, following the gold rush to California in 1849.

The Indian hostilities of the 1860s brought terror and fear to travelers and settlers. Treaty after treaty with the Indians was broken by the white man. As white settlement continued, restrictions on the Plains Indians increased. The climax came in 1864, when the Indians raided the small settlements along the trails bounded by the South Platte River. Wagon trains were attacked, telegraph lines cut and towns were burned, including Julesburg, which was attacked and burned twice. The end came with the battle at Summit Springs, causing much death and destruction to the Indians. This act removed the Indians from the prairies of northeastern Colorado.

Railroads steamed into Colorado, bringing permanent settlement to the High Plains. Farms sprang up, providing fresh vegetables and livestock to the mountain mining camps. In time, the transcontinental railroad brought a network of rails across the state. Population and prosperity came to the Eastern Plains.

Ranchers such as John Wesley Iliff and Jared Brush built cattle empires along the South Platte River, becoming two of the wealthiest men in Northeastern Colorado. Iliff, who started out buying crippled cattle from migrating travelers, commanded high prices for his grass-fed cattle. Thus inspired, Charles Goodnight brought the first herd of Texas longhorn cattle to Colorado in 1868. The Goodnight-Loving Trail is still visible in many spots across eastern Colorado. With great population growth during the 1870s and 1880s, and the arrival of the railroad, the cattle industry boomed, supplying towns, mining camps, military forts and later, the Indian reservations.

Many towns were a direct result of the railroad, yet the High Plains became a stockman's empire. In 1862, the Homestead Act was enacted, allowing 160 acres to any settler willing to live and improve upon the land within five years. This was the prelude to the western migration that within twenty years, caused one of the greatest population movements in American history.

Agriculture also played a large part in northeastern Colorado. Inflated food prices, led many to try their hand at growing crops. The Native Americans had success with corn, squash and beans. With irrigation, crops began to grow in abundance on the prairie. The feed grain industry of Colorado began in the northeast portion of the state. Large cattle feeders contracted to feed and market the ranchers' cattle, while meat packing plants such as Sterling Beef and Monfort became the mainstay for world-wide beef sales, while creating local employment.

With ingenuity of people such as Charles Boettcher, and John C. Campion, the new industries were founded. Boettcher introduced the sugar beet to Colorado and eastern Colorado provided the perfect soil and climate for its growth. By the turn of the century, sugar beet factories were a primary business in many towns.

Northeast Colorado suffered a blow during the winter of 1885 – 1886. Blizzards killed whole herds of cattle, children died of disease, and business, for a time, came to a screeching halt.

Yet with determination and tenacity, farming, ranching, and industry, has prevailed. The early pioneers of the "Great American Desert" built communities, family life and a foundation for future generations.

— — —

Interstate – 76 West
The South Platte Road

JULESBURG

HILLSIDE CEMETERY
LOCATED ONE-HALF-MILE SOUTHEAST OF TOWN. IN THE TOWN OF JULESBURG, TAKE HIGHWAY 385 EAST ONE-QUARTER-MILE.

This small corner of Colorado has more long ranging history, legend and lore in its prairie setting than the entire rest of the state. The South Platte River is the life-blood of this land. The Indian tribes, for some ten thousand years called this area home. The Spanish explored the area as early as 1738. The covered wagons of the westward migration in the 1840s created a flood of Easterners along the trails that became known as the Overland, the South Platte, and the famed Pony Express routes. The first transcontinental telegraph reached Julesburg in 1861. It would not extend to Denver for over two years.

They were all here: Native Americans, fur traders, outlaws, the U.S. Calvary, Oregon and Mormon Trail travelers, Pony Express riders, and finally the telegraph and the Union Pacific Railroad builders.

Most of the major players of the western migration traveled through or stopped by one of the four sites known since the 1850s as Julesburg.

Julesburg was the prominent town in the region. While history moved through this tiny corner, Julesburg moved as well. The first settlement grew around Jules Trading Post. Established in 1859, and named for Jules Beni, a one-time station manager for the Overland Stage, the site was located at the crossing of the South Platte River and Lodgepole Creek.[1]

In 1865, Julesburg was burned by the Indians. The community relocated to Fort Sedgwick, north of present-day I–76. A flagpole stands on the location of the fort, and a red flag marks the cemetery where the soldiers are buried. The Union Pacific Railroad came through north of the site and Julesburg moved again. Known as the "Wickedest City in the West," Indian raids, railroad feuds, gangs and thieves dominated the area. The railroad built a line to Denver in 1880, and again Julesburg moved. In time, the town settled in, grew and prospered, remaining dominant in the history of this tucked away section of northern Colorado prairie.

The first cemetery was located northwest of town on land owned by a George Johnson, near the old water tower. A Southerner by the name of Kitchen, had homesteaded south of the town of Julesburg. In an effort to raise money, he proposed a land deal to the city for a new cemetery. In the meantime, Kitchen shot and killed a man named Runner. The two had been in competition of one sort or another, and a feud developed. Runner became the first official burial in the new Hillside Cemetery.

The Hillside Cemetery was created in 1888, an unprecedented seven years after the founding of Julesburg. It is well laid out, with wide avenues, gracious space and is well maintained. Native sandstone and a few wooden markers can be seen. Prairie grass and sage brush cover many of the tombstones. Many stones are the work of area stone mason, Uberto Gibello. A few markers are dated 1886, indicating existence prior to incorporation. Many deaths are attributed to the Scarlet Fever epidemic of 1899.

Aguayo, Marciano O. (1897 – 1979)

A descendant of the Chichimeca Indians, Marciano Aguayo was raised by his father, Geronimo Aguayo, to live off the land, a respected native tradition. He ran away at age sixteen. He became a stable boy for Pancho Villa of Mexico. Following the war between Villa and the U.S. Army, young Aguayo made his way north into the United States. He worked in the fields and the coal mines of southern Colorado, was robbed and deprived of equal justice before he hid on a freight train headed north. He jumped off at the Union Pacific railroad tracks at Sedgwick, Colorado, where he worked in the beet fields for several years, saving his money.

In 1929, he married Javita Ortega and bought a home in Sedgwick. Small as the shack was, it was home to the couple and the birthplace of their children. Aguayo continued his work in the beet fields. The long hard hours were necessary to provide for his many children. All of his children were able to attend college, earning degrees and many honors. The hard work of Marciano Aguayo provided education and leadership for his family as well as his community.

The stone marker in the Hillside Cemetery gives tribute to the great dedication of a pioneer. It reads: "El Destino Esta En Tus Manos." "Destiny Is In Your Hands."

Brown Family Plot

The Thomas Brown family arrived in Julesburg in 1902, where they farmed and provided general labor, eventually establishing one of the finest farms and a pioneer heritage unsurpassed.

Thomas Brown crossed the ocean from his native Ireland to America as a stowaway. He took labor jobs, saving his money and returned to Ireland, working for his passage. In Ireland, he married Mary Marshall, started a family and returned to America. He would cross the ocean twice before his family joined him in the United States. In time, he managed to provide passage and passports for his wife and children to cross to America. Settling first in Michigan, he arrived in Julesburg in 1902, where Thomas joined a brother and eventually opened the Brown Hotel.

William Marshall Brown, son of Thomas and Mary, was born in 1836, in Ireland, and came to America in 1886. He eventually settled in Sedgwick County in 1902. William brought with him, his wife, Phoebe and their three children. While William ran the family farm, Phoebe taught school in Julesburg. In 1909, William bought his own ranch in Logan County, near Merino. Here, he built one of the finest ranches in the county and became a very wealthy rancher. In 1917, William and Phoebe returned to Julesburg, where they bought a home in town for their retirement years.

William died in 1927 at age ninety. Phoebe followed him in death in 1946 at age 101. They are buried together in the family plot.

George Thomas Brown, the third generation of the pioneer Brown family, was born to William and Phoebe in 1888. As a child, he came to Julesburg with his parents and sisters in 1902. He and his sisters made the move to Merino, and the new family farm in 1909.

In 1910, scandal erupted when George and his sisters Catherine and Mary, stole off to Denver and had a triple wedding. George married Ella May Zimmerman, Catherine married Charles A. McSay, and Mary married Clarence W. Heckert. The Logan County sheriff was called in when the young Browns were discovered missing. Following a brief Denver honeymoon, the three couples returned home and began their own lives.

George and Ella Brown homesteaded a half mile from his parents, just inside Morgan County. In 1917, George and Ella bought land four miles east of Julesburg, near the South Platte River. Here, the family raised livestock and produce. George later became a member of the school board, while Ella taught Sunday school for twenty-five years, and as a midwife, delivered some thirty babies in the community.

George died in 1948, Ella died in 1976. They are buried together in the Brown family plot, in Section 28, Lots 16 through 24.

Dye, Robert S. (1869 – 1940)

Robert Dye settled in Julesburg in 1886, where he opened a hardware store with other family members. Family-owned for over a hundred years, the store is still operating. Their skills were in such demand, that the brothers also built tin roofs and siding for the community.

Robert was active in business and the politics of the young community, serving a term as mayor. Through the years, the Dye hardware store became a cornerstone in the business community. Robert managed to keep the store operating during the Great Depression. He attributed this to being an honest businessman and having good friends and neighbors. The Dye family helped establish the Methodist Church, organized in the spring of 1886.

Dye is buried with his wife Emma. There is a large stone marker in the Dye family plot in Section 13, Lot 39.

Eeckhout, Adolph (1855 – 1943)

A native of Belgium, Adolph Eeckhout arrived in Sedgwick County with his bride, Ethel, in 1889. The couple homesteaded land near Julesburg, where they built a sod house, planted wheat and oats, and raised milk cows. As his farm grew, he employed the legendary Julesburg character, Uberto Gibello.

Adolph and Ethel were instrumental in the founding of the Catholic Church at Julesburg, and active in the early formation of the town.

He is buried in Section 11, Lot 12. There is a marker.

Gibello, Uberto (1840 – 1910)

Of Italian descent, Uberto Gibello became one of Julesburg's most colorful residents. Upon his immigration to the United States, in the 1880s, he worked for the Union Pacific Railroad until 1887. Shortly thereafter, he homesteaded land just outside of Julesburg. The land was some of the rockiest in the area, and even his ingenious irrigation system could not make the ground fertile. He turned to stone work for his living. He cut, engraved and hand carved many of the tombstones found in the cemetery.

In his spare time, he began digging and carving an extravagant cave dwelling. He built three buildings into the massive rock on his land. From there, he carved the rock into steps leading up and down to various rooms. The steps eventually led down to a cave of rock rooms a half-mile long.

Uberto died suddenly in 1910 and was laid to rest in the cemetery among the stones he had carved. His own stone reads: "Holy Name Society of Julesburg." The headstone was a gift from a local group of nuns.

His small upright stone monument is located in Section 4, Lot 1.

Johnson, Mercy Elizabeth Pike (1848 – 1927)

A native of Tioga County, New York, Mercy began her teaching career following the death of her father.[2] When her mother died some time later, she and her sister Sarah, came west to seek relief for Sarah's consumption. The two women traveled across the great prairie by covered wagon, accompanied for a time by their younger brother. Alone, they made the journey to Garden City, Kansas and eventually to North Platte, Nebraska. Mercy taught school to make ends meet before she met and married Christopher Johnson of Julesburg, in 1885. The couple had three sons.

Christopher worked for the railroad. The family in various section houses for the first few years. Mercy opened a millinery shop in Julesburg and became quite prosperous.

Mercy's sister Sarah, died in 1886 and was buried on land over-looking the South Platte River. The land later became Hillside Cemetery, Christopher Johnson being an original board member and cemetery promoter.

Mercy and Christopher bought a ranch south of town which burned in 1910. They relocated for a time to the abandoned cave house of Uberto Gibello. Christopher died in 1921. Mercy carried on the ranch duties until her death in 1927.

The two are buried together, in Section 28, Lot 14. There is a marker.

Randall, Frank (1886 – 1965)

Born in Hayes, Kansas, Frank Randall grew up in Tologa, Oklahoma, where he attended the college at Norman, Oklahoma. Following his education, he joined the Longhorn cattle drives from Mexico to Montana. He was a member of the Teddy Roosevelt Rough Riders and rode in Buffalo Bill Cody's Wild West Show.

In 1918, he brought his family to Julesburg by wagon pulled by a team of mules. He operated a farm near Julesburg, where the family home was a sod house. His wife Ethel, earned a Colorado teacher's certificate and taught school in Sedgwick County for sixteen years.

The Randalls moved to town when Frank accepted the position of deputy sheriff in 1940. He served in this capacity for seventeen years.

He is buried in Section 26, Lot 16.

Sowder, Martha J. (1839 – 1897)

The mother of World Champion Rodeo Rider Thad Sowder, Martha married Daniel Sowder in 1860. The young couple lived in Kentucky and Iowa, where their ten children were born. Daniel died in Derby, Iowa, in 1886. Following the death of Daniel, Martha brought her children to Sedgwick County, in the same year. She filed on a homestead south of Ovid and called it the Lazy D. There, she raised her family and sold her fine livestock throughout the county.

She is buried in the Hillside Cemetery. There is a marker.

OVID

OVID CEMETERY

LOCATED NORTHEAST OF THE TOWN OF OVID. FROM TOWN, GO NORTH ACROSS THE RAILROAD TRACKS. TURN EAST ON HIGHWAY 138, FOR ONE MILE. AT THE FIRST INTERSECTION, TURN LEFT ON THE GRAVEL ROAD. THE CEMETERY IS ONE AND ONE-HALF MILES ON THE RIGHT SIDE OF THE ROAD.

The land was deeded to the Ovid Cemetery District in 1895. The cemetery records also list the name as the Valley Cemetery and Prairie Center Cemetery. Formal records were not kept for many years and therefore are incomplete.[3]

Cannady, George Washington (1844 – 1940)

Born in Danville, Illinois, George Cannady was orphaned at eighteen months of age, when his mother died. He spent his childhood in various family homes until he enlisted in Company G of the Union Iowa Volunteers, at age seventeen. During the Civil War, he saw action at Corinth, Shiloh, Jonesboro, and met President Abraham Lincoln on one occasion. Wounded in duty, he served until the war ended, being mustered out in 1865.

He married Maria Ellen Douglas in 1866. Ten children were born to this union. He brought his family to Ovid in 1907, where he farmed and became a blacksmith in town. He participated in local politics and attended the state Republican conventions as a representative of Sedgwick County. Following the death of Maria in 1916, he married Amelia Ward Johnson in 1921.

There is a military stone marking his grave.

Dawson, James A. (1859 – 1935)

His ancestors came to America from England in 1700, settling in Maryland. James Dawson was born in Beaver County, Pennsylvania, where his father was a farmer and active in politics. He married Margaret Linda Barclay in 1885. The couple traveled west, eventually locating at the Sedgwick military post in 1887. A sod house was their home on the prairie for several years.

In an effort to improve the living conditions of the westward immigrants, Dawson introduced a bill in Congress to open the Fort Sedgwick land to homesteading. The bill passed and homesteaders, including Dawson, were allowed to purchase the government land. Unfortunately for Dawson, the railroad built through his land, and he was forced to purchase it twice.

Very active in town politics, he was director of the sod schoolhouse built in 1890, and served on the Sedgwick County School Board until 1930.

He is buried in the Ovid Cemetery. There is a marker.

Sowder, Martin Thadeus (1874 – 1931)

Perhaps Sedgwick County's greatest claim to fame is World Champion and Cowboy Hall of Fame member, Thad Sowder. He came to Colorado as a boy, with his mother and siblings. Mrs. Martha Sowder took a homestead south of Sedgwick, where she raised livestock. At the Lazy D Ranch, young Thad learned to ride, rope, and break horses.

By his early twenties, Thad was competing in rodeo events as far away as Cheyenne, where he met Anna Ferrel. Over her parents objections, the couple eloped and made their home in Ovid. Thad continued his rodeo competition, winning the World Champion Bronco division in Denver, in 1901 and again in 1902.[4]

In 1903, Sowder suffered a head injury when he was thrown from the notorious bucking bronco, "Midnight." A metal plate was placed in his head during the many surgeries he endured. However, he never fully recovered from this injury.

Denver Public Library

Martin Thadeus Sowder,
Pro-Rodeo Hall of Fame

Thad and his wife Anna rode with Buffalo Bill Cody's Wild West Show in Europe, during its heyday. While Anna rode sidesaddle during demonstrations, Thad rode the bucking broncos. The couple returned to Ovid and eventually separated.

Thad Sowder was the first person to be inducted into the Cowboy Hall of Fame in Oklahoma.

When he died in 1931, Thad's grave at the Ovid Cemetery was marked by a simple stone. Later, a beautifully engraved monument to this accomplished man was placed at his final resting place.[5]

Zorn, Philip J. (1865 – 1927)
Zorn, Maria K. (1873 – 1940)

A native of Ohio, Philip ventured west with his brother Casper, in 1880. At Oshkosh, Nebraska, he met and married Maria Kerzenthia Hartman. Maria, nicknamed "Santa," was the social belle of Oshkosh, yet set aside all admirers for Phil Zorn.

In 1903, Philip Zorn brought his family to northeast Colorado, settling on a farm between Ovid and Sedgwick. Their ranch house became a stopover for travelers along the westward trails. Their ranch produced some of the finest livestock in the area.

The family later moved to Julesburg, where Philip opened a bowling and billiards hall. In 1915, Zorn bought the first Model T Ford in the area. In 1922, they bought the Hippodrome Theatre, which Philip operated until his death in 1927. Santa and her oldest sons ran the businesses and both farms. The Oshkosh ranch is still in the family.

Philip and Santa Zorn are buried together. There is a marker.

SEDGWICK

SEDGWICK CEMETERY

LOCATED NORTHEAST OF THE TOWN OF SEDGWICK. FROM TOWN, CROSS THE RAILROAD TRACKS, AND GO NORTH ON ROAD 165. THE CEMETERY IS APPROXIMATELY THREE AND ONE-HALF MILES JUST OFF COUNTY ROAD 15.

The cemetery was formed by Sedgwick citizens in 1908. To pay for the land, burial lots were sold for ten dollars each, during the first promotion. Thus, cemetery records are listed by name of purchaser, rather than burial name. The cemetery was turned over to the city in 1947. Early burials prior to 1908 do exist, the oldest being 1888.

Crowfoot, John (1839 – 1915)
Crowfoot, Lydia (1846 – 1939)

John Crowfoot, born and raised in New York, moved to rural Wisconsin with his family. He entered the Civil War in 1861, serving with Company I, 29th Wisconsin Regiment. Following the war, he returned to his Wisconsin home, where he married Lydia Thayer in 1867.

Due to John's ill health, the family, including seven children, moved west, in search of a healthier climate. (A war injury left John with one lung.) They first homesteaded at Lodgepole, Nebraska. Diphtheria tragically struck the family in 1882, claiming four of the Crowfoot children. The family left for California and a new beginning.

By 1895, the family returned to the Plains, settling in Sedgwick, temporarily living in a dugout. John farmed and raised crops on his homestead and later built a sod house for his family. Following John's death in 1915, Lydia tended the household, the children and raised hens for eggs, produce and oats. An ardent member of the Sedgwick Methodist Church, she served her community humbly.

The pioneer couple are buried together. There is a marker in Block 2, Lot 5.

Darling, Leanzer (1845 – 1916)

Born near Wheelock, Vermont, young Leanzer Darling moved with his father to Indiana and on to Iowa, where he received his education. He went to Nebraska, where he became a schoolteacher. He met and married Anna Marie Adams in 1878.

He brought his family to Sedgwick in 1886, homesteading some five miles west of town, where he built a dugout. He installed his wife's pump organ, the first in the community, in their new home. The Darlings were able to work the land, providing staple crops for sale in the community. Maria died in 1887, leaving Leanzer to raise the children. He saw to their schooling and encouraged them to attend church, being a charter member of the Methodist Episcopal Church. He became secretary of the first school board in 1886. Darling managed to build a sizable herd of cattle, which he bred and sold throughout the country.

There is a marker to the pioneer Darlings in Block 4, Lot 3.

Jankovsky, Adolph (1863 – 1930)

A native of Prague, Bohemia, Adolph Jankovsky attended the Melk Monastery near Vienna, Austria. At age eighteen, he emigrated to America, where he stayed with an uncle in Des Moines, Iowa. He moved farther west, finding work in various towns such as Casper and Cheyenne, Wyoming. He married Eleanor Jenik in 1893. The couple owned a general store in Lodgepole, Nebraska.

In 1906, he surveyed the South Platte Valley and the new town of Sedgwick. With new opportunity and ample irrigation from the new Jumbo Reservoir, Jankovsky moved his family across the prairie in three wagons. Supplies and merchandise for his general store were shipped by train. His daughter Rose, was the first baby born in the town of Sedgwick.

The general store, the first business in Sedgwick, was such a success, that a second store was opened in Ovid in 1917. It was eventually handed down to the next generation. Jankovsky built a large two-story home for his family in Sedgwick. Through his business, this pioneer merchant provided the farmers of Sedgwick with hardware, wagons, pumps, butter, eggs, grain and feed. Active in the community, he served on the town board, fire department and cemetery board.

He and his wife, Eleanor are buried in Block 3, Lot 16.

McKinstry, Charles B. (1868 – 1945)

One of the first pioneers of Sedgwick, McKinstry arrived with his wife Ottie, and seven children, in October 1906. He became cashier of the Sedgwick County Bank in 1907. He helped many homesteaders and farmers in the early years of the community.

His bank remained solvent during the depression years and continued to aid the community. Active in the school district and town activities, he helped the irrigation district and the cemetery association.

Charles McKinstry is buried next to his wife, Ottie, in Block 4, Lot 11.

Vernon, William (1850 – 1912)

Born and raised in East Liberty, Ohio, William Vernon married Arminta Drydan on Christmas Day, 1879. Six children were born on their farm near Churdan, Iowa. Vernon brought his family to Colorado, by train. He settled on a homestead three and a half miles northwest of Sedgwick, where he built a grand two-story home in 1901.

One of Sedgwick County's earliest pioneers, he was instrumental in the agricultural growth of the county. He helped with the planning and ditching of Jumbo Reservoir, providing his time and machinery for the project.

Arminta became active in the town as well. She offered her home as the base for the phone company. The company operated out of the Vernon home for several years.

William and Arminta Vernon are buried together in Block 4, Lot 1. There is a marker.

STERLING

RIVERSIDE CEMETERY
LOCATED WEST ON HIGHWAY 6, TWO MILES SOUTHWEST OF TOWN ON THE NORTH SIDE OF THE HIGHWAY.

The earliest records of Riverside Cemetery date from 1903. The Logan County Cemetery Association operated Riverside until 1942, when the city of Sterling took control. The original cemetery was two miles north on Sidney Avenue. According to cemetery records, all bodies were exhumed and reinterred at Riverside, including the first children born in Sterling. Edgar and Eva Smith were the twins of pioneer Richard Smith and his wife. They died at birth.[6]

Davis, Horace B. (1860 – 1938)
Davis, Sarah Elizabeth Powell (1863 – 1934)
Horace Davis, an early settler of the area, started the B.B. Colorado Colony Company, responsible for much of Logan County's early growth. He was an agent of the Union Pacific Railroad, advertising the great land opportunities.

He married Sarah Elizabeth Powell in 1885. While Mr. Davis promoted the land and built the town of Sterling, Mrs. Davis improved the culture by teaching piano and art. Both were active in the First Presbyterian Church, she serving as choir director until her death.

They are both buried in Section 1-72, Block 0009.

Hadfield, William S. (1838 – 1927)
Hadfield, Charity Sanders (1834 – 1914)
Mr. Hadfield was reportedly Logan County's first permanent white settler. A native of England, he had been in America about eight years before arriving in what would become Logan County. It was 1871, when he pitched a tent on an island at the mouth of Pawnee Creek, and the South Platte River.[7]

He filed a land claim under the Homestead Act, and began raising sheep and cattle. He became a prominent stockman of the area. He built a sod house for his bride in 1878, the former Charity Sanders, sister of Allen Sanders, another pioneer of the area.

Denver Public Library
Portia Lubchenco
Pioneer Doctor of Logan County

"Uncle Billy" and "Aunt Charity" were favorites of the community for years. They are buried together in Section 1-140, Lot 0109.

Harris, William C. (1870 – 1940)

William Harris was five years old when his father, W.H. Harris, left Nebraska and traveled by covered wagon to the Sterling area. His schooling was occasional, yet he was one of three who graduated, at age twenty, with the first class of Sterling High School, in 1890.

He was the first in northeastern Colorado to custom feed his cattle, buying waste pulp from the Great Western Sugar Factory. By 1913, he was feeding 3,000 cattle and 20,000 sheep. In 1936, he was listed as the largest feed lot operator in the United States. He was elected to the Colorado Legislature and was instrumental in organizing the North Sterling Reservoir Project, bringing irrigation to much of Logan County.

William Harris is buried in Section 1-72, Lot 0007. His large granite stone, designed by noted sculptor, Fred Torrey, notes his pioneer status.[8] It is the most impressive monument in the cemetery.

Lubchenco, Portia M., M.D. (1887 – 1978)

Portia Lubchenco, a native of South Carolina, was the first woman to earn a medical degree from North Carolina College in 1912. She married Russian agronomist Alexis Lubchenco, living for a time in Russia, where she practiced medicine. In 1918, she and her husband returned to the states, narrowly escaping the Russian Revolution.

By 1930, she and her husband had moved to Haxtun, Colorado, where Portia practiced medicine with her brother. She moved to Sterling in 1936, where she became the first chief of staff at Logan County Hospital. Her husband Alexis, died in Sterling in 1941.

In 1967, she moved to Denver where she practiced in the geriatric department of the Denver clinic at age eighty.

She was the 1954 Colorado Mother of the Year, and received the Colorado Medical Society Award in 1962.

She is buried with her husband in Section ES, Lot 2103.

Propst, Sidney (1846 – 1924)

A Confederate Army veteran, Sidney Propst came west at age twenty-seven, on an excursion of the Colorado Territory. Impressed with the land and possible prosperity, he returned to his native Alabama to get his family. He returned to the Sterling area in 1874, with a bride and her family. By 1876, his parents and nine brothers and sisters had made the journey to Sterling.

Engaged in buffalo hunting, he soon operated a stage line from Sidney, Nebraska to Greeley. By 1881, he had homesteaded 160 acres of land near Sterling.

He was influential in building the new Sterling and encouraged landscaping of the new "city." Generations of the Propst family have made the Sterling area their home.

Sid Propst is buried in the family plot in Section 1-72, Block 022.

Smith, Richard E. (1840 – 1886)

Smith originally settled at Greeley, with the Union Colony.[9] Dissatisfied with the organization of the colony, Smith moved on to Old Sterling in 1873.

With the coming of the railroad, Smith is credited with relocating the town three miles south to the rail line. He started a general store and helped build the town. By 1881, Sterling was incorporated, with Smith being instrumental in writing the city charter, laws and regulations.

Smith died in the city he founded. He is buried in Section 1-72, Block 035.

Weir, James (1831 – 1912)

James Weir came to the Sterling area from Canada in 1865, to work for the railroad. By 1866, he was a foreman, and moved his family to the area. The settlement was called Weir, when Julesburg #3 was founded in 1881.

Later, Weir moved his family to Sterling, along with several of the Weir buildings, including the family home, which was moved in sections.

The Weir family founded several business in Sterling, becoming prominent citizens of the community. Andy Weir's building was the first post office and his sister Edna, the first postmaster.

The Weir family plot is located in Sections 1-40 and 1-70.[10]

Denver Public Library

Indian burial site.
Eastern Plains, about 1860.

Wilson, Victor S. (1866 – 1932)

Victor, along with his brother John, published the newspaper at Atwood, during the county elections of 1887. When Sterling won the county seat, the Wilson brothers moved their *Advocate* newspaper to Sterling. It is still in existence today.

Very personal in style, the Wilsons were adamant in writing the news as it was, without slant. They did not pander, nor did they favor. However, in 1892, the brothers waged a war of words through their paper, against the new Populist Party, accusing local politicians of stealing money.

In the end, it seems all the wrath was caused over competition concerns.

Victor Wilson is buried in Section 1-140, Lot 0064.[11]

OFF THE BEATEN PATH:

SUMMIT SPRINGS BATTLE SITE (JULY 11, 1869)

THE SUMMIT SPRINGS SITE IS APPROXIMATELY SIX MILES SOUTH OF ATWOOD, ON HIGHWAY 63, AND FIVE MILES EAST ON COUNTY ROAD 60, (THE LOGAN/WASHINGTON COUNTY LINE).

The Cheyenne Dog Soldiers went on a violent rampage following the Sand Creek Massacre in 1864. Telegraph lines were cut, wagon trains attacked, settlers burned out and towns along the trails threatened.

General Carr was charged with ending the raids, which included the kidnapping of two women. Army scout Buffalo Bill Cody led the troops on the mission to rescue the women.

The Cheyennes were taken by surprise at their camp near Summit Springs, on July 11, 1869. Chief Tall Bull was among those killed. While one of the kidnapped women was recovered, the other died. The unfortunate battle ended the Indian conflict in northeastern Colorado.[12]

In 1969, Richard Tall Bull, Chief Tall Bull's great-grandson, headed an Indian Centennial ceremony at the site.

A natural rock monument with a plaque was erected in 1933. It reads :

Our lands are where our dead lie buried.

BRUSH

J.L. BRUSH MEMORIAL CEMETERY

LOCATED NORTH OF BRUSH, JUST OFF INTERSTATE 76. TAKE THE HOSPITAL ROAD *EXIT FROM THE INTERSTATE. TURN RIGHT AT THE INTERSECTION. FOLLOW HOSPITAL ROAD TO MILL STREET, TURNING LEFT ON MILL STREET. THE CEMETERY IS APPROXIMATELY ONE-QUARTER-MILE.*

The cemetery is divided into two sections. The oldest, known as the Northside Cemetery, was established in 1893. The land was donated by town father, Jared L. Brush, a one-time state lieutenant governor. The cemetery became a reality in 1895. White marble stones mark the burials in the First Addition. The oldest section, located next to the road, is very prominent. White marble military stones mark the burials of U.S. War veterans. Among the veterans, is a memorial to Jeff Reece who died December 7, 1941, at Pearl Harbor, Hawaii. On the south side of the cemetery, in Section 8, is the Baby Section. The northeast corner is known as the Potters Field. At the west end of the cemetery is a section for the tuberculosis patients of the Eben Ezer Hospital.

The Southside Cemetery, located across the road, was established in 1929. The following biographical sketches are those of burials in the oldest section, or Northside Cemetery.

Christensen, John C. (1860 – 1944)

Born Jens Kristjian Christensen, near Thisted, Denmark, he faced forced enlistment in the Danish army at age twenty. Refusing to serve in the army, he booked passage to America, settling in Chicago in 1880. He struggled to learn the English language and changed his name to John C. Christensen. Within seven years, he saved enough money to return to Denmark and marry his childhood sweetheart, Juliane Howe-Pedersen. Returning to America in 1894, Christensen became a naturalized citizen.

In Chicago, John learned of the Homestead Act, and applied for a section of land in Washington County, Colorado. On the open prairie, the family built a home and started a farm among the jackrabbits, rattlesnakes and ever-present wind.

He moved his family to Brush in 1889, homesteading three miles west of town. A two-story rock home was built with hand quarried rock. It stands today. The farm produced fruit, potatoes, grains, alfalfa, and sugar beets.

John Christensen is buried beside his wife Juliane, in the family plot, in the Third Section, Block 4, Lot 39. There is a marker.

Danielsen, Daniel (1855 – 1926)

A native of Denmark, Daniel Danielsen left his homeland for America at age sixteen. He lived for a time in Illinois, before moving to South Dakota. In May 1882, he married Anna Martha Norby, an immigrant from Norway. Nine children were born to this union. One child died in infancy, in 1886.

Daniel and his oldest daughter traveled by covered wagon to Colorado in 1900. He homesteaded north of Brush, where he had a house built for his large family. In time, the entire Danielsen family arrived, complete with their livestock. While the children worked the farm and cared for the livestock, Daniel raised his prized bee colony. He became the local authority, writing journals on bee raising, and selling his queen bees throughout the county. The Danielsen fruit orchard, produced cherries and apples. Daniel's honey, was also well-known.

Ardent members of the St. Ansgar's Lutheran Church, north of Brush, the Danielsens were very involved in their community. When the country church dissolved, they became members of the First English Church of Brush. They also became supporters and worked for the establishment of the Eben Ezer Lutheran Mercy Center in Brush.

Anna Danielsen died in 1919, followed by Daniel in 1926. Daniel's funeral was held at the Eben Ezer All Saints Chapel, in the Danish language. A second service was held in English, at the First English Lutheran Church.

Daniel and Anna Danielsen are buried in the Third Section, in Block 3, Lot 43. There is a marker.

Davis, Robert Dent (1876 – 1934)
Davis, Katie Farrar (1877 – 1976)

One of the earliest Brush pioneers, Dent Davis, as he was known, came to Colorado in 1896, with his wife Katie, and their family.

Both were born in Lexington, Missouri, and were childhood sweethearts. Dent and Katie both attended college in Missouri. Katie studied music, while Dent graduated with a degree in pharmacy, and passed the Farmers Pharmacy Board of Missouri.

The Davis family first settled in Sterling, where Dent was employed at Dr. Chipman's pharmacy. A year later, he moved his family to Brush, where he worked at the McAllister Drug Store. For a time, the family lived in the Shudloskey house on Clayton Street. The telephone office was in the house, and Katie became the operator. Along with her telephone duties and raising her children, she managed time to operate a successful hat shop.

Dent opened his own drug store in 1903, and became very involved in the community. He was instrumental in the construction of the armory building for the National Guard in Brush. In 1905, he expanded his pharmacy business by building the first two-story brick building in the town. The business was on the first floor, while the family living quarters were on the second level.

Katie worked long hours in the drug store and eventually became an apprentice pharmacist. Together, the couple made a success of their business.

Dent was involved in the local baseball team, becoming team manager and financial supporter. Katie, a talented artist, taught music and oil painting.

Following Dent's death in 1934, Katie went to Denver, where she became a clerk for the state Legislature. At age sixty, she passed the examinations for admission to the Industrial Commission. She worked in the commission for the next twenty-three years, retiring at age eighty-three. She returned to Brush, where she died at age ninety-nine.

Robert Dent Davis and Katie Davis are buried in the First Addition, in Block C, Lot 24. There is a marker.

Joslin, Riley S. (1860 – 1937)

A native of Clayton, New York, Riley Joslin came west in 1880, at age twenty. First settling in Illinois, he married Ada McIntosh. A year later, he continued west, staying in Iowa, Nebraska, and Kansas, before permanently settling near Brush, in 1899. He purchased a large parcel of land outside Brush, where he raised cattle. He built a fine home in town for his family, which still stands at 402 Carson Street. His cattle were shipped to eastern markets by rail.

Involved in all aspects of local business and town promotion, Joslin built a grain elevator in 1906. It is still in operation as the Cox Grain Company. That same year, he made John Needham a partner in the business. This partnership expanded to sheep feeding, oil stations, and the formation of the Farmers State Bank in 1915.

He served on the board of directors for the bank, as well as a director of the Carnegie Library, contributing funds for the lighting system.

Riley Joslin is buried next to his wife Ada, in the North Section, Block E, Lot 35. There is a marker.

Kimsey, James P. (1844 – 1921)

Born in Perry County, Illinois, James served with the Illinois Infantry during the Civil War. In 1865, he settled at the Union Colony near Greeley. He worked as a miner, Indian fighter, buffalo hunter, and rancher.

In 1877, he married Anna S. Nelson in Greeley. That same year, he formed a partnership to buy land near Brush. He moved his family to Brush in 1882. Their first home on Railroad Street still stands. Electricity was installed in 1935.

The first church service was conducted in the Kimsey home in 1883. Involved in the community development, James Kimsey led the organization of the Brush School District, becoming school board president.

The Kimsey family plot is located in the First Section, in Block D, Lot 2. James and Anna are buried next to Anna's father, Thorkel Nelson, who crossed the Plains on the Oregon Trail to California and back.

Raugh, Samuel (1842 – 1904)

A native of Pennsylvania, young Sam was raised in middle of the Allegheney Mountains. In 1864, he traveled west with a team of oxen, eventually arriving in the Colorado Territory. He worked as a miner in Black Hawk for several years. In 1871, he came to the eastern Plains to raise cattle.

In 1883, he purchased land six miles south of Brush, where he built a home and raised cattle and horses. His prized livestock was sold throughout the state, with several head being purchased by Buffalo Bill Cody. He married Sarah M. Johnston in Yuma, in 1894. The couple had one child, Mildred, born in 1895. Samuel Raugh died in February 1904. Sarah managed the ranch and the cattle business. She built a home in Brush in 1911, where she frequently entertained. She was an active member of the community the Presbyterian Church. Their daughter, Mildred, a graduate of the Brush school system, died at age thirty-four. Sarah died of a heart attack in January 1934.

The Raugh family plot is located in the Original Section, in Block 2, Lot 11.

Samples, John Knox (1860 – 1929)

Born to a prominent Kentucky family, John Samples began his journey west with his parents, as a boy. The family farmed in Missouri. In 1878, at age eighteen, he ventured out on his own. He worked as a ranchhand and cowboy on the Colorado Plains near Deer Trail. While working as a foreman at the Shaefer Deer Trail Ranch, near Weldona, he met and married Daisy May Vedder, in 1893. "JK," as he was known, homesteaded in the Weldona area, where his children were born.

In 1910, he moved his family to Brush, where he opened a butcher shop. He later operated a ranch northwest of Snyder.

A leading member of Morgan County, Samples served several terms as county commissioner and was active in the building of the Carnegie Library at Brush. In 1924, Governor Sweet appointed him State Water Commissioner.

John Samples is buried next to his wife Daisy, in the Original Section, in Block 2, Lot 38.

EBEN EZER CEMETERY

LOCATED WEST OF BRUSH, JUST SOUTH OF HIGHWAY 34. THIS IS A PRIVATE CEMETERY AND PERMISSION TO VISIT IS REQUESTED.

This Lutheran Seminary, established in 1905, was the life-long work of Pastor Jens Madsen. A Danish immigrant with a passion to help those in need, he persuaded the Deaconess Motherhouse to purchase land west of Brush for a sanatorium. Many tuberculosis patients were advised to seek the high, clear, dry climate of Colorado for relief. Pastor Madsen and his wife provided care and medical attention. His dedication is self-evident in the name he chose for his sanatorium. Eben Ezer means "Stone of Help." At first a small sanctuary of tents, by 1905, a two story building had been constructed and served as the first hospital for the surrounding area. Within the year, the institution had nearly 1,000 patients.

The beautiful architecture and landscaping was designed by Pastor Madsen. The private cemetery, located near the church, is the final resting spot for the many pastors and nuns who dedicated their services to the care of others.[13] Near the Cross of the Calvary, the pastors are buried, while the nuns lay in the shadow of the cross, watched over by the life-size statues of Mary and John. Jens Madsen is buried in Section 8. The outer edge of the cemetery is reserved for the burials of the administrators.

FORT MORGAN

SITE OF OLD FORT MORGAN

This military post was established in 1864, a mile from the South Platte River on the Overland Trail. Originally called Camp Tyler, in honor of Captain Clinton M. Tyler, the name was eventually changed to Morgan.[14] The United States government established the post because of the many Indian attacks on travelers, and the continuing unrest following the Sand Creek Massacre.[15]

Just east of the site of Fort Morgan lies the city's first burial ground; the military cemetery of Old Fort Morgan. The graves of thirteen unknown soldiers are buried here, as well as what are believed to be civilian travelers. Incomplete government records do not reveal the names of those interred.[16]

This historical site is now adjacent to the United Presbyterian Memorial Garden.

RIVERSIDE CEMETERY
601 W. 8TH AVENUE

This cemetery, established in the early 1890s, contains many of the reinterred bodies of the soldiers of Fort Morgan. The oldest marked burial is that of a reinterred soldier, dated 1864. The land is believed to have been donated by founding father, Abner S. Baker. Early records are not available. There are several religious and fraternal sections, and many burials are recorded by block and plot.

The landscape of the cemetery takes on a unique shape, that of a flower, or wagon wheel. Winding walkways and flowers grace the area. Sections A through H are part of the original cemetery. Section I (1-2-3) is the original Potter's Field. According to the records, all lots are filled, although, there are few visible headstones. Grand evergreen trees, shrubs and flowers grace the winding paths, and stone benches adorn the grounds.

The Veteran's Section is located in Section D, with a monument dedicated to those who served in the Civil War. Of note is a monument in Section G, memorializing General Jarres Jewel, one-time Commander-in-Chief of the Grand Army of the Republic. He is buried in the Arlington National Cemetery.

Baker, Abner S. (1841 – 1898)

A Civil War veteran, Baker came west to pursue a new beginning at the Union Colony of Greeley, Colorado, becoming one of the original members. There he learned irrigation and ditch building techniques, and eventually married.

In 1884, he settled in the area of what would become Fort Morgan. He built the Morgan Irrigation Canal, accessing the Platte and Bijou rivers as a water supply to the community, opening over 25,000 acres for agriculture, bringing more settlers to the area.

Baker surveyed and filed a plat in 1884. He promoted the town's growth and assured the support of the Burlington Railroad.

He is buried next to his wife, Sarah, in the family plot, in Section C , Block 3, Lot 11.

Clatworthy, Kate Maria Baker (1856 – 1937)

Kate was a sister of town founder, Abner S. Baker. Along with her husband William, Kate was instrumental in laying the foundation of Fort Morgan. From naming the streets, to planting trees, to forming the first school, she also set the social standards. She was deeply involved with the Women's Christian Temperance Union, serving a term as state secretary. Her association with this group allowed her to make Fort Morgan a "dry town," free of alcohol.

She also started the Riverside Cemetery Association and was a charter member of the DAR.

She is buried in the family plot in Section C, Block 3, Lot 12.

Clatworthy, William H. (1856 – 1944)

William Clatworthy was an infant when his parents immigrated from England, settling in Wisconsin. In 1883, he brought his young wife and baby daughter to the Union Colony at Greeley, Colorado, where his brother-law was engaged in irrigation. From there, he followed his brother-in-Law, Abner Baker, to Fort Morgan. Within a year, he had invested his life savings of fifty dollars in hardware and a brick building. He opened the first hardware store on Main Street.

He went on to be the first postmaster and served as mayor in 1897. He fostered town improvement including parks, hospitals and the fire department.

He is buried in the family plot in Section C, Block 3, Lot 12.

Dick, Philip K. (1928 – 1982)

A writer of science fiction, Philip Dick wrote some thirty-five novels. He received the Hugo award in 1962 for his writing. He gained national fame when his novels were made into Hollywood movies, including *Blade Runner,* and *Total Recall,* starring Arnold Schwarzenegger.

In his memory, the annual Philip K. Dick Award was established for best original paperback novel. One biographer said Dick "lived in obscure poverty until his untimely death." Philip Dick died of heart failure following a stroke, in Santa Ana, California.

He is buried in Section K, Block 1, Lot 56. Beside him lies his twin sister, Jane, who died in infancy.

Fort Morgan Museum
Mary Katherine Weimer
Killed in crossfire.

Eyser, Charles P. (1856 – 1916)

Charles Eyser served as marshal of Fort Morgan for four years and was a life-long resident. Following a tip on bootlegging occurring in the "dry town," Marshal Eyser went to the upper living quarters of the Godfried Weimer's Manhattan Cafe on Main Street. Confronting one of the bootleggers, gunfire ensued. Eyser was killed and the bootlegger, John Swan was wounded. During the shoot-out, Mrs. Godfried Weimer was hit by a bullet and died instantly. All three bootleggers were arrested. John Swan was convicted of both murders; however, he managed to saw through the bars of the jail, escaped and was never heard from again.

Marshal Eyser is buried in Section B, Block 3, Lot 5, next to his second wife, Louisa.

Miller, Lewis E. (1867 – 1936)
Miller, Mattie L. (1872 – 1963)

Lewis and Mattie were the parents of famed band leader Glenn Miller. They raised their four children in Fort Morgan, where Glenn played football, the tallest player on the team of 1921. He was voted the best left end in the state by the Colorado Sports Association.

Yet music was his true love. After graduation from Fort Morgan High School, he went on to Colorado University at Boulder for one year, majoring in music. Glenn Miller went on become one of the most popular big band leaders in America, with such hits as *Chattanooga Choo-Choo*, and *Moonlight Serenade*.[17]

The parents of Glenn Miller are buried in Section I, Block 5, Lot 22.

Weimer, Maria Katherine Becker (1864 – 1916)

Maria and her husband, Godfried Weimer, owned the Manhattan Café on Main Street. In the fall of 1916, she rented rooms above her cafe' to three men, including John Swan.

Marshal Eyser confronted the trio above Mrs. Weimer's cafe, looking for evidence of bootlegging. As gunfire rang out, Maria Weimer was shot in the forehead as she peeped out her door, and was killed. She left behind a husband and two small children.

Maria Weimer is buried in Section I, Block 2A, Lot 75.[18]

— — —

US Highway 6 West

PLEASANT VALLEY

PLEASANT VALLEY CEMETERY

LOCATED TWO MILES WEST OF THE COLORADO STATE LINE. FROM HIGHWAY 6, TURN SOUTH ON COUNTY ROAD 61 APPROXIMATELY TWO AND ONE-HALF MILES. THE CEMETERY IS ON THE EAST SIDE OF THE ROAD.

Established in 1885, the cemetery is also known as the State Line Cemetery. Evidence of an old wagon trail, leading west from Nebraska, angles north of the cemetery. A few of the cemetery burials are family members of those who traveled the old trail. While the cemetery is well maintained through volunteer efforts, there are few actual records of burials.

There are several family plots, including the Martin family. Robert F. Martin, born in 1851, brought his wife Charity, and nine children to Colorado in 1886. The family homesteaded in Phillips County, some twelve miles east of present-day Holyoke. Robert worked his farm, while Charity raised the children. The family was well respected in the community.

Robert died in 1925, followed by Charity in 1950. They are buried in the Martin family plot with their sons, Harry, Joseph, Lester, and other family members. There are markers to their memory.

HOLYOKE

HOLYOKE CEMETERY

LOCATED ONE MILE EAST OF THE JUNCTION OF HIGHWAYS 6 AND 385. TURN SOUTH ON COUNTY ROAD 41. THE CEMETERY IS THREE-QUARTERS-MILE ON THE RIGHT SIDE OF THE ROAD.

The cemetery was formed and laid out in 1888. One hundred dollar shares were issued to pay for the land. Burial records date to 1889, although several unmarked graves exist. The land is well landscaped, with pruned trees and grass. The layout is circular, with diamond shaped plots. It is enclosed by a wrought iron fence, linked by brick pillars. The obvious community pride makes this one of the most beautiful resting spots in northeast Colorado.

Evans, Scott C. (1857 – 1949)

The first permanent settler in the Phillips County area, Scott Evans drove a team and spring wagon from Chichasa County, Iowa, in 1886. He homesteaded and built the first house in the area, just east of present-day Holyoke. The lumber was hauled from Julesburg, across the South Platte River by boat and then loaded on a wagon for the final journey to the homestead. For water, Evans built the first well by hand, which was 180-feet deep. The well was later used by the railroad workers during construction.

As the population increased in those first years, Evans opened the first school, held in his home. Later, after he had proved up on his land, he returned to Iowa, in 1888, to bring out his bride, Mattie Mabel. Their son was the first child born in Phillips County.

The couple worked as teachers in the town of Holyoke, while continuing to farm. There was no undertaker in Holyoke, so Mr. and Mrs. Evans laid out many of their neighbors. Their efforts were simple and primitive, but served the community need.

Following the founding of Holyoke, Mr. Evans served as deputy clerk, while Mrs. Evans spearheaded social activities. Evans was a true founding father and pioneer of the Holyoke area.

He is buried in Circle T, Section E.

Goddard, Samuel D. (1857 – 1931)

Sam Goddard homesteaded land about twelve miles north of the site of Holyoke, in 1886. The following year, his wife Mary, and his two young sons, Clifford and Roy, traveled west by train.

No water was available on the homestead, it was hauled from a nearby farm. Food during those first hard years consisted of rabbits, snow birds and doves. Sam spent the harvest months in Greeley, digging potatoes to make ends meet, until his farm matured. Eventually, water was provided by ditching, and crops were raised. A fine cattle herd was acquired and the family began to prosper.

Sam invested in stock at the struggling Paoli State Bank and helped organize the Phillips County State Bank in Holyoke. He was president of the Paoli Bank and vice president of the Holyoke bank at the time of his death in 1931, at the height of the Great Depression.

Following Sam's death, both banks failed, Mrs. Goddard suffered the losses, and was forced to sell her home and land.

Sam and Mary are buried together in the family plot in Circle C, Section F.

Heginbotham, John B. (1849 – 1936)

A native of Manchester, England, Heginbotham arrived in America with his parents in 1861. The family settled in Ohio, where John grew to manhood. He married Melissa Happy in 1887.

A building contractor, he came to Holyoke when the Lincoln Land Company advertised town lots for sale.[19] He built the original grade school building, and was instrumental in the formation of the First Methodist Church.

He was a financial backer in the first bank in Holyoke, the Farmers and Merchant Bank, in 1888. In subsequent years, other banks were formed, only to succumb to the power of Heginbotham's bank. In 1901, the bank was nationalized under federal regulations and became the First National Bank.

A stalwart of the community, he financially helped many farmers through his bank, and served as treasurer of Holyoke for twenty years. One of the wealthiest of Holyoke's pioneers, he died in 1936.

He is buried in the family plot in Circle T, Section N.

Heginbotham, William E. (1879 – 1968)

The son of John and Melissa E. Heginbotham, William grew up in the early years of Holyoke's existence. He graduated from Holyoke Public School in 1896 and received a registered pharmacist certificate in 1900. In 1901, he entered the banking business with his father and was president of the Holyoke First National Bank for many years.

He married Catherine Sellers in 1916. The lavish wedding was followed by a honeymoon in Hawaii. While the couple were the envy of Holyoke, the community did not agree with the extravagance, given the atmosphere of World War I.

Following his return, William became manager of the Phillips County Fair, a position he held for several years. The present fairground was built under his supervision. He served as town clerk and city manager from 1918 until 1932. During this time the water, electrical and sewage systems were installed.

In addition to his public service, he gave privately as well. During World War I, he organized the Holyoke Enlistment Board and headed the War Bond and food rationing drives. He gave large donations to the churches, American Legion, and funded the Melissa Hospital in Holyoke, named for his mother.

During the Depression, his wealth was greatly enhanced. Many family homes and farms facing foreclosure, accepted quit claim deeds from Heginbotham. The destitute were relieved of their burden and had cash for a new start. Heginbotham became a millionaire in real estate acquisitions.

At the time of his death in 1968, his will stated that his fortune
was to be used "for the betterment of Phillips County." Through the
years, the Heginbotham Trust has provided a school auditorium, a
nine-hole golf course, low income housing, ambulance garages, and
the cemetery fence, just to name a few.

He is buried Circle T, Section N.

Helland, William G. (1856 – 1922)

A native of New York City, William Helland was diagnosed with
"consumption" at age twenty-one. Following his doctor's advice, he
traveled west for relief of his condition.

He first worked in Nebraska and Baggs, Wyoming. He married Ada
Annetta Adair in 1882 and worked in North Bend, Nebraska, before
moving his family to a homestead three miles east of Holyoke, in 1886.
Their small prairie home was a dirt dugout. The following spring, a
daughter was born, but died ten days later. In 1892, one-year-old
Ethel died from a snake bite.

While the Helland family struggled with tragedy, the drought and
no livestock, they somehow managed. After nine hard years on the
prairie, they were able to sell their land and purchase a place in town.

William became the first justice of the peace, first town assessor,
county judge and clerk of the district court for twenty-four years. He
was the driving force, and contributed monetarily to the building of
the Methodist Church of Holyoke. Unfortunately, he died before the
church was completed.

He is buried with his wife Ada, who died in 1924. Their graves are
located in Circle C, Section D.

Wilcox, George Sr. (1857 – 1938)

A native of Pennsylvania, George Wilcox first settled in Minden,
Nebraska. There he met and married Mary Ana Andrews in 1884.

George and Mary Ana traveled to Colorado in 1886, after learning
of the homestead opportunities. They claimed land in Phillips County,
but registered the claim in Sterling, as Holyoke did not yet exist.
George built his farmhouse with materials hauled from Julesburg.

When the town of Holyoke was built, George opened the first blacksmith shop in the town. During the disaster years involving the
drought, blizzards, grasshoppers, prairie fires and the Depression,
George barely managed to keep his farm and his business.

The hardship of the pioneer life nearly got to him. He once said he
would have left, but he did not have the money to go.

He is buried in Circle C, Section C.

HAXTUN

HAXTUN CEMETERY

LOCATED ON THE WESTERN EDGE OF HAXTUN, JUST NORTH OF HIGHWAY 6.

Anderson, Andrew J. (1853 – 1925)

A native of Sweden, Anderson came to America in 1887. He homesteaded six miles southeast of Haxtun. He built a sod house for his wife and four children who came to America in 1888.

During the drought years, Andrew and his sons made ends meet by digging potatoes in Greeley. Over the years, the family proved up on the homestead and bought a second farm near the Fairfield Community. Andrew raised Percheron horses, while his wife Edla, aided in community affairs, although she spoke little English.

The Anderson family is buried Block 5, Lot 45. There is a marker.

Edwards, Kate C. Fletcher (1860 – 1942)

As a child, Kate migrated west with her family to Kansas in the early 1880s. The drought conditions and grasshopper plagues discouraged the family and they returned to Iowa. Undaunted, Kate returned to the West with friends in a covered wagon.

Settling in Phillips County, Kate homesteaded on the land that would become the site of Haxtun. She later sold her land for a fancy price to the Lincoln Land Company, when the railroad was building toward Haxtun. She bought a homestead about six miles northeast of town, and built a fine ranch.

Albert Edwards arrived in the Haxtun area in 1891. He homesteaded some seven miles northeast of Haxtun. He supplemented his income by logging in the Colorado mountains.

In January 1894, Albert and Kate Fletcher were married. The two joined their homesteads which became one of the foremost ranching operations in the area.

Kate died in 1942, and Albert died in 1956.

The two are buried together in Block 4, Lot 21.

Hendrix, Andrew H. (1856 – 1901)

Andrew and his wife Lydia settled in Phillips County, Colorado in 1886. It was a lonely existence on the desolate, windy prairie. Six months passed before Lydia saw another woman.

Andrew and Lydia operated a general store, and offered room and board. A small farming community developed around the Hendrix business, but was destroyed by fire in 1901.

The couple were among the founders of Haxtun and were instrumental in the growth of the town.

They are buried in Block 3, Lot 15.

Nelson, Christina Skold (1845 – 1913)
Skold, Carl F. (1840 – 1888)

Of Swedish decent, Skold served in the Swedish Army. He married Christina Carlson in 1872. He brought his family to the United States in 1880, first settling in Iowa.

In 1886, the family came to Colorado where they were forced to camp near Julesburg for over a month, due to the high water of the South Platte River. They eventually homesteaded just south of Paoli. Carl died in 1888, leaving Christina to tend the land and raise their four sons.

Christina married John S. Nelson in 1891. Together, they operated a cattle ranch, with the help of the Skold boys. Later, the couple moved to Haxtun where Mr. Nelson was custodian at the grade school and caretaker of the Haxtun Cemetery.

They are buried together in Block 4, Lot 47. Carl Skold is also buried here.

Wood, James L. (1847 – 1917)

James Wood and his wife Mary, brought their four children to Colorado from Illinois in 1887. They took a quarter section of land approximately seven miles southeast of Haxtun. Here they lived for several years, in a one-room sod house. Mr. Wood was known throughout the county for his cattle and quality horses. During the drought years of eastern Colorado, he drove his livestock near Scottsbluff, Nebraska, where grazing conditions were better.

Among the earliest of Haxtun's pioneers, the Wood family left a precious heritage. James is buried in Block 3, Lot 54.

— — —

Highway 34 West

WRAY

GRANDVIEW CEMETERY

LOCATED SOUTH ON MAIN STREET, APPROXIMATELY THREE-QUARTERS-MILE.

Grandview Cemetery is located on a hill overlooking the Republic River Valley. The land was donated from a portion of William J. Dorman's homestead in 1886. The site contains the graves of one or more of the Dorman children, however there is no marker. The first marked grave is that of the Shinabarger baby, buried in 1886.

Until 1913, Mr. Dorman held control of the cemetery, at which time it was sold to a group of businessmen. The city of Wray took ownership in the 1920s.

Landscaping began under a WPA project, along with the efforts of the local Boy Scouts. Today the cemetery is a beautiful resting place.

Brown, Josephus (1840 – 1924)

One of the original pioneers of Yuma County, Josephus and his wife Sarah Bell Brown, homesteaded just north of Beecher Island in 1885. He and Sarah had twelve children. They were respected as good farmers, active in the community and involved in church functions.

They are buried together in Range 7, Lot 1.

Conway, Margaret Teresa Minahan (1859 – 1939)

Born in Illinois, Margaret moved to Ogden, Iowa with her parents in 1870. Following her education, she opened a dress shop in Ogden, which she operated successfully for several years.

She married William Clayton Conway in 1884, at Boone, Iowa. The couple eventually settled on a homestead near Armel in Yuma County, in 1886. As pioneers, they did their share to help with the formation of the community, while raising their children and tending their farm. Margaret suffered a double tragedy in 1927, losing her father and her husband.

Margaret was a driving force in promoting the Beecher Island Memorial Association. Largely due to her work, it is now one of Colorado's registered historical sites.[20]

Margaret died in 1939 at age seventy-nine. She is buried in Range 1, Lot 27, beside her husband who proceeded her in death.

Dorman, William J. (1839 – 1916)

William Dorman was born in Illinois and served in the Civil War with Company E, Tenth Illinois Cavalry, where he advanced to Second Lieutenant.

Following the war, he married Martha Stults of Illinois and traveled west for a new beginning. By 1887, the couple had settled in Yuma County where they raised their thirteen children. Their farm was located just south of Wray.

Dorman was instrumental in the town's founding and active in the community. He was the founder of Grandview Cemetery and held ownership for many years, selling just prior to his death.

He is buried beside his wife Martha, who died in 1926. They are buried in Range 2, Lot 22.

Jennings, Thomas C. (1857 – 1925)

Born in Virginia, Jennings left his home state for the West, arriving in Texas sometime in the late 1870s. He took a job on a cattle drive, making several trips on the Texas-Ogallalla Trail. As a cowboy, he led drives across Texas, Oklahoma, Kansas and Colorado. In Colorado, he became foreman of the old Bar 11 Ranch, west of Wray.[21]

In 1891, he married Mattie E. Davenport of Wray, moved to town and raised his family. He was active in community affairs, serving as marshal for a time and was elected mayor in 1921. He served as county judge, and was in his ninth year as United States Commissioner at the time of his death.

He is buried with his wife Mattie, in Range 2, Lot 31.

Parker, L.R. (1838 – 1906)

A Kentucky native, Parker served in the Civil War. Following the war, he became a Methodist minister. He married Sallie E. Wade in 1857. They settled in the Wray area in 1886, becoming one of the earliest pioneer families.

Through his ministry, he became known as one of the founders of the town of Wray. A pillar in the community, he stood for all that was moral and right, a foundation on which the town grew.

The town of Wray suspended business for Reverend Parker's funeral. The two rooms in the church were filled to capacity as the citizens paid tribute to their beloved pioneer. Burial was at the Grandview Cemetery.

His impressive family tomb is located in Range 5, Lot 20. His wife Sallie, who died in 1912, lies beside him in eternal peace.

Smith, Allen S. (1845 – 1927)

At age twenty-one, Allen Smith left his native Illinois with his new wife, Sarah for the West. By 1886, he had homesteaded some six miles southwest of Wray. Here, he farmed and made a home for his wife and nine children.

In 1907, he and his wife moved to the town of Wray where he ran a successful blacksmith shop for the next twenty years. He and his wife Sarah were active in community affairs, the Christian Church, and school activities.

Allen died in 1927 and Sarah in 1937. The two are buried together in Range 3, Lot 12.

OFF THE BEATEN PATH:
BEECHER ISLAND BATTLE SITE
(SEPT. 17, 1868)

LOCATED EIGHTEEN MILES SOUTH OF WRAY, ON COLORADO HIGHWAY 385, THEN EAST ON COUNTY ROAD 22.

Indian retaliation for the 1864 Sand Creek Massacres was swift and brutal.[22] A reported 800 settlers had been killed by 1868.

A military force of about fifty soldiers and civilian scouts was sent out to find the hostiles. The detachment, led by Major George A. Forsyth, and twenty-eight-year-old Lieutenant Frederick Beecher, followed Indians to a narrow valley near the Arikaree and Republican Rivers, in present-day eastern Colorado, (south of Wray.)

Denver Public Library
Roman Nose
The famous Cheyenne chief
was killed at the Battle of
Beecher Island in 1868.

The next morning, the soldiers were attacked by over 700 Cheyenne and Sioux warriors, led by Tall Bull, and Roman Nose, reputed killer of the Hungate family.[23] The soldiers and scouts reacted quickly, taking cover on an island in the riverbed, suffering a few casualties. Chief Roman Nose was among the first of the Indian deaths, badly damaging the morale of the warriors.[24]

The battle lasted eight days. Two soldiers finally slipped past the Indians, crawling on hands and knees for over a mile. They fled to deliver the news of the attack and get reinforcements. The soldiers on the island were forced to live on horse and mule meat. The whites held out until reinforcements arrived. In the end, the Indians retreated.

Twenty-two soldiers, and seventy-five Indians died in the fight. The Indians carried off their dead under cover of night, although several dead warriors remained, and were later buried at the site.

The memorial to the Battle of Beecher Island was erected in 1935. Today it is designated as a National Historic Landmark.

ECKLEY

ECKLEY CEMETERY

LOCATED SOUTH OF TOWN. THE CEMETERY IS ON THE SOUTH SIDE OF HIGHWAY 34.

The land for the cemetery was deeded to the city of Eckley by the Catchpole family in 1917, with additional land donated by family members in 1931 and 1932. The first known burial is that of infant, Alice E. Rice, who died in 1908.

Andrews, Loren A. (1859 – 1934)
Andrews, Mary Ann (1866 – 1959)
The couple were married in Peoria, Illinois in 1885. The following morning, the Andrews began their honeymoon in a covered wagon headed west. For the next twenty years, they farmed in various areas of Nebraska until Mary Ann filed on a homestead sixteen miles southwest of Eckley. The family settled at Eckley and started a cattle ranch.

Ranching at Eckley proved profitable for the Andrews as they eventually expanded to farming and horse breeding. Mr. Andrews was involved in the town's prosperity, while Mrs. Andrews was involved in community affairs.

They are buried together in Block 4, Lot 22.

Catchpole, Charles L. (1877 – 1965)
When Charles brought his wife Emma to Eckley, their first home was a one-room cabin about seven miles southeast of town. It was later discovered that their land was once Indian hunting grounds, as arrowheads and buffalo skulls were found throughout the area.

With time, Catchpole improved his homestead, providing a water well to the kitchen for his wife and family. In later years, he trained stallions, and wild horses.

He is buried with his wife Emma, in Block 2, Lot 8.

Coffman, Lafe E. (1884 – 1958)
From Kansas, Lafe Coffman brought his family to Eckley in 1916, where he homesteaded and did blacksmithing for the town. By 1930, he had moved into town and ran his blacksmith business until his death.

He is buried in Block 3, Lot 20.

Neuschwanger, David (1884 – 1966)
Of German descent, David Neuschwanger's parents settled in Canada and eventually came to the United States. David brought his bride Lowetta to a homestead near Eckley.

They endured the farming life, using cow chips for fuel and constantly battling the elements. They lost a daughter to dysentery in 1911. By 1941, four of their sons were in World War II.

Devoted to family and community, they were involved in church and social affairs.

They are buried together in Block 5, Lot 44.

YUMA

YUMA MUNICIPAL CEMETERY

LOCATED ONE-HALF-MILE EAST OF TOWN, ON COUNTY ROAD 39.

There is an interesting story to the naming of this community. During the building of the railroad in the 1880s, a teamster named Yuma, fell ill and died some three miles east of the present town. The area was a railroad switching point and became known as Yuma. In the 1920s, during the construction of a road, pioneer Wilber Chrismer witnessed a grave being unearthed. Knowing the site and occurrence of Mr. Yuma's earlier burial, his investigation revealed human bones, along with Yuma's rifle dated 1873.

The original community cemetery was located somewhere north of the railroad depot. The exact spot is unknown. In 1888, John B. Wescott donated a portion of his homestead, a mile east of town, to the city of Yuma as a cemetery. The graves from the old cemetery were moved to the new Yuma Cemetery. There are records of burials as early as 1886, and many unmarked graves.

Landscaping began in the early 1920s, making many improvements. Today the cemetery is a lovely park-like memorial site.

Abbott Family Plot
Abbott, John M. (1842 – 1913)

John Abbott came to Yuma County from Illinois in 1885, where he settled his family and opened the first law office in the county.[25] In three short years, his achievements led to his nomination for attorney general in 1888. He became mayor of Yuma in 1906, while serving as deputy district attorney. It is said he was a friend of Abraham Lincoln, while the two attended law school in Illinois.

John Abbott is buried with his wife Drusilla, in Lot 79.

Abbott, John G. (1880 – 1955)

The son of John M. Abbott, John G. Abbott arrived in Yuma County with his parents at age five. He became a teacher, and earned his law degree. He served on the school board, was a newspaper editor and town trustee. He entered politics, following in his father's footsteps. He too, served as mayor for a time and was elected state senator in 1932.

He is buried in Lot 79.

Bushner, Frederick W. (1860 – 1965)

One of eleven children, by the age fifteen, Frederick Bushner was working in the Pennsylvania coal mines, supplementing the family income. For the next fifty years, he worked as a farmer, drilling for water, and locating mines from Pennsylvania to New Mexico.

By 1916, he had located in Yuma County with his wife and three children. He operated a successful farm northeast of town. Following the death of his wife Marie Eva in 1931, he sold the farm and moved to town, where he married Jennie Cummins in 1934.

During these years, he read and educated himself, staying keenly alert and active until his death in 1965, at age 105.

He is buried in the new section of the cemetery, in Lot 149.

Chrismer, Charles C. (1862 – 1934)

Charles Chrismer was born at Gettysburg, Pennsylvania when the Civil War was raging literally in his backyard. His parents were forced to seek refuge in the basement while battle raged above their heads.

At age sixteen, Charles journeyed west, taking up the trade of cigar maker. He traveled from Missouri to work on the Mississippi river boats and finally settled in Yuma County in 1884. He homesteaded, started a ranch, married and raised a family.

He served as county commissioner and was founder of the Farmers State Bank, serving as director until his death.

He is buried with his wife Jennie Margaret, in Lot 123.

Fletcher, Ernest (1867 – 1941)

The Fletcher family traveled by wagon from North Carolina to Texas, a two-year journey ending in 1870. They lived on the old Chisholm Trail. At age fourteen, Ernest was persuaded by cowboys along the trail to join a cattle drive.

He worked the trails to Dodge City, Liberal, Kansas and to Colorado and Arizona. At age twenty-three, Ernest was sentenced to the Colorado Penitentiary for ten years. He was convicted of stealing a cow worth twenty dollars from a ranch that owed him money and refused to pay. He served five years before being pardoned by the governor in 1895.

Roaming from ranch to ranch, he settled in Yuma County in 1905. He started a ranch of his own, several miles southeast of Yuma. By 1910, the very successful Fletcher married and raised a family.

He is buried in Lot 37, next to his wife Carrie, who preceded him in death in 1933.

Schramm, Raimon von Harrum (1846-1907)

Involved in the cattle business in Texas, Schramm was quite well off when he arrived in Yuma in 1887. He was instrumental in building the commerce of the young town and provided many of the first brick buildings still standing today.

"Herr" Schramm, as he was known, wanted to run for mayor, but the townfolk were against it, as he was a foreigner, despite his generosity. So Schramm moved a couple of his buildings six miles east of Yuma and start a new town. He said the town of Schramm would put Yuma out of business. Yuma town leaders called an emergency meeting. Schramm was unanimously elected mayor of Yuma!

Stepanie Wommack White Photo

Grave of George J. Shopp, Civil War Congressional Medal of Honor recipient.

As for the town of Schramm, it lingered for several years, largely due to Herr Schramm's ranch. At one time, his ranch was one of the largest in the county. Parts of the ranch remain today.

The drought and grasshopper plague of the early 1890s hit Yuma County particularly hard. Schramm became the benefactor, providing jobs and creating business opportunities for the community.

He is buried in Lot 64, next to his wife, Mary, who died in 1916. The beautiful family crest adorning their monument is a testament to the family nobility and stature he claimed.

Shopp, George J. (1834 – 1924)

A French immigrant, George Shopp came to America in 1853, settled in New York, married and started a family. He fought for the Union during the Civil War, where he was wounded and cited for bravery in 1865, receiving the Congressional Medal of Honor.

He arrived in Yuma in 1890, with his family, where he worked for the railroad as a steam engine operator. He was active in community affairs and helped to build the Methodist church in 1911.

He is buried with his wife, Mary Adaline, who preceded him in death in 1906. They are buried in Lot 48. There is a military marker.

OTIS

OTIS CEMETERY
LOCATED ONE MILE SOUTH OF OTIS ON DADE STREET.

The land was deeded to the city of Otis, by James H. Stewart in 1888. Not uncommon to the many eastern prairie cemeteries, this cemetery was the victim of several grass fires. The common wooden markers of the day have long since burned or decayed, leaving many of our Otis pioneers to memory and quiet solitude. Records of the cemetery were lost in the 1890s, around the time the community almost collapsed from the hard economic times of that decade. We know the first recorded burial was Raymond R. Middlecoff in 1888.[26] However, the earliest dated tombstone is that of three-year-old Bertie Smith dated 1875. We know he was reburied at this site. Because of the lack of records, occasionally a sexton would dig a grave, only to discover an earlier burial.

Chapman, Calvin C. (1839 – 1896)

A doctor, Calvin Chapman arrived in the Otis area in 1888, where he set up his medical practice and later formed a farm loan business. He built a two-story home on the corner of Second and Arapahoe. In 1890, he purchased the First Bank of Otis.

A prominent businessman, he died suddenly in 1896, leaving a pregnant wife and a daughter.

He is buried in the southeast corner of the middle section, beside his wife, although she has no marker.

Dungan, George W. (1838 – 1935)

An early pioneer of Otis, the Reverend Dungan served in the Civil War and saw duty at the Battle of Gettysburg.

He began his pastor service in the town of Otis in 1886. He organized the Congregational Church and led the worship at the Hope School.

He retired, moving to Oregon in 1930. Upon his death in that state in 1935, his body was taken to Otis for burial.

He is buried with his wife, in the center section.

Fackrell Family Plot

George Fackrell, born in 1863, and Mabel Whitehurst Fackrell, born in 1881, were married in the Whitehurst family home north of Otis, in 1903. Their first child, John, died as an infant in 1904.

George worked odd jobs around Otis, including well digging, ditch work, and dray man. Mabel was active in social functions and the Methodist Church.

George died in an accident involving a runaway team of horses in 1906. Mabel died in 1967.

The family plot is located in the northwest section of the cemetery.

Hoopes, Samuel Y. (1822 – 1893)

Samuel Hoopes built a two-story building in 1896 that became the first drug store in Otis. He was caught in the middle of the real estate war between the west and eastside Otis merchants, led by the Lincoln Land Company. He was forced to relocate his business to the northeast corner of Second and Washington.

He and his wife Marilla were prominent early pioneers, engaged in social and business events in the community. They owned several pieces of property in the town.

They are buried together in the southwest corner of the cemetery.

Shedd, Charles (1866 – 1953)

Charles Shedd arrived in Otis in the fall of 1887, homesteading eight miles south of town. He built a frame house. Lacking a barn, his horses were stabled in the house for a time. The house burned the first winter he lived there.

He moved to town for a time following the fire, to teach school and raise money to rebuild his home. There he fell in love with one of his students. When Rean Lee turned twenty-one, in 1893, the couple were married. Several children died at birth, before a son was born. The couple remained in the town of Otis, where Shedd became heavily involved in the community, serving as school principal for several years.

He and his wife are buried side-by-side. There is no marker.

Whitehurst, William (1854 – 1938)

Born in Lancaster, Ohio, Whitehurst arrived in the Otis area in 1886, via Kansas. The following year, five additional families related to Whitehurst settled in the area. The families owned adjoining homesteads ranging from two miles north of Otis to three miles west. This became one of the largest land shares in the area.

By 1895, William had proved up on his homestead and moved to the town of Otis with his wife, Elizabeth, and daughter, Mabel. In 1901, he owned the general merchandise store and the town's only coal operation. He served Otis as justice of the peace for several years. He is also known unofficially as the pioneer historian, for it was through his efforts that much of the history of Otis is preserved.

He is buried in the center section of the cemetery, next to his wife, Elizabeth who preceded him death in 1897.

AKRON

AKRON CEMETERY

LOCATED ONE-QUARTER-MILE WEST OF TOWN, JUST NORTH OF HIGHWAY 34.

The first cemetery to serve Akron arose out of necessity, rather than planning. It was located south of the railroad track. The bodies were later moved to the new cemetery, established in 1885. However, most graves are unmarked. The oldest marked grave is that of Winnie V. Curtis who died in 1887.

The cemetery is well laid out with named lanes, a handsome fence and beautiful landscaping.

Andrews, Nathan (1853 – 1934)

A native of Ohio, Nathan Andrews grew up in the railroad industry, working construction from Ohio to Iowa. He married Eva Rilla Sturdivan of Iowa in 1883. Here they farmed for a few years, before journeying west by covered wagon. They followed the Burlington Northern Railroad route into Colorado, arriving in Akron in 1886.

At that time, Akron was a young community, with many growth possibilities because of the railroad.

Nathan and Eva established a homestead some twelve miles southwest of Akron. They lived in their covered wagon until Nathan completed their sod house, where they raised their family. They grew vegetables, and raised beef, pork, chicken and eggs, selling them in town. The Andrews family soon became a welcome and needed addition to the community.

Nathan expanded his farm to ranching, breeding cattle and horses. He was a member of the Colorado Stockman's Association. His land holdings grew to three ranches at the time of his death, although he moved to town in his declining years.

He is buried with his wife Eva, in Block 1, Section 6.

Annable, Dallas H. (1848 – 1924)

Dallas Annable brought his family to Akron in 1886, in two covered wagons. Husted Ebenezer Annable, the father of Dallas, made the long journey, only to contract pneumonia shortly after his arrival. He died a few days later and was buried in the original cemetery south of the railroad track. His was the third body interred in the cemetery. He was later removed to the new Akron Cemetery. There is no marker.

The Annable family first stayed in the back room of the E. E. Dey barber shop, as there were no accommodations in the busy young community. Later, a two-room house was built in the northwest section of town, where the family made their home.

Dallas made his living raising thoroughbred horses, and worked in the draying and hauling businesses. He also worked for the railroad and was a part-time deputy sheriff of Washington County. He was a member of the town council for many years.

He and his wife Margaret, are buried together in the original section, in Block 25, Lot 1.

Dey, Enoch E. (1861 – 1935)

A native of Cedar Rapids, Iowa, Enoch Dey settled in the Akron area in 1885, at age twenty-four. He filed on a tree claim two miles east of town. A year later, he opened a barber shop in the Commercial Hotel. There he met and later and married Belva Curtis in 1895. He later operated his own barber shop on Main Street, a business he maintained until his death.

He was very active in the church and was a member of the I.O.O.F. and Modern Woodman Associations. He was a member of the first board of trustees of Akron in 1887. He was a chief of the volunteer fire department and served as the county coroner for several years.

In April 1935, Dey became ill and closed his barber shop for the first time. He died two months later. The funeral was held at the family home, due to the frail health of Mrs. Dey.[27]

Interment was in the family plot in Block 1, Section A.

Ferry, Richard C. (1843 – 1933)

Ferry was a native of New York and served in the Union Army with Company K, 1st Regiment of Ohio. He married Naomi Stockwell of New York in 1871. They lived in Pennsylvania and Ohio, before coming to Colorado in 1886, where the couple filed on a preemption claim northwest of Akron.

He was employed by the Burlington Northern Railroad. He served as mayor of Akron for several years, and served on the school board. He was a member of the local I.O.O.F. lodge and was active in the church functions of the town community.

He is buried with his wife, Naomi, in Block 2, Section B.

Little, William (1835 – 1914)

Born in Virginia, William's parents were early American pioneers. It is said his father was with General George Washington during the American Revolutionary War, and was a friend and neighbor of the nation's first president.

William made his way west by covered wagon, through Ohio and Iowa, where he met and married Elizabeth Worley. The couple moved on to Nebraska, where their seven children were born. In the spring of 1885, all the three daughters died of diphtheria. The family chose to move away from the "plague."

By train, Little brought his family to Washington County, where they settled near Hyde. Their first home was a soddy. After proving up on the preemption, the family moved to town, where Little became involved in real estate. He was instrumental in many of the political functions of early Washington County.

Years later, he and his wife Elizabeth, moved back to the family homestead, where Elizabeth died in 1910. William continued on until his health failed. He died in 1914.

He is buried next to Elizabeth, in Block 4, Section B.

Pickett, Horace Greeley (1844 – 1939)

H.G. Pickett was born in Peoria, Illinois, where his father was a newspaper editor. In Peoria, Horace grew up and learned the printing trade. During his childhood, he accompanied his father on several trips to the law office of Abraham Lincoln, his father being a personnel friend of Lincoln's.

When he was seventeen, Horace joined the 37th Illinois Volunteers and fought in the Civil War. He was later appointed principal musician. He was involved in battles at Pea Ridge and Vicksburg. Following the war, he held several positions including railroad work, and mail clerk.

The pioneer spirit took hold and he headed west. At Lincoln, Nebraska, he married Miss Margaret Hennessey.

In 1885, Pickett was persuaded by a land agent to come to the prairie town of Akron, Colorado. There, he and his family filed on a preemption claim. When ownership requirements were met, the family moved into the town of Akron. Pickett became editor of the *Pioneer Press* in 1886, purchasing the paper ten years later.

When the town of Akron was incorporated in 1887, Pickett served as the first mayor. He served on the district court from 1896 to 1908, was justice of the peace from 1914 to 1921, an Elder of the Presbyterian Church, and a member of the Akron Lodge. He was a personnel friend of Colorado's first governor, John L. Routt. He attended the seventy-fifth anniversary reunion of the Civil War Veterans in 1938. He was ninety-four years old when he made the trip to Gettysburg, Pennsylvania.

He died a year later in Akron, Colorado. He is buried with his wife, Margaret, in Block 1, Section A, Lot 8.

Yeamans, John E. (1857 – 1936)

A native of Iowa, John Yeamans came to Akron by way of Nebraska in 1885. He was among the first pioneers to settle permanently in the area. Anticipating the coming of the railroad, he built a brick building, opened a merchandise store, and promoted the town of Akron. He later bought and sold cattle.

He became the first town clerk, served on the town board for seventeen years, and was a founder and board member of the Washington County Hospital. He served as county coroner, and for a brief time was town marshal.

His social activities included a large contribution to the building of the Methodist Church, which he served as superintendent of the Sunday School for many years.

He is buried with his wife Sadie, in Block 4, Section 8.

KUNER

GERRY CEMETERY

LOCATED TWO MILES NORTH OF THE ORIGINAL SITE OF THE KUNER PICKLE COMPANY, THEN EAST ONE-QUARTER-MILE ON ROAD 388.

Colorado Historical Society

Elbridge Gerry
Colorado's "Paul Revere"

The Gerry Cemetery is the final resting place of Elbridge Gerry and his family. Known as "Colorado's Paul Revere," Elbridge Gerry deserves a prominent spot among our pioneers. He may have single-handedly prevented total destruction along the South Platte River Trail during the Indian raids of 1864 and 1865.

A colorful character, he is believed to have been the grandson of Elbridge Gerry, one of the signers of the Declaration of Independence. A trapper, Gerry came west in the 1830s. He became an agent at the Fort Laramie trading post during the gold rush of 1849. He married four times, all Indian women. He had four children by Kate Smith, a half breed, and many more children by his other wives.

He established the Gerry Trading Post at the confluence of Crow Creek and the South Platte River, some ten miles east of Greeley, later the site of a farming community and pickle factory called Kuner. He maintained peace with the Indians, acting as a negotiator for the government until war broke out.

In August 1864, more than 100 Indians gathered for an attack along the South Platte River Trail, heading west into Denver. An Indian relative of Gerry's wife alerted him to the attack. Gerry left immediately on his "Paul Revere" ride to alert the governor in Denver.

Along the way, he spread the news, changed horses and made the trip in record time. He arrived at Governor Evans' home the following midnight. The governor sent warnings via the telegraph to the east, along the trail, and troops were mobilized.

The Indians, realizing their plan had been thwarted, changed direction. Stage stops, ranches, homesteaders and travelers were assaulted, burned out and murdered. Denver and Fort Latham were protected, due to Gerry's warning.

Gerry became a local hero, but suffered at the hands of the Indians. They ran off his livestock, and constantly threatened and attacked his ranch. He lost everything and petitioned the government for financial aid. Eight years later, he received compensation – about half of what he had lost.

Gerry died at his home at age fifty-seven. He was buried on his ranch, on a knoll overlooking his land. His headstone reads:

First permanent white settler in Weld County.[28]

The community erected an iron fence in the 1930s and has since maintained the area.

LATHAM

FORT LATHAM CEMETERY

LOCATED ON THE NORTH SIDE OF HIGHWAY 34, JUST ACROSS THE SOUTH PLATTE RIVER BRIDGE, SOUTHEAST OF GREELEY.

The first known burial was in 1861, the last in 1873. Most of the bodies were removed when Highway 34 was built.

The small community grew around a fort-like stage station along the South Platte River. Because of the sturdy fortress, the site was used to shelter settlers during the turbulent Indian wars in the 1860s. The "100-Day Volunteers" trained here in 1864, prior to the Indian campaign. Latham was once the county seat of Weld County.

This tiny cemetery is all that remains of the once important fort along the mighty South Platte River. Abandoned, the cemetery contains a stone that reads:

Only known buried here
Magdalena Simon 1809 – 1861 and two infant sons
Several others unknown

A marker erected in 1927 at the corner of a nearby house reads:

Site of Latham Station at junction of Denver and California Overland Stage routes 1859 – 1870. Refuge from warring Indians. Camp of Colorado 100-day volunteers 1864. U.S. Post Office, store and school 1864-1870. County seat of Weld County, Colorado Territory 1865 – 1876.[29]

— — —

Highway 36 West

ARMEL

ARMEL CEMETERY

LOCATED THREE MILES NORTH OF HIGHWAY 36, AT THE TOWN OF ARMEL. FROM ARMEL, TAKE COUNTY ROAD 15 NORTH. THE CEMETERY IS AT THE INTERSECTION WITH ROAD PP.

The cemetery was established at the turn of the century. The first recorded burial was in 1905. The cemetery is still in use and maintained to a degree.

Beck, William (1849 – 1900)

A native of Pennsylvania, Beck arrived in Yuma County in 1889, one of the earlier pioneers. He ran the general store at Lansing and was instrumental in the town's prosperity.

He is buried in Row 7, Grave 14.

Breninger, Armel S. (1857 – 1932)

Born in Ohio, Armel Breninger came to Yuma County by way of Iowa and Nebraska, filing a homestead in 1889. He was the founder of the the small farming community known as Armel. Heavily involved in politics, he was also highly respected for his social and moral commitments, which were the foundation of the town.

He served as an Elder of the Church of Christ until 1910, and donated a portion of his land for the town cemetery.

He is buried in Row 4, Lot 27.

Chase, Jacob Armstrong (1854 – 1930)

Jacob Chase was born in Meigs County, Ohio, where he grew up and was educated. He began teaching at age sixteen and later became a Baptist preacher.

He came to Armel by way of West Virginia, arriving shortly after the turn of the century. It was here that he chose to make a home for himself and his orphaned niece. He never married.

He farmed his land and became a valuable part of the community for twenty-three years, where he was known fondly as "Uncle Army." He is buried in Row 4, Lot 6.

Harding Family Plot (May 31, 1935)

Josiah F. Harding, his wife Harriet and twelve-year-old son Roland Jay, lost their lives in the flood of the Arickaree and Republican Rivers in May 1935.

They had settled in Southeast Yuma County just two years previous to their deaths. Nine children survived their death.

They are buried in Row 9, in the family plot.

Pleis, Gottlieb (1860 – 1934)

Escaping the military of nineteenth century Germany, Pleis came to America. He settled in the Lansing Valley in 1893. He built up his homestead and became a respectable part of the community.

Regarded as one of the early pioneers of Armel, he is buried in Row 6, North Section Number 5.

IDALIA

SAINT JOHNS EVANGELICAL CEMETERY

FROM THE IDALIA JUNCTION AT HIGHWAY 36 AND 385, GO SOUTH ON HIGHWAY 385 TO COUNTY ROAD 7, THEN WEST FOR ONE AND ONE-HALF MILES TO THE CEMETERY.

The land for the cemetery was deeded to the church in the 1880s by Franz Helling. The first recorded burial was the Franz's infant son in 1888.

Bettex, Edward (1865 – 1930)

Born in Germany, Edward Bettex left for America at age fifteen. At St. Louis, Missouri, he entered the Theological College. There he married Hulda Hoeberle, daughter of the college president.

He settled his family at Idalia in 1903, where he became pastor of the German Evangelical Church. He was a prominent figure in establishing Idalia's social and moral values.

He is buried in Block 5, Lot 4.

Boden, Margaret Grecha (1862 – 1923)

At age twenty-four, Margaret and her new husband, Nanne Boden, left Germany for the United States. Eventually homesteading near Idalia in 1888, the couple raised ten children.

Mrs. Boden, a pioneer to the area, was strong in social and moral leadership. Respected in the community and active in school functions, she was also an instrumental part of the community church.

She is buried in Block 1, Lot 8.

Lehman, Henry S. (1854 – 1923)

Henry Lehman was born in St. Joseph, Missouri. As an infant, he began his journey west with his mother, following the death of his father. He was raised in Kansas and eventually settled near Idalia with his own family, in 1885. A dedicated farmer and loyal to his neighbors, he was a leading citizen in the community.

He is buried in Block 1, Lot 7.

Moellenberg, Casper H. (1858 – 1931)

Young Casper migrated from his German homeland, arriving in Idalia in 1888. One of the town founders, he was respected throughout the community as an honest business leader. He married Mary Fisher in 1892. Ten children were born to the union.

He is buried in Block 4, Lot 2.

Warner, Olaf Johnson (1870 – 1936)

A native of Sweden, Warner migrated to America in his youth. He eventually settled in Yuma County in 1889. He owned a store about three and a half miles south of Hale in the southeast corner of the county.

A lifelong bachelor, he was known to read by lamp light into the night. In August 1936, a fire destroyed the store. Mr. Johnson could not be saved.

Funeral services were held at the Evangelical Church near Idalia, with burial at the St. Johns Evangelical Cemetery.

He is buried next to his brother Andrew in Block 1, Lot 10.

LUCAS MEMORIAL CEMETERY

LOCATED THREE MILES WEST OF IDALIA ON HIGHWAY 36, THEN ONE-HALF-MILE NORTH ON COUNTY ROAD AA.

The land was donated to the community by Andrew Lucas. His intent was to provide a resting place at no charge for anyone regardless of race, religion or creed. That policy remains in effect today. The cemetery is landscaped to a degree and volunteers perform the maintenance.

Davisson, Augusta Shields (1864 – 1956)

Augusta left her native Germany for America, arriving in 1889. She found work in Denver, Leadville and Grand Junction. She married Daniel Shields of Yuma County and there, made her home.

She helped Shields raise his two sons and run the Wineglass ranch on the Arickaree River near Idalia. Following the death of Daniel in 1892, Augusta ran the ranch on her own. By 1921, she had leased the ranch and lived with her daughter. A true pioneer and faithful to the community, she died at age ninety-two.

She is buried in Row 1, Number 23, just north of the entrance gate.

Dieckman, Adolf August (1897-1922)

Twenty-five-year-old Adolph was the oldest son of Mr. and Mrs. J.F. Dieckman, who owned a homestead near Idalia. He was killed instantly when lightening struck at the home of his parents.

The funeral was held in the family home, with burial in the Lucas Memorial Cemetery, Row 8, Number 4.

Fox, Emmett A. (1887 – 1928)

Emmett Fox was considered a pioneer of the Idalia area. He and his brothers Bud and John, operated the Fox Brothers Ranch, one of the largest ranches in Yuma County.

His death was due to an illness resulting in paralysis.

He is buried in Row 2, Grave 5.

Nash, James O. (1849 – 1934)

An early settler of the Idalia community, James Nash came to the area from his native Illinois, by way of Kansas. He homesteaded near Idalia in 1916. He was very active in town affairs, and a faithful member of the Baptist Church.

Funeral services were held at the home of his daughter on Sunday March 25, with the burial following at the cemetery.

He is buried in Row 4, South Number 1.

JOES

JOES "NEW HOPE" MENNONITE CHURCH CEMETERY

LOCATED ONE AND ONE-HALF MILES EAST OF JOES ON HIGHWAY 36. THE CEMETERY SITS JUST EAST OF THE CHURCH.

The land was deeded to the Mennonite Brethren Church of New Hope by Abraham Heinrichs in 1916. The oldest recorded burial is that of infant Katherina Krause in 1896.[30]

Klassen, Abraham (1852 – 1900)
Klassen, Katherina (1854 – 1941)

Born in Russia, Abraham Klassen fled with his wife Katherina to America in 1876, to escape religious persecution. Settling in Kansas for seventeen years, they moved family and belongings by covered wagon to the Joes area in 1896.

Abraham homesteaded land near Joes and built a sod house for his wife and nine children. His farm later became one of the most prosperous in the county at the time of his death in 1900.

Katherina continued the operation of the family farm with the help of her surviving children. An adjoining homestead was later purchased.

This pioneer woman was highly respected in the community. She was laid to rest next to her husband in 1941. They are buried in the west half of Row 2.

Klassen, Henry (1896 – 1951)

The son of Abraham and Katherina, Henry was born in Colorado a few years after his parents settled here from Russia.

Following the death of his father in 1900, typhoid fever swept the county, taking the life of one of his older sisters. Young Henry soon contracted the illness. His mother and sisters nursed him through a difficult recovery.

Henry filed on a homestead just north of Kirk, married Agnes Braun of Nebraska, and brought her to Yuma county to make their home. The family struggled and endured the ravages of the prairie; fire, dust storms and drought.

He was a prominent member of the Mennonite Brethren Church, a member of the school board, serving as president for several years.

He is buried with his wife Agnes in the Klassen family plot in the west half of Row 2.

Nikkel, Henry P. (1881 – 1920)

Born in Kansas, Henry Nikkel came to Yuma County as an infant with his parents in 1882. Completing his education in the Yuma schools, he started his own cattle ranch. In 1908, he married Miss R. Belle Earl. In 1913, the couple bought the White Brothers' store at Joes.

Moving his family to town, Nikkel became a valuable member of the Joes business district. He was instrumental in town developments, and the town grew and prospered largely due to his leadership.

He is buried in the west half of Row 1.

Tedder, George W. (1853 – 1924)

A long time resident of Joes, George Tedder was an inventor, working on a new gasoline engine when he died. His family, including his wife, resided in Kansas at the time of his death for reasons unknown.

He is buried in the east half of Row 5.

COPE

COPE COMMUNITY CEMETERY

LOCATED EAST OF TOWN, ON HIGHWAY 36. TURN SOUTH ON COUNTY ROAD 59. THE CEMETERY IS ONE-THIRD MILE.

The land for the cemetery was sold to the Cope Cemetery Association in 1899 by James F. and Elizabeth C. Beezley. The quit claim deed reveals the price as one dollar. Organization of the cemetery included the sale of family plots at a cost of one dollar to provide landscaping and erect a fence.

The earliest marked graves date to 1890. The oldest may be that of fourteen-year-old Bertie I. Brown, who died March 10, 1890.

The Cope Cemetery is a wonderful prairie setting for the departed. It is enhanced by the great volunteer work of the community residents. While there are cemetery records, they are not complete, therefore block and plot numbers are not listed.

Cope, Jonathan Calvin (1835 – 1921)

Born in Indiana, his father raised thoroughbred horses. Jonathan Cope married Mary Ann Neil in 1859. He fought for the Union during the Civil War. A war injury left him with a disabled hand.

Following the war, he came west, staying several years in Nebraska, before settling in Washington County in 1886. He filed a tree claim on the Arikaree River. By 1887, he had moved his family to the area in three covered wagons.

In the meantime, other settlers had moved into the area. Cope founded the town named in his honor. The land was surveyed, plots were staked out, and stores opened for business.

Cope's town grew slow, but steady. Sound business prevailed and morality was the rule for Cope. Soon, churches were built and a school was started. There was was no doctor in those formative years, so Mrs. Cope took on the duties. She handled the sickness, emergencies, and most of the births in those early days.

Mr. and Mrs. Cope are buried side-by-side.

Laybourn, David (1841 – 1922)

David and his wife, Nancy Jane Snodgrass Laybourn, came to Nebraska from Ohio in 1883. The family stayed in Franklin, Nebraska for a few years. They traveled by train to Cope, Colorado in 1887.

Mr. Laybourn started the first Sunday School in Cope, operating out of his home. He became the first Notary Public of Cope. His sheep herd was known to be the finest in the county.

He died in 1922 after a long illness, his wife, Nancy, died in 1932.

Mack, William Adelbert Sr. (1855 – 1944)

Born in Illinois, young William went to work at age twenty-one. He was among the many railroad workers who built the Rock Island Railroad in 1876.

In 1887, he brought his wife Sarah, and their four children to the Cope area. The family homesteaded in Washington County, approximately ten miles north of Anton.

While Mack managed a fair living from his farm, the drought years forced him to seek better conditions. In 1895, the family moved to Iowa and then to South Dakota, before returning to the Cope area in 1906. With modern farming equipment, he employed a crew of men and operated a successful threshing business for several years, retiring in 1920.

William Sr. is buried in the family plot, next to his wife Sarah, who died in 1930. Their sons William Jr. and Melvin E. are also buried in the cemetery.

Wrape, John P. (1864 – 1947)

From Ackley, Iowa, John Wrape came to Cope with his father William and brother James, in 1887. His mother had died some years earlier, in New York. John homesteaded with his father and brother about five miles northwest of Cope.

To supplement his income, John worked mule teams in Denver, constructing streets and alleys. During his free time in Denver, he took in theater at the Tabor Opera House and had many stories of seeing H.A.W. Tabor and the lovely Baby Doe in the balcony.

A very versatile individual, he also worked in Cripple Creek and Victor during the "Gay Ninetys," working for the railroad, and even hauled buffalo bones to Nebraska for fertilizer. For four years, he hauled the mail between Seibert and Cope.

In time, John improved his homestead, expanding it to include a large cattle herd. His round pen was the finest in the country.

Ranchers all over the county used his pen for breaking horses and branding cattle.

He is buried with his wife Bessie, in the Cope Cemetery. There is a marker.

Last Chance

Swan Cemetery

From the town of Last Chance, go eight miles on Highway 71 to County Road 20. Turn left and go three miles west to County Road D. Turn right and go one mile north. Turn right at the junction and go one mile east to the cemetery.

This sad, neglected prairie cemetery once served the proud pioneer families of Last Chance in southwestern Washington County. The land is located on the Swan family ranch. Early pioneers in the area, the Swan family offered a portion of their land for a cemetery. The land remains in the possession of the Swan family.

Coles, George (1831 – 1914)

One of eastern Colorado's earliest pioneers, George Coles was a well-known and greatly respected businessman. He and his daughter operated a general store in the farming community of Abbott, located some seven miles northeast of Last Chance. Coles became postmaster serving until the town folded in the 1920s.

Coles made regular trips to Akron for supplies. It was common to see him and his team of mules travel the forty-five miles north into town and back to Abbott, loaded with supplies.

Coles died at age eighty-two. His tombstone is mixed in with a few of the veteran markers.

Kirby, William (? – 1934)

One of the most unusual tombstones in the cemetery is that of William Kirby. Engraved on the marker are the words "Unknown Sheepherder." It is a mystery as to why these words were placed on his tombstone. His obituary in the *Akron News-Reporter*, dated June 21, 1934, gives an accounting of who William Kirby was.

According to the paper, Kirby, a black man, worked as a sheepherder for a man named Joe Raska. He was in the field with his sheep, south of Last Chance on June 12, 1934, when a sudden hailstorm hit with great force. His body was found three days later, lying face down near a fence. An examination revealed no fractures, but several bruises were found, suggesting he died from the hail or lightening strikes. Around his body were sixty dead sheep. No inquest was held.

Author's photo

Fairview Cemetery, Burlington, Colorado

William Kirby was immediately buried in the nearby Swan Cemetery.

— — —

Interstate 70 West

BURLINGTON

FAIRVIEW CEMETERY

LOCATED ON THE NORTHERN EDGE OF TOWN. TAKE 15TH STREET NORTH, CROSSING THE RAILROAD TRACKS AND PAST THE FAIRGROUNDS. THE CEMETERY IS ON THE RIGHT SIDE OF THE ROAD.

In August 1888, the town of Burlington, located on the old Smoky Hill Trail, was laid out and platted. By September of that year, the board of trustees accepted a donation of ten acres of land for the cemetery. The land was fenced and recorded as the Fairview Cemetery.

The cemetery is neatly laid out and well maintained. As with many cemeteries, the older stones are generally located toward the center.

Boger, Andrew (1836 – 1920)

A native of Bald Eagle, Pennsylvania, Andrew Boger left his home for the West at an early age. First settling in Illinois, he married Abigail Brown, in 1860. In August 1862, he joined the 102nd Illinois Infantry Volunteers, serving as a Union soldier throughout the war. Following the war, Andrew returned to Illinois, where he owned a farm and raised his six children.

In 1900, at age sixty-four, he and his wife Abigail, came to Kit Carson County, where two of their sons, Frank and Ed lived. Andrew liked the country and built a home for he and Abigail, some fifteen miles north of Seibert. Andrew farmed the land for most of the next twenty years of his life.

Andrew and Abigail are buried together. There is a marker.

Boger, Ed (1866 – 1908)

The third born son of Andrew and Abigail Boger, Ed came to Colorado with his brother Frank, in 1885. They worked as cowboys on several different ranches, and did some mining in the gold fields of Leadville and Cripple Creek. The brothers also ran a freight wagon between Colorado Springs and Cripple Creek.

In 1890, they took squatters rights on land in Kit Carson County, just west of Vona. They lived in a small dugout for the first few years. Both brothers married in the 1870s and built homes of their own on the family ranch. The Boger ranch was primarily a mule ranch.

Ed Boger died in 1908, from injuries received in a horse accident.

Andrew and Abigail Boger both died in 1920, just months apart. They are buried together, in Block 12, Lot 2. Ed is buried near them in the Boger family plot.

Davis, Elias G. Sr. (1841 – 1913)

Elias Davis came to Colorado in 1886. He filed on a preemption and tree claim along the Republican River in Kit Carson County. One of the first settlers in the area, he built a sod house and made improvements on the land before bringing his family to the homestead a year later.

Times were tough in the beginning. Their only income for the first year was from gathering buffalo bones from the prairie, which they sold for eight dollars a ton. Davis managed to purchase some cattle, and eventually had a fine ranch. Before the town of Burlington was established, the post office was at the Davis ranch, with Elias serving as postmaster.

When the town of Burlington was established, and later the county of Kit Carson, in 1889, Davis was one of the first county commissioners.

Elias G. Davis died in 1913. He is buried beside his wife, Leah, in the Davis family plot.

Davis, John J. (1857 – 1943)

John was the son of Elias Davis Sr. He came west by covered wagon with his mother, grandfather and brothers and sisters in 1887.

While helping his father start his farm, he also worked in the coal fields a hundred miles away, to help the family.

He later purchased his own land near Kirk, where he built a two-story sod house. In 1900, he married Anna Homrighaus, a member of a pioneer Kirk family. After five months of marriage, Anna died of diphtheria. A few years later, John married Amelia Homrighaus, Anna's sister.

John moved his new family back to the Davis farm in 1913. He built a large frame house and established an irrigation system from the river. His produce of fruits and grains were the finest in the county. He later contracted for haying and established a blacksmith shop.

John J. Davis is buried near his parents, Elias and Leah in the Davis family plot.

Glass, John (1812 – 1892)

A native of Wales, John Glass arrived in Kit Carson County in 1887, at age seventy-four. He helped his son-in-law, Elias A. Davis, Sr. start his ranch and worked for him until his death. He became the foster father to John J. Davis.

John Glass spent his last days in Burlington, with his family and their dreams. He is buried next to his daughter, Leah Glass Davis, the wife of Elias Sr., in the Davis family plot, in Block 17, Lot 25.

Guthrie, Peter (1849 – 1916)

Born in Scotland, Peter and his wife Clementina, sailed to America, in 1886. Peter joined his brother, already established in Philadelphia. The two worked together as contractors and carpenters.

Another brother, James, had filed on a homestead near Burlington, Colorado. In 1888, Peter received word of the death of James and traveled by train to Colorado. Arriving in Burlington, Peter soon learned his brother had been murdered in his claim shack. The body was buried on the homestead. With the help of a Burlington lawyer, S.D. King, Peter had the body of his brother exhumed and a formal inquest was made into the cause of death. The inquest revealed the cause of death as a severe blow to the back of the head. There were two suspects, but no charges were ever brought. Because his land was next to the new railroad line, and therefore very valuable, greed was rumored to be the motive behind the murder of James Guthrie.

Peter Guthrie decided to make Burlington his home. He brought his wife Clementina, eight children, and their possessions to Burlington in 1889. Filing a homestead of his own, he built a small frame farmhouse. Water had to be hauled from a well a mile away, until a well could be dug. The Guthrie farm became the largest pro-

Author's photo
John J. Pugh
An early pioneer of Burlington.

ducing farm during Burlington's early growth.

Clementina became the mother of the first set of twins in Kit Carson County. Sara and Clyde Guthrie were the pride of all of Burlington. People came from miles to see the beautiful babies. Three years later, a second set of twins was born to the already large Guthrie family.

Peter Guthrie helped make the bricks used for the first schoolhouse in Burlington, and helped to provide the moral and ethic foundation upon which the town was built and still operates to this day, the testament of a true pioneer.

Peter and Clementina Guthrie are buried in Block 15, Lot 25. There is a marker.

Hoskin, Henry G. (1871 – 1948)

Born in Cornwall, England, Hoskin set sail for America with his parents at age five. The family located in Wisconsin in 1876. When new land in eastern Colorado was opened for settlement in 1887, the Hoskin family came to the Burlington area by train. They homesteaded eight miles south of Beloit. Seventeen-year-old Henry filed for the adjoining land. Henry spent the next ten years farming the land and making a successful farm for himself and his father.

In 1904, Henry moved to Burlington, where he became clerk of the first county court. A year later he became affiliated with the Stock Growers State Bank and married Nannie B. Yersin. He purchased the Kit Carson County Abstract Company in 1916, a business he successfully ran until his death. He managed the Kit Carson County Fair for ten years and served in the State Legislature in 1927 and 1929.

Henry G. Hoskins is buried in Block 14, Lot 1. There is a marker.

Pugh, John J. (1857 – 1913)

A native of Wales, John Pugh worked in the coal mines as a youth. Completing his apprenticeship, he booked passage to Liverpool, England, and on to America, arriving in 1878. He stayed in Pennsylvania for a time, and then moved to Iowa, where he found work on the Richards farm. He moved on to New Mexico, where he learned the cattle business.

In February 1886, he returned to the Richards farm, where he married Jane Richards. The couple homesteaded land near Burlington in 1886. Shortly after their arrival, Jane gave birth to the first white child in Kit Carson County.

The Pugh homestead, located near the Republican River, became one of the most prosperous farms in the area.

John Pugh is buried in Block 15, Lot 20. There is a large granite tombstone, handsomely engraved.

Ragan, Burt (1868 – 1916)

Born in Iowa, young Burt's mother died when he was four years old. His father sent him to live with his grandparents. At age sixteen, he left Iowa on horseback, bound for the adventurous West. He stayed in Oberlin, Kansas for a year, and walked to Colorado with a wagon train.

At the small settlement of Burlington, he found work as a cowboy on a ranch north of town. Later he became foreman and earned enough money to attend two winter terms at the Franklin Academy in Nebraska. In 1899, Ragan was elected county clerk and recorder. He became president of the Republican Cattle Company, and was instrumental in the founding of the Stock Grower State Bank.

He is buried in Block 16, Lot 22. There is a marker.

OFF THE BEATEN PATH:

On a high bluff above the Republican River, just west of the Bonney Reservoir, is an Indian burial ground. A circular layer of stones marks the tomb of Cheyenne Chief Roman Nose. Roman Nose was killed on the second day of battle at Beecher Island, in September 1868. Following the battle, the Cheyennes took their dead, including their chief, southwest of the battlefield, toward the bluffs, a traditional Cheyenne custom. Changes in the course of the river, and floods, have uncovered several skeletons over the years.

LIMON

PERSHING MEMORIAL CEMETERY

LOCATED AT THE NORTHERN EDGE OF THE TOWN OF LIMON. FROM TOWN, TAKE HIGHWAY 71 NORTH TO 7TH STREET. TURN LEFT ON 7TH STREET. THE CEMETERY IS A SHORT DISTANCE FROM THIS POINT.

This cemetery is well maintained with pruned bushes, flowers and trees. The oldest known burial is dated 1896. There are several sections, all laid out in an orderly manner.

Haug, John W. (1854 – 1946)

One of the first pioneers of the area, John Haug, a native of Pennsylvania, began his mining career at age nine. He worked in the coal mines of Pennsylvania until age seventeen, when he came west with his parents by covered wagon. The family first settled in Shelton, Nebraska, where John married Mary Oliver in 1884. The couple had twelve children.

In 1889, John brought his family to Colorado, and filed a homestead twenty miles west of Genoa, in Lincoln County. In 1891, the family moved again, eighteen miles north of Limon, to what became known as the Walks Camp District. At the time of Haug's arrival, the business section of Limon consisted of one store.

During the first years at Limon, Haug worked in the mines of Walsenburg and the smelters of Denver, while Mary worked the homestead and raised the children. Within a few years, he was able to turn his homestead into a thriving cattle operation.

Following the death of his wife Mary, in 1910, Haug moved his family to the town of Limon.[31] He was a member of the Lincoln Lodge, the Masonic Lodge, and the El Jebel Shrine.

He is buried in Section 3, Lot 6.

Jenkins, Ulysses S. (1867 – 1941)

A native of Woodson County, Kansas, Ulysses Jenkins moved to the Indian Territory of Oklahoma. He herded cattle for several years and witnessed the opening of the Indian land to homesteaders. He came to Colorado in 1887, where he worked as a cowhand for several ranches in Lincoln County. Jenkins married Laurena Beadle in 1905. The couple had two children, and later homesteaded on Steel Fork Creek. He became foreman of the Hamlick Ranch near Boyero, a capacity he held for several years. During President Teddy Roosevelt's visit to Hugo in 1903, Jenkins topped the list of entertainment with his expert horse riding during the chuck wagon feast.

Active in the community, he worked to bring a school to the area and served on the first board.

Ullysses S. Jenkins is buried in Section 3, Lot 18. There is a marker.

Newberry, Daniel (1869 – 1942)

Born near Jerseyville, Illinois, Newberry brought his family west in 1910. He filed on a homestead in Lincoln County, some twenty miles northeast of Limon.

He was persuaded to run for county commissioner in 1924. Elected on the Democratic ticket, he served four consecutive terms.

Being quite active in the Methodist Church, Daniel was instrumental in establishing the Walks Camp Church, and taught the Sunday School class for three years, before moving to Limon. At Limon, he was superintendent of the Methodist Sunday School for seventeen years.

Daniel Newberry's tombstone is located in Section 5, Lot 7.

Pershing, William S. (1852 – 1942)

A native of Indiana, Pennsylvania, William Pershing was only a year old when his parents moved to Rock Island, Illinois. In 1867, he settled near Omaha, Nebraska, where he operated a ranch. He married Eliza Jane Beistline in 1873. The couple had thirteen children.

In 1885, Pershing brought his family to the Yuma area, where he was engaged in the real estate business. The grasshopper plague and floods caused him to relocate to Hugo in 1890. At Hugo, was employed with the United States government and the Union Pacific Railroad, as a land appraiser and surveyor.

He moved to Limon area in 1906, where he purchased the townsite of Limon Station from the railroad. Sectioning the land into lots, he sold the property and promoted the "new" town of Limon. Known as the founding father of Limon, he became the first mayor, serving two terms from 1906 to 1910. He served as Lincoln County surveyor from 1891 to 1907.

A recognized authority on dry farming techniques, Pershing became a consultant for colleges and national agriculturists. He planted trees throughout the town for both beauty and conservation.

More than any other individual, William Sansom Pershing promoted, and developed not only the town of Limon, but the agricultural promise of Lincoln County.

His funeral in July 1942, held at the Methodist Church, was the largest ever held in Limon. He was laid to rest in the Limon Cemetery, which he organized. The name was later changed to the Pershing Memorial Cemetery in his honor.

He is buried next to his wife Eliza, in the family plot. Their daughter, Stella is also buried in the plot, as well as members of the John Guy family. The Pershing family plot is located in Section 3, Lot 2. There is a marker.

Quist, Hans P. (1878 – 1942)

Born in Denmark, Hans Quist came to this country as a boy. The Quist family settled at Ruthland, Iowa. In 1907, Hans left Iowa and filed on a homestead south of Hugo. He married Epes Minnie Thompson, in 1909. After proving up on the homestead, he moved his family to the town of Hugo, where he opened a blacksmith shop. He later owned a hardware store.

In 1923, he moved to Limon, opening a blacksmith shop. The partnership with C.H. Holmes in 1927, allowed Quist to expand his business. The partnership lasted until Quist died in 1942.

Quist served on the town board of trustees. He was a member of the Hugo Lodge and the Modern Woodmen of America.

He is buried in Section 5, Lot 8. There is a marker.

Stevens, Howard W. (1874 – 1941)

A native of Poweshiek County, Iowa, Stevens ventured west at an early age. Working on various ranches in Oklahoma, he finally settled in Colorado in 1906. He proved up on a homestead in Lincoln County, then traded the land for a claim at Rye, Colorado, in 1926. In 1929, he bought a gas station and store at Punkin Center. Two small cabins attached to the property, were rented to travelers.

Known as a quiet, gentle man, Stevens worked hard at his business and kept to himself. He never married. For fifteen years, he operated his business at this isolated highway junction. He faced more than his share of attempts at robbery. In 1930, two young teenagers rented a cabin from Stevens. On that cold night, the kind-hearted Stevens invited the boys into his warm home for a hot meal. One of the youths went outside and proceeded to fire a gun into a window. A bullet hit Stevens in the shoulder. He managed to grab his rifle and hold the second youth. The boys were eventually sent to the reform school in Buena Vista. In July 1937, someone entered his store through a broken window, struck Stevens in the head, and tied his hands and feet together. The thief or thieves made off with a hundred dollars in cash, several items, and gasoline.

On August 29, 1941, Howard Stevens was attacked again. This time his luck ran out. Family members, Mr. and Mrs. Sears Stevens, found the body of Howard Stevens inside his store. The coroner's inquest revealed two bullet wounds to the chest and liver. He was buried two days later in the Pershing Memorial Cemetery.[32] Following the sheriff's investigation, Alfred Madsen, Jr. of Otero County, and Frank Madill of La Junta, were charged and eventually convicted of the murder.

Cemetery records concerning the interment of Howard Stevens do not record his burial location.

RIVER BEND CEMETERY

LOCATED FIVE MILES WEST OF LIMON. TAKE INTERSTATE 70 WEST FROM LIMON TO EXIT 354. FOLLOW THE DIRT ROAD NORTH, AROUND THE SMALL

*HILL. THE CEMETERY IS ON THE TOP OF THE HILL OVERLOOKING THE HIGH-
WAY.*

This small prairie cemetery served the one-time railroad town of
River Bend, in Elbert County. The cemetery is all that is left of the
once thriving community. Prairie grass and a few trees, are nature's
landscaping in this final pioneer resting spot. The oldest marked
grave is that of Susanna Mooney, who died in 1880 at age eighteen.
She was the sister of John Edwards.

There are several unmarked graves in the cemetery. Some are said
to be shooting victims killed in the many saloons in the railroad town.
A local story is told of a railroad worker who went on a drinking spree.
In a drunken brawl, he was struck on the head, and passed out. Still
unconscious, the following day, his buddies, thinking he was dead,
climbed the hill and dug a grave at the cemetery. As the supposed
dead body was lowered into the grave, the man regained consciousness and refused burial.

Of particular note is the grave of Lizzie Hudson, a nurse in the
Spanish American War, who became the first female postmaster of
River Bend. She died at age ninety-five in 1955.

Edwards, John (1865 – 1945)
Edwards, Katherine (1879 – 1943)[33]

Born near Janesville, Wisconsin, John Edwards moved west with
his family, eventually settling at River Bend in 1872. Edwards worked
at the section house for the railroad until age twenty. He filed on a
homestead four miles north of River Bend. While he ran a successful
farm and ranch, he faced constant danger from the Indians. In time,
he was able to make peace with the natives, and even traded with
them.

He married Kate Monahan Middlemist in 1899. Kate is said to be
the first white child born in the area. The couple had ten children.
Kate's parents, Mr. and Mrs. John Monahan, came to River Bend by
covered wagon, prior to the arrival of the Kansas Pacific Railroad,
(now the Union Pacific.)

Kate was born in a log cabin her father built on the family homestead. At a young age, she married William Middlemist. A son was
born to this marriage. William died in 1897, and is buried in the River
Bend Cemetery.

Following her marriage to John Edwards in 1899, Kate Edwards
became involved in the community and school functions.

John and Kate Edwards are buried together, next to Kate's parents, the John Monahans. John Edwards' brother, Walter, is buried
nearby. The family plot is enclosed with a wrought iron fence.

Monahan, John (1840 – 1904)

The first pioneers of the River Bend area, the John Monahan family arrived by covered wagon in 1874. Their children, Michael and Kate, were the first white children born in the area. John became the first section boss with the construction of the railroad.

John and Katherine Monahan are buried together. There is a marker.

DEER TRAIL

EVERGREEN CEMETERY

LOCATED ONE-QUARTER-MILE EAST OF TOWN ON CEDAR STREET. THE CEMETERY IS UP THE HILL, OVERLOOKING THE PRAIRIE.

With a backdrop of the enormous eastern prairie, this cemetery is quite grand in stature. Surveyed and platted in 1875, the year Deer Trail was founded, the first recorded burial occurred in 1876. The cemetery is well landscaped. Beautiful trees offer shade and a sense of protection.

The oldest section of the cemetery is to the north and east. It is believed this burial section existed prior to 1876. While a few markers remain, most are gone, if they existed at all. The site has been set apart for protection and respect to the unknown pioneers of the area.

The oldest marked grave in the cemetery is that of Leonard A. Stanley, dated February 28, 1876, age twenty-seven years. Mystery surrounds his death. While herding horses at a nearby ranch, he and his partner were separated. When his partner returned to camp for dinner, Stanley was dead. The accepted theory was that his horse stumbled in a hole, throwing Stanley off the horse, and that he died on impact with the ground. Following his death, as the story is told, for thirty years, a mysterious woman visited his grave, leaving a rose.

Benham, Jay (1853 – 1916)

Born in Batavia, New York, Benham was the son of famous Pony Express rider Alex Benham, who was stationed at the Julesburg exchange in 1860 and 1861. Alex Benham received the telegraph news of Abraham Lincoln's presidential election in November 1860 and carried it west on horseback.

Jay Benham spent his childhood in the East, while his father made his way in the West. He joined his father near Deer Trail in 1886, operating a cattle and sheep ranch. By 1900, the ranch was widely known, with cattle being shipped by rail as far as Chicago.

In 1910, Jay Benham was one of the founders of the Byers State Bank and established the Benham school in 1911.

He is buried beside his wife Louise, in Section 5. There is a marker.

Brown, Otto (1852 – 1898)

An immigrant of Prussia, Otto Brown ran a sheep ranch north of Deer Trail. In the fall of 1898, he suddenly disappeared. A neighbor notified the authorities of Brown's absence and began his own surveillance of the Brown ranch, while sheriff's posse searched the area. Meanwhile, the neighbor noticed that Brown's dog constantly wandered between the cabin and the creek. The neighbor followed the dog to the creek a few days later. Poking around the area, he discovered the hidden body of Otto Brown.

The murderer was eventually apprehended while attempting to herd Brown's sheep over the Laramie Bridge in Wyoming.

Otto Brown is buried in the north section of the cemetery, in Section 4. There is a large brown headstone.

Deter, Philip (1865 – 1966)

Born in La Grange, Indiana, Deter left home at an early age. In Texas, he joined a cattle herd headed for Akron, Colorado. He made his home in Deer Trail in 1882, working as a cow puncher for several ranchers. He became a cook on the trail drives, earning twice the wages of a cowboy. Over the years, he was known as a barbecue specialist, heralded all over the county.

In 1891, he married Julia O'Conner, who worked at the White Hotel in Deer Trail. The couple took squatters rights on 160 acres, four and a half miles north of Deer Trail. They filed homestead rights in 1901. Ten children were raised on the homestead. In time they expanded their land holdings and became one of the largest ranches in the county.

Philip Deter personally knew the likes of Buffalo Bill Cody, Governor Billy Adams, outlaws Sam Bass and Billy The Kid, from whom he claimed he once bought a horse.

One of the earliest pioneers of Deer Trail, he was honored in 1962, receiving an engraved certificate from the Homestead Centennial Association. This was in honor of the 100th Anniversary of the Homestead Act. On his 100th birthday in 1965, Brown served as grand marshal in the annual Deer Trail Parade, riding a horse and holding his own.

He is buried in Section 3, beside his wife, Julia, who died in 1929. There is a marker.

Scott, James Ambrose (1865 – 1932)

A native of Ohio, James Scott left home at age twenty-one. Near Kearney, Nebraska, he signed on with a cattle drive serving as the cook.

By 1866, he had settled in Julesburg where he engaged in horse trading. He served as the first sheriff of Sedgewick County. He married Henrietta Wamsley in 1891. The couple moved to Deer Trail, where six children were born. The marriage ended in divorce and Scott was left to raise the six children. In time, he expanded his horse ranch to include several acres west of Deer Trail, and east of Agate. In 1908, he married the pretty schoolmarm, Jeanette H. Aukema. Two children were born to this union.

The Depression years were extremely hard for Scott and his family. He lost everything except a small ranch near Deer Trail and a house in town. For the first time in many years, he was forced to look for work. He was an assistant manager at the Singleton Resort near the mountain town of Bailey, where he was shot to death in June 1932.

His assailant, Robert Proudfeet had at one time been employed by Scott and held an unknown grudge. Proudfeet was judged insane by the courts and spent the rest of his life in the Pueblo State Hospital for the insane.

James A. Scott is buried in Section 5. There is a marker.

Sniff, William N. (1859 – 1941)

Born in Fort Madison, Iowa, William Sniff migrated west with his parents following the Civil War. At age fifteen, he set out alone for Colorado, where he hoped his fragile health would improve.

Arriving in Deer Trail, he went to work for the Union Pacific Railroad, a position he held until age eighteen. His brother Alonzo, who arrived in Deer Trail after William, was also employed by the Union Pacific.

William went to work for the Bo-Peep Ranch for twenty-six dollars a month. During his six years at the ranch, he did not spend any of his earnings. He saved to buy land for a ranch, which he was able to do in 1891.

The land was located approximately twenty-seven miles east of Deer Trail, near the banks of the Little Beaver Creek. It was a three-day round trip drive by wagon to Deer Trail for supplies. He had 1,000 head of sheep, and was very prosperous until the 1930s.

In 1899, Sniff married at age forty. He and the former Miss Minnie Grace Masters had three children. Minnie died in 1911, leaving William to raise the young children.[34] In 1918, Sniff married his housekeeper, Alpharettia Kramer.

One of the earliest and most prosperous pioneer ranchers of the Deer Trail area, Sniff died at the home of his daughter in 1941. He is buried beneath a stone marker in Section 3.

BYERS

BYERS CEMETERY

LOCATED AT THE SOUTHERN EDGE OF TOWN, ACROSS THE RAILROAD TRACKS, SOUTH ON OWENS STREET.

This quiet resting spot lies on the western edge of the Colorado prairie. One of the better organized cemeteries, it is laid out in neatly arranged rows. The blocks are alphabetical beginning at the eastern edge, progressing to the west gate entrance. The landscape is carefully pruned and very attractive.

Unfortunately, the cemetery records were lost in a fire in December 1930. It is known that the oldest part of the cemetery is in the eastern section, located in Blocks F1, G1, and H1. The majority of the pioneers listed in this sketch are located in the eastern section.

Bitzer, John (1861 – 1913)

A native of Germany, John Bitzer arrived in America at age seventeen, in 1878. He made his way to the gold mines of Colorado, where he found work in Central City, Black Hawk and the boom town of Cripple Creek. In 1886, he married a native German, Margaret Moeck. She had arrived in America in 1874, at age nineteen. In the next two years, two sons were born, Louis and John, both dying in infancy. In 1893, their two-year-old daughter Katie died. Just five years later, Margaret gave birth to a healthy daughter named Anna. Two additional children were born to the union.

Miner's consumption caused John Bitzer to seek a better climate and way of life for himself and his family. In 1907, he homesteaded land seven miles northeast of Byers. It took the family three days to make the journey by wagon from Central City to their new home at Byers. John worked on the farm that spring and summer, returning to Central City and the mine work in the winter. This routine was followed for several years. The farm eventually proved successful through the hard work and determination of John Bitzer and his family.

John died in January 1913. He was buried in the Bitzer family plot, located in Block E1, Lots 28, 29 and 30. His wife Margaret died in 1949 and is buried with her husband.

Clark, John (1860 – 1947)

A native of Dumfries, Scotland, John Clark married Euphemia Grant in 1881. The couple arrived in America in 1883. One of the earliest pioneers of Byers, Clark built the second home in the young community.

John worked for the railroad, eventually loosing his sight to snow blindness. Euphemia was active in the social affairs of Byers and a member of the Presbyterian Church.

The couple are buried together in Block C, Lot 7.

Gaudot, Mary Hurst (? – 1931)

A widow with four young children, Mary came to Denver from McComb, Mississippi, in 1896. She took work at a local cotton mill and worked nights at a hotel as a cook to support her children. She married Jean Gaudot in 1900. Mr. Goudot, a widower, had four children of his own. The newlyweds added two children to the family.

In 1907, the family took a homestead five miles southeast of Byers. They lived in a tent until the lumber was hauled to the site and their wooden frame home was built. The children attended the Ludwick school. The farm was a marginal success, but was leased in 1919, when the Goudots moved to town.

Following the death of Jean Goudot in 1924, Mary ran the local hotel for a time, while raising the youngest of her children. She died in 1931, leaving the farm to her children, where it remained for many years.

She is buried in Block C, Lot 2.

McDonnell, Leonard (1844 – 1896)
Monroe, Linnie McDonnell (1864 – 1950)
Monroe, John A. (1885 – 1920)

One of the first pioneers of Byers, Leonard McDonnell was born in Halifax, Nova Scotia. He came to America, first settling in Missouri, where he taught school. By the early 1880s, he was in Colorado, where he took a quarter section of land south of the railroad at Byers. In 1888, he and his partner, John Fetzer, gave the northwest section of their claim to the township of Byers for development.

McDonnell married Linnie E. Jewell in 1885. Linnie, born in Ohio in 1864, came to the Byers area in 1882. Twenty years Leonard's junior, she bore him six children. The couple raised their family on the homestead, while Leonard ran a mercantile store in town to supplement their income. He served the town of Byers as postmaster during the period of 1885 to 1892.

Leonard McDonnell died of pneumonia on February 13, 1896. Burial was in the Byers Cemetery. Twelve days later, the widowed Linnie McDonnell gave birth to her sixth child. The following year was a trying time for Linnie. She struggled with the homestead and her six children. She disposed of the mercantile store in town.

In October 1897, Linnie married John Alexander Monroe, nineteen years her junior. Monroe was a ranch hand, employed at the McDonnell ranch. Five children were born to the Monroes, making Linnie the mother of eleven children. The children all attended the one-room Ludwick school.

Linnie and John Monroe moved to the town of Byers in 1918, where they purchased a home at the south end of what is now Fetzer Street.[35] Linnie was a charter member of the Byers Presbyterian Church in 1910 and devoted much of her time to the church once she moved to town. The majority of her time, however, was spent running a popular hotel and restaurant she had opened.

John Monroe passed away in September 1920. He was laid to rest in the Byers Cemetery. Linnie, now twice a widow, went to Denver, where the younger children finished their education.

Linnie Jewell McDonnell Monroe died in Denver on March 24, 1950. She was eighty-six years old. She was buried in the McDonnell burial plot at the Byers Cemetery, with both her husbands, and other family members.

The McDonnell-Monroe family plot is located in Block A1, Lots 31 through 38.

Paine, Edward S. (1871 – 1947)

Born in Seneca County, New York, Edward Paine graduated from the New York City Trade School. He married Cora Travis in New York, in 1895. The couple came to Colorado in the early 1900s in search of a better climate.

In 1905, Paine homesteaded five miles northeast of Byers, where he and Cora raised their four children. To make ends meet, Edward found work in Denver in construction and carpentry. He rode the train to Byers on Saturdays, bicycling to the homestead, returning to Denver on Sunday. This routine lasted for four years, while Cora cared for the children, the livestock and the homestead.

Edward Paine was the first farmer to experiment with summer fallowing with success. His wheat crop of 1912 was over forty bushels per acre, by far the best in the county. The success was partially due to his engineering of farming machinery. He designed a dry auger rig, as well as advanced drilling wells, all of which were used in his wheat fields.

He and Cora were involved in community affairs and the Presbyterian Church. Edward designed and contracted to build the new church in 1910. He served several years as elder of the church.

He is buried beside his wife in Block C, Lot 8.

— — —

North/South Highways
Highway 85 South

GREELEY
LINN GROVE CEMETERY
1700 CEDAR AVE.

The cemetery was established in 1874 from land purchased by J.C. Shattuck. It was named Linn Grove in honor of his home town in Missouri. Bodies from the original cemetery southwest of town were reinterred in Linn Grove by 1882. Strict rules were enforced, including a ten dollar fine for riding a horse or any other animal in the cemetery.

Markers of significance include the Babyland Marker located in Block 10 on the north end, dedicated in 1958. The Soldier's Field is located in the northeast section in Block 29.

The Linn Grove Cemetery has taken great care to provide historical accuracy in its records, and maintain the historical significance of the grounds. A white granite monument, four feet high, near the office was erected in 1984. It reads simply:

This is a Cemetery.

Brush, Jared L. (1835 – 1913)

One of the largest pioneering cattle barons in northeast Colorado, the town of Brush was named in his honor. Jared L. Brush made his money in the cattle industry, establishing and promoting northeast Colorado as prime cattle land.

Brush was born in Clermont County, Ohio and arrived in the Colorado Territory in 1859. He worked the gold mines of Russell Gulch before farming in Weld County in 1860. As one of the original 59ers, his name is associated with nearly every aspect of early life in Colorado. He became one of Colorado's greatest empire builders, in the same company of John Iliff.[36]

Despite his large cattle enterprise, he took time to shape the politics of a young country growing to statehood. He served Weld County as sheriff in 1870, county commissioner in 1874, and became a member of the first state Legislature in 1876. A three-time delegate to the Republican Convention, he also served twice as lieutenant governor.

He and his wife Ada, made their home in Greeley, where they raised two children, Walter and Adna. Jared Brush served as president of the Greeley National Bank for twenty-one years and served on the State Board of Agriculture for several years.

He was instrumental in forming an irrigation system serving the upper and lower Platte River regions.

He is buried in Block I, Lot 12.

Denver Public Library
Benjamin H. Eaton
Governor of Colorado 1885-1887.

Crozier Family Plot
(July 7, 1917)

Forty-year-old Bessie Crozier murdered her four daughters, Lois, age eleven, ten-year-old Emily, Mildred, age six, and two-year-old Martha. Bessie then killed herself. The whereabouts of the father, then and now, is unknown.

Eaton, Benjamin H.
(1834 – 1904)

Prominent pioneer and promoter of the Greeley area, the nearby town of Eaton was named in his honor. He became the fourth governor of Colorado, serving from 1885 to 1887.

He is buried in Block H, Lot 10.

French, Wilbur (1846 – 1888)

Wilbur French had a history of violence and was hanged in 1888, in front of the courthouse, for beating his wife.

He is buried in Block A, Lot 64.

Humphrey, William & Rosanna (Died 1876)

Unfortunately, nothing is known of their history. The young couple were struck by lightening in July 1876. Their bodies were burned, and

Denver Public Library
Oliver T. Jackson
Prominent black businessman.

so locked together, they were buried that way.

They lay together in Block L, Lot 6, Grave 3.

Jackson, Oliver T. (1862-1948)

The son of a prosperous black businessman, Oliver T. Jackson was educated in northern Ohio. O.T. Jackson entered the restaurant and catering business. At age twenty-five, he settled in Boulder in 1887. Moving into the black business community, Jackson successfully operated the Stillman Cafe and Ice Cream Parlor on Pearl Street, becoming a respected community leader. Jackson was staff manager at the Chautauqua Dining Hall in 1898. He went on to own and operate a restaurant at 55th Street and Arapahoe, where today's Boulder Dinner Theatre is located.

Oliver Jackson was heavily involved in the Democratic campaign of 1908. In a period of history when few black men were involved in politics, O.T. Jackson made a name for himself. Democrat John Shafroth was elected governor of Colorado, and to show his appreciation to Jackson, he helped in securing a 320-acre land title in rural northeast Colorado.

Jackson's new land, thirty miles east of Greeley, became the nucleus for the black colony of Dearfield.[37] Jackson and his wife Minerva, organized the Negro Townsite and Land Company in 1909. With advertising and persuasion, Jackson inspired sixty settlers of color to join in his agriculture colony. He established the Dearfield Lodge, complete with the fashionable false front of the period.

Along with the farming, Jackson planned canning factories and a college. While these dreams never materialized, the community did prosper for a time, with a peak population of 700. Even Booker T. Washington visited the small community. Within five years Dearfield had forty-four wooden cabins and over 600 farm acres. The community had two churches, a school, a boardinghouse, blacksmith shop, cement factory and a filling station.

The Great Depression hit the rural communities of Colorado exceptionally hard. As times grew tough, the people left for the larger towns. By 1940 Dearfield's population was down to twelve, including O.T. and Minerva Jackson. Minerva died in 1942, and O.T.'s niece, Jenny Jackson came from Chicago to care for her now elderly uncle.

Oliver Toussaint Jackson died in 1948. He was buried in an unmarked grave in Greeley's Linn Grove Cemetery.[38] For twenty-five years, Jenny tried unsuccessfully to raise funds to mark her uncle's grave. Thanks to the Weld County Historical Society and Linn Grove Cemetery, O.T. Jackson's final resting place is now marked in Block H-L, Lot 1.

Meeker, Nathan C. (1817 – 1879)[39]

Upon moving west from Ohio, by 1870, Meeker founded the Union Colony on the Cache La Poudre River, called "Greeley," after his personal friend, journalist Horace Greeley.

Genuinely interested in the Indian struggle, he became agent of the White River Ute Agency, in Northwest Colorado, in 1879.[40]

He was killed in an Indian uprising at the agency in September 1879.[41] His wife and daughter, (also buried here), were held captive by the Indians for some twenty days.

Originally buried at the agency near Meeker, he was reinterred in the family plot in Greeley, in Block O, Lot 37. A large pink marble stone marks his grave.

Monfort Family Plot

Patriarch of the Monfort dynasty was Warren H. Monfort. Returning from World War I, Monfort started a cattle ranch north of Greeley. During the Depression of the 1930s, he pioneered crop surplus as a way of feeding cattle. This allowed him to produce premium cattle year round, a first in the industry.

The Monfort Meat Company expanded to 3,500 head by World War II, and 100,000 head of cattle by the late 1960s. It was the largest family owned cattle operation in the nation, until it was acquired by ConAgra in 1987.

Warren H. Monfort is buried in the family plot in Block 14, Lot 50.

— — —

Ghost Notes, Mysteries, & Other Related Findings

There are several Indian burial grounds located on the Eastern Plains of Colorado. Some eleven miles northwest of Burlington, on the bluffs of Landsman Creek, is an old Indian burial spot, marked by the

Nathaniel Meeker
Indian agent of the White River
Utes. His policies resulted in
the 1879 Meeker Massacre.

traditional pyramid of stones. The stones a particularly high, a sign of the burial of a high chief or warriors.

Unfortunately, many of these burial spots have been destroyed by homesteaders and farmers. Clearing their land, many did not realize what the stones represented.

Indian confrontations broke out once again in 1886, when the land was opened for settlement. Hell Creek, just north of Seibert, was the scene of an Indian attack on a group of roving cowboys. The bodies were buried near the old Kit Carson Trail. Several years later, soil erosion uncovered the bodies and they were reinterred on higher ground.

* * *

Franklin H. Baker had a small homestead northeast of Burlington. Baker became enraged at the growing traffic crossing his land during the second westward movement in the 1880s. He went so far as to build a a sod barrier overlooking the traveled course, with the intent to shoot anyone who crossed his land. In April 1888, he did just that.

Three ranchers traveling in a buckboard, crossed Baker's land., stopping at a gulch close to the Baker cabin. Baker leveled his shotgun and fired at the trio. John C. Morrison and E.B. McConnell were shot several times in the back.

Deputy Sheriff Jerry Barnes arrested Baker as the two victims lay between life and death. The deputy, under a clever rouse, attempted to take his prisoner to the safety of the jail at Arapahoe, but was intercepted by a vigilante mob at Cheyenne Wells. The mob grabbed Baker and hanged him from the water tower. That night, Baker's victims also died.

The body of F.L. Baker dangled in the moonlight until dawn. A coroners jury cut the body down the following day, pronounced death and hastily buried Baker in the cemetery at Cheyenne Wells.

Two weeks later, Baker's body was dug up from the cemetery, and taken to Burlington. It is rumored that the bones were used for medical research.[42]

— — —

Additional Cemeteries Listed by County

Adams County

Cemetery	1st Burial
Bennett Cemetery	1880
Leader Cemetery	?
Saron Luther Scandinavian Cem.	1918 – Abandoned

Kit Carson County

Cemetery	1st Burial
Beaver Valley Cemetery	?
Beloit Cemetery	?
Bethune Cemetery	?
Calvary Cemetery	?
Clairmont Cemetery	?
Flagler Cemetery	?
Hope Cemetery	?
Immanuel Cemetery	?
New Friedenburg Cemetery	?
Prairie Home Cemetery	?
Siebert Cemetery	?
Settlement Cemetery	?
Shiloh Cemetery	?
Smit Cemetery	?
Vona Cemetery	?

Lincoln County

Cemetery	1st Burial
Arriba Cemetery	1911
Arriba Old Cemetery	1898
Bovina Cemetery	1888
Genoa Cemetery	1908

Logan County

Cemetery	1st Burial
Barber Cemetery	1907
Fleming Cemetery	1897
Kelly Cemetery	1914
Leroy Cemetery	1892
Lynch Cemetery	?
Merino Cemetery	1916
New Haven Cemetery	1915
Peetz Cemetery	1917

Cemetery	1st Burial
Rockland Cemetery	1890
St. Petersburg Cemetery	1914
Willard Cemetery	1912

Morgan County

Cemetery	1st Burial
Adena Union Church Cemetery	?
Frost Ranch Cemetery	?
Hoyt Cemetery	?
Weldona Cemetery	?

Phillips County

Cemetery	1st Burial
Amherst Cemetery	?
Bryant Cemetery	?
Dunkard Cemetery	?
Fairfield Cemetery	?
Jarvis Cemetery	?
Paoli Cemetery	?
Posegate Cemetery	?

Sedgwick County

Cemetery	1st Burial
Weir Cemetery	1887
Woodhams Cemetery	1887

Washington County

Cemetery	1st Burial
Abbott Cemetery	1913
Burdett Cemetery	1890
Curtis Cemetery	1894
Elba Cemetery	1911
Glen Chapel Cemetery	1905
Hope Cemetery	1880
Hyde Cemetery	1882
Indian Burial Ground	?
Thurman Cemetery	1888

Weld County

Cemetery	1st Burial
Ault Cemetery	1914
Briggsdale Cemetery	1911
Brush-Daniels Cemetery	1868

Buckingham Cemetery	1917
St. Vrain Cemetery	1875
Coleman Cemetery	1906
Eaton Cemetery	1887
Evans Cemetery	1863
Fort St. Vrain Cemetery	?
Fort Vasquez Cemetery	?
Highland Lake Cemetery	1878
Hillside Cemetery	1881
Home of the Peace Cemetery	1894
Indian Burial Ground	?
Johnstown Cemetery	1901
Keota Cemetery	1911
Lakeview Cemetery	1880
Mizpah Cemetery	1873
Mount Pleasant Cemetery	1883
Hudson Cemetery	1888
New Raymer Cemetery	1888
Pilgrim Cemetery	1917
Pleasant View Cemetery	1915
Saint Francis Cemetery	1878
Sligo Cemetery	1888

Yuma County

Cemetery	**1st Burial**
Delto Cemetery	1895 – Abandoned
Downey Cemetery	? – Abandoned
Friend Cemetery	?
Glendale Cemetery	1889
Hanshaw/Lakeview Cemetery	1919 – Abandoned
Idalia Cemetery #1	?
Idalia Cemetery #2	?
Lansing Valley Cemetery	1887 – Abandoned
Mildred Cemetery	1912 – Abandoned
Olivet Nazarene Cemetery	1915
Pleasant Valley Methodist Cem.	1909
Spring Valley/Landsman/ Lutheran Cemetery	1888 – Abandoned
Triangle/Wauneta Cemetery	? – Abandoned

— — —

Sources

Blevins, Terry – Lincoln County Historical Society
Carroll, Joan – Eastern Colorado Historical Society
Eldringhoff, Susan – Deer Trail Historical Society
Glenn, Arlene – East Yuma County Historical Society
Logan County Museum – Sterling
Oestman, Pat – Historian Phillips, Yuma and Washington
Counties
Smith, Cathy – Brush City Clerk's Office
Stephens, Maggie – Fort Morgan Museum
Van Buskirk, Thomas, Superintendent – Linn Grove Cemetery
Yuma County Historical Society

Newspapers

Akron News-Reporter
Burlington Call
Cheyenne County News
Cheyenne Wells Gazette
Colorado Patriot
Deer Trail Tribune
Denver Catholic Register
Denver Times
Denver Post
Denver Republican
Eastern Colorado News
Eastern Colorado Leader
Eastern Colorado Plainsman
Fort Morgan Times
Logan County News
Rocky Mountain News
The State Herald
The Strasburg News
Wray Gazette
Wray Rattler
Yuma Pioneer

Interviews

Mr. and Mrs. William Dye – Julesburg
Mr. Richard Austin – Austin Funeral Home – Julesburg
Mrs. Jean Williams – Julesburg
Mr. Wallace McClary – Sexton, Sedgwick Cemetery
Mr. Terry Blevins – Limon, Hugo, River Bend Cemeteries

— — —

Chapter Two Notes

[1] History records the long-standing feud between Beni and the notorious Jack Slade who murdered Beni and cut off his ears. Beni's burial site was never recorded.

[2] Mercy claimed to be a distant cousin to Zebulon Pike. Pike is buried in New York, not far from Mercy's birth place.

[3] All biographies listed are burials in the Ovid Cemetery. However, cemetery records list only one of the burials in this documentary.

[4] According to records kept at the Pro Rodeo Hall of Fame, Sowder is the only man to win this honor two consecutive times.

[5] Thad's brother, John F. Sowder is buried in Woodhams Cemetery south of Sedgwick. Most of the Sowder children left the county.

[6] Logan County records, date unknown.

[7] Three miles south of Sterling, the island called Hadfield, is also known as Sarinda.

[8] Mrs. Mabel Landrum Torrey grew up in Sterling, graduating with the class of 1904, and was a famous artist in her own right.

[9] Union Colony, an early settlement later became Greeley, Colorado.

[10] James Weir's first grandchild, Maude Elizabeth, was one of the first children born in the area. She is buried in Section 1-72, Block 048.

[11] I have only found one source stating John Wilson is buried at Riverside Cemetery. The cemetery has no records of his burial.

[12] The grave of Mrs. Susanna Alderice lies near the monument. She was killed by a jealous squaw on July 11, 1869.

[13] Much of the original architecture has been replaced.

[14] See C.M. Tyler, Chapter 3.

[15] See Sand Creek Massacre

[16] Federal Archives, Denver, Colorado

[17] Glenn Miller joined the war effort in 1942. In December 1944, his plane went down over the English Channel. There is a memorial marker in Cambridge, England.

[18] Godfried Weimer died in 1930. He is buried in Section 1, Block 3, Lot 18.

[19] The Lincoln Land Company worked with the Burlington Railroad in land promotion.

[20] See Beecher Island.

[21] Still in operation, this ranch is now known as the T-Triangle.

[22] See Sand Creek

[23] See Hungate Family.

[24] See Off the Beaten Path, Bonney Reservoir, this chapter for burial of Roman Nose.

[25] At the time, the area was located in Arapahoe County, one of the original counties created during statehood proceedings.

[26] Middlecoff's grave is located in the southeastern corner of the cemetery, on the other side of the hill.

[27] Following the death of her husband, Mrs. Dey moved to Denver. She was buried in Crown Hill Cemetery in 1942.

[28] Gerry's personal papers are on file at the Colorado Historical Society. An item listed is dated South Fork, Platte, 1857. In another paper, he gives his DOB as 1818.

[29] Latham became the county seat in 1868. In 1870, the honor went to Evans, Colorado.

[30] Daughter of Abraham and Katherina Klassen.

[31] Mary Haug is buried in Shelton, Nebraska.

[32] Eastern Colorado Ledger, 9/5/41.

[33] Her obituary in the Eastern Colorado Leader, lists her DOB as 1880.

[34] Minnie Masters Sniff is buried in the Evergreen Cemetery at Deer Trail.

[35] The home still stands and for years, remained in the Monroe family.

[36] See Iliff, John Chapter 2.

[37] The site is located on Highway 34, between Greeley and Fort Morgan.

[38] A cemetery was never established at the Dearfield colony.

[39] Meeker's headstone incorrectly gives DOB as 1814.

[40] See Meeker Massacre.

[41] The bodies of all Greeley men killed in the Meeker Massacre were reinterred to Linn Grove Cemetery.

[42] Cheyenne Wells Gazette, May 5, 1888.

Chapter Three

Metro Denver

G old was discovered at the confluence of the Platte River and Cherry Creek in 1858 by William Green Russell. The event created a mass population movement the likes of which the Rocky Mountain region had never seen. Tent cities, and eventually log cabins, were erected on both sides of Cherry Creek. The town of Auraria lay on the west bank, while Denver City lay on the east. By 1859, Denver City became the stopover for gold seekers on their way to the Rocky Mountain mines.

Prior to settlement, the area that would become the city of Denver, was in the middle of the region known as "The Great American Desert." The area, largely ignored by the Spaniards, and Europeans, was deemed worthless and hardly worth any effort to settle the land or challenge the Cheyenne. Yet with the discovery of gold, Denver's destiny was sealed.

As the original gold strike at the Platte and Cherry Creek played out, the men still flooded the area, stopping in Denver City long enough for supplies and moving on to the hills and the riches.

In the midst of this frenzy, a town was created. Merchants and businessmen gave the bustling tent town a sense of permanence. Businesses opened, log cabins were built and trees were cleared. William Larimer laid out the town of Denver City with a futuristic eye. Denver, "The Queen City," as she would come to be called, was situated closer to the Platte River with plenty of room for growth. By 1859, William Newton Byers had printed the first edition of *The Rocky Mountain News*, and Edward Wynkoop became the first sheriff. In time, the railroad would bring "Manifest Destiny" to Denver and the Rocky Mountain region, while gold, silver, copper and lead would help Colorado Territory become the thirty-eighth state in the Union.

Denver Public Library
Criminals were among the first burials in Denver's City Cemetery. This hanging took place in the 1860s in what is now downtown Denver.

The Old City Cemetery

Larimer chose an ideal spot for the city's cemetery, close enough to town, yet far away to allow future development. At least that was the idea in the beginning.

The site selected was a gently sloping hill two miles from the heart of Denver City. Covering one hundred and sixty acres, in an L-shaped area, the Mount Prospect Cemetery, or City Cemetery, as it was later known, spread from today's 13th Avenue to 8th Avenue south, and from York Street to the city ditch on the west.

The land was sectioned off by the early pioneers, headed by General Larimer in the spring of 1859. The Catholic section, called Mt. Calvary, and the Jewish section, named Hebrew Cemetery, were organized in 1865. What was referred to as the pauper's section or Boot Hill, was alloted eighty acres.

Abraham Kay, twenty-six years old, suddenly died of an infection of the lungs in March 1859. He became the first burial of Denver's Mount Prospect Cemetery. A few weeks later, a fifteen year-old named Marywall died when he was thrown from a horse. Young Marywall became the second burial. The next two burials were in April 1859. John Stoefel and Arthur Biengraff were buried in the same casket for reasons unknown.

The cemetery, a desolate place on the windblown prairie with no water, soon became unsightly, overgrown with tumbleweeds and wild thistle. A fitting setting, for the first years of Denver's existence, but not to Larimer's vision. The majority of the burials were the results of various criminal activities, including murder, gunfights and hangings.

City Cemetery, as it was known after 1873, became so dilapidated and unseemly, Denver residents preferred to bury their loved ones in the new stately Riverside Cemetery.

In 1890, Senator Henry Teller proposed turning the cemetery into a park. By 1893, bodies were removed to Riverside. Out of the some twelve thousand bodies, only about five thousand were actually moved. More bodies were moved in the 1950s when grading began for today's Botanic Gardens; this was the Mount Calvary Catholic section. Many bodies still lie under Cheesman Park.

To receive government appropriations for the new park, Senator Teller named the park "Congress Park." In 1907, a deal was struck with the widow of Walter S. Cheesman to change the name to "Cheesman Park." Her part in the deal was a new pavilion, dedicated in her husband's honor. The pavilion stands to this day.

Author's photo

Ornate monuments decorate Denver's oldest operating cemetery, Riverside.

Visiting the beautiful park area today, while the soft wind rustles the tree branches, one wonders; are these sounds from the past? Or could it be the loneliness and unrest of the broken bodies and forgotten souls laying under Cheesman Park?

RIVERSIDE CEMETERY
5201 BRIGHTON BLVD.

Denver's oldest operating cemetery was founded in 1876, the year Colorado was admitted to the Union. The Riverside Cemetery Association consisted of leading businessmen, providing the city of Denver with an appropriate burial site, complete with landscaping and trees, near the South Platte River. With access to water, Riverside Cemetery was the first in the state to incorporate an adequate irrigation system in a park-like surrounding.

Establishing Riverside Cemetery meant the end of the "graveyard," and the beginning of peaceful burial settings. The association promised to spare no expense in making the new cemetery a place that Denver could be proud of. In doing so, there was a list of rules to be followed. All markers had to be approved by the association, and there would be no fencing of graves or family plots, without approval. Landscaping included carriage roadways and walkways, as well as trees, flowers and shrubs. With the improved water system, green

Author's photo
Pioneer James Archer is remembered
with a life-size bronze statue.

lawns eventually grew, covering the spacious land. The first of Denver's fashionable "park" cemeteries, Riverside still operates today.

Archer, Colonel James (1824 – 1882)

An innovative man with a keen sense of the future, Archer brought the gas light to Denver in 1871. He went on to bring powered gas works to the city. His greatest achievement was the much needed innovative piped water system, later the Denver City Water Company. His pioneer contribution was undoubtedly one of the greatest services to Denver. His monument is one of the most impressive of all in the cemetery. A white marble base holds the bronze life-size statue of Archer. One of the most prominent monuments in the cemetery, it is located in Block 13, Lot 256.

Brown, Clara (1800 – 1885)

Clara Brown was inducted into the Society of Colorado Pioneers just before her death in 1885. This high honor was even more special for Clara and the Society, for Clara Brown was the first black woman to be so honored.

Born a slave, she was given her freedom by her Kentucky slave owner in 1859. During her slavery, her husband and daughter, Liza Jane, were sold separately to other plantations. Clara later learned of her husband's death, but was unsuccessful in locating her daughter.

After Clara was freed, she went to Leavenworth, Kansas to join a wagon train headed for the California gold rush.

Stopping in Auraria, on the banks of Cherry Creek, she worked at a bakery, earning enough money to push westward. She then headed for Central City after gold was discovered in Gregory Gulch. Posing as hired help for a prospector, even though she paid her own way, Clara earned her way to the gold camps.

Clara set up a laundry service for the miners of Central City. Eventually, she had saved enough money to purchase land and mining claims. By the close of the Civil War, Clara had saved enough money to return to Kentucky, and look for her daughter, Liza Jane. During her search, she spent all her savings helping as many of the slaves as she could, escape out of the South. She eventually united with her daughter, just before her death.

Following her death in 1885, Clara was recognized with a stained glass window in the State Capitol.

Clara Brown is buried in Block 25, Lot 185. A recently-placed granite stone marks her grave.

Clifton Bell Children (1879, 1881, and 1887)

This is undoubtedly the most touching plot in the cemetery. It is marked by three marble statues, which include the images of a girl with a doll, a boy on a rocking horse, and a sleeping babe. The images tell of the tragedy of young death. The parents, Clifton and Lizzie are buried at the head of the path leading to the children's memorial.

Clifton Bell, a distraught father, eulogized his children with the following poem on one of the markers:

> *This lovely lad so young and fair*
> *Called home by early doom*
> *Just came to show how pure a flower*
> *In paradise could bloom*

The sorrow lies in the close dates of the childrens' deaths: Baby, 1879, Gracie, 1881, Stella, 1881, and Harley 1887.

According to the *Rocky Mountain News* of 1891, Clifton's death left the grieve-stricken Lizzie . . . "so over-come with bereavement that it was hard to get her to the side of the coffin." The graves are located in Block 5, Lot 59.

Evans, Dr. John (1814 – 1897)

An esteemed doctor from Illinois, Evans was the first to form the theory that cholera was a contagious disease, and lobbied Congress to establish a national quarantine system. He founded the Northwestern Methodist University of Illinois. Involved in politics, he was a member of the delegation nominating Abraham Lincoln as the presidential candidate in 1860. It is said Evans was responsible for suggesting slave emancipation to Lincoln.

In 1862, Lincoln personally asked Evans to take the Territorial Governorship of Colorado. Evans proved to be the right choice for Lincoln, and Colorado.

Govornor Evans was instrumental in securing Colorado statehood, became a leader in bringing railroads through the state. He was the founder of Denver's first seminary in 1864, now known as Denver University. Mount Evans is named for him.

He is buried with his wife, in Block 13, Lot 257. (Records show he was moved from the original family plot at Lot 68.)

Denver Public Library
Barney Ford, a runaway slave, became a very prosperous Denver pioneer.

Ford, Barney (1822 – 1902)

A fugitive slave, Ford settled in Denver in 1865. He used his trade as a barber, opening a shop on Market Street. With his earnings, he became a successful businessman, opening the Inter-Ocean Hotel at 16th and Blake. He entered politics, lobbying for Colorado statehood, and the black right to vote. He died of a stroke in 1902.

The honors followed his death. His building at 1514 Blake Street is listed on the National Register of Historic Places as a Denver landmark. Several public buildings including a Denver school, have been named for him. In 1982, Governor Richard Lamm recognized him for his "significant role" in Colorado history and dedicated a stained glass window in his honor at the State Capitol.

An original 59er, Barney Ford is buried in Block 20, Lot 40. There is a natural stone marker.

Marcelle, Oliver E. (1890 – 1949)

Born in New Orleans, Oliver Marcelle grew up to play the game he loved as a child. He played professional baseball in Atlantic City, Brooklyn, New York, Baltimore, and Detroit, before coming to Colorado in 1934. Known for his uncontrollable temper, his nose was bitten off in a fight. The first black baseball player in Colorado, he was one of the many responsible for bringing black professional baseball to Colorado.

He later became a house painter and died in poverty. His unmarked grave is in Block 29.

Murat, Katrina Wolf (1824 – 1910)

Countess Katrina Murat is noted by many as the "Betsy Ross" of Colorado. True pioneers, having arrived in Denver in 1858, Katrina and her husband, the "Count" Henri Murat, set up a barbershop and laundry operation. Haircuts were one dollar and a laundered shirt cost fifty cents.

When celebrity journalist, Horace Greeley visited early Denver, he was outraged at the five dollars Count Murat charged him for the haircut.

Patriotic Katrina Murat, a member of the Daughters of the American Revolution, fashioned the first American flag to fly over the territory of Colorado. The materials were from her own clothing, including a red flannel petticoat and a blue ball gown.

The Count was said to be related to Napoleon, however, their meager existence suggests otherwise. In 1881, Katrina divorced the Count and lived alone in a small cabin at Palmer Lake. For nineteen years, Katrina was supported largely by the Pioneer Ladies Aid Society.

Katrina Murat was buried in Riverside Cemetery, near Henri, in March 1910.

In Block 4, Lot 41, the Count's grave is a small flat marker, while Katrina's is a natural stone boulder, donated by the DAR. The crudely fashioned inscription reads: "In memory of the maker of the first United States flag in Colorado."

Oakes, Daniel C. (1825 – 1887)

Known in Colorado history as the perpetrator of the "great gold rush hoax," Daniel Oakes led a party of men west from his Iowa homeland in 1858, seeking fortune in the Colorado Rockies. Having participated in the California gold rush of 1849, he had some placer mining experience, or so he thought. Oakes explored the mountains and prospected in various areas. Becoming discouraged, he returned to Iowa within a year.

In Iowa, he wrote and published a Colorado guide book with the elaborate title; *Discoveries on the South Platte River by Luke Tierney To Which is Appended a Guide To The Route by Smith and Oakes.* Highly exaggerating his own gold panning expertise, the book was circulated widely in the East. The glorified report caused a migration of some 150,000 people. "Pikes Peak or Bust" became a national slogan.

The following year, Oakes returned to Colorado Territory. Not for the gold, but for the business opportunities. Hauling a sawmill by wagon, he crossed the prairie trail, where he was met by thousands of men returning to the East. Shocked, he saw his name marked in effigy on many different spots along the trail. Mock tombstones carried the epitaph "Here lies D.C. Oakes, Who started this damn hoax." With his life also being threatened, he wisely chose to avoid Denver City.

Locating thirty miles south of Denver City, Oakes set up his sawmill in the midst of fine timber land at Riley's Gulch along Plum Creek. It was the first mill in the area. He soon had a thriving business, filling orders as far away as Denver City. He started the small communities of Oake's Mill and Huntsville in Douglas County.

With a successful business, and high demand for his lumber, Oakes regained favor among the Colorado pioneers. In 1865, he was appointed as Indian agent by President Andrew Johnson, and became involved in the movement for Colorado statehood. In the winter of 1867 – 68, he and friend Kit Carson, along with Lafayette Head and Hiram P. Bennet, escorted Chief Ouray to Washington D.C. The trip was a formality for Ouray's benefit, an exchange for yet another peace treaty that would not be honored by Washington.

Returning West, Carson fell ill. Oakes personally took Carson to Fort Lyon in southeastern Colorado, where the famous frontier scout later died.[1]

Oakes later moved to Denver, where he continued to serve in the political arena. He organized the Society of Colorado Pioneers in 1866 and was its first president.

He is buried in Block 5, Lot 70, next to his wife, Olivia, a cousin to William F. "Buffalo Bill" Cody.

Routt, John L. (1826 – 1907)

Appointed territorial governor in 1875, John Routt became Colorado's leader in the drive to statehood in 1876. He made several contributions in legislative action for the new Centennial State and was Colorado's first governor after statehood, in 1876, serving two terms. He also served one term as Denver's mayor from 1883 – 1885. Among Routt's accomplishments were the first organizations of city managed police and fire departments, replacing volunteer departments. Colorado's Routt County is named in his honor.

He is buried next to his wife, Eliza, in Block 6, Lot 14.

Tabor, Augusta Louise Pierce (1833 – 1895)

She was a grand lady, this matriarch of Colorado pioneers. The first wife of H.A.W. Tabor, married in 1857, Augusta was abandoned by Tabor, when he struck it rich in Leadville.[2]

Augusta accompanied her husband and infant son, Maxcy, to Colorado's gold country in 1858. While Horace prospected for gold, Augusta provided the family income. For eighteen years Augusta took in boarders, cooked meals, provided laundry services for the miners, baked goods and eventually ran a general store, while Tabor dug for gold. Moving from mining camp to mining camp, Augusta was often the first white woman in the area, her domestic services were a needed commodity.

Denver Public Library
Agusta Tabor
First wife of H. A. W. Tabor.

The Tabors eventually settled in Leadville in 1878, after the discovery of silver. Tabor grub-staked two miners for a third of their find and became rich overnight. The Tabor wealth grew while the Tabor marriage came apart. Tabor became flamboyant, while Augusta withdrew. Tabor was now involved in real estate and politics, and socialized in circles Augusta wanted no part of.

The marriage turned dismal for Tabor, as his wandering eye caught sight of young divorcee Baby Doe.[3] Following a scandalous affair, Tabor sued for divorce, which Augusta eventually granted in misery, claiming, "Not willingly, Oh God, not willingly."

The divorce settlement left Augusta a very wealthy, yet heartbroken woman. Yet she managed to build on her assets until her death in California, in 1895. Services were held February 7, 1895 at the Unity Church in Denver. Her only son, Maxcy had her interred at Riverside Cemetery.

Augusta served on the first committee of Colorado Pioneers and has since been known as the "First Lady" of Colorado's pioneers.

Her original small, flat grave, perhaps indicative to her simplistic ways, is located in Block 7, Lot 78. The new granite monument was erected in 1995, by the Colorado chapter of the DAR.

FAIRMOUNT CEMETERY
430 S. QUEBEC

Located some five miles southeast of downtown Denver, Fairmount Cemetery became incorporated in 1890. The original acreage was selected far enough from the city, to accommodate growth. The landscaping provided for winding, tree-lined walkways, and beautiful flower arrangements.

A little over six months later, the cemetery board refused the first fifty applications for burial, according to the *Rocky Mountain News*. The board claimed the cemetery was not yet ready. The citizens of Denver were infuriated. The board hurried their tasks, and soon had a fine cemetery.

The architecture at Fairmount Cemetery is unprecedented in the city. Monuments by Italy's greatest artists grace the grounds. The Gate Lodge, used for the office and superintendent, was designed by H.T.E. Wendell, a leading architect of the time. The roadway into the cemetery passes through the archway of this magnificent structure. The impressive mortuary chapel, built in 1891, is French Gothic and is ninety feet high.

Byers, William Newton (1831 – 1903)

William N. Byers was one of the original 59ers. Without the insight of this man, it is fair to say the city of Denver might never have come about.

William Newton Byers was one of many of thousands who followed the rush of gold seekers west for opportunity. From Omaha, he and two partners were among the first to arrive at the confluence of Cherry Creek and the South Platte River, in the spring of 1859. Their wagon load included a printing press. Within three days of his arrival, Byers put out the first newspaper of the region. He called it *The Rocky Mountain News*. Byers set up his printing press on the top floor of "Uncle" Dick Wootton's saloon, on the Auraria side of Cherry Creek.[4]

With the strong voice he had in the region's most-read paper, Byers became obsessed with building the greatest town in the West. His voice begged for progress, pleaded for tolerance, and most importantly spoke the truth, as he saw it. His Colorado loyalty is apparent in his activities concerning railroad expansion, miners equality, agriculture, politics, and women's rights.

Byers sold the newspaper and lived an active life, until his death in 1903. Among his pallbearers were D.H. Moffat, John L. Dailey, Rodney Curtis, and William G. Evans, son of Colorado's first, governor, John Evans. The Denver Chamber of Commerce said, "Byers was Denver's most loyal and best beloved citizen." Historian Jerome

Smiley said, "not a single page of Denver history could be written without Byers being mentioned."

William Newton Byers is buried in Block 3, Lot 87.

Chase, Ed (1838 – 1921)

Twenty-two-year-old Ed Chase arrived in Denver in 1860. The handsome blue-eyed man became well-known in Denver as a knowledgeable man in games of chance. Several leading citizens of early Denver talked him into opening his own gambling business. Jerome B. Chaffee, who later became a U.S. Senator, helped Chase acquire the funds.

By the late 1860s, Chase had built a two-story brick building across the street from the Progressive Club and called it

Denver Public Library
"Big" Ed Chase
He built a gambling empire in Denver.

The Palace, and later purchased the Cricket Club. One of Ed Chase's biggest money makers turned out to be the Interocean Club, located in an old mansion at 1422 Curtis Street. Within ten years, Chase had built a gambling empire. He became known as the "Boss" of Denver's underworld. A shrewd businessman, he ran Denver's gambling circuit, while deepening the pockets of Denver's politicos, including Mayor Speer.[5]

Chase once said; "All the chances are with the man who owns the house, I thought they might as well lose to me as to someone else, and did the best I could to accommodate them." Ed sat on a bar stool with a shotgun on his lap and keenly eyed his customers for signs of cheating. He ran a "smooth" operation.

Ed Chase died in 1921, at age eighty-three. The once gambling "Boss" of Denver left his third wife, Frances, over $600,000, in Denver real estate, stocks and bonds.

He is buried in Block 63, Lot 9. There is a large granite tombstone.

Chivington, John M. (1821 – 1894)

A Methodist preacher from Ohio, John Chivington came to Colorado in 1860. Although he taught salvation and righteousness, his career would end in disgrace.

Denver Public Library
Colonel John M. Chivington
He led the attack on the Cheyenne
village at Sand Creek.

Sue Oswald photo
Tombstone of John M. Chivington
Fairmont Cemetery, Denver.

As colonel and commander of the First Colorado Regiment of 1864, Chivington won praise for his leadership during the battle of La Glorieta Pass, Colorado's only Civil War battle. Under Chivington's command, the Confederate advance for the West's gold supply was stopped. Yet on a cold November day of that same year, he led the Third Colorado Regiment on a brutal, murderous attack at the camp of Cheyenne and Arapaho Indians, known as the Sand Creek Massacre. The unsuspecting Indians, mostly women and children, were dead within a matter of hours. Official government records put the count at nearly 600 dead. Eyewitness accounts stated it was a heartless, brutal massacre, and inhuman in concept.[6]

Chivington was condemned by a congressional committee and attempted to live out his life privately. He left Colorado during the winter of 1865 – 66 and went to Nebraska, where his son drowned tragically. His wife died soon after. He later married his daughter-in-law, it is said in an effort to gain his son's estate. His wife accused him of forging her name and thereby stealing her property. She later dropped the charges. Chivington returned to Denver in the 1880s, where he lived out the remainder of his life.

When he died in 1894, Chivington was buried with full Masonic honors in the Fairmount Cemetery. His grand funeral procession included members of the Grand Army of the Republic, as well as the Colorado Pioneer Society.

His gravesite is located in Block 2, Lot 143. There is a fine granite monument to his memory.

Griffith, Emily (1880 – 1947)

Emily Griffith came to Colorado with her parents from Nebraska, in 1895. Living in Denver, she secured a teaching position at the Central School, at age fourteen. In 1904, she joined the State Department of Education and was the Deputy State Superintendent of Schools from 1910 to 1912. Returning to teaching, in 1914, she started a night school program for Denver's working poor, and foreign speaking immigrants. By 1916, The Emily Griffith Opportunity School gained national recognition as an institution providing thousands with a second chance at learning.

Emily Griffith retired in 1933, living in a secluded mountain cabin with her sister. Tragically, in June 1947, she and her sister were slain by unknown assailants. Her legacy, the Emily Griffith Opportunity School, lives on today, a model of adult education.

The grave of Emily Griffith is found in Block 61.

Hill, Nathaniel P. (1832 – 1900)

Professor of Chemistry at Brown University, Nathaniel P. Hill was asked by the mine owners of Colorado to look into the problem of extracting gold from embedded quartz. Surface gold by 1864 was virtually nonexistent. Placer mining had played out; the ore lay in deeper combined rock formations. The Colorado mining industry faced financial ruin if a method could not be developed. Hill's research in Europe ultimately led to a solution and Colorado's mines boomed once again. Hill built the first successful smelter in Black Hawk. The people were so grateful, he was elected mayor of Black Hawk in 1871.

Later elected U.S. Senator, he was a supporter of the national gold standard. In Denver he established the Argo Smelter.

Nineteenth century Colorado depended on the mining industry; Nathaniel P. Hill single-handedly made that a reality.[7]

He is buried in Block A, Lot 14.

Hungate Family (Murdered 1864)

During the height of the Indian wars around Denver, members of the Nathan Ward Hungate family were found murdered by Indians at their farm some twenty-five miles southeast of the city, along the Running Creek, in Douglas County. The mutilated bodies were brought to Denver for public show, being placed in a local business window. The bodies were reported as horribly mutilated and scalped, by the *Rocky Mountain News*.[8] The outrage among the citizens of

Sue Oswald photo
Hungate Family
monument.

Denver led to the final war against the Indians in Colorado Territory, known as the Sand Creek Massacre. The murdered family members were first buried at Mount Calvary Cemetery, and later reinterred at Fairmount several years after their deaths, with a single stone marker at the family plot. The granite stone marker, placed at the time of the reinterment, lists the names of parents Nathan and Ellen, and children Laura and Florence. Block 6, Lot 10. There is an additional marker inscribed with the words, "Killed by Indians 1864." This marker, originally placed at the Mount Calvary burial site in 1864, was moved to Fairmount in 1892.

Iliff, John Wesley (1831 – 1878)
Iliff, Elizabeth Sarah (1845 – 1920)

John W. Iliff grew up on the family farm in Ohio. Seeing promise in the lad, John's father offered to help him in starting a farm of his own. John asked for $500 and the opportunity to go west. He operated a store in Kansas from 1856 to 1859, when the gold rush of 1859 lured him further west. With a wagon loaded with canned goods, house-hold items, and clothing, he headed toward Colorado Territory, opening a store on Denver's Larimer Street.

Instead of finding his riches in the Colorado gold mines, Iliff looked east, to the grazing land of the Colorado prairie. He sold his store in Denver, eventually moving near Lodge Pole Creek in the northeast corner of Colorado. Within three years, Iliff had assembled the greatest cattle herd in the West. Known as the "Cattle King" of Colorado, he ran up to 7,000 head of cattle on land stretching for 100 miles from Julesburg west to Snyder.

By 1870, Illiff shipped beef by the carload in iced railroad cars, to Chicago. The winter of 1871 – 1872 was extremely harsh, killing almost half of Iliff's herd. Iliff recovered and by the 1880s, his herd of over 50,000 head, roamed 20,000 acres.

Iliff was known as the most powerful rancher in Colorado, and highly respected. In 1868, he organized the Colorado Stockmans Association, an obvious gesture of unity to the smaller ranch owners.

In his personal life, he married Sarah Elizabeth Smith in Kansas, in 1865.[9] In October of the same year, Sarah returned to her parents home in Kansas, to await the birth of their child. Sarah died from complications following the birth of their son.

In 1868, Iliff met a young Denver business-woman, Elizabeth Sarah Fraser. An adventurous saleswoman, Elizabeth came to Colorado alone, by stagecoach from Chicago, opening a Singer Sewing Machine Shop, and became one of the first women in Denver's business circle. Two years later, she married John Iliff. The couple had three children.

John Iliff died from alkali tainted water in 1878, at age forty-six. The business of running his cattle empire fell to his widow, Elizabeth. She managed to increase the business and her wealth over the next twenty-five years. At the time, she was the wealthiest woman in Colorado.

Author's photo
The Iliff Family marker was moved in one piece from Riverside to Fairmont Cemetery.

Elizabeth Iliff married Methodist Bishop Henry Warren in 1884. The couple built the famous mansion on South Cook Street, in Denver, known as Fitzroy Place. Elizabeth and her children established the Iliff School of Theology, completed in 1893. One of the finest universities in Denver, it is still in existence.

Elizabeth died in 1920, and is buried in the Iliff family plot next to her first husband, John, in Block 63, Lot 31.[10] Bishop Warren is buried nearby.

Moffat, David H. (1839 – 1911)

David Moffat began his career working in a bank at the age ten, in his home state of New York. At age seventeen, he accepted the post of cashier, at a bank in Omaha.

Forming a partnership with C.C. Woolworth in 1859, Moffat joined the tide of westward migration, setting out for the Pikes Peak country. Arriving in Denver in 1860, Moffat opened a shop on Larimer Street, selling stationery and business supplies. He became cashier of the First National Bank in 1867. Working his way up to president of the bank, he launched a new career and a loyalty to Colorado that became legendary. He guided Colorado's economy through the Silver Panic of 1893, allowing the state to emerge as one of the strongest in the nation.

As stockholder in nearly one hundred ore mines, he enhanced the mining industry by providing financial backing and keen foresight in building nine Colorado railroads. His greatest undertaking was the Moffat Road, a railroad over, rather than through the mountains.

Sue Oswald photo
The grave of Martha Redy
Better known as Madam Mattie Silks.

Built over Rollins Pass, the railroad chugged to an altitude of 11,660 feet and was Colorado's first leg on the transcontinental route.

Completion of the railway and subsequent Moffat Tunnel, was a dream Moffat did not live to witness. His death in 1911 ended an era of opportunity and growth made possible by one man's great vision.

His impressive granite monument is located in Block A, Lot 2.

Sabin, Florence R. (1871 – 1953)

Unlike many of Colorado's pioneers, Florence Sabin was a Colorado native. She was born to a struggling Central City mining family in 1871.[11]

A pioneer nonetheless, she was the first female professor at John Hopkins University, a position she held for twenty-three years. She was known worldwide for her study of human cells, and her research in public health and sanitation programs.

For her humanitarian achievements, including health care, she received fifteen honorary degrees, and was the first woman to be elected as a lifetime member of the National Academy of Sciences.

To her honor and dedication, a bronze statue was placed in the Hall of Statuary in Washington D.C. She is Colorado's single representative.[12] She retired in 1950.

Florence Sabin died in 1953 while standing up for a seventh inning stretch while watching a Dodgers game on television.

She is buried in the mausoleum, in Column D, Section 1058.

Silks, Mattie (Martha Ready) (1848 – 1929)

Mattie Silks was considered the "Queen of the Row" in Denver, during the 1880s. Twenty-nine-year-old Madam Silks, as she preferred to be called, first arrived in Georgetown, from Dodge City, in the 1870s. By 1877, she had made the move to Denver, where she soon made newspaper headlines.

Mattie and competitive madam Kate Fulton, held the first female duel in Denver history. Kate became too friendly with Cortez Thomson, considered Mattie's man. Mattie called out Kate to a duel. Both fired their pistols; both missed their targets. Ironically, Mattie's bullet nicked a bystander; her beloved Thomson.

Establishing her parlour house on Denver's "Row," (Holladay Street, later named Market Street), Mattie ran her establishment for twenty years, while other houses came and went. The service and atmosphere were first rate, yet discreet. Denver's finest "carriage" clientele were her customers, including government officials, and leading businessmen.

Mattie was temporarily dethroned when beautiful madam Jennie Rogers opened her "House of Mirrors."[13] After the death of Jennie Rogers in 1909, Mattie bought the House of Mirrors from Jennie's estate, for

Denver Public Library
Denver Mayor Robert Speer

$14,000. Reclaiming the crown of "Queen" of the Red Light District, Mattie laid "M. Silks" in tile at the doorstep, putting the cap in her new crown. There now was no question who ruled Market Street. For another twenty years, Mattie ran her business, invested in real estate, traveled and married at age seventy-six.

Mattie died from complications suffered from a fall, at Denver General Hospital in 1929. Only a handful of mourners attended her service.

She is buried next to Cortez Thomson, her only true love, in Block 12, Lot 131. There is a flat stone marker. [14]

Speer, Robert W. (1855 – 1918)

Speer was a "common people's" man and did much for the ordinary citizen of Denver, as well as the city itself. He often ran into opposition from his political associates for following his non-conformist philosophy.

Elected mayor of Denver in 1904, he put forth his "City Beautiful" plan, reshaping the city by building parks, a modern sewer system, erecting statues depicting Denver history and designated tree lined boulevards. The Civic Center is one of his finest contributions.

One of the most controversial politicians, Speer nevertheless was elected three times. He worked hard for the city, yet believed in the rights of the people, often breaking a political "fine line" by siding with the gambling establishment and his empathy for business in the red light district. Critics called Speer corrupt, claiming his plans for city beautification were a cover up for political underhandedness. In the end, it was the city that benefited.

The Speer monument is in Block 24, Lot 76.

Teller, Henry M. (1830 – 1914)

Teller set up his law practice in the booming mining town of Central City in 1860, and is responsible for erecting the magnificent Teller House in 1872. The Teller House was the finest hotel in the West. By 1864 he was in politics, joining with John Evans in the movement for Colorado statehood. He was elected to the United States Senate in Colorado's first election following statehood in 1876, and was reelected four times. He left the Senate over the gold standard controversy in 1876, only to be reelected by the other party. He also owned gold mines, was president of the Colorado Central Railroad, and nominated for Secretary of the Interior.

Teller is buried in Block 10, Lot 6.

Wood, Leah J. (Jennie Rogers) (1843 – 1909)

Jennie Rogers, was the most spectacular madam in all of Denver. Arriving from St. Louis in 1879, she was known legally as Leah Fries. She opened a house on Denver's notorious Market Street red light district.

The madams of early Denver competed for each other's business and often became rivals. Such was the case with Jennie and Mattie Silks.[15] Jennie's beauty and commanding presence soon took business away from Mattie Silks. By 1889, Jennie was the undisputed queen of Denver's "Row."

Mirrored in scandal, Jennie built the grandest parlour house ever. Rumors of blackmail, deceit, and murder abounded around a questionable loan Jennie had acquired for her "House of Mirrors." Yet, her new parlour house was the talk of the West. The magnificent wood, the mirrors, the furniture, the food and service were unmatched. The exterior brick was adorned with facial sculptures said by some to resemble the members of the scandalous blackmail and murder plot.

The "House of Mirrors" was the envy of all the other madams on the Row. Business was booming. Entire business conventions arranged entertainment at Jennie's, including the Colorado Legislature.

Her business thrived until the politicos campaigned to close down the Row at the turn of the century. Business slumped, and Jennie apparently lost interest. She leased the House of Mirrors to a fellow madam and began investing in Denver real estate. Stricken with Bright's disease, her health deteriorated.

Once a vivacious, handsome and smart businesswoman, a frail, broken down Jennie Rogers died of uremic poisoning on October 17, 1909. Jennie's funeral was well attended by the madams, their girls, and several Denver businessmen.

Jennie was laid to rest next to her only love and one-time husband, John Wood, in the oldest section of stately Fairmount Cemetery, in Block 2, Lot 76. Her memorial simply says Leah J. Wood, her legal name.

Author's photo

Mary Chase, who wrote the award-winning play "Harvey," is buried near another tombstone bearing the name of her famous invisible rabbit.

CROWN HILL CEMETERY
W. 29TH AVENUE AND WADSWORTH BLVD.

John Olinger and his wife Emma came to Denver in 1890, opening an undertaking business in downtown Denver. Within ten years, their company had expanded into a chain of Olinger mortuaries; the first and only such chain in the industry. When George W. Olinger inherited his father's chain of mortuaries in 1890, he built a fine white mansion west of Denver, then plotted Crown Hill Cemetery across the road. This new suburban cemetery, opening in 1907, became the crown of the Olinger empire. Innovative advertising was another of Olinger's traits. In 1958, he constructed an enormous 398-foot tall electric cross at the top of Mount Lindo, west of the city, still visible today. Atop Mount Lindo lies another cemetery owned by the Olinger family.

Crown Hill Cemetery became west Denver's premier resting place in 1907. The immaculate Tower of Memories, constructed in 1925, is now on the list of historical sites. At a cost topping a million dollars, this four-story tomb for the dead is an example of architecture at its best. The sanctuary is built of hand-honed and polished marble. Rosa Aurora, Arkansas Crystal Rose, Georgia Cherokee and Tennessee Pink marbles glisten throughout the magnificent structure. The "Hall

Denver Public Library

This group of brewery workers includes young pioneer Adolph Coors,
founder of the Coors Brewing Company. Adolph is the man in the
second row from the bottom, wearing a white hat.

of Pioneers" is a main attraction, with magnificent marble variety and
adorned with Lexson overlay photography.

The cemetery grounds are laid out with wide driveways, turn
arounds, and landscaped beautifully.

Chase, Mary Coyle (1901 – 1981)

An award-winning writer, Mary Chase was the author of the crit-
ically acclaimed novel *Harvey*. A wonderful story made into a New
York play, she wrote this while living in Denver.[16] The play became a
major Hollywood production, starring the late James Stewart.

Ironically, her red marble gravestone lies just a few feet from a
family stone with the name HARVEY.

She is buried in the southeast edge of Block 35, Lot 324.

Coors, Adolph (1847 – 1929)

An emigrant from Prussia, Adolph Coors came to America in 1868.
Working on various railroads, he arrived in Denver in 1872. His background was as apprentice in several European breweries. He joined a

Frank Zaputil photo

The Tower of Memories Mausoleum and Crown Hill Cemetery.

partnership in a Denver bottling company, buying out his partner within a year.

The dream of Adolph Coors was to own his own brewery. He purchased land east of Golden, on the edge of Clear Creek where the cool spring water was pure and perfect for brewing beer. By 1880, the Coors Brewery was profitable, and Adolph soon became very wealthy. Keeping the business in Golden, Mr. Coors never lost sight of the community needs, or his employees, yet kept the business in the family.

Today, the Coors Brewery is known internationally as one of the finest, and is run by Adolph's grandson, Peter Coors.

Adolph Coors is buried next to his wife in the family plot located in the northwest corner of Block 41.

Garson, Augusta (1874 – 1892)
Garson, Mabel (1899 – 1907)

The Garson sisters were the first burials in Crown Hill Cemetery. Nothing is known of them, except the fact that they were moved from Fairmount Cemetery in 1907 to the new Crown Hill Cemetery.

They are buried in Block 25, Lot 150, at the north end, near the gray stonemason.

Manley, George V. (1901 – 1968)

Involved with boxing from an early age, George Manley worked his way into national fame, during the great Golden Era of boxing. A

Golden Gloves winner several times over, his ultimate dream of winning the belt was not to be. He lost by decision in a close fight.

His tall red monument, a tribute from his children, is in Block 30, Lot 28.

Olinger, John W. (1851 – 1901)

John Olinger arrived in Denver in 1890, and started an undertaking business in downtown Denver. So successful was his business, he expanded into a chain of Olinger mortuaries. It was the first and only such chain in the industry.

Turning philanthropic with his money, he built several low income housing projects in west Denver and contributed to the political future of the city. A family-operated business, the fortune he acquired passed to his sons.

The Olinger family memorial is located on the first floor of the Tower of Memories mausoleum, in the private Room 83, Tier E.

Veterans of the Spanish American War Memorial

This impressive memorial is dominated by a large marker built of soft granite, holding the statue of a soldier. The hundreds of soldiers buried in this plot are all identified with the traditional white marble government issue stones.

The veterans of World War I and II are memorialized in the traditional manner, including a statue, and the American Flag paying tribute.

The Spanish American War Memorial is located in Block 26, while the World War Veteran's Memorial is in Block 27.

LITTLETON CEMETERY
6155 S. PRINCE STREET

Littleton Cemetery sits on the west edge of downtown Littleton, the oldest of suburban Denver hamlets. Set on a hill overlooking the city to the east, and commanding a spectacular view of the Rocky Mountains to the west, a more majestic spot could not have been found. Land was donated by Mr. R.S. Little, one of the original 59ers and founder of Littleton. The first recorded burial occurred in 1864; a five-year-old child. Over thirty veterans of the Spanish American War, World Wars I and II are buried here, in a place of honor at the north end of the cemetery.

Ames, Lewis B. (? – 1913)

A "Jack of all Trades," Ames worked his way west taking jobs in various towns along the way. He worked as a clerk recorder, a farmer, and a shoe salesman. He settled in Littleton, starting a farm just south of R.S. Little's farm, along the Platte River. His fruit growing success endeared him to the young community. He soon became the local justice of the peace, providing early day law and order.

Littleton's School District No. 6 was formed in 1865, with Ames as the first teacher. The following year, his wife took over the duties in the small log schoolhouse, teaching for several years. The evolution of today's Littleton public school system started over 100 years ago with Mr. Ames.

Lewis B. Ames is buried in Block 3, Lot 26. His small granite tombstone also contains the name of Bixby.

Bemis Family Plot

Fred A. Bemis arrived at the small community of Littleton, with his new bride in the fall of 1883. Bemis brought the first registered Jersey cows to Colorado from Massachusetts in 1884, the beginning of his great farm. Their first home was on the site of today's Valley Feed and Supply store, on West Main Street, stretching north and west, along the river (approximately South Santa Fe Drive). He later sold the land to the Santa Fe Railroad. When a road was cut along the tracks, Bemis named it Santa Fe.

Renowned in the cattle and horse breeding industry, Bemis was instrumental in creating the National Western Stock Show Association, a major contributer to Denver's economy today.

Elected justice of the peace in 1932, he held this office until his death in 1947.

— — —

Following in his father's footsteps, Edward A. Bemis, born in 1887, continued to work for and give back to the city of Littleton. He headed projects providing for the improvements of the city, such as street work and sanitation.

He bought the struggling *Littleton Independent* newspaper in 1919, and turned it into a profitable city paper, and promoted the town of Littleton. He was director of the Colorado Press Association, and devoted his life to journalism. Ultimately, the *Littleton Independent* became one of the nation's most respected small town newspapers, achieving high honors.

Littleton's highly-acclaimed public library was named in his honor in 1965.

The Bemis Family Plot is located in Block 6, Lots 28 and 29.

Author's photo

The grave of cannibal Alfred Packer
is covered by a concrete slab
to prevent vandalism.

Bowles, Joseph W.
(1835 – 1906)

Bowles came west from North Carolina, first settling in the Nevada mining district, serving two terms as sheriff. He moved to Littleton and bought land just west of the South Platte River in 1862. Bowles brought the tiny farming community to new heights. He improved the land, raised the finest livestock in the area, and became a backbone to the community. He sat on several town committees, devoted to the enrichment of Littleton. Bowles Avenue is named after the pioneer pillar of the city.

The Bowles family plot is located in Block 3, Lot 34.

Little, Richard S. (1829 – 1889)

A farmer from Grafton, New Hampshire, and an educated civil engineer from Vermont, Little moved west in 1860, surveying land claims along the Platte River. Little saw the advantages of a water-powered mill along the Platte River, and sold the idea to the politicos of the territory, including William N. Byers. Little turned to agriculture, building the Rough and Ready Flour Mill. A town soon sprang forth, on land owned by Little, and named Littleton, in his honor.

Littleton, designated by the U.S. Post Office in 1869, lay ten miles south of Denver, and was considered a farming community. The town grew and prospered because of Little's promotional ideas. Little was elected to the state Legislature in 1872. Involved in real estate, Little donated land to benefit his beloved city, including the city's cemetery and one of the first churches.

His grave is located in Block B, Lot 31. There is a marker.

Packer, Alfred (1842 – 1907)[17]

Just the mention the name, Alfred Packer conjures up gruesome thoughts. Packer is the only man in United States history to be convicted of cannibalism.

An epileptic, Packer drifted west for his health, eventually scouting for gold prospectors in the Rocky Mountains. Just before the win-

Author's photo
Fort Logan National Cemetery, with Loretto Heights in the background.

ter of 1873 – 1874, Packer led a party of six men from Montrose into the San Juan Mountains. A blizzard hit, forcing the party to camp above Lake City. What really happened during the encampment has never been proven, yet Packer was the lone survivor.

On April 6, 1874, Packer arrived on foot at the Los Pinos Agency, some seventy-five miles from his winter camp. Suspicious officials eventually arrested him on murder charges. The remains of his five companions were found above Lake City, with body parts missing.[18] Escaping from jail twice, he was eventually caught, tried, and sentenced to forty years in prison in 1886. Packer was released in 1901. He died six years later.

This horrendous tale should end here, but curious historians seeking the truth have uncovered further evidence. In the summer of 1989, a party of researchers from George Washington University, examined the graves of the five men buried on the hillside in Dead Man's Gulch south of Lake City. Their findings were sent to a lab at Arizona University and the results were revealed in August 1989.

The researchers found no evidence to suggest a gunshot wound on any of the five remains, leaving us to question Packer's testimony of shooting Bell in self defense.

Cemetery records list his cause of death in 1907, as stomach trouble. Packer's grave is covered with three feet of concrete, to protect against vandals. His grave is located in Block 3, Lot 65. It is marked with a white marble military stone.

Veteran's Section

The grand Veteran's Section is a testament to those who served in the Spanish American War, and both world wars.

Located in the north end of the cemetery, this memorial is marked by a tall flag pole, with the government issue white marble tombstones circling the flag pole.

FORT LOGAN NATIONAL CEMETERY
3698 S. SHERIDAN BLVD.

This military post was established by Congress in 1887. General Phil Sheridan selected the site, then far west of Denver. The facility, originally called Fort Sheridan, located on the bank of Bear Creek, was a tent camp for the Eighteenth Infantry. The post was renamed Fort Logan in 1889. Two reasons are given for the renaming: General Sheridan selected another site in Chicago to be named in his honor, thus snubbing Colorado. The second reason was General Order #11, issued in 1888, by General John A. Logan. The order set aside a national veteran decoration day, now known as Memorial Day.

During a Memorial Day celebration, on the brink of World War II, a speaker asked of the audience:

> *Have we kept faith with those who are buried here and whom we honor today?*

Activity was high during both World Wars. In peacetime, the facilities were used for military training. At one time, two railroads served the post.

Fort Logan is recognized as the birth place of the Air Force. In 1894 it was the base of the Signal Corps balloon. The balloon was developed for use in Cuba, to observe the enemy during the Spanish American War.

Today, Fort Logan National Cemetery is a monumental resting place for all branches of the United States armed forces. It became a national cemetery in 1950, the eighth largest in the country.

Fort Logan has two Medal of Honor Holders: Major William E. Adams, located in Section P, Grave Number 3831, and First Sergeant Maximo Yabes, located in Section R, Grave Number 369.

Robert "Bob" Caron was the tail gunner on the Enola Gay on August 5, 1945, when his plane dropped the atomic bomb over Hiroshima, Japan. It was his camera that captured the image of the mushroom cloud of explosion that flashed around the world.

Robert Caron died in June 1995, and was buried with honors in Section 8, Grave 1106.

LORETTO HEIGHTS CATHOLIC CEMETERY
3001 SOUTH FEDERAL BOULEVARD

The Academy was established in 1875 by the Sisters of Loretto, under the famed Catholic Padre Father Machbeuf.

In the northwest corner of the beautiful campus, now called Teikyo University, lies a small cemetery. Its setting is unique as it is tucked away among Denver's southwest bustling communities.

Approximately fifty Sisters from the Academy are buried in this tiny corner, surrounded by a high wrought iron fence. With the exception of one marker, all bear beautiful white marble stones, surrounding a large white marble statue of the Sacred Mother Mary.

The large dark granite tombstone, bears the name of Mother Mary Pancratia Bonfils.[19] Born in 1851, her dream was to establish a Catholic Academy for women.

She became the founder of Loretto Heights Academy. Mother Mary died in 1915.

MOUNT OLIVET CEMETERY
12801 W. 44TH AVENUE

If ever a more ordained burial site by circumstance exists, it must be matched with Denver's Mount Olivet Cemetery.

Father Joseph P. Machbeuf came from Santa Fe, New Mexico, to hold religious services in the Colorado gold country. An original 59er, he traveled from camp-to-camp, preaching the religious word. He slept under the stars, in the snow drifts, and in the wind, until he reached Denver. Continuing his work in Denver, Father Machbeuf became a bishop of the Holy Church, the first in Denver.

The site of Mount Olivet Cemetery is Machbeuf's original 400-acre farm, which he donated to the Denver diocese as a sacred Catholic burial ground, consecrated in 1892. A special car carried hundreds of visitors daily to the cemetery, by way of the Union Pacific Railroad.

This new cemetery graciously allowed burial transplants to be received from the Catholic Section of the old Mt. Calvary, then undergoing reconstruction.[20]

Features of Mount Olivet include eight mausoleums, the Priests Section, Sisters Section, Calvary Section, Stations of the Cross, a memorial to the Mother Cabrini Orphanage, and the Pioneer Section. The Chapel is five individual chapels in one, completed in 1969.

Father Tihan, at a Memorial Day Mass, urged his listeners to visit the cemetery often and bring a picnic lunch, to enjoy the quiet beauty and inspiration.

Dietemann, Henrietta (? – 1868)

In 1868, Henrietta Dietemann, and her five-year-old son Johnny, were found dead at their ranch in Elbert County. Their bodies were riddled with Indian arrows, and their scalps removed. Seeing a band of Indians taking horses out of the corral, Henrietta, her sister, and hired hands took as many possessions as possible, and with her son and daughter, began to walk to the stage line, some two miles away. The Indians rode toward the group, and they scattered. Henrietta, heavy with child and pulling her young son, did not get away. Henrietta and young Johnny were shot full of arrows, scalped, and their bodies horribly mutilated.

John Dietemann, Henrietta's husband, had the bodies of his loved ones interred at the Mount Calvary Cemetery in Denver. Henrietta and young John's remains were removed to Mount Olivet Cemetery in the 1950s.

There is a marker in Section 16, Block 4, Space 23.

Gallagher Memorial

The Gallagher Memorial Sanctuary was erected in 1937 by Mrs. Patrick R. Gallagher in memory of her husband. "Reddy" Gallagher was a wrestler and boxer from back east. He stopped off in Denver while in route to a match and decided to stay. He worked as a cub reporter for the *Denver Post* and promoted boxing and wrestling in the Denver area.

The chapel is erected of pink marble walls and holds the crypts of the bishops of Denver. Among those entombed are Bishops Machebeuf, Matz, (both reinterred) and Tihen.

The memorial is located in Block 7.

Gilpin, William (1813 – 1894)

The Gilpin burial site is one of the oldest plots at Mount Olivet. William Gilpin was a West Point graduate, a member of the Fremont Expedition, and a major of the First Missouri Cavalry in the Mexican War of 1846. In 1861, President Lincoln appointed him the first governor of Colorado Territory. He convened the first Territorial Legislature and formed the Colorado Volunteers. Marred by controversy, his term barely lasted a year. Gilpin championed Colorado's interests, being involved in the fight for statehood, railroad transportation and local government.

The weathered tall marble pillar marks the grave of the Gilpins' son Willie, who died in 1892 at age seventeen, with William and his wife Julia buried on each side of their offspring, in the southeast corner of Section 9, Block 1.

Moon, Catherine (1865 – 1926)

Born aboard a ship along the French coast, Catherine grew up on the family farm in Ireland. A daring young lass, she left Ireland on her own for America. She first arrived in Wisconsin, where she married Frank Gartman. The couple moved on to Colorado, locating near Fort Collins. Gartman took several odd jobs, while Katie took in laundry.

One of Katie's customers was Cecil Moon, a young wealthy Englishman. When Moon fell ill, it was Katie who nursed him back to health. The two developed a romance. Some say Moon paid Gartman to divorce Katie. Another version has it that a scorned and bitter Gartman divorced his wife, leaving her nothing. In any case, Katie married Cecil Moon in July 1888.

Within a year of the marriage, Cecil's father and grandfather died. Shortly after, his two older brothers died in the English army. Thus, the family fortune was passed to Cecil who became Lord Cecil Moon. Katie, the hot tempered Irish laundress, suddenly became a rich aristocrat, and gained the title of Lady Moon. Yet she was ostracized by her English in-laws, and snubbed by Colorado society.

The Moons purchased the Elk Horn Ranch near Fort Collins, where they lived out their days comfortably, yet lonely.

Lady Moon became the inspiration for the longest running radio soap opera, "Our Gal Sunday." The show ran from 1937 to 1959.

There is a monument to her memory in the south end of Section 18, Block 1.

Mullen, John K. (1847 – 1929)

One of the most grandiose of family section is the J.K. Mullen plot. Christian symbolism is prominent in most of the monuments, headed by the Mullen Pillar, adorned with the bronze statue of Our Lord, in the center of the exedra. Markers are placed in a semi-circle around the center plot, marking the family members and descendants.

A mill worker at age fourteen, Mullen settled in Denver in 1871, finding work at a flour mill for room and board. Within four years he owned his own mill, which evolved into the Hungarian High Altitude Flour Mill. Expanding the mill, he also purchased wheat fields and grain elevators, establishing a multi-million dollar mill empire from the west coast to Kansas, making Denver the milling capitol of the Rockies.

Having made his fortune, Mullen turned to philanthropic causes. He built the Home for the Aged, and the Boys Home, both in Denver. He contributed to Mayor Speer's "City Beautiful" by donating bronze statues for the Civic Center in downtown Denver. He helped build the Immaculate Conception Church, the Mullen School for Boys at Ft.

This marble mausoleum, built
in Italy at a cost of $250,000,
is the final resting place of
Verner Z. Reed and his wife.

Logan, and helped establish Colorado's
first employee profit-sharing plan.

The J.K. Mullen plot is located at the
north end of Section 9, Block 10.

Reed, Verner, Z.
(1863 – 1919)

A Chicago newspaperman, Reed
moved to Colorado, settling in Colorado
Springs during the Cripple Creek gold
rush of 1891. Successful in real estate, he
bought into several ventures including
fruit orchards, ranch land, and mining
interests such as the Midwest Refining
Company. As a lawyer, he was responsible for the multi-million dollar sale of
W.S. Stratton's Independence Mine in
Cripple Creek, earning a million dollar
commission, a first in the industry.[21]

Reed contributed unconditionally to
the war effort during World War I, and to
several religious causes including
Denver's Catholic Church quarters at Colfax and Logan. His estimat-
ed wealth at death was twenty million dollars.

His wife Mary continued his philanthropic causes. She was instrumental in the founding of Colorado's Community Chest, later the
national United Way Foundation. She also co-founded Bonfils Theater
and was named Outstanding Woman of the Year in 1942. Mrs. Reed
opened one of her husband's Cripple Creek mines during the depression, so that men would have jobs.

The Reed monument is a stunning castle-like mausoleum, resem-
bling an almost life size chapel. Built of white marble, delicate carvings, and ornate sculpture, it is also adorned with statues and stained
glass. Built in Italy, the memorial and crypt were transported to
Mount Olivet in 1923 at a total cost of $250,000.

The Reed Family memorial is in Section 15, Block 1.

Swigert, John "Jack" (1931 – 1982)

Colorado University graduate, U.S. Air Force aviator, and one of
the original Apollo astronauts, Swigert was one of four civilians chosen for the Apollo Space Program in 1966. He became backup command module pilot of Apollo 13 in 1970. The mission suffered a major
accident when an explosion damaged the life-support system. The

moon landing was canceled by NASA, focusing on a safe return to earth. The astronauts reduced power consumption, conserving the life-support systems. After a six-day ordeal, the space craft splashed down in the Pacific Ocean. Swigert's work was praised by President Nixon.

Colorado voters elected Swigert to the U.S. House of Representatives 1982. He was never sworn into office. Swigert died at age fifty-one of bone cancer. His fellow Apollo astronauts attended the funeral, planting a memorial tree near his grave. A bronze plaque on the tree marks the astronaut's remembrance to Jack Swigert, astronaut.

In the spring of 1997, a statue of Jack Swigert became the second representative of Colorado to grace the Hall of Statuary, in Washington D.C.

Author's collection
Elizabeth "Baby Doe" Tabor
She was the second wife of Horace
Tabor, died alone, in poverty.

The stone monument to Jack Swigert is in Section 15, Block 1.

Tabor, Horace Austin Warner (1830 – 1899)
Tabor, Elizabeth Bonduel McCourt Doe (1854 – 1935)

A greenhorn miner and one of the original 59ers, Tabor became Colorado's own "rags-to-riches-to-rags" legend. Looking to cash in on Colorado's gold riches, Tabor prospected for eighteen years, finally finding fame and fortune in Leadville.

In Leadville, Augusta, Tabor's first wife, ran a general store and post office, while Horace was elected first mayor and postmaster. Grubstaking two miners in 1878 was the turning point in Tabor's life. The duo struck it rich and Tabor received a third of the claim. With overnight wealth, Tabor invested in other mining ventures, all of which added to his wealth. Tabor improved Leadville with an opera house, the first bank, a fire hose company, law enforcement, and a telephone company, then moved to Denver to hobnob with the rich and pour money into the Republican Party. His money bought him a temporary position as lieutenant governor in 1878, and he later served a thirty-day term as U.S. Senator, in 1883. Yet his further political ambitions were dashed by a scandalous affair with divorcee Elizabeth (Baby Doe.)

Tabor eventually divorced his wife, Augusta, and married Baby Doe in Washington D.C., while still in his Senate term, with President Arthur in attendance.

The repeal of the Sherman Silver Purchase Act of 1893, caused the value of silver to plunge, and so too, most of Tabor's mines. He subsequently squandered his remaining fortune, dying penniless in 1899. His last words to his beloved Baby Doe were; "Hang on to the Matchless Mine, it will make millions."

Many called Baby Doe the "Belle of Oshkosh." Elizabeth Bonduel McCourt came to the Colorado gold fields with her new husband, Harvey Doe in 1873. The two worked their honeymoon claim, known as the Fourth of July, in Central City, for two years. Harvey had mismanaged the mine from the beginning, forcing Elizabeth to take over. She acquired the nickname "Baby Doe" from the miners as she took on all the responsibilities of mining in a man's world. Eventually divorcing Harvey, Baby Doe headed for Leadville, where she set her sights on the rich H.A.W. Tabor. They were married in 1883.

Baby Doe gave Horace two daughters before their world fell apart. Within ten years, Horace lost his fortune and died penniless, leaving Baby Doe destitute. Clinging to his dying words, "Hang on to the Matchless Mine, it will make you rich," she moved into a shack at the Matchless, determined to make the mine run. Baby Doe worked the mine alone, and walked the bitter cold mile to town for food and mail, covered in burlap and newspaper. She borrowed money only when she had to, to keep the mine working. For thirty-five years she tried to make the dream of the Matchless Mine come back to life; she died trying.

Elizabeth Bonduel McCourt Tabor was found frozen in the shape of a cross, to her shanty floor on March 1, 1935. Her long lonely vigil had finally come to an end, and so too had the saga of the Tabors.

Baby Doe Tabor is buried at Mount Olivet in Section 18, Block 6. Horace's remains were moved from the Mount Calvary Cemetery and reinterred next to his beloved Baby Doe.

— — —

Ghost Notes, Mysteries,
& Other Related Findings

Some say the heartbroken ghost of Augusta Tabor roams the Mile High Building in downtown Denver. This is the site of her twenty-seven-room mansion, shared with Tabor and awarded to her in the divorce settlement. Augusta never wanted the lavish mansion, or the social lifestyle wealth brought, or the eventual unhappiness that left her miserably alone.

* * *

To make way for the new Denver Botanic Gardens, some 7,000 bodies were moved from the Mount Calvary section of City Cemetery to Mount Olivet. Supposedly, all remains were identified, with the exception of a young Irish maiden. Her coffin was opened and the delicate scent of roses filled the air. The workmen were overcome with the eerie feelings they experienced. Concern immediately prevailed among the Mount Olivet staff; this could be a Saint! The sanctity must be proven before removal, or doom abounded. The Catholic Registry immediately stepped in, researched the unfortunate woman's past, yet found nothing.

* * *

While the majority of bodies were moved from Mount Calvary Cemetery, many of the bodies from Mount Prospect were not moved. Burial contractors pocketed the city's money, rather than move all the bodies to make way for the Cheesman Gardens. The beautiful landscape and floral abundance of today's Cheesman Park may be due to those who lie below the surface.

* * *

In 1979, a gruesome discovery was made in the dark, dingy basement of the Colorado state capitol. As workmen cleared the basement and sorted the dusty boxes and files, one of the men opened a wooden box. Inside the box was a cloth wrapped carefully around two human male skulls. Several weeks of tests and research were conducted. The conclusion, although not positive, was that the skulls were that of the infamous Espinosas, tracked and killed by famed scout and mountain man, Tom Tobin.[22]

Tobin was asked by Governor John Evans and Colonel Tappan of Fort Garland to apprehend the murderous Espinosa gang, and offered him a reward of $25,000. Tobin tracked and killed two of the gang, and for proof, he cut off their heads. Delivering the heads of the Espinosas to the governor, Tobin demanded his reward money.

Tobin claimed he never received the money, although it is now apparent, Governor Evans received proof that Tom Tobin kept his part of the deal.

* * *

Captain Silas Soule was from a prominent abolitionist family. During the Civil War, his orders brought him west, where he marching with the First Colorado Regiment to New Mexico, to stop the Confederates from stealing western gold. His efforts were rewarded in the defeat of the Texan Army at Apache Canyon and Glorieta Pass, in March 1862. Captain Soule was fond of his regiment commander, Colonel John M. Chivington, offering informative letters to the colonel on many occasions. Soule was present at the Indian talks at Camp Weld, as well as witnessing Major Wynkoop's promise of peace to the Indians. When Chivington announced his plan to attack the Indians at Sand Creek, in 1864, Soule was horrified and argued with Chivington that such an attack upon peaceful Indians would be dishonorable. When Chivington proceeded as planned, Soule refused to order his men to open fire.

Following the massacre and subsequent congressional hearing, Soule testified to the horrors he had witnessed at the hands of Chivington and his men. His testimony may have cost him his life. A few months after the hearings concluded, condemning Chivington for his actions, Soule, serving as Provost Marshal in Denver, was found murdered. Although never proven, it was believed that the assassin, Charles Squier, had been hired by Chivington.

— — —

Additional Cemeteries Listed by County

Adams County

Cemetery	1st Burial
Elmwood Cemetery	1895
Indian Burial Ground	?
Pioneer Cemetery	1864
Platte Valley Congregational Cem.	1872 – Abandoned
Rose Hill Cemetery	
- Commerce City	1892
St. Clair-Ross/Wolpert Cemetery	1872
Wesley Chapel Cemetery/	
Quimby Cemetery	1889
Woolsey/Leader Cemetery	1918 – Abandoned

Arapahoe County

Cemetery	1st Burial
Melvin-Lewis Cemetery	1880 – Abandoned[23]
Mount Nebo Cemetery	1902
Running Creek/Salam Cemetery	1905

Denver County

Cemetery	1st Burial
Acacia/Masonic Cemetery	1867
All Souls Walk	1920
Lowry Field Graves	1896 – Abandoned
Regis College Cemetery	? – Abandoned

Jefferson County

Cemetery	1st Burial
Arvada Cemetery	1863
Ault/Reid Old Mill Cemetery	1889
Buffalo Creek/ Little Chapel Cemetery	1881
Lehow Cemetery	1870
Ralston Cemetery/Osborn Hill	1869
Rockland Cemetery	1880

— — —

Sources

Black American West Museum
Colorado Historical Society
Colorado State Genealogical Society
Denver Public Library – Western Section
Fairmount Cemetery Records
Littleton Cemetery Records
Mount Olivet Historical Records
Riverside Cemetery Records

Newspapers

Denver Post
Denver Republican
Littleton Times
Rocky Mountain News

Interviews

Byer, Vicki – Consultant, Arapahoe County

Gallagher, Dennis – Former state Senator, and member of Historic Denver, Inc.

Grueles, Ronda – Fairmount, Riverside Cemeteries

Houser, John – Littleton Cemetery sexton

Noel, Tom – History professor, Denver University

Sales, Scott – Crown Hill Cemetery sexton

— — —

Chapter Three Notes

[1] See Fort Lyon, Chapter 4.

[2] See Tabor, H. A. W.

[3] See Tabor, Elizabeth Bonduel McCourt Doe.

[4] See Wootton, Richens.

[5] See Speer, Robert.

[6] See Sand Creek Massacre Historical Site, Chapter 4.

[7] The Hill family burial plot also includes Hill's wife, son Crawford, and his wife, Louise, who was Denver's socialite and founder of the "Sacred 36."

[8] Rocky Mountain News, June 15, 1864. However, an interview with Mrs. Ruth V.W. Oettinger, daughter of ranch owner Isaac Van Wormer, by Dr. L. F. Hafen, of the Colorado Historical Society, states the bodies of her father's ranch hand and family were not scalped. Interview with CHS dated January 29, 1935.

[9] Sarah E. Smith Iliff was a descendent of John Smith, of Pochahontas fame.

[10] John Iliff was originally buried at Riverside. His remains, along with the large white Obelisk were later moved to the Fairmount Cemetery.

[11] Her childhood home still stands in Central City.

[12] A second statue, honoring Coloradan Jack Swigert was erected in the spring of 1997.

[13] See Wood, Leah J. (Rogers, Jenny).

[14] Her husband, John "Handsome Jack" Ready, is buried in an unmarked grave.

[15] See Silks, Mattie.

[16] Her home at 532 W. 4th Avenue, still stands.

[17] "Alfred" is the name listed on birth, Civil War, trial transcripts, and the death certificate. In his second written transcript, Packer spelled "Alfred," yet signed "Alferd."

[18] See Lake City, Chapter 5.

[19] She was the first cousin to Frederick G. Bonfils, co-founder of the Denver Post newspaper.

[20] See The Old City Cemetery.

[21] See Stratton, W.S., Evergreen Cemetery.

[22] See Tobin, Thomas, and the Espinosa Gang.

[23] Burials removed to Fairmount Cemetery in 1910.

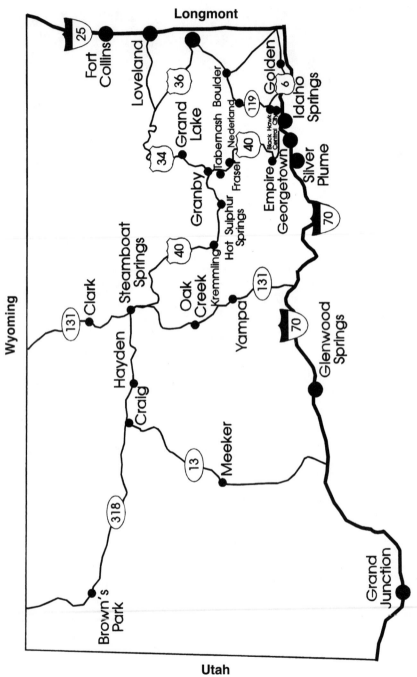

Chapter Four

The Western Plateaus

The Ute Indians were the first inhabitants of northwestern Colorado. The Ute ancestry goes back to the Anasazi of the Four Corners area, sometime prior to 1300 AD. At that time, the Utes became a separate tribe and were pushed into the mountains by the dominant Plains Indians. They were the first known tribe to call the Rocky Mountains home.

Early in the seventeenth century, the white man appeared. Explorers, trappers and traders crossed the area. In time, the area opened for settlers. The Utes resisted and fought for their land. In the end, the Utes were forced onto a reservation.

In 1859, the foothills of northwestern Colorado experienced a frenzy of growth. Gold was discovered at Russell Gulch. Known as the gateway to the Rockies, thousands of pioneers flocked to the foothills and the great mountains beyond. Gold camps evolved into towns, creating a demand for railroads. The Colorado Central built a narrow gauge line up Clear Creek to Central City in the early 1860s. Within ten years, railroads were built to Boulder, Longmont, Fort Collins, and Loveland, crossing Colorado west to the Utah line, by the 1880s. Railroads did more than aid existing towns, they provided a venue for new towns and population growth.

The western portion of northern Colorado saw the beginnings of permanent settlement in 1870. Several treaties with the Indians were made and broken during that period. The Indians retaliated, waging war. The climax was the 1879 Meeker Massacre. In the aftermath, the Indians were moved to reservations in Utah. And the westward migration continued.

Farmers and ranchers staked their claims across northwestern Colorado. Cattle and horse breeding were the primary businesses. Sheep herding, fruit orchards and mining, were among the major industries.

Northwest Colorado has a unique terrain. Foothills lead to the majestic Rocky Mountains. The western slope of the Rockies dips into many valleys and meadows, that stretch west to the Utah border. At the border, Colorado's terrain becomes rugged and quite rocky. It is here that famous outlaws such as Butch Cassidy, found refuge at a place called Brown's Park.

With such diversity, northwest Colorado offers it's own brand of pioneer history. It is a story rich in legend and lore, triumph, and defeat, fortune and loss.

— — —

Highway 34 West

GRAND LAKE

GRAND LAKE CEMETERY

THE CEMETERY IS LOCATED ONE-HALF-MILE NORTHWEST OF THE TOWN OF GRAND LAKE. FROM HIGHWAY 34, FOLLOW THE ROAD THROUGH TOWN, FROM THE CHAMBER OF COMMERCE BUILDING, TURNING LEFT AT THE SECOND ROAD. TURN RIGHT ON WESTERN ROAD, JUST PAST THE GOLF COURSE ROAD. THE CEMETERY IS JUST AHEAD.

This cemetery, recorded at the Grand County Courthouse, began in 1875. The location was the Harbison Ranch and contained ten tracts. The early cemetery records are not complete. Cemetery lots were free, therefore, formal records were not necessary. Area residents often buried their dead themselves, following a quiet service in the home. Many of the original tracts contain the remains of the unknown loved ones, due to either lack of records or because the graves were never marked.[1]

The oldest marked grave is that of Minerva Simonds. Her remarkable original wooden marker is dated 1879. State and county land records record the land as the Grand Lake Cemetery, however records of 1915, place the land as part of the Rocky Mountain National Park. A special government permit has been extended "in perpetuity" by a Senate bill, signed into law in November 1996. This bill gives the city of Grand Lake legal title to the cemetery.[2]

A cemetery on the Lehman Ranch and two cemeteries near Shadow Mountain existed prior to the Granby Reservoir and Shadow Mountain Lake. The graves were moved to the Grand Lake Cemetery when the lakes were created in the 1940s. The cemetery is maintained in its natural setting by the Grand Lake Women's Club.

Baker, John Jack (1809 – 1891)

A native of Fort Wayne, Indiana, John "Jack" Baker came to the Grand Lake area in the mid 1850s. An explorer, hunter and trapper, he is known as the first pioneer of the Grand Lake area. He is believed to be the first white man to climb the 12,000-foot mountain north of Grand Lake that bares his name.

Baker was a relative of fellow pioneer and founder, Joseph Wescott, and spent many years in his company. He was a friend to the Indians, and instrumental in negotiating peace in the formidable years of Grand Lake's existence.

Baker's death in 1891, was the first burial in the Young family plot.

Duty, E.R. (? – 1883)

One of the earliest pioneers in the Grand Lake area, E.R. Duty arrived in 1879. A miner at the Wolverine Mine, he was caught in a snow slide in the winter of 1883. Mike Flynn was found barely alive four hours later. Flynn stated he heard the cries of Duty for hours, but was unable to help.

Duty was found hours later, frozen to death in a seated position, a few feet from Mike Flynn's location.

According to cemetery records, he was the fifth interment in the cemetery. There is a marker.

Mills, John G. (1849 – 1883)

A native of Northern Vermont, it is curious that Mills became involved with the radical movements of Southern reconstruction, following the Civil War. He was named in two violent deaths in Mississippi and immediately left for the untamed West.[3] Following a stint in Wyoming, where he was an agent for two newspapers, Mills came to Teller City, Colorado, in the early 1880s. At Teller City, he speculated in mines and toll roads and eventually became a self-proclaimed mining lawyer.

Mills was elected county commissioner in 1880 and served as the board chairman. When he lost the re-election to E.P. Weber of Hot Sulphur Springs, the one-time close friends became bitter political enemies. Following the election, Grand Lake became the county seat, winning in a hot political dispute against Hot Sulphur Springs.

Mills headed the mining faction of Hot Sulphur Springs and proceeded to overturn the voters of Grand County and return the county seat to Hot Sulphur Springs.[4] Fellow commissioners, all from Grand Lake, now joined forces in opposition to Mill's activities. E.P. Weber, Barney Day, and T.J. Dean, held secret commissioner meetings, without the knowledge or presence of Mills. The result of these secret meetings undermined Mills' authority, allowing Weber to gain political control of the county and return the county seat to Hot Sulphur Springs. Mills, aware of the obvious sabotage, was unable to get legal action from the authorities.

The climax came on July 4, 1893, when Mills, frustrated by a jury summons served by the commissioners for his removal, convinced two of his cronies to help in a "scare" as he called it, to oust the three commissioners from Grand Lake.

On the morning of the fourth of July 1883, Mills and his associates laid in wait on the hill above Mrs. Young's Fairview House, where the holiday celebration was taking place. Weber, Dean and Day approached the boardinghouse on foot, expecting to join in the holiday festivities.

The Mills' faction opened fire, hitting Weber first. Dean was hit next. Day, falling to the ground, returned fire, hitting a masked man. Dean was shot again. Within seconds, the gunfire was over, and four men lay dead or dying.

Several men from Mrs. Young's holiday gathering rushed to the scene. Barney Day lay dead in the lake. Weber and Dean, near death, were taken to Mrs. Young's boardinghouse.[5] Dean's blood soaked into the hardwood floors of the boardinghouse, and was never removed, despite the efforts of Mrs. Young.

The fourth victim was John G. Mills, identified as the masked killer who perpetrated the ambush. The coroner's report stated that all three died of gunshots by parties unknown.[6] The two masked men with Mills were never identified, or apprehended. Many historians believe they were Sheriff C.W. Royer, and Undersheriff William Redman.[7] Thus ended the long political feud of Grand County and the worst episode in Colorado politics.

For all his mighty, and self-imposed political hierarchy, Mills received a small funeral, scantly attended. There is a marker to his memory.

Plummer, Robert (? – 1882)

A miner, Robert Plummer worked at the Ruby Mine above Grand Lake. On December 31, 1882, he attended the New Year's Eve Ball at the Grand Lake House. This establishment was built by Wilson Waldron, in 1878. It was Waldron who hosted the party.

During the party, Waldron became quite drunk, and in a mean spirited way, teased his infant child and wife. Mrs. Waldron, becoming frightened, asked an innocent Bob Plummer to get Waldron away from the baby.

Plummer dutifully responded. When Waldron refused to leave, Plummer got tough. Waldron grabbed his gun from the wall, and Plummer left the party. Waldron pursued and shot Plummer. Waldron was immediately arrested and placed in jail, where he later escaped, and was never heard from again.

Robert Plummer is buried in the Grand Lake Cemetery. There is a marker.

Wescott, Joseph L. (? – 1914)

A native of Nova Scotia, Wescott fought as a Union cavalryman in the Civil War. Mustered out of the army in 1865, he moved west. Looking for a cure for his rheumatism, he first settled at Hot Sulphur Springs. He is known as the first white settler of Grand Lake, arriving in 1867. A life-long bachelor, he spent his time hunting and fishing, earning his living off the land. Through the seasons, he could catch over 100 trout a day from Grand Lake. The fish, packed in ice, were then sent by stage to Georgetown and Hot Sulphur Springs. He hunted for rabbit, shot deer, elk, and bear for local families, stage stops, and restaurants. A great friend to the Indians, he helped manage the peace in the area.

In 1877, he became Grand Lake's first postmaster. He is known in local history as "Judge" Wescott, although there is no documentation regarding the title. In his later years, he became a recluse of sorts, occasionally spending time fishing with the children of the area. He wrote poetry, much of which centered around the history of Grand Lake.

A legend of Grand Lake, Joseph Wescott died of natural causes in 1914. There is a marker.

Young Family Plot

Mary Jane Young came to Middle Park in the 1870s, a widow with two children. Her father, John Jack Baker, had settled in the area several years prior to Mary Jane's arrival. To support her family, Mary operated a neglected hotel and boardinghouse on the west edge of Grand Lake. She later purchased the enterprise, which she had turned into a profitable business, known as Fairview House and made it the most popular boardinghouse in the area. It was her establishment at the lake where the historic shoot-out involving four county commissioners took place on July 4, 1883. She married Al Hanscomb in 1889, who won the election of 1888 to county treasurer.

Mary Jane Young is buried in the Young family plot.

Christian F. Young, the son of Mary Jane, ran a freighting and stage operation before he and his wife, Josie started the Rustic Inn in

1899. Four children were born to this union. Christian was known as the best caller for the many social dances held at Grand Lake. In 1896, he was calling a dance when Ben Mitchell stabbed a man to death. In early 1905, following the calling of a dance social, Christian Young died in his sleep.

Christian is buried near his daughter Mary Vesta Young, who had died the previous year, at age fourteen.

Josie Young Kalsey Langley is the final member of the pioneer Young family to be buried in the family plot. She came to Grand Lake as a child, with her parents, the Nute Coffeys.[8] She met Christian Young at a social dance held at his mother's Fairview House and Hotel.

In 1889, Christian and Josie built their own hotel, the Rustic Inn. While Josie ran the hotel and tended the children, Christian drove a stage between Grand Lake and Georgetown. The Youngs were later an instrumental part of the Grand Lake Yacht Club Association.

Tragedy took its toll on Josie. Her daughter, Mary Vesta died at age fourteen in 1904, and her husband Christian, died in 1905. A strong woman, Josie kept her family together, running the Rustic Inn on her own. Josie had a very astute business reputation. People either liked or disliked her, there was no medium.

In 1906, Josie married a newcomer to the area by the name of H.C. Langley. Together, they ran the hotel for several years until Langley died, at which time the property was sold.

The stern, disciplined and unemotional Josie Young Langley lived her last years in lonely solitude. Her former daughter-in-law, Nell Young Pauly, seemed to be the only member of the family to care for her in her last years.

At the time of her death, it was Mrs. Pauly who handled all the arrangements. In a soaking rain, Mrs. Pauly and her second husband dug through the wet, clammy, clumped dirt, to make the grave. They fortified the dirt sides with timbers and laid Josie Young to rest. A handful of citizens later paid their respects. As the rain fell again, the couple were left alone to cover the grave.

— — —

Highway 36 West

BOULDER

COLUMBIA CEMETERY
LOCATED IN DOWNTOWN BOULDER, AT 9TH AND COLLEGE AVENUES.

This old pioneer cemetery served as Boulder's first graveyard in 1870. The land was purchased by the Masons from pioneer Marinus Smith. Originally a cow pasture, the location was far away from the infant town at that time. Within six months of the purchase, the local I.O.O.F. Lodge took over ownership of the cemetery. Prior to the establishment of this cemetery, burials occurred near the mining camps or on private ranch land. The first burial occurred in May 1870, that of Redmond C. Fisher, although there is no marker. The first designated section was the Potter's Field, in the corner now bounded by College Avenue and the school yard. As the cemetery grew, a fence was erected to keep out the cattle.

Just south of the potter's section, is the small veteran section. Only a dozen military stones dot the area. There are four main roads winding through the cemetery, now cut off to automobile traffic. Large trees grace the area, their limbs shadowing broken stones and weathered markers. A rock-lined canal flows east through the grounds.

Today, the cemetery in the heart of downtown Boulder, is in sad disorder. Many burials were reinterred in the new Greenmount Cemetery in 1904, in favor of a more attractive resting spot. The Park Cemetery Association took over management of the old "Pioneer" cemetery, as it had come to be known, in 1910. Both the grounds and general record keeping were so bad, the association could not recover and eventually turned the grounds over to the city of Boulder.

Unfortunately, there has not been much improvement. There have been few interments since 1964. Cemetery records are now kept by the Carnegie Library in Boulder, and do not appear in any better shape than they were in 1910. There are no records for the first seven years or for the first three years following 1910. Among the records dated 1914, are notes mentioning the need to show who owned plots and monies due for burials. A burial abstract showed empty plots where tombstones were known to exist.

Block and plot records are sketchy at best, therefore, a general location is offered for the following pioneer burials.

Arnett, Anthony (1819 – 1903)

One of Boulder's founding father's, Arnett, a Frenchman, came to Colorado in search of gold. Arriving in 1859, he worked in the Central City mines before operating a successful freighting business between Central City and Golden. In 1864, he moved his family to Boulder, where he operated the Boulder House Hotel for several years, and later bought the Brainard Hotel.

Arnett became involved in Boulder real estate, owning several large tracks of land. In keeping with his early day mining career, he

Denver Public Library
Tom Horn

invested in several mining properties at Gold Hill and Ward.

In 1865, he built the Black Hawk and Central City Wagon Road, followed by the construction of the Caribou and Central City Wagon Road. With the incorporation of Boulder in 1871, Arnett sat on the first town board.

Arnett donated some of his land for the site of the University of Colorado, in 1887, as well as a cash contribution to the building fund. It is said that Arnett swayed members of the Legislature toward voting for Boulder as a university site, in return for a few of his prized horses.[9]

During all of this activity, apparently Arnett found time to bring a herd of 100 cattle across the Plains from Illinois. The cattle did well in the winter climate, and Arnett is credited with Boulder's agricultural beginnings.

He is buried with his wife, Mary, in the northwest section of the cemetery. There is a marker.

Cheney, Charles H. (1873 – 1938)

The son of Boulder pioneer Lewis Cheney, Charles was born in Illinois and came to Colorado with his parents in 1877, when he was four years old. He received his education in the Boulder schools and went on to graduate from the State Preparatory School.

Charles worked as a bookkeeper in the First National Bank of Boulder, the bank his father founded in 1877. He became president of the bank in 1919, a position he held until the time of his death.

He is buried in the center of the north section along Pleasant Street. His tall white marble obelisk is the most prominent marker in the cemetery.

Horn, Thomas (1860 – 1903)[10]

One of the West's most notable characters, Tom Horn was born in Memphis, Missouri. At age fourteen, he headed west, away from his abusive father. He found work in Newton, Kansas, then went to Santa

Fe, where he hired on as a stage driver for the Overland Mail Company, in 1874. In 1876, he worked for the U.S. Army, succeeding Al Sieber, as chief of scouts.

For the next ten years, Horn tracked for the Army, fighting many battles against the Apache, under General George Crook. During this time, his biggest accomplishment was in tracking Geronimo. By 1890, he was living in Arizona, occasionally working as a lawman, when he joined the

Author's photo
Tom Horn's grave in Boulder's
Columbia Cemetery.

Pinkerton Detective Agency in Denver. He worked cases in Colorado and Wyoming, which included theft of livestock. He rid the Brown's Hole area of rustlers Madison Rash and Isom Dart, although suspicion of his character was first raised at this incident.[11]

Before age thirty, Horn had gained the reputation of the most fearless lawman in the territory. From this point, his story becomes one of simple corruption.

Horn was hired by the Swan Land and Cattle Company of Wyoming, in 1894, technically as a horse breaker. His real duties included tracking rustlers and encroaching homesteaders. Now a hired killer, he bushwhacked his prey. Any evidence would be carefully removed, and two small rocks would be placed under the victim's head. In this manner, the vigilante warning would be served.

Horn was paid handsomely, receiving $600 for each elimination. For the next several years, he continued his killing spree. The end came on a fateful day in 1901. Fourteen-year-old William Nickell was shot in the back, mistaken for his father. The boy was found the following day, with a single rock under his head.

Famed Pinkerton agent Joe Le Fors, was sent to hunt down Horn. He tracked Horn to Denver. At a saloon, he reportedly got Horn drunk and coerced him into confessing to the murder of the youth. Agents secretly wrote down Horn's confession.

Horn was arrested and stood trial in Cheyenne, where he was pronounced guilty of murder and sentenced to hang in October 1892. Horn managed to escape from the Cheyenne jail, but was promptly apprehended. Before his death, he wrote a biography of his life, in which stated he did not commit the murder of the boy. The cattleman's lawyers made a feeble attempt on Horn's behalf. It is possible they were involved in the murder, a way to get the "Killer Horn" out of the way.[12]

On November 20, 1903, the day before his forty-third birthday, Horn was executed with the modern gallows system. The trap door sprang open automatically and Horn dropped four feet. In thirty-two seconds, he was dead.

Tom Horn is buried east of the Veterans Section, across the road, beside his brother Charles. There is a small red granite marker. [13]

Kingsley, Marietta (? – 1910)

Marietta Kingsley ran a very popular parlour house on Walnut Street, Boulder's "Red Light" district. From the 1880s until the early 1900s, the Boulder newspapers were spiced with stories of Madam Kingsley and her "White House" of ill-repute. Fights would break out, raids were a regular occurrence, and even murder happened under Kingsley's domain.

A colorful character despite her profession, Kingsley was rarely seen without her two small pug dogs. During the flood of 1894, Kingsley was rescued from the rushing waters by a Doctor Jay. Emerging soaking wet, she managed to hang on to both pug dogs.

Marietta Kingsley is buried in an unmarked grave in the eastern section, in the corner bounded by the gravel road to the west, and just south of the Casey monument.

Nichols, David H. (1828 – 1900)

Born in Hardwick, Vermont, David Nichols left home at age twelve, following the death of his father. He learned the lumber trade in Minnesota and Wisconsin. Leaving his wife Elizabeth, and children in Illinois, he fought in the Mexican War in 1847. Following his discharge in 1848, he returned to his family.

He brought his family to Colorado during the gold rush of 1859, where he located in Boulder. He opened a sawmill and later went into business with the Tourtellet and Squires sawmill operations.

In 1864, he joined the 100-Day Volunteer Service, commissioned by Governor Evans and led by Colonel John M. Chivington. He served in the battles at Buffalo Springs, Beaver Creek and the infamous Sand Creek Massacre.[14]

He returned to Boulder and served in the first Territorial Legislature in 1864 – 1865, and was elected Speaker of the House in 1873. He became lieutenant governor in 1892.

David and Elizabeth Nichols are buried in the southern end of the cemetery, just east of the Tom Horn monument. There is a marker.

Rippon, Mary (1850 – 1935)

A native of Detroit, Mary Rippon graduated college, earning a teaching degree. In 1877, she was offered a teaching position at the new Colorado University at Boulder. Intrigued with the West and Colorado wildflowers in particular, she accepted. Rippon became the third Colorado University faculty member and the first woman in the United States to teach men at a state university. She spent the next fifty-seven years as professor of French and German and in 1895, was instrumental in establishing a public library in Boulder.

Mary Rippon led Boulder women in several organizations, including the political Better Boulder Party, and a women's organization to beautify the Columbia Cemetery. A true pioneer, the Boulder campus theater is named in her honor.

In 1888, Mary fell in love with one of her students, twenty-five-year-old Will Housel. By the spring of 1888, Mary found herself pregnant. Victorian convention did not permit female teachers to marry, so the young lovers left Boulder separately, bound for St. Louis, where they were married in secret. From St. Louis, Mary went on to New York and set sail for Germany. Housel returned to Boulder. Mary gave birth to a baby girl, Miriam, and returned to her teaching post shortly thereafter. Mary and Will eventually divorced.

Mary was reunited with her daughter in the 1920s. Miriam had a family of her own and came to Boulder, where she too, became an instructor at CU. When Mary Rippon died in 1935, Miriam was listed in her obituary as Mary's "closest friend." Mary Rippon is buried in the north section, near the Tourtellot monument.

Sturtevant, Joseph B. (1851 – 1910)

Known as "Rocky Mountain Joe," by the time he arrived in Boulder in 1876, Joe Sturtevant was raised by Indians in Wisconsin, joined the circus in Illinois, and fought with the 4th Wisconsin Calvary in the Civil War. He fought Indians with General Custer in 1873, narrowly missing the massacre at the Little Big Horn.

Arriving in Boulder in 1876, this colorful character first worked as a paperhanger and house painter. He married Anna Lyckman in December 1876. Finding a photograph of Boulder taken in 1866, he turned his interests to photography. For the next twenty years, Sturtevant took thousands of photographs around Boulder. With his long hair, prominent goatee, and buckskin clothing, the dashing "Rocky Mountain Joe" was a well-known personality and premier photographer. Much of Boulder's early photographic history is due to this great pioneer.

Joseph Sturtevant is buried in the west end of the cemetery, across the road, and south of the tool shed next to the fence. There is a marker.

Todd, William (1842 – 1887)

A native of North Cumberland, England, William Todd sailed to New York Harbor in 1861. He worked on the Brooklyn Bridge. A miner at heart, he soon left for the copper fields of Michigan.

The Colorado gold rush of 1859 lured William. He arrived at the gold camps of Nevadaville with his wife Eliza Jane, in 1862. Todd's background in Cornish mining served him well in America. After mining a few years in Gilpin County, Todd moved his family over the mountain to the silver camp of Caribou, in 1872.

He built a large two-story, twelve-room house for his growing family.[15] Eliza Jane raised her children, kept the family home, and helped with her husband's many business ventures. A practiced mid-wife, she helped many young mothers in child-birth. Todd operated a freighting business and a meat market. He later became a mining superintendent. In that capacity, he was trained to set bones, pull teeth, treat gunshot wounds and anything else his miners might require. In a mining cave-in, Todd rescued two miners and retrieved the body of A.J. Maxcy's nephew.

William Todd died unexpectedly in 1887. He was forty-four years old. His widow, Eliza Jane, sold their Caribou holdings in 1892, following the demonetization of silver, and moved the children to Boulder. She later married James A. Francis. However, William Todd and Eliza Jane are buried next to each other, in the Columbia Cemetery. Their simple granite markers are located just south of the water canal, near the Austin obelisk.

Tourtellot, Jonathan (1813 – 1870)

A native of Providence County, Rhode Island, Tourtellot came west with his family, first settling in Cincinnati, Ohio, where he received his education. He returned to Rhode Island, where he operated a mercantile establishment and married Miss Miranda Wade in 1836. He was a member of the Rhode Island Legislature in 1842.

In 1851, he brought his wife, Miranda, and family to his parents farm in Illinois. There he met F.A. Squires. The two became life-long business partners. Squires married Mrs. Tourtellot's twin sister, Maria Wade.

The Colorado gold rush lured Tourtellot and Squires in 1860. Arriving at Boulder, they purchased the log cabin hotel known as the Boulder House. The wives cut willow branches for brooms and used horse blankets to protect everything from the leaky roof. They were the among first white women to settle in the area. The two families expanded the hotel to include a mercantile shop before selling to Anthony Arnett in 1864. A year later, the two brothers-in-law built a home large enough for both families. Constructed of native rock and stone, it is the oldest home in Boulder today.[16]

Tourtellot and Squires opened a lumber yard, and the first general store in Boulder. The business flourished and the partnership lasted until 1871, when Jonathan Tourtellot died.

Jonathan Tourtellot is buried in the northwest section. A tall obelisk marks his burial spot.

Tyler, Clinton M. (1834 – 1886)

Clinton Tyler packed his wagons with his possessions and a stamp mill and headed for the goldfields of Colorado, in 1860. Along with his wife Sarah and her parents, the Nelson K. Smiths, he arrived in the booming gold camp of Black Hawk, where he set up his stamp mill.

During the Indian uprisings in the early 1860s, Tyler organized a volunteer calvary company at Black Hawk. Tyler and his men joined Colonel John Chivington at Sand Creek in 1864. Following this battle, Tyler received the rank of captain from Territorial Governor Evans.

Captain Tyler headed the military unit on the South Platte, providing protection for the wagon trains on the Eastern Plains. A fort at the junction of the Platte and Bijou rivers was named in his honor.[17]

In 1865, Tyler and his brother-in-law, James P. Maxwell, organized a wagon toll road to Central City from Boulder. With the discovery of silver at Caribou in 1869, Tyler and Maxwell built a road to Nederland and through the Narrows to Caribou.

His success at roadbuilding gave Tyler a high ranking in the Boulder community. He invested in real estate and became a political figure, although he never held office. The sawmill firm of Tyler and Maxwell operated quite successfully until Tyler's death. A very wealthy landowner, at one time Tyler owned all the land from Tyler Hill east to Alpine Avenue. He donated a portion of his holdings for the future site of the University of Colorado, and was an integral part in the founding of the university.

Captain Clinton Tyler is buried in the central portion of the cemetery, just south of the water canal, and west of the Chase monument. There is a marker. The Nelson K. Smith memorial is across the road to the west.

Author's photo
Toombstone art in Boulder's Green Mountain Cemetery.

Whitely, Richard H.
(1830 – 1890)

Born in Ireland, Richard's father died when he was six years old. His mother immigrated to America in 1836, with her three small children. She settled in Augusta, Georgia, where Richard attended school for a short time. He quit school in 1841 to help his mother. He found employment in a cotton mill at age eleven. He joined the Confederate Army in 1861, serving throughout the war, and earned the rank of major. Following the war, he returned to Georgia and took up the study of law. Admitted to the state bar, he went on to be elected to the United States Congress in 1868, and served as a state senator in 1870.

In 1877, Whitely left the South, convinced his work in politics would not change the current opposition to reformation. He arrived in Boulder in that same year. He opened a law practice, and by 1880, he was Boulder's leading attorney. He was an authority on mining law and also became a regent at the university.

Boulder society was shocked with scandal in 1884, when Whitely divorced his wife, Margaret, after thirty-three years of marriage, for a younger woman. His political career was severely damaged, his social integrity was ruined.

Richard Whitely is buried in the center of the west section, just south of the fence.

GREEN MOUNTAIN CEMETERY
290 20TH STREET

This cemetery replaced the old dilapidated pioneer Columbia Cemetery in 1904. Many burials at Columbia were moved to Green Mountain Cemetery. The cemetery sits on a high hill overlooking the city below. In stark contrast to Columbia Cemetery, Green Mountain Cemetery is resplendent in landscaping beauty. Luscious grass lawns and flowers grace the tombstones, while tall pine trees offer shade and protection. The wide lanes wind their way up the hill and around the many sections of graves.

Brookfield, Alfred A. (1830 – 1897)
Brookfield, Emily Lorton (1821 – 1914)

One of the earliest pioneers of Boulder County, Alfred Brookfield was a native of Morris County, New York. He clerked in his father's mercantile store and later became a partner in the business. He came west in 1856, first settling in Nebraska City, Nebraska, where he opened a grocery and became mayor in 1857. That same year, he married Emily Lorton, a native of Augusta, Georgia.

In the spring of 1859, rumors filtered back of gold discoveries in the high Colorado Rocky Mountains. Brookfield left his wife and business to seek new opportunity, joining a party of men including Thomas A. Aikins. Brookfield spent that fall prospecting along the rivers. With winter approaching, he moved down the creek and built several cabins for himself and the party. Disgusted with the area, and discouraged by the small quantity of gold, he wrote letters to his wife, saying he would return in the spring.

Evidently, he changed his mind. Before the winter was out, he had organized a town and sectioned off lots. A stake was driven for the center of the town, the present intersection of Broadway and Pearl streets. He called it Boulder for the number large rocks moved to clear the land. The following spring, he found gold bearing quartz on Gold Hill, above Boulder. His mood suddenly changed.

With a gold producing mine and a town established, Brookfield left for Nebraska to bring his wife to Colorado. Emma, as she was known, was the first white woman to settle in Boulder.

Emma Brookfield arrived in the frontier town of Boulder and quickly adjusted to her new surroundings. She became involved in social functions of the town and entertained from her home at 1840 Walnut, which still stands. Emma and her husband Alfred were instrumental in founding the Presbyterian Church at Valmont, in 1867. Affectionately known as "Auntie" Emma, her death in 1914, marked the passing of the last of the 59ers in Boulder.

The town of Boulder grew at a steady pace. Brookfield was elected president of the town company, initiating building codes and city plans. In 1864, he became a lieutenant in Governor Evans' "100-Day Volunteer" army, led by Colonel John M. Chivington.[18] Under Chivington's command, Brookfield participated in the Indian battle at Sand Creek.[19]

Following his brief military service, Brookfield returned to Boulder and resumed his civic duties. In 1874, he led a committee proposing the building of a reservoir, extending Boulder's water supply. He later moved to Ward, Colorado, where he opened a hotel. Six years later, he returned to Boulder and purchased the Colorado House hotel, located at Pearl and 13th Street.

Alfred and Emily Brookfield are buried in Section D, Block 251. There is a gray stone monument facing the road.

Butsch, Valentine (1827 – 1905)

Butsch arrived in Boulder from Indianapolis, Indiana in 1878. He went into the newspaper business with his son-in-law, Lucius Paddock. In 1892, the two bought the year-old *Daily Camera* newspaper, expanding the paper to a daily publication within a year. Butsch and Paddock published their paper from one of the first brick office buildings, still standing at 11th and Pearl. The beautiful home at 1105 Spruce Street was built by Butsch in 1894. It is now used as apartments.

The Butsch family plot is located in Section D, Block 384. There is a large gray granite family memorial, while each individual stone is flat.

Davis, Joseph A. (1855 – 1931)

Joseph and his wife Elizabeth, arrived in Boulder in 1878, where Joseph got a job with the Bradley and McClure Mercantile Company. Serving as secretary-treasurer of the Mercantile, he later joined W.W. White in purchasing the company. This successful business continued well into the next century.

Heavily involved in town promotion. Davis was instrumental in establishing several community associations, including the Boulder Chamber of Commerce, serving as president for many years. He was an officer of the Colorado Chautauqua Association for many years, and served twenty-eight years on the board of education.

He is buried next to his wife, Elizabeth, Section D, Block 252. There is a marker.

McClure, George (1843 – 1915)

A native of Vermont, George McClure came to Colorado in 1873, first settling in Denver. In partnership with Jay Joslin, the two opened a dry goods store that would eventually branch out all over Colorado. George opened a Joslin store in Boulder in the fall of 1873, and made Boulder his permanent home.[20]

He is buried with his wife in Section D, Block 253. There is a marker.

Paddock, Lucius C. (1859 – 1940)

Born in Grand Rapids, Michigan, Lucius Paddock arrived in Colorado in 1878, at age eighteen. His father owned the Mountain Lion Mine at Magnolia, where he worked for a time. Being the only high school graduate living at Magnolia, he was asked to teach the children of the mining community. After a few years of teaching, he moved to Boulder, where he worked for the *Boulder News* weekly paper. For a time, he went back to mining in Leadville and Aspen.

Paddock returned to Boulder in 1888 and started a weekly paper of his own, called the *Boulder Tribune*. In April 1892, in partnership with his father-in-law, Valentine Butsch, he purchased the *Daily Camera* newspaper. A weekly paper, within a year, Paddock raised advertising levels to bring the paper to a daily publication.

For the next forty-nine years, he served as editor of the pioneer paper. His spicy and witty editorials became well-known throughout the state. He made the paper what he said it would be, "free, fearless, newsy and independent." During his powerful editorial term, he received many awards and honors, as well as being recognized by the Dean of Colorado editors.

The legacy of this pioneer survives today in the pages of the *Boulder Daily Camera*.

Lucius C. Paddock is buried in Section D, Block 384. There is a marker.

OFF THE BEATEN PATH:

NEDERLAND CEMETERY

THIS OLD MOUNTAIN MINING CEMETERY LIES SOUTHWEST OF BOULDER ON COLORADO HIGHWAY 119.

The cemetery was established within a year of the silver strikes at Nederland and Caribou, in 1869. There are many broken and weathered tombstones, as well as several unmarked graves.

Brown, Nathan W. (? – 1898)

Nathan Brown, the first homesteader in the area, arrived in 1858. He homesteaded and built a cabin near the future site of Nevadaville. The cabin developed into an inn, called Brownsville. The location was a natural stop-over for prospectors and hunters.

Nederland's first pioneer, Nathan W. Brown, is buried next to his wife Virginia. There is a large white marble marker. Their three year-old son, Roy lies nearby.

Bryant, William (1828 – 1890)
Known as "Billy" to all who knew him, he and his brother "Pike" were hard rock miners in the silver mines of the Nederland area.
Billy died unexpectedly in 1890. There is a marker.

Tanner, Clay Arnett (1906 – 1907)
Little Clay Tanner was the infant son of pioneer grocer, Wallace L. Tanner. Wallace and his brother Ira, operated the Tanner Brother's grocery, the most popular establishment in Nederland.

– – –

Colorado Highway 40 West

EMPIRE

EMPIRE CEMETERY
LOCATED SOUTHEAST OF THE TOWN OF EMPIRE. FROM HIGHWAY 40, (MAIN STREET,) TURN SOUTH ON BARD CREEK ROAD. THE CEMETERY IS APPROXIMATELY ONE-HALF-MILE PAST THE BRIDGE ON THE EAST SIDE OF THE DIRT ROAD. IT IS SITUATED BEHIND THE BALL FIELD AND IS DIFFICULT TO SEE FROM THE ROAD.

This cemetery lies just a mile south of the east slope of Berthoud Pass. The few trees whistle in the ever blowing mountain air, as the sage and prickly wild bushes dance around the tombstones. A quaint wooden bridge allows entrance to the graveyard, surrounded by a high wired fence.

The first known burial dates to 1863.[21] A nineteenth century burial custom at Empire Cemetery was to pile rocks on the freshly covered grave, in an effort to protect the remains from the mountain wildlife. Unfortunately, there is no remaining evidence of this caring gesture.

Free from the restraints
of life the spirit soars
An Empire Cemetery Epitaph

Cowles, Henry D.C. (1815 – 1888)
Henry De Witt Clinton Cowles was one of the founding fathers of Empire. A native of Genessee County, New York, he arrived in Colorado Territory with the Gold Rush of 1859. He had a strong family background, one that would prove beneficial to the mining town of Empire. Cowles grandfather, George Clinton, was the first governor of New York, and vice president of the United States under President

Thomas Jefferson. In his memoirs, Cowles stated the drumsticks he played with as a boy, were used by his grandfather at the battle of Bunker Hill, during the American Revolutionary War. Young Henry married Katherine Bradford, the daughter of the governor of West Virginia.

Cowles arrived in Empire in 1860, where he prospected and worked in the mines. In October of that year, he located the Ida Silver Lode, named for his oldest daughter. It was the first fissure silver lode in Colorado. It assayed at 100 ounces of silver per ton. With his education and background, he soon took up the concerns of miners. He was the first judge of the miners court in Clear Creek County. He presided in the first criminal case in the district in 1861.

He wrote for the *Georgetown Courier*, championing the miners' plight. He was instrumental in the foundation of Empire and the mining laws of Clear Creek County.

His large rose colored marble stone is located at the south edge of the cemetery, on the hill. It is the tallest monument in the cemetery.

Geary, Peter (1829 – 1864)

Peter Geary was a miner in the Empire District. Unfortunately, he crossed the path of Gallant V. Hunter. An incident occurred when Hunter felt his oxen were being threatened by Geary's dogs. In anger, Hunter shot the dogs, turned and shot Geary point blank. Geary died instantly. The shooting took place in front of the Town Hall in Empire, with several witnesses. Geary's wife ran into the street shouting, "What made you kill my husband?"

Hunter was brought to trial in 1865. He was found not guilty. Legend has it that Hunter deeply regretted the incident and paid for the tombstone marking Geary's grave, spending long hours at the gravesite. The stone is a small sandstone carved marker, discolored with age.

Huet, Fred (1826 – 1916)

Born in Paris, Fred Huet attended one of the best art schools in the city, the Gobelin Institute. He came to America in 1848, working in textile mills before working as an artist in Boston. Frank Leslie, publisher of *Leslie's Weekly* in Boston, hired Huet to make sketches of the Colorado gold camps, miners and Indians for his publication.

Upon his arrival in the Colorado Territory, Huet prospected and sketched art in Breckenridge and Georgetown. Near Empire, he staked a claim and spent years driving a tunnel toward his mine. This was the beginning of today's Union Pass. His La Belle Parisienne mine never yielded ore. He was forced to paint pictures to make a living. The town encouraged his work, even selling raffle tickets for his paintings. Fellow Frenchman Louis Dupuy of Georgetown held raffles to benefit Huet.[22]

An eccentric fellow, Huet dressed in as army overcoat and black skull cap. His gray beard was never trimmed. He once said soap was a luxury, used sparingly, but tobacco was a necessity. A beloved character of Empire, when his sight began to fail, he was found helpless in the street and forced into the county poorhouse. Several citizens set up a room for Huet, providing the supplies, so he could continue his painting.

When he died in 1916, he was buried in an unmarked grave. In 1964, Louise C. Harrison, on behalf of the Empire Conservation Society and the Log Cabin Foundation, erected a memorial marker as a tribute to Fred Huet.[23]

Maire, Margaret Josephine Leahy (1865 – 1930)

Margaret was born in Mountain City, Colorado. She came to Empire with her second husband, Julius Caesar Maire, where they operated a livery and stable business. Following the death of Mr. Maire, she ran the business quite successfully. Margaret was the only businesswoman in Empire. She expanded the business by getting a government contract to carry the mail.

Margaret Maire was a small woman. She always wore a black hat with her jet black hair tucked underneath. Dressed in black, she was fondly nicknamed "Black Diamond."

She was involved with the town politics of Empire and was instrumental in the business developments of the community.

A small sandstone tombstone memorializes her life.

Mellis, S. Harvey Reverend (? – 1866)

Harvey Mellis was a traveling missionary staying in Central City in the fall of 1865, when he attended a seminary held by the Reverend William Crawford. The group, looking for support for the Congregational Church, did not meet with much enthusiasm when Empire was mentioned as the location of a new church. Mellis volunteered to go.

In January 1866, the Congregational Church was organized in Empire, at the direction of Mellis. There were eight members. Mellis built a house for himself which doubled as a chapel. He worked with the community and built his congregation around support and values necessary to the founding of Empire.

Within three months of his new appointment, he was diagnosed with a heart problem, by a doctor in Central City. He immediately left for the East, for further tests and treatments. He made it as far as Denver but was too sick to continue. In July 1866, he died in Central City, in the rooms of his colleague, the Reverend William Crawford.

His body was escorted by horsemen to Empire and the chapel home. The funeral was held the following day, a Sunday. Masonic Lodge #8 officiated the largest ceremony ever held in Empire. The services were in the town hall. As the mourners gathered in the hall, there was a crash from above. The masons had been upstairs, changing into uniform when the floor gave way. The mourners rushed for the door in hysterics. Order was reestablished, the ceiling held and the service was conducted.

The years and weather eroded the tombstone of Reverend Mellis, if he ever had one. A memorial monument was erected 100 years later.

Nelson, Fred (1852 – 1931)
Cowles, Kate (1855 – 1954)

Fred Nelson came to this land from Denmark, first settling in Minnesota, where he changed his given name of Nielson to Nelson, because there were so many Nielsons in area. He migrated west shortly after the Pikes Peak Gold Rush, settling in Empire. He worked in the mines of the Empire District.

In 1880, he married Kate Cowles in Empire. Kate was the youngest daughter of Empire founder, Henry D.C. Cowles. Fred and Kate Nelson had seven children, two dying of diphtheria as infants. The Nelsons carried on the founding tradition of giving to a supporting community.

They are buried together. There is a stone marker.

Vivian, Charles J. (? – 1880)

Charles Vivian is first mentioned in Colorado history with the discovery of the Neath Mine near Empire. He and his brother George, located the mine sometime prior to 1876. The mine was on the north side of Clear Creek, just below the town of Empire. Ore samples assayed at seventy-three ounces per ton, above average for the area.

Vivian bore a tunnel, hoping to reach richer ore and built a stamp mill for processing. For four years he worked his mine in an effort to make it profitable. In 1874, mining magnate John M. Dumont bought the Neath from Vivian and his brother for $64,000. The work of Charles Vivian had finally paid off.

Unfortunately, he would not live long enough to enjoy it. The following year, he died of pneumonia. His tombstone states he was twenty-nine years old.

His sandstone marker sits next to an infant of the same surname.

COZENS RANCH

COZENS RANCH CEMETERY

LOCATED ONE-HALF-MILE WEST OF WINTER PARK, ON HIGHWAY 40. THE COZENS RANCH MUSEUM IS ON THE NORTH SIDE OF THE HIGHWAY. THE FAMILY CEMETERY IS LOCATED BEHIND THE RANCH HOUSE.

This small family cemetery is also known as the Maryville Cemetery, located on the ranch property once owned by William Zane Cozens. It is enclosed by a wire fence.

Cozens, William Z. (1830 – 1904)

He is best remembered as Gilpin County's finest and feared sheriff. Although Canadian by birth, his parents were natives of New York, where he spent his youth. After completing his education, William Zane Cozens went on to apprentice in the carpentry trade. He left his homeland in pursuit of his own adventures in the West, arriving in Denver in 1858. The gold rush of 1859 energized Cozens, as it did thousands of men. He left Denver on foot, bound for the first major gold camp later called Central City. Bartending for a time, he soon became deputy sheriff.

In December 1860, he married Mary York, the first white woman in the mining camp of Central City. Their wedding was the first performed in the area.

When "Billy" became sheriff of Gilpin County in 1862, his first act was to erect a jail. The first public building, it still stands on Eureka Street in Central City. Known as a tough lawman, he held crime and murder to a minimum in Gilpin County. He personally intervened in many of the mine controversies. He put his life on the line on numerous occasions, all in the name of law and order.

In January 1864, Cozens apprehended a man by the name of Van Horn, for murder. Van Horn, held in the new jail, soon became the object of a lynch mob. Threatened with death, Sheriff Cozens stood his ground and held his prisoner. The man stood trial, was convicted and sentenced to hang. Billy Cozens led his prisoner to the first legal hanging in Colorado Territory.[24] Known as a great lawman, he knew the likes of Father Machebeuf, Kit Carson, and the notorious Charlie Wilson.[25]

In 1876, he and his wife Mary, purchased 320 acres of prime ranch land on the Fraser River in Colorado's Middle Park. He raised fine livestock and became a prominent citizen. Cozens was elected as commissioner of Grand County in 1878, and served as postmaster of Fraser for nearly twenty-eight years. He, like many ranchers of the area, faced Indian scares, and rode with the posse on several occasions.

A wayward carpenter with three of his buildings now designated as historic sites, William Zane Cozens died on his ranch in 1904. His funeral is recorded as one of the largest in the ranching community.

Almost symbolic of the time, this legendary pioneer and lawman passed on, just as the future passed through his land, with the completion of the Moffat Railroad.

Cozens, Mary York (1830 – 1909)

Of Irish Catholic descent, Mary York arrived in America at age twelve. Three months later, her parents died, leaving young Mary an orphan. She spent the next seventeen years in orphan asylums and in domestic service. When news of the Pikes Peak Gold Rush reached Baltimore, her employers urged her to join them on their journey to the frontier West. Mary accepted.

The trip by covered wagon turned into an eye opening experience for Mary, as they reached the Platte River. Her employer, Mr. McGee began making unsuitable advances toward Mary. She soon learned she had been brought along to sell herself to the miners. Mary struggled with her religious conscious, but soon chose death over immorality.

At the banks of the river, she prepared to throw herself in, when she spotted a stranger. Pleading for help, he came to her aid. His name was William Green Russell, the man responsible for the gold rush of 1859. It was Russell who had found the gold in Gregory Gulch, near the new mining camp of Central City. Mary made the rest of her journey in the company of Russell and his men, who carefully guarded her. The first woman in the Gregory diggings, the men built her an a joining room to their cabin, complete with a bolted door. In return, she cooked, did the laundry and cleaned for Russell and the miners.

Mary's cooking became legendary, bringing many to her evening supper table, including the dashing sheriff, William Z. Cozens. Billy spent his evenings with Mary, helping with chores and doing odd jobs around the cabin. One particular Saturday evening, Billy brought a special guest to dinner, catholic Father Machebeuf. Billy stumbled in his marriage proposal, and Mary cried, while the good father offered to perform the services.

William and Mary were married in Central City on December 30, 1860.[26] It was a celebration of firsts. Mary, the first woman in the gulch, and William, the first sheriff of Gilpin County, were married in Central City's first wedding by the first Catholic missionary in the area.

Legend has it that the wedding night included prisoners chained to the bed, as there was no jail. True or not, a jail was soon built by Billy, no doubt at Mary's insistence.

Mary became a devoted wife and mother, while continuing her dedication to the church. She was instrumental in the founding of the Catholic Church in Central City, and gave equally of her time to charities in the Fraser Valley.

She is buried with her husband, along with children William, Jr., Mary and Sarah.[27] An infant, Bernard V. Zahn is also buried in the family plot.

FRASER

FRASER CEMETERY

TURN SOUTH AT THE ONLY STOP LIGHT IN FRASER. THE CEMETERY IS LOCATED ONE-HALF-MILE SOUTH DOWN THE GRAVEL ROAD, ON THE LEFT.

The Fraser Cemetery is part of the original land owned by pioneer Captain Louis Gaskill. When Gaskill's wife Nellie died in 1910, she was buried on the Gaskill family property, near the road, with a wooden marker. With Gaskill's generosity, this portion of his land grew into a cemetery. Eventually, the land was sold to Charles Johnson and Frank Carlson.

In 1975, Frank Carlson Jr. deeded the land to the new Fraser Cemetery Association. A non-profit organization, the group, now headed by Glenn Wilson, maintain the records and the integrity of this pioneer resting spot. Cemetery records are not recorded by block and plot, however, are meticulously maintained by Alta Gesellman.

The first recorded burial in Grand County occurred in 1876. Nathan Stockton Bangs was found frozen in the Fraser Valley. The name and location of the burial was not recorded.[28]

With no access to water, the cemetery is somewhat unique in its' natural setting. Wild flowers, trees, and mountain juniper, offer their natural landscaping.

Clayton, Charles C. (1884 – 1931)

Born in Ohio, where he spent his youth, Charles Clayton married Ethel Jones in 1902. Two children were born to this union. He brought his family to Colorado in 1916, first living in Trinidad.

The Clayton family moved to Fraser in 1924, where Charles found work at a local sawmill. An accident at the mill injured his arm, causing Clayton to seek other opportunities. He opened a grocery store, which he ran successfully until his death in 1931.

He is buried in a small family plot next to his wife, Ethel. There is a gray granite marker.

Gaskill, Captain Louis Dewitt Clinton (1840 – 1915)

Perhaps the leading pioneer of Fraser, he not only built for himself, but more importantly, championed the community of Fraser.

A native of New York, where he received his education, Louis Gaskill later attended the Auburn Business College. In May 1861, he enlisted with the 28th Regiment of New York Volunteers and entered the Civil War. An engagement at Cedar Mountain gave him the title of captain. He was honorably discharged in June 1863, having attained the rank of 2nd Lieutenant.

Following the war, he married Nellie C. Rogers of Rochester, New York. In 1868, he came to Colorado on behalf of several Auburn, New York bankers to operate the gold mine properties of the company. He located and developed the highly profitable Saco Mine near Idaho Springs, in 1872.

Gaskill relocated to the Middle Park area in 1874, where he took on the task of building a road over Berthoud Pass. The project took sixty days at a cost of $50,000. In addition, he built a bridge over the Grande River, which opened the Middle Park for settlement. During this time, he and his family lived in a roadhouse he built at the top of the pass. Many travelers, trappers, and hunters stopped for refuge at his home, where he lived for nine years.

Under Superintendent E.P. Weber, Gaskill became the first foreman of the Wolverine Mine.[29] With his mining and surveying abilities, Gaskill expanded, investing in his own mine holdings. In 1885, he moved his family to one of the first quarter sections of government land opened for homesteading, south of Fraser.

Gaskill served the community as justice of the peace for twenty-five years, six years as county commissioner, and four years as county surveyor. He became Democratic chairman of the county commissioners in 1896. The mining ghost town of Gaskill, at the north fork of the Grand River, was named in his honor.

Nellie Gaskill died at the ranch near Fraser in 1910. She was buried with a wooden marker on the family property. Captain Gaskill died in June 1915. His funeral, conducted by the local GAR, was held in Denver. Interment took place at the Crown Hill Cemetery in Denver. It was one of the largest funerals held at the cemetery. Nellie Gaskill's remains were removed to Crown Hill following the Captain's burial. Years later, the Gaskill's daughter, Bertha Gilbo, had the remains of her parents reinterred in the Fraser Cemetery. The Fraser

Cemetery Association placed a memorial marker at the graves of the Gaskills in 1995.

Gardner, Mabel (1887 – 1914)

Born in Indianola, Nebraska, Mabel came to the Middle Park area with her parents, in 1905. The Ferguson family settled on ranch land on Ranch Creek, near Fraser.[30] At the ranch, nineteen-year-old Mabel Ferguson married Charles Roy Gardner in May 1906. The couple had three children, their first dying in infancy.

The members of the Gardner family were long time residents and early pioneers of the Fraser Valley. C.R. Gardner's father, David, a descendent of the legendary Davy Crockett family, brought his young family to the Fraser area by covered wagon, in 1875.[31]

C.R. Gardner worked on the family ranch and eventually, filed on his own homestead, in 1905. Located on the old Midland Trail, he built a cabin for his bride, shortly before their marriage. The cabin still stands near the gravel pit, land that once belonged to the Gardners. In 1910, he purchased a grocery store in Fraser. He played a minor role in the death of the infamous outlaw, "Texas" Charlie Wilson, being a witness to the demise of Wilson.[32]

Mabel died at age twenty-seven, in 1914. With her death, she left her husband, Charles Roy, to raise their two daughters, Florence, age five, and Nona, age three. Charles later left the area for California.

The grave of Mabel Gardner is marked with a gray monument to her memory, surrounded by a wrought iron fence.

Just, Carl Sr. (1842-1924)

A native of Vienna, Carl Just came to America, settling in the Fraser Valley of Colorado. He married Adelia Lehman of Grand Lake, in 1880. Homesteading land, he built a ranching enterprise known throughout the county for the quality of his livestock. He and his family contributed greatly to the Middle Park area and the community of Fraser.

He is buried in the Fraser Cemetery. There is a marker.

Lindsey, Edith M. (1916 – 1930)

The daughter of Frank and Bessie Lindsey, and granddaughter of Hot Sulphur Springs pioneer, P.H. Smith, Edith was fourteen when she met her tragic death. Her father worked on the construction crew during the building of an adjacent tunnel near the famous Moffat Tunnel. Young Edith often accompanied her father to the tunnel.

On April 27, 1930, while playing near the tunnel, Edith was electrocuted by a live wire.

She is buried in the Fraser Cemetery. There is a marker.

Newman, John M. (1869 – 1936)

Born in Clayton County, Iowa, John was adopted as a baby and given their family name, Newman. At age twelve, he came west with his family, stopping briefly in Colorado, before settling in Utah. He later returned to Colorado, where he lived for several years in Evergreen. He married Eliza Bell Halls in Georgetown, in 1897. The couple had nine children.

In 1898, Newman accompanied W. H. Woods on an exploring venture, to Grand County. The two returned in 1904, following the completion of the railroad. Newman operated a timber mill and hauled coal for the railroad, as well as ore for the mines. He later owned two sawmills. During the winter months, he helped open Berthoud Pass, using hand shovels and horse teams.

When his wife, Eliza died, he raised his last two daughters on his own. He followed his wife's example, sending them to school and insisting they attend church. He became quite active in the school and community events of Fraser.

He is buried beneath a white marble headstone. The marble is from the Marble, Colorado quarry, with lettering done by his grandson.

HOT SULPHUR SPRINGS

HOT SULPHUR SPRINGS CEMETERY

LOCATED ONE MILE EAST OF THE GRAND COUNTY MUSEUM ON COUNTY ROAD 55. THE CEMETERY IS ON THE LEFT SIDE OF THE ROAD.

The land for this cemetery was donated by Solomon Jones in 1892. The cemetery has expanded over the years. Several graves were moved to this site in 1895. The oldest stone is dated 1878.

Day, Barney (1832-1883)

Born in Ohio, Barney Day was raised in Illinois. A Civil War veteran, he served with the 35th Illinois Infantry. Following the war, he worked for the Kansas Pacific Railroad as it moved west. In September 1868, he served as a scout for Colonel G.A. Forsythe and witnessed the Battle of Beecher Island.[33]

By 1875, he had settled with his wife Sophronia, in Middle Park, where he built a cabin. It was here that Sophronia gave birth to their only child, a son. It is said young Barney Hulse (Judd) Day was the first white child born in Middle Park.

Barney Day established a sheep ranch and soon became well-known and trusted among the settlers. Instrumental in the founding of social and government policies of Grand County, he was appointed county commissioner in 1882, by acting government official, H. A. W. Tabor.

Shortly after the appointment, Day found himself caught in the fallout of a nasty election in Grand County. A political difference became a personnel vendetta, resulting in the worst political tragedy in Colorado history.

Early on the morning of July 4, 1883, Day along with E.P. Weber, and county clerk T.J. Dean, were walking toward the boardinghouse of Mary J. Young, where a holiday celebration was under way. Just a few yards from the boardinghouse, the three men were ambushed by three masked men. All three men were shot down in the first round of fire. Commissioner Day managed to get a shot off, hitting his mark before he fell to the ground. The masked man Day killed was ex-commisioner John Mills.

Barney Day tried to get to Mrs. Young's boardinghouse, but fell dead on the shores of Grand Lake. Commissioner Barney Day, caught in a political war, never had the chance to serve his voters in the honest way he gained the election.

He is buried in the Hot Sulphur Springs Cemetery, next to his wife Sophronia N. Day, who died in 1907. There is a marker at the top of the hill on the west side.

Dean, Thomas J. "Cap" (1826 – 1883)

A native of New York, Thomas Dean traveled west, spending time in Kentucky, where he married his wife Nancy. He served with the 5th Michigan Cavalry and was wounded at Gettysburg. He was taken prisoner by the Confederates, where he remained until the end of the Civil War. He got his nickname from his former army rank. He is known to have been in Colorado as early as 1871, and in Grand County by late 1875. He acquired a homestead for his family near Hot Sulphur Springs and was a saloon keeper in that town. He was involved with the Indian Wars and rode with the posse following the murder of Abraham Elliott in 1878.

He was elected judge of Grand County in 1877, and took part with Commissioner E.P. Weber in recovering the county records stolen when Hot Sulphur Springs replaced Grand Lake as county seat.

Dean was at the center of the famous county seat controversy in 1880. A vote was put to the public changing the county seat from Hot Sulphur Springs to Grand Lake. Evidence of an inaccurate vote count and the fact that many Grand Lake votes were later discounted, caused a political battle that would be settled with murder.

In the election of 1882, Dean, along with E.P. Weber, won the Republican nomination and were elected county commissioners of

Grand County. John Mills, who lost the election, set out to undermine the Republican control of Dean and Weber. The political fight heated in the local papers. The *Prospector Newspaper* printed an open letter accusing Dean and county clerk Barney Day of perjury and theft. Secret committee meetings were held without Mills.

On the morning of July 4, 1883, John Mills, and two other masked men, ambushed Dean, Day and Weber at the Fairview boardinghouse on the west shore of Grand Lake. The gunfire lasted a few minutes. In the aftermath, both Barney Day and John Mills lay dead. Edward Weber and Cap Dean were carried into the boardinghouse, where Weber died a few hours later.

Dean had been shot in the bridge of the nose, the bullet lodging in his brain. A second bullet hit him in the right hip. He remained conscious and watched as the two surviving attackers got their horses and fled the scene. From his testimony, the survivors of the shooting were believed to be sheriffs Royer and Redman.

Thomas J. Dean lingered between life and death for thirteen days at the Young's Fairview House. Conscious almost to the end, he joked that "there wasn't a bullet made to get me." In fact he was right. Infection set in and Judge Dean breathed his last, dying on the night of July 17, 1883.[34]

Following a formal funeral ceremony, his body was buried next to Barney Day on the top of the hill at the west end of the cemetery.

Elliott, Abraham (? – 1878)

Born in Kentucky, Abraham Elliott spent time in Missouri and Montana, before settling in Colorado.

He and his wife, Nannie, operated two separate ranches. The winters were spent on their cattle ranch near present day Colorado Springs, while the warmer months were spent near Hot Sulphur Springs. Although not well-known in the community, he had a good reputation among the Grand County farmers and ranchers.

On the evening of September 2, 1878, a band of Ute Indians, led by a young chief named Piah, camped on the Blue River within sight of Elliott's home.[35] Elliott kept an eye on the Indians while cutting wood, and eventually sent his son for help. Shortly thereafter, in an eruption of gunfire, Elliott was hit by three bullets, dying instantly. The Indians ran off the Elliott horses.

The murder of Abraham Elliott was the culmination of a bloody Indian feud in Grand County. Chief Piah had earlier led a band of braves in a raid at the fenced area known as Junction Ranch.[36] The local sheriff's posse forced the Indians to leave. As the Indians departed, a member of the the posse shot into the group, killing a brave named Tabernash. The Utes, in retaliation, killed Abraham Elliott.

Abraham Elliott was buried in an unmarked grave. A marker was placed in his memory in 1967. The grave is located in Block 2, Lot 6.

Jenne, Daisy Button (1886 – 1979)

The daughter of a local retailer, Schuyler J. Button, Daisy was very active in school and church functions, and very popular at the winter ice skating carnivals.

She encouraged her younger brother, Horace Button, in his ambition to compete in ski jumping, the new sporting sensation. He went on to be one of the first elected to the Ski Hall Of Fame.

As a young socialite of Hot Sulphur Springs, Daisy left a legacy of community history. Throughout her life, she recorded town history, developments and changes. These journals provide an incredible first-hand account of the early history of Hot Sulphur Springs.

She is buried in Block 2, Lot 31, next to her husband, Charles, who died in 1940. There is a marker.

Jones, Solomon (1847 – 1916)

Solomon Jones arrived in Grand County in 1880. He opened the first blacksmith shop in Hot Sulphur Springs, where he was immediately successful. By 1899, he was one of the leading businessmen of the community. He brought his wife Mary, to Colorado from Ohio and made a home for his family in Hot Sulphur Springs.

Elected sheriff on the Democratic ticket in 1893, he served the county as commissioner in 1895, and was re-elected in 1897. He served in this capacity for twenty years, losing once in 1906, during the Republican reform years. His successor was charged with several crimes of corruption, causing Jones to be re-elected again, this time in a landslide, in 1908.

A founding father and community leader, he died in 1916, and is buried in Circle 1, next to his wife Mary, and son John.

Pettingell, Jacob N. (1860 – 1941)

A law student from Boston, Jacob Pettingell settled in Hot Sulphur Springs in the 1880s. He did some mining, but soon tired of the labor and turned his attention toward town politics. Practicing law, he became very influential among the town leaders, as well as the general population.

He was elected postmaster, county clerk, judge and appointed interim commissioner, following the commissioner deaths in the Grand County War of 1883. During his tenure, he was instrumental in securing the land rights at Hot Sulphur Springs for David Moffat's dream railway over the Continental Divide.

He is buried next to his wife Laura, in Block 2, Lot 27. There is a marker.

Pharo, Thomas E. (1848 – 1903)

Thomas E. Pharo, an Englishman from Surrey, arrived with his large family in 1880. One of the earliest settlers in the area, he bought a ranch not far from the young community of Hot Sulphur Springs, on the Blue River. In time, he was known throughout the county for his fine horses and cattle.

He was active in community and political concerns. Following the Grand County War of 1883, he was appointed sheriff, a position he declined. He was an active member of the Middle Park Stockgrowers Association and fought for the control of water and land rights for the ranchers and farmers.

He is buried with his family members in the Pharo plot, in Circle #2.

KREMMLING

KREMMLING CEMETERY

LOCATED EAST OF THE TOWN OF KREMMLING. FROM HIGHWAY 40, TURN SOUTH ON EAGLE AVENUE. THE CEMETERY IS AT THE JUNCTION OF EAGLE AVENUE AND 14TH STREET, ON THE LEFT SIDE OF THE ROAD.

The land for this cemetery, also known as Riverside Cemetery, was owned by Willis Call, who donated a portion of his homestead for burial purposes, in 1905. The first recorded burial is dated 1906, however, there is a tombstone dated 1895. The Cemetery Association was formed in 1926. The city of Kremmling has maintained the grounds and records since 1980. Early records do not list block and plot.

There are several family sections, including the Lee family plot. The five people in this plot all died between September and December 1931. Francis H. Lee died in December 1931, at age thirty-nine. The other four graves are those of children, ranging in age from three months to twelve years.

Call, Willis C. (1845 – 1936)

A Canadian, Call came to Colorado in 1870, at age twenty-five. He settled in the Middle Park area in 1881, after serving as cook on a railroad grading operation. By 1890, he owned one of the prime pieces of bottom land in the Kremmling area.

Aggressive in politics, he became county assessor in 1884. He improved his social status with his marriage to Mary Rohracher, a member of the Grand County social elite. He and his wife were active both socially, and politically.

The two are buried together. There is a marker.

Kimball, William (1844 – 1909)

An early pioneer to Middle Park, William Kimball homesteaded near Kremmling. In 1875, he got the government contract to carry the mail. His general route ran between Empire and Hot Sulphur Springs, a route he ran daily and year round. It is said he carried up to seventy-pound loads, through the snow drifts, on foot, and was seldom late for delivery.

He helped open the Kremmling area for settlement. Kremmling was somewhat remote, due to the lack of of transportation, and inadequate access. The Grand River ran fierce and high. Kimball built a ferry, allowing better access to the town and valley.

One of Kremmling's first pioneers, he is buried in the Kremmling Cemetery. There is a marker.

Martin Family Plot

A very distinguished pioneer family, there are several graves in this resting place. Among the burials, is that of Patrick J. Martin, (1864 – 1939). A prominent member of the Kremmling community, he served as mayor in 1913, and was instrumental in the founding of the Grand County Fair.

Samuel Martin (1857 – 1945), one of the early pioneers, filed on a homestead, yet continued to blaze the trails across the West. In 1923, he and Ute Bill Thompson ran the last cattle drive into Middle Park. By 1923, cattle were shipped by rail. Martin and Thompson, in an effort to avoid freight charges, chose to herd the cattle themselves. In wages and time, the effort did not pay off. That ended the cattle drives.

Martin's ranch on the Muddy River became a stop-over for the railroad, and the Martin Post Office was established. The area was popular for a time, but died out by World War I.

He is buried in the Kremmling Cemetery. There is a marker.

STEAMBOAT SPRINGS

STEAMBOAT SPRINGS CEMETERY

LOCATED ONE-HALF-MILE NORTHWEST OF THE TOWN OF STEAMBOAT SPRINGS ON THE NORTH SIDE OF HIGHWAY 40.

The earliest recorded burials are I. Belle Cantrell and Nannie Leola Woolery, both in 1882. The cemetery is well laid out and maintained with a fine mountain landscape. Much of the history of Routt County lays at rest in this serene mountain cemetery.

Several bodies were reinterred here from the original cemetery, dating to 1879. Known as Dream Island Cemetery, it was situated on an island in the Yampa River which ran through the town of Steamboat Springs.

Campbell, Henry T. (1859 – 1952)

A native of Ontario, Canada, Henry Campbell came to America, working as a ranch hand in Wyoming and mining in Colorado before arriving in Routt County in 1885.

Working at the mines near Hahns Peak, he also served as under sheriff from 1906 to 1908, and later became sheriff of Routt County.

He is buried in the First Addition, Block 5, Lot 21.

Crawford, James H. (1845 – 1930)

Crawford, a native of Missouri, served with the 7th Missouri Cavalry at age sixteen. In May 1865, he married Margaret E. Bourn. The couple journeyed west with their three children in 1873.

In the summer of 1874, James built the first cabin at Hot Sulphur Springs. He also claimed land near the area that would become Steamboat Springs. Crawford became the first entrepreneur in the area and is considered the founding father of Steamboat Springs. His homestead had a gassy pool of water that blew spray every few seconds, reminding Crawford of the Mississippi steamboats in his old home town. Thus, he named his new town Steamboat Springs.

Crawford established the foundation of the town and through his leadership and contributions, Steamboat eventually became the commerce center of Routt County. He was the first county judge, first postmaster, and first mayor. He established the Routt County Pioneer Association, and served as the first president. He also served in the state Legislature.

James Crawford and his wife Margaret, are buried together in the First Addition, Block 2, Lot 117. A beautiful stone monument marks their graves. It is a likeness of the pioneer cabin Crawford built over 100 years ago. Above the cabin replica are etched words: "The End of the Trail."

Clutter, P.A. (? – 1910)

An early settler in the Trull area, Clutter operated a ranch with his wife and thirteen children. History does not record the family's travels prior to arriving in Routt County.

According to a 1910 article in the *Steamboat Pilot* newspaper, Mr. Clutter was shot to death at his ranch during an argument of unknown nature. The article, entitled "The Funeral," goes on to say: "Out in the cemetery is a fresh grave. In the potter's field rests all that was mortal of P.A. Clutter. A board gives his name and date . . . the mother and her family of little ones will now have to depend upon themselves for an existence."

The gravesite is no longer marked. The majority of the sixty-odd graves in Potter's Fieldare not marked.

Foster, Fred (? – 1981)

A native of Pennsylvania, Fred Foster worked in the mines of Idaho Springs before arriving in Routt County in 1901.

He drove a four-horse stage from Yampa, hauling passengers and the mail. He was elected sheriff in 1928, serving until 1935. He was re-elected in 1937, serving another six years.

He is buried in the First Addition, Block 3, Lot 21.

Woolery, Nannie Leola (? – 1882)

Nannie was the first wife of James Milton Woolery, who came to the area with his brother Harvey and his family, in 1881.

The two families homesteaded three miles apart on opposite sides of the Yampa River. The easiest form of communication for the families was tying a note to a rock and throwing it over the river.

On the morning of May 16, 1882, the thrown rock contained bad news. Nannie had died suddenly the previous night. A crude casket was made from the side of a wagon. Mrs. Woolery was laid to rest on the island in the river, at the edge of the town of Steamboat Springs. This was the first burial in the community. It became known as Dream Island Cemetery.[37]

Six years later, the remains of Nannie Woolery were removed to the present cemetery. This probably occurred at the same time Woolery's second wife, Melissa May was laid to rest at the Steamboat Cemetery. She died in 1887.

A single stone marks both graves in the Original Section, Block 3, Lots 3 and 4.

OFF THE BEATEN PATH:

CLARK CEMETERY

LOCATED JUST EAST OF THE TOWN OF CLARK, ON COUNTY ROAD 129, ONE-HALF-MILE SOUTH OF THE CLARK STORE.

The Clark Cemetery lies on the hillside east of town. It was originally part of the Whitmer Ranch. The first recorded burial was in

1895. It is enclosed by a metal fence. Listed as a Colorado Historical Site, the National Association for Cemetery Preservation recently placed a historical marker at the location.

The Norman-Whitmer families were early pioneer ranchers and instrumental in settling the Clark area. There are fourteen graves.

Clark, Hannah E. (? – 1898)

Hannah and her husband Rufus, homesteaded a ranch in Routt County, and Hannah was appointed postmaster in 1889. She designated the location as "Clark," and the small town grew under that name. She remained postmaster until her death in 1898.

Both Hannah and her husband Rufus W. are buried in the west end of Section A, Lot 6.

Franz, George H. (1861 – 1937)

Franz and his wife Lyda purchased the Kinney Resort in 1913. They renamed it Glen Eden in honor of the natural surroundings. George added a general store. He also rented a building to the government, which was used for the post office. The charming resort was a tourist destination for years.

George and his wife Lyda are buried together in Section D, Lot 3.

Norman, Mark (1841 – 1911)

Mark Norman arrived by covered wagon in northeastern Colorado in 1895. With him were his eight children. He previously had lost his wife and five other children. A devoted family man, he worked a homestead near Clark, to support his children.

A hard worker, despite the loss of an arm in an earlier accident, he was popular in the community of Clark. He was postmaster at the time of his death.

He is buried in Section A, Lot 3.

HAHNS PEAK CEMETERY

LOCATED ONE-QUARTER-MILE SOUTHEAST OF THE TOWN, ON ROUTT COUNTY ROAD 129.

Flanked by stately pine, fir and aspen trees, this cemetery is truly cast in a charming mountain setting. Wild mountain flowers, red roses and tall columbine serve as nature's landscaping. It is believed to be the oldest public cemetery in Routt County, dating to 1870. However, it has always been on private land. Official records were never kept, yet due to the effort of Roger Cusick and the National Association for Cemetery Preservation, fifty-seven burials have been identified.

Condelin, Michael (1851 – 1911)

An early prospector of the Hahns Peak area, Michael Condelin was also trained in the Catholic priesthood. He was known throughout the community as a kind, caring, and giving man.

Following his funeral, his body was transported to the cemetery by toboggan, a tradition at Hahns Peak.

Cross, George W. (1843 – 1907)

George Cross is one of the Civil War veterans buried in the cemetery. His grave is enclosed by a wooden fence.

Larson, Charles J. (1858 – 1909)

Larson was one of the earliest pioneers in the area. The Larson monument is one of the largest in the cemetery.

Mahler, Herman F. (1824 – 1901)

An early pioneer to the Hahns Peak region, Herman Mahler was instrumental in the town's development, as well as establishing and preserving the cemetery site. His tombstone marks the oldest record- ed grave in the cemetery.

Wallace, R.G. (1839 – 1912)

Wallace was an early pioneer. He held several public offices, including county judge. The *Routt County Republican* dated February 23, 1912, stated that he ". . . was classed among the old timers of the county."

HAYDEN

HAYDEN CEMETERY

LOCATED AT THE EAST END OF THE TOWN OF HAYDEN. GO SOUTH ON ROUTT COUNTY ROAD 37 APPROXIMATELY ONE-QUARTER-MILE.

The first recorded burial was in 1891, although several burials occurred previously on the then privately-owned land. A portion of the land owned by B.T. Shelton was obtained by the government in 1891. The cemetery was plotted in 1900. Today the cemetery is well main- tained and enclosed by a metal fence.

There are several sections, including a large cross in memory of the Hispanics buried there, as well as a monument to the Japanese. A sep- arate section listed as "colored" is now in the process of receiving a memorial marker.

Clark, John F. (1859 – 1944)

Born in Munich, Germany, at age fourteen, John Clark shipped on a merchant vessel to South America. Two years later, he arrived in Colorado, working for the Colorado Cattle Company in Pueblo.

In 1880, at age twenty-one, he took a desert claim in Routt County. He married Georgia Drusilla Smith in 1882. In December 1907, over a dispute involving water rights, Clark shot George McFarland. He was confined in the jail at Hahns Peak for nine months while awaiting trial. He was found not guilty.

Clark went to work at the Cory Ranch, and later became foreman. He bought a pool hall in town, which he ran successfully for many years.

Following the death of Georgia in 1937, John Clark was never the same. On the night of June 4, 1944, he bathed, put on clean clothes and shot himself.

He is buried in Lot 138.

Shelton, Ezekiel (1833 – 1927)

A native of Ohio, Shelton brought his family to the Breckenridge area in 1879. He worked as a land surveyor before being sent to the Yampa Valley by Denver businessmen, in search of coal deposits.

By 1882, he had made a home for his family near Hayden. One of the earliest pioneers in the valley, he contributed much to early Hayden. He was superintendent of schools for Routt County from 1888 to 1890, Routt County commissioner from 1892 to 1895 and a United States Congressman for thirty years.

As Routt County surveyor, he made over 500 surveys, including the Hayden Cemetery, which he laid out on land owned by his son, B.T. Shelton.

He is buried in Lot 15.

Solandt, John V., M.D. (1869 – 1916)

A native of Canada, John Solandt received his veterinary degree from the McGill University in Toronto, in 1884. An asthmatic, he came to Colorado, receiving further medical training at the University of Denver in 1898.

He started a medical practice in Hayden and was elected coroner in 1904. Active in all functions of Hayden society, he was a member of the school board, town board, and later elected mayor of Hayden. The Solandt Memorial Hospital was named in his honor.

He is buried in the I.O.O.F. Section in Lot 52.

Wadge Mine Explosion (1942)

A few miles east of Hayden a small community known as Mt. Harris served the miners of the Wadge Mine. A few of the miners who made Mt. Harris their home and lived with their families were Maximo Bustos, Antonio Adame, and his brother, Plutarco "Joe." In his few hours away from the mine, Joe studied to receive his naturalization certificate. Through dedication, Joe Adame became a United States citizen.

Disaster struck on January 27, 1942, when an explosion rocked the Wadge Mine. Thirty-four men died, including Max Bustos, and brothers Antonio and Joe Adame.

The three are buried together, along with other miners from the explosion, in Lot 18. A stone monument was erected in the memory of all who died.

Whyte, John T. (? – 1888)

John Whyte taught school at the log cabin on Joe Kircher's homestead, just east of Hayden, in 1884 and 1885. He was elected superintendent of the public schools in Routt County in 1887, but died at the home of Ezekiel Shelton, before serving in that capacity.

He was buried on the Shelton land, on a hill over-looking the town of Hayden. It is believed he was the first to buried in today's Hayden Cemetery.

His burial site is unknown.

HAYDEN PIONEER CEMETERY
LOCATED EAST OF HAYDEN ON HIGHWAY 40, APPROXIMATELY FIVE MILES ON ROUTT COUNTY ROAD 69. THE CEMETERY IS A LITTLE OVER ONE-HALF-MILE ON THE SOUTH SIDE OF THE ROAD.

The cemetery is also known as the Stanton Family Cemetery. Still in use, it is somewhat maintained.

Aigner, Joseph (1853 – 1887)

Very little is known of Mr. Aigner. From his obituary, he died from injuries resulting in a horse accident. He must have been a prominent citizen, as Aigner Mountain, north of Hayden is named for him.

Marshall, A.J. (1833 – 1902)

A pioneer of Routt County, Marshall arrived in 1876. He purchased his ranch near Hayden in 1879, where he became quite successful. He and his wife raised their children in the Hayden community and were active in the affairs of the town.

Smith, Kate (1870 – 1910)

The daughter of A.J. Marshall, Kate died at age thirty. At age fourteen, she married to C.J. Smith. Three children survived her, one died at birth.

Stanton Family Plot

Henry Stanton was born in Cornwall England, in 1840. He and his wife Martha Crago, born in 1841, left for America in 1866. They lived in several mining towns in California and Colorado, before settling in the Hayden area in 1881.

In the spring of 1883, the five Stanton children contracted diphtheria. Daughters Minnie, age twelve, and Salina, age three, both died. Son Henry died in 1890.

CRAIG

FAIRVIEW CEMETERY

FOLLOW 7TH STREET EAST TO THE END OF TOWN.

The cemetery lies on the east end of town, on the hill, overlooking the Yampa River. The oldest known grave is dated 1876, however the cemetery was not officially recorded until 1889, when the town of Craig was established.

The cemetery is beautifully landscaped and irrigated, for such a dry climate. Trees and flowers are found throughout the cemetery. The older section receives care, unique to the majority of cemeteries, where this portion is often neglected.

The veteran section, to the south, has markers primarily dated from World War II. It is very neat, and well laid out.

Breeze, Lemuel L. (1852 – 1923)

A graduate of Iowa Law School, Lemuel Breeze came to Colorado in 1881, eventually settling near Craig in 1883. He was the first attorney of the area and justice of the peace at the time of his death. He was a member of the I.O.O. F. and a Freemason.

His funeral was held at his grand home on Yampa Avenue.

He is buried next to his wife, Rosella in Block 2, Lot 13.[38] Unfortunately, the graves are unmarked.

Durham, Almon L. (1857 – 1931)

Almon Durham left his native Minnesota for the West in 1879. He found work as a stage driver, covering the territory from Rawlins, Wyoming to Meeker, Colorado.

By 1880, he had earned enough to start a ranch and homesteaded the Circle Bar Ranch. He went to Iowa and returned with his bride, Martha Jane, in 1888.

A prominent stockman, he owned several ranches. He was director of the Craig National Bank, a member of the Masonic Order, and a great benefactor to the town.

The Masonic Lodge held his body in state and performed the last Masonic Rites at the interment.

His fine marker is located in Block 38, Lot 5.

Farnham, Ethan Allen (1859 – 1908)

Ethan Farnham was deputy sheriff of Routt County in 1897, where he took part in the capture of escaped prison inmates Harry Tracy and David Lant, at Hahn's Peak. He later became sheriff, serving the community for two terms. He moved to Grand Junction where he died of cancer.

His body was returned to Craig. The funeral was held under the direction of the I.O.O.F. His funeral was the largest ever attended to date at Fairview Cemetery.

He is buried in the Farnham family plot, at the south end, in Block 8, Lot 19. There is a small pink marble stone.

Ledford, John S. (1860 – 1937)

A pioneer of Moffat County, John Ledford arrived in 1886. He began his career as a stage driver, handling the mail from the old Pony Express stop at Rawlins, Wyoming, to Meeker, Colorado. Later, he opened a livery business, where he kept horses and buggies for hire, serving most of the county. He was also the county game warden and was appointed sheriff in 1912. At the time of his death, he owned a large ranch west of town.

He was buried next to his wife Ella, who proceeded him in death in 1933.

They are buried in Block 18, Lot 1.

McLachlan, Archibald (1847 – 1917)

McLachlan arrived from California's gold fields with his widowed mother in 1883. He started a ranch near Craig under the Homestead Act, where he became one of the area's largest cattle breeders.

He started one of the first sawmills in the area, north of town, supplying the new community with lumber. He went on to serve the county in the state Legislature for a number of years.

He is buried in Block 7, Lot 15.

Mack, John Sr. (1857 – 1945)

Leaving Germany in 1871 to avoid military service, John Mack was one of the earliest settlers along the Yampa River.

Arriving in America, Mack traveled the country, working in Ohio, Wyoming and several towns in Colorado, before coming to Moffat

County in 1883. He homesteaded what would become the oldest operating ranch in the valley at the time of his death.

He is buried next to his wife Effie, in Block 3, Lot 25.

Rose, William H. (1844 – 1930)

A veteran of the Union Army, William Rose came west from New York in 1868. He first settled at Leadville where he used his knowledge of civil engineering in the bustling mining camp.

He came to Moffat County in 1882, continuing his search for gold. He stayed, filed on land and started a ranch. He built the first residence, which still stands today.

He was active in laying out the townsite, city politics and was a charter member of the I. O.O.F. He was director the the First National Bank of Craig for several years. He also served as the U.S. deputy mineral surveyor and U.S. commissioner. There is a street named in his honor.

A fine tombstone marks his burial, next to his second wife, Julia, in Block 11, Lot 13. The original government issued headstone was removed to the foot of the burial plot by family members.

Tucker, William H. (1848 – 1941)

A native of Ohio, William Tucker originally settled in Colorado Springs in the 1880s. By 1889, he had brought his bride of two years, and her brother, Willard Teagarden, to the infant town of Craig.

Tucker was the man responsible for the plotting of the Craig townsite. He was heavily involved in the city's first charter and became the town promoter. He sold lots for the town, planted trees, and opened the first mercantile store.

He later owned a ranch and was a strong member of the I.O.O.F. Until his mid eighties, he was still selling real estate and promoting "his" town. A street in Craig is named in his honor.

Mrs. Flora Tucker was active in Craig's social activities, and volunteered with home health care. She was a charter member of the Craig Christian Church.

Both are buried in Block 2, Lot 14. There is a large marker.

— — —

Colorado Highway 318 West

BROWN'S PARK

BASSETT FAMILY CEMETERY

LOCATED ONE MILE NORTHWEST OF THE BROWN'S PARK SCHOOL, AND ONE-HALF-MILE NORTH ON HIGHWAY 318. THE BASSETT FAMILY PLOT IS ON PRIVATE LAND, ORIGINALLY THE SITE OF THE BASSETT RANCH.

Herbert and Elizabeth Bassett brought their family to Brown's Hole, along the Green River, in 1878.[39] Bassett started a horse and cattle ranch, unaware of the growing hostilities in the area. Cattle barons and small ranchers including Bassett, were soon in an all-out range war that lasted years. Bassett's children inherited the ranch and the land wars.

Outlaws frequented Brown's Park and the Bassett ranch in particular. The rugged terrain and close proximity to three state lines, made this an area in which difficult to track lawbreakers. The area became known as "Hole in the Wall," a stretch of the Robber's Roost in Utah, a hide-out for Butch Cassidy and the Wild Bunch.[40] In this atmosphere, it was inevitable that the Bassett children would be caught up in the turbulence of the times. Daughters Josie, and Ann inherited the family ranch.

Bassett, Elbert (1880 – 1925)

Elbert Bassett was the son of Herbert and Elizabeth, and the brother of Ann and Josie Bassett. An amateur outlaw, Elbert, known as "Eb," was more of a nuisance to residents of Brown's Park. He committed suicide at the family ranch.

Elbert Bassett is buried in the Bassett Family Cemetery. There is a marker.

Bassett, Elizabeth (1855 – 1892)

Sixteen year-old Elizabeth Chamberlain married Herbert Bassett, twenty years her senior, in Arkansas, in 1871. The couple settled in Brown's Park in 1878. Their daughter Ann, later known as Queen Ann, was the first white child born in the park. An excellent hand with horses, Elizabeth in fact, ran the ranch, along with raising her children. During the years of ranch wars, and cattle barons, she became known as a rustler, and a cohort to the famous outlaws that hid out in the area.

Elizabeth died in December 1892, at age thirty-seven. Daughter Josie claimed her mother died of appendicitis, while Ann always maintained she suffered a miscarriage.

Elizabeth Chamberlain Bassett was laid to rest in the Bassett family cemetery. Her grave is marked.[41]

Bassett, Josephine "Josie" (1874 – 1964)

A daughter to Elizabeth and Herbert Bassett, Josie and her sister Ann took over the family ranch, and fought the cattle baron take-over. Josie's life was a hard one, facing danger and death threats. She married five times. Josie was rumored to be a one-time sweetheart of

Butch Cassidy. Josie married James MacKnight in 1893. There were two sons, Crawford and Herbert (Chick.) James and Josie took over old Sam Bassett's homestead, near Isom Dart's place, in 1897.[42]

Josie knew Butch Cassidy quite well from his outlaw days in Brown's Park. She claimed to have visited him in Nevada in 1928, and in Baggs, Wyoming, on several occasions in the 1930s, long after he was reported killed in South America. Josie's remarkable life became a feature story in *Life* magazine, and the subject of a movie starring Doris Day.

Denver Public Library
Ann Bassett Willis
Cattle queen

Josie spent her last years in a lonely cabin on Diamond Hill, on land now occupied by the Dinosaur National Monument. The cabin still stands.

Josie Bassett died at age ninety. There is a marker.

Willis, Ann Bassett (1878 – 1956)

Born to Herbert and Elizabeth Bassett in 1878, Ann was the first white child born in Brown's Park. Following the deaths of her parents, Ann became known as the "Cattle Queen" of Brown's Park. She took over the ranch and fought the cattle baron attempts to take over her land. Rumors flowed of her activities in cattle rustling, and as leader of the Bassett outlaw gang, harboring fugitives, including Elza Lay of the Wild Bunch, and possible murder.

She successfully drove off the cattle barons, faced death threats, and is rumored to have committed murder herself. She claims in her memoirs, a large cattle company contracted with Tom Horn to have her killed.[43] Shortly before her death she answered a reporter's question with this statement:

"I've done everything they said I did and a helluva lot more."

Ann died in Leeds, Utah. Her cremated remains were in the possession of her husband Frank, until his death in 1963. Following Frank's death, Ann's ashes were buried in an unmarked spot in the family cemetery. Today, there is a marker to her memory, next to her sister Josie.

Willis, Frank (1883 – 1963)

The husband of Ann Bassett, Frank was a rancher and had numerous dealings with the outlaw gangs of Brown's Park.

He is buried just outside the Bassett Family Cemetery, at his own request, stating he was not a church member. There is a marker.

BROWN'S PARK CEMETERY
LOCATED NEXT TO THE LODORE SCHOOL.

The cemetery began in 1880, on land owned by Valentine Hoy, and officially dedicated as a cemetery in 1890. The oldest known burial is that of Juan Catrino, who died of pneumonia, in 1880. Louie Carro, a ranch hand for the Bassetts, is buried in an unmarked grave. His pine box coffin was lined with satin from Ann Bassett's wedding gown.

There is a large red sandstone boulder in the northeast corner of the cemetery. The east face shows Indian petroglyphs. There is a plaque on the stone commemorating the site of Fort Davy Crockett, built in 1837, and a rendezvous site for traders and trappers in the 1840s.

Bassett, Samuel C. II (1836 – 1910)

The brother of Herbert Bassett, Sam left his native home of New York, following the death of his mother in 1839. Sam's father, Samuel, remarried and brought his family to Illinois.

Young Sam left his home while still a teenager. He served as a government scout on the Overland Trail. He joined Lincoln's Volunteers in Springfield, Illinois, in 1861. In 1870, Sam filed one of the first land claims in Brown's Park. He left the park before proving up on the land, turning it over to his niece Josie, and her husband.

After spending several years in Montana and Baggs, Wyoming, Sam returned to the park in 1905, where he lived out his final years.

Samuel C. Bassett was seventy-four years old when he died. There is a marker at his gravesite in the Lodore Cemetery.

Bennett, Jack (? – 1898)

An outlaw hiding out at Brown's Park, Jack Bennett rode with Harry Tracy's gang. Bennett, Tracy, David Lant, and Patrick Johnston, were caught stealing cattle from Brown's Park pioneer Valentine Hoy. Hoy swore out a complaint and organized a posse. The outlaws split up in Lodore Canyon, outside Brown's Park. The posse followed Tracy and Lant. Harry Tracy shot and killed Valentine Hoy.

Meanwhile, Jack Bennett went to his friend Eb Bassett at the Bassett Ranch. Vigilantes nabbed Bennett and hanged him from the crossbar of the Bassett Ranch gate.

His grave is unmarked.

Jarvie, John (1844 – 1909)

A pioneer of the Brown's Park area, John Jarvie, a Scotsman, arrived in the area in 1880. He owned a general store, river ferry and ran the post office on the Utah side of the park. His ranch was a regular stopping place for travelers through the park. Jarvie knew and hosted the likes of Butch Cassidy, the Sundance Kid, Matt Warner, Isom Dart, and was a friend to Ann Bassett.

He was killed when two men robbed his store in July 1909. The robbers then tied his body to a boat and shoved it into the Green River. His body was discovered downstream months later.

He is buried in the Brown's Park Cemetery with a marker.

Rollas, Jack (? – 1882)

A victim of murder at the Bassett Ranch, his killer was never identified.

OFF THE BEATEN PATH:
Dart, Isom (1855 – 1900)

A black cowboy with a shady past, Isom Dart came to Brown's Park from Texas in 1884. He was born a slave in Arkansas, his real name was Ned. He took the last name of Huddleston following the Civil War. He left the war-torn South, and headed west, where he performed in rodeos and engaged in horse stealing, and cattle rustling. He worked for various ranchers, including the Bassett family. He was jailed off and on for cattle rustling and was believed to have stolen cattle hidden on his remote ranch. He reportedly rode with Butch Cassidy from time-to-time.

Hired gun, Tom Horn, stalked Dart and shot him in cold blood, in the early morning at his cabin. Brown's Park residents buried Isom Dart near his cabin at Cold Spring Mountain.[44]

— — —

Highway 6 West

GOLDEN

GOLDEN CEMETERY
LOCATED AT 6TH AVENUE AND ULYSSES STREET IN GOLDEN.

> *A Cemetery is a history of people, of community, of family
> . . . A record of yesterday.*
> From a plaque located at the Golden Cemetery.

Nestled at the mouth of Clear Creek Canyon, the town of Golden provided access for the miners to the rich mining districts . The short-lived capitol of the Colorado Territory was founded by William A.H. Loveland. As a gateway to the Rocky Mountain riches, the town boomed from the early 1860s. Competing for the state capitol, Golden lost to Denver in 1867, yet remained a necessary asset to mining.

The Golden Cemetery was formed in 1874 by the city of Golden, headed by the founder, W. A. H. Loveland. The original cemetery was called Cemetery Hill, situated on a hill north of town. It is believed this land was once an Indian burial ground, but was sold by the government to private individuals. The grounds were divided into customary sections, including the Catholic, I.O.O.F. Lodge, and Masonic Order. By the 1950s, the majority of the Catholic Section had been moved to Mount Olivet Cemetery in Denver.[45] The Veterans Section was deeded in 1910.

Smallpox devastated the community in 1895. Several graves of epidemic victims dot the cemetery. Yet it is a testament to the times and tragedy, that a separate block was sectioned around 1946, called the Babies Section.

The monuments express the deep sorrow of the loss of a child. The carvings depict the grief of the young life lost.

The Babies Section is located in Block 255, in the northwest portion of the cemetery, approximately half way up the hill.

Berthoud, Edward L. (1828 – 1908)

Edward Berthoud came to America from Geneva, Switzerland with his parents in 1830. Young Edward grew up in central New York and entered Union College in 1845. He received his degree in civil engineering in 1849. He served as an engineer on the Panama Railroad in South America in 1851. He returned to America in 1855, settling in Leavenworth, Kansas. A Civil War veteran, Berthoud found a route through the Rocky Mountains for the Colorado Central Railroad, with famed guide Jim Bridger. The route became known as "Berthoud Pass."

As chief engineer of the Colorado Central Railway, Berthoud built several lines from Denver to Golden, Cheyenne, Black Hawk, Central City, and Georgetown, to name a few.

He settled in Golden and became one of the founders of the Colorado School of Mines, teaching until 1887. He served as city engineer and mayor of Golden in 1890.

He is buried in Block 63, Lot 2. The family gravestone is flanked by two military stones.

Palmer, Matila J. (1837 – 1910)

A pioneer of Golden, Matila Palmer traveled by covered wagon west from Kansas, arriving in Golden in 1860. Remarkably, she made the majority of the trip on foot, and gave birth to a healthy young boy, just weeks after her arrival.

She is buried beside her husband and family in Block 243, Lot 2.

Vivian, John C. (1887 – 1964)

John Vivian served as governor of Colorado from 1943 to 1947. He governed the state through the end of World War II, and did his best to see Colorado through a national crisis. Unfortunately, he is best known as having given one of the longest inaugural addresses in Colorado history.

He is buried next to his wife in Block 7, Lot 2. The Colorado Seal is engraved on his tombstone.

West, George (1826 – 1909)

Born on a farm near Claremont, New Hampshire, young George had little opportunity for schooling. In 1840, he became an apprentice at the local weekly newspaper office. At age seventeen, he moved to Boston to continue his printer trade. With the onset of the Civil War, George joined Company H of the Massachusetts regiment, as captain. Later, West, with a group of men headed for the Pikes Peak region, where they settled at the base of the Rocky Mountains. George West built the first home on the land that would become Golden. He was one of the founders of Golden. In 1866, he started the *Colorado Transcript*, one of Colorado's oldest, and still operating newspapers.

He was appointed adjutant general of the Colorado National Guard. Camp George West is named in his honor.

He is buried in Block 68, Lot 1. Two stones mark his gravesite; the family marker, as well as a military stone. To the right is a Woodman of the World memorial to George West.

WHITE ASH MINERS MEMORIAL

LOCATED JUST WEST OF MAPLE STREET, ON 12TH AVENUE.

This memorial is dedicated to to ten miners who lost their lives when the White Ash Mine flooded in September 1889. In June of that same year, a mining inspector reported the coal mine, fifteen years old, too dangerous for operation. The report cited rotten timbers and possible flooding from the nearby Loveland Mine, already condemned from flooding. The miners signed a letter, pleading for their jobs, and the mine remained open.

On September 9, 1889, ten miners, working 730 feet below the surface, were drowned when the Loveland Mine gave way. Air was pumped down the shaft, but by morning, the water had risen sixty-five feet. Any hope for survivors was gone. Recovery of the bodies was impossible. The mine closed permanently, with the ten men entombed.

In 1936, Golden Mayor Burt Jones, whose father was mine foreman at the time of the disaster, raised funds for the monument. Originally placed at the entrance to the mine, near 2nd Street, the monument was later moved to its present location.

BLACK HAWK

DORY HILL CEMETERY

LOCATED APPROXIMATELY FIVE MILES FROM TOWN. FOLLOW HIGHWAY 6 WEST TO HIGHWAY 119 NORTH. CONTINUE NORTH ON HIGHWAY 119, PAST THE TOWN OF BLACK HAWK. APPROXIMATELY FIVES MILES. TURN RIGHT AT THE INTERSECTION WITH HIGHWAY 46. TURN RIGHT ON THE FIRST ROAD TO THE RIGHT. THE CEMETERY IS ON THE RIGHT SIDE OF THE ROAD.

This quiet, remote mountain graveyard sits at the base of a chain of mountains that produced Colorado's first gold rush in 1859. Gilpin County produced millionaires and legends with its vast mining and smelting industries. The miners were the backbone of this community. Many are buried in this cemetery, along with their families. The epitaphs on the tombstones speak of the hardships of the mining life.

The cemetery is enclosed with a wrought iron fence and two gate entrances. While the enclosed land is quite large, the tombstones are widely scattered throughout.

The oldest tombstone dates to 1862, that of Susannah B. Hoopes. According to Gilpin County historians, there are a couple of stories with regard to the origins of the cemetery. One claims a John Hull, hunting on the Dory Ranch property, was accidentally shot and killed. He was buried on the property, and the cemetery eventually was established. Another story is that of a family traveling west by wagon. Along their journey, a child died and was buried on the spot. Other burials eventually followed.

There are no records of the early burials, although a memorial on the property dates the cemetery to 1859. The cemetery does not list burials by block and plot.

Golden, Jennie (1841 – 1921)

Born a slave in Missouri, Jennie Golden came to Colorado with the gold rush of 1859, reportedly with her master. She arrived in Black

Hawk in 1860, the only black woman in the mining camp. Shortly after her arrival, Jennie witnessed a funeral procession winding up the road to the Dory Hill Cemetery. It was the rites for a young woman who had died in childbirth. From that time on, Jennie practiced her mid-wife skills in Black Hawk, delivering hundreds of babies over the years.

When she died in 1921, Jennie's headstone was graced with her photograph, the image of a large jolly woman with a basket of clothes under one arm. The photograph disappeared years ago. A copy is being restored and will be placed on the monument, an effort of the Gilpin County Historical Society.

Smith, Maude (1866 – 1867)

The infant daughter of Lucien K. and Mary Smith, Maude died of unknown causes in her first year of life. Her father, Lucien Smith, a wealthy businessman, built the famous Lace House for his wife, in 1863. The family occupied the home for only two years. Their life in the Lace House was a sad one. Mrs. Smith lost a child in childbirth, followed by the death of their first born, Maude.

There is a marker to Maude's memory.

Steva, Gus (1830 – 1900)
Welsh, Joseph (1840 – 1900)

Both men were guests at the Colorado House in Black Hawk, when a fire broke out in the early morning of October 16, 1900. Their burned bodies were found in the aftermath of the fire.

Seventy-year-old Gus Steva was a ranch man, and Joseph Welsh, sixty, was a miner. Neither had relatives and both were buried in unmarked graves.

CENTRAL CITY

MASONIC CEMETERY

LOCATED SOUTHWEST OF THE TOWN. FOLLOW NEVADA STREET SOUTHWEST ONE-HALF-MILE. THE CEMETERY IS LOCATED ON THE HILL TO THE NORTH OF THE NEW CASINO PARKING LOT.

The setting for this rustic cemetery overlooks the once Victorian hamlet of Central City. Established in the early 1860s, this cemetery contains many old stones of native sandstone, and granite. Several family plots are enclosed with wrought iron fencing. The number of deaths during childbirth is staggering.

The infant child of Gilpin County Sheriff William and Mary Cozens is buried here.

Cameron, John E. (1859 – 1887)

The only child of Robert and Catherine Cameron, John Cameron's parents left their native home of Canada, when John was a year old. The young family drifted in the Midwest, before arriving in Gilpin County in 1866.

John received his education in Central City, and later joined the Central City Fire Department. In 1886, he received an award for valor following a rescue of trapped miners.

Socially, he was known as the city's most eligible bachelor. He attended social gatherings and dances, yet never courted.

Suddenly, in the late fall of 1887, Cameron fell ill. On November 1, John cried out for his mother and collapsed dead at her feet. The doctor said he died of paralysis of the heart.

His funeral, conducted from the First Presbyterian Church, was an crowded affair. The somber black plumed hearse carried his body up the hill for burial in the Masonic Cemetery. Members of the Central City Fire Department, in dress uniform, followed the hearse in parade form.

John Cameron was buried beside his father. The graves are marked with a tall marble obelisk and includes the name of John's mother, who died several years later, in 1912.

Harvey, Richard (1826 – 1897)

A native of Cornwall England, Richard Harvey immigrated to America in 1845. He lived in Wisconsin and Illinois where he married and started a family. He brought his family to Central City in 1863. Harvey found work as a carpenter, and invested in a few mining claims. Well-liked and admired in town, he was elected to the city council in 1873. In 1878, he was elected to the state Legislature, Colorado's second General Assembly. President Hayes appointed him as head of the United States Land Office in Central City, in 1879. He served as clerk of the district court from 1889 until his death.

He and his family lived in a fine Victorian home on historic Casey Street, where his children were raised.

He is buried in the family plot next to his wife Rebecca H., who died in 1893. Included in the plot are the graves of his sons, Chris H. (1852 – 1885) and James H. (1857 – 1909). James died in an avalanche at the Homestake Mine in Leadville.

Kruse Family Plot
Kruse, Hinrich Henry (1814 – 1898)

The patriarch of the Kruse family, Hinrich Kruse migrated from Germany in 1870. His son, Henry J., had already established himself in Central City by 1862. In 1871, Henry J. brought his mother, Frerich, to Central City from Germany. Born in 1806, she died in 1883.

Also buried in the family plot are Hinrich and Frerich's children, Hinrich, Jr. and infants Clara, and Henry C.[46]

There is a large gray granite obelisk marking the family plot.

Lorah, Samuel J. (1834 – 1909)

The son of a probate lawyer who lived in Pennsylvania, and later Iowa, Samuel Lorah was born and raised in Iowa. He graduated from Jefferson College in Pennsylvania, in 1855. He was employed as book-keeper at the Darby and Barksdale Bank in St. Louis.

Gold fever hit Lorah in 1860. He arrived in the gold fields, near Idaho Springs, in the fall of 1860. With his leg broken in a mining accident, he obtained a clerking position at the Mountain City Post Office, above Central City.

Returning to Central City, he worked for the banking firm of B.K. Frink. He joined the Third Colorado Regiment in 1874, commissioned by Governor Evans, to fight the Indians. Following his enlistment, he returned to Central City, where he became a bookkeeper for several mining companies. He later served as city clerk. In 1878, he became ticket agent for the Colorado Central Railroad.

He owned mining property in the area, and held a majority share of the Saratoga Mine stock.

Although his burial spot is not marked, there is a stone monument marking the burial of his wife, Olive, and nine-month-old Samuel Lorah, Jr.

Rudolph, Sarah E. (1872 – 1899)

Sarah, the daughter of J. McCullom, grew up in Gilpin County. She married William Rudolph, a miner, and part owner of the Cricket Tunnel. The couple lived near Apex, in the Pine Creek mining district, where William worked and Sarah raised her three children.

On the early morning of January 29, 1899, the family had just finished breakfast. William left the home on an errand with a neighbor. As Sarah cleared the table, and the children played, a sudden avalanche crushed the cabin in an instant. William turned toward the cabin at the sound and rushed back. Help came immediately. The cabin was buried in ten feet of snow.

After several hours, Sarah's body was recovered under a roof beam. Eighteen-month-old Stella was found close by, crushed under the timber. Young George and James were found pressed together against a wall. Both were alive. George later died, but James, the oldest escaped with minor injuries.

Sarah and her children, Stella, and George are buried in the Masonic Cemetery. There is a marker.

I.O.O.F. CEMETERY

FOLLOW EUREKA STREET UP THE HILL PAST THE TELLER HOUSE. CONTINUE ON THE DIRT ROAD. THE CEMETERY IS THE FIRST ON THE LEFT, IN A GROUP OF CEMETERIES.

On a hill above the town once known as "The Richest Square Mile On Earth," lies a series of cemeteries. All established in the 1860s, today the many tombstones are weathered and decayed. While portions of the cemeteries have sunk over time, the rich pioneer history remains.

The layout of the cemeteries is most interesting. Typically, mountain cemeteries in the mining towns were contained to one section of land, with various religious and lodge associations designated within the grounds. Not so at Central City. Each group was deeded its own land from Gilpin County. While close in proximity, the distinction is apparent in the layout.

Each cemetery had a chapel, all of which are now gone. The cemeteries are primarily filled with the miners and merchants of the area. Central City gold made mine owners rich. They often moved on to spend their fortunes.

The cemetery on the left side of the fork, is the I.O.O.F. Rocky Mountain Lodge No. 2 Cemetery, founded in 1865. The remains of a stone building stand near a metal archway. It is a small structure and may have been either a separate building or adjoined the chapel that once graced the cemetery. There are several family plots, enclosed by wood fencing, or wrought iron. There are many victims of the flu epidemic of 1918.

The most elaborate and unusual tombstone in the cemetery is that of William R. Walter. He died in 1899 at the age of twenty-one years, three months and ten days. His tombstone, made of soft sandstone, is a remarkable replica (to scale) of a log home. Detailed with logs, windows and doors, it is not to be missed.

The tombstone of Sarah Stevens is unique in the fact that she is the earliest pioneer in the cemetery. Born in 1796, she died in 1872. She is buried with John M. Stevens, born in 1830 and died in 1870.

Beaman, Joseph (1833 – 1911)

Born in Germany, following school Joseph Beaman went into the beer brewing business. He migrated to America with his parents in

1851. He worked and furthered
his education, while moving from
Louisiana to Kentucky, to Ohio.
He arrived in Central City in
1859.

As a miner, he worked in the
various mines of Gilpin County
until 1875, when he opened his
own bottling business. His successful business expanded to
include bottled water, the retail
rage of the time.

Author's photo

Tombstone of Joseph S. Beaman

His marker states "Pioneer
arrived in 1859."

Jenkins, David (1827 – 1884)

David Jenkins and his wife, Anna, came to Central City in 1869.
Jenkins owned a profitable mine in the Gilpin County Mining
District. His son, Evan died in 1886, from an accident involving a
horse. Evan left a wife and young son.

David died in 1884, followed by his wife in 1893. The three are
buried in a small family plot. There is a marker.

Lemkuhl, William (1849 – 1903)

Born in Germany, William Lemkuhl apprenticed in the brewery
trade at age fourteen. He came to America, eventually settling in
Central City, in 1863. He later built the first brewery in Gilpin
County. Many social events were held at his establishment. A stockholder in several mines, he was prominent in the business and social
circles of Central City.

An original 59er, William is buried with his wife Mary, and five
children in the family plot. There is a marker.

CITY CEMETERY

*LOCATED ON THE RIGHT SIDE OF THE EUREKA STREET DIRT ROAD, JUST
SOUTH OF THE CATHOLIC CEMETERY.*

Enclosed by a wire fence, the entrance is marked with a large
wrought iron arch. Tombstones are scattered about and extend back
into the trees and the overgrowth. The Knights of Pythias Cemetery,
to the south, once separated, has now grown to join the City
Cemetery.

Copeland, Josiah (? – 1864)
? , Van Horn (? – 1864)

The first legal execution in Colorado Territory occurred in Central City in 1864. A man known only as Van Horn was hanged for the murder of Josiah Copeland. Van Horn owned a whiskey shop and lived with a woman he had brought with him to the mining district. Copeland was the chief clerk of the Massasoit House, and well-known in the community.

Discovering an affair between Copeland and Van Horn's live-in woman, Van Horn followed the two on a cold night in October 1863. Van Horn confronted the pair and shot Copeland. Copeland, although hit, managed to run away, with Van Horn in pursuit. Van Horn shot again, and Copeland fell dead.

Van Horn was immediately arrested and taken to jail by Sheriff Cozens. A lynch mob formed. Cozens dispersed the crowd.

Van Horn, convicted of first degree murder, was led to the scaffold by Cozens, and hanged.

Although the local papers reported both the shooting and the hanging, there are no obituaries. Cemetery records of Gilpin County do not include Copeland or Van Horn. There are many unmarked graves in Central City cemeteries. The City Cemetery seems to be a logical burial place. Although burial is uncertain, their spirits are not.

Covington, Samuel (? – 1896)

A miner and a drifter, Samuel Covington first became known in Central City in 1895. Always armed, he was known as unfriendly, and reportedly an outlaw from New Mexico.

Due to an illness, he sought medical attention from one Doctor Thrailkill. The doctor billed Covington an outrageous price of sixty-one dollars for his services. Covington refused to pay. Doctor Thrailkill turned collection of the debt over to his attorney, James M. Seright.

On the morning of April 15, 1896, a desperate Sam Covington climbed the stairs to Seright's office above Eureka Street. Pulling a gun, he demanded of Seright, a receipt for sixty one dollars. Covington fired his pistol, the bullet deflecting toward the floor. Hearing the shot, Marshal Keleher ran to the scene, followed by Sheriff Dick Williams.

Making their way through the crowd, Keleher and Williams were confronted by Covington. Descending the stairs, Covington opened fire, hitting Marshal Keleher and mortally wounding Sheriff Williams.

Covington ran from the scene of the murder, with armed citizens in hot pursuit. Near the end of Nevada Street, Covington turned and fired at his pursuers. A wagon pulled up with Henry Lehman, armed with a rifle. Following Covington, Lehman jumped from the wagon as Covington shot again. Lehman calmly aimed his rifle and fired, hitting Covington. He was put in the wagon, taken to the sheriff's office and died an hour later. His body was laid out for public display in the front room of the Ed Harris undertaking building.

Samuel Covington, murderer of Sheriff Dick Williams, was buried in an unmarked grave in the City Cemetery.[47]

Kruse Family Plot

Among the burials in this plot are several children, including the children of Henry and Mary Kruse. Henry, very prominent in Gilpin County, served as mayor, owned a bank and was in the first state Legislature.

Four-month-old Theodore and eight-month-old Victor Kruse are buried here. Their graves are enclosed with a wrought iron fence.

KNIGHTS OF PYTHIAS CEMETERY
LOCATED NEXT TO THE CITY CEMETERY.

This cemetery was established in the early 1860s. The oldest known marker dates to 1880. The cemetery is filled with unique headstones. Several once held photographs, since removed by vandals.

Magor, Elizabeth J. (1846 – 1922)

From her native England, Elizabeth crossed the Atlantic Ocean with her husband Richard, in 1865. In New York, Richard worked in the iron mines for several years. In 1876, the family including six children, left New York for the Colorado gold fields.

Leaving most of their possessions behind, the family traveled by covered wagon, crossing the Mississippi River, through the Midwest, and into Colorado. Along the journey, a daughter, Liza was born. Entering Colorado, another daughter, five-year-old Bell, died of measles.

The Magor family arrived in Central City in 1880. Richard went to work for the Gunnell Mine, where he eventually became a foreman. A son, Jonnie was born in 1882. He died the following year.

During the scarlet fever epidemic of 1884-1885, the Magor's lost six of their children, Amelia, Louisa, Caroline, Liza, Richard, and Frank. Lester was born in 1886 and died six years later. Hattie, born in 1890, lived two months.

Elizabeth's husband, Richard, died in 1894. Of her eleven children, only Ellsworth lived to adulthood.

The sad, tragic life of Elizabeth Magor ended with her death in 1922. Her grave is marked with a large monument erected by the Knights of Pythias. Vandalized in years past, it is still visible.

Mitchell, William (1851 – 1927)

A native of England, William Mitchell learned the trade of blacksmithing at an early age. He sailed for America at age twenty-one. He came to Gilpin County, where he prospected and worked in several mines, including the Gregory and Bobtail mines.

He served three terms as sheriff of Gilpin County, and participated in local politics. He married Elizabeth J. Stephens in 1874.

He is buried next to his wife, Elizabeth. There is a marker.

Welch, Isaac (1869 – 1910)

Born in England, Isaac Welch had limited education. At age twelve, he worked on a farm to support his family. At age eighteen, he migrated to the United States. He worked in New York and St. Louis long enough to save money to return to England. He wed his childhood sweetheart in 1894. The couple returned to America the following year and settled in Gilpin County.

Working various jobs, Welch eventually became a reporter with the *Register Call* newspaper, a position he held for fourteen years. He worked as a correspondent for the *Denver Post* and did part-time work as an insurance agent.

On the morning of July 19, 1910, Welch went to the *Register Call* office. The morning was spent in writing and research. Shortly before noon, two insurance agents entered the office, reportedly to audit the books. Welch made arrangements with the men to meet in an hour, so that he could retrieve the accounts from his home. He stopped by his house, and as lunch was not ready, he told his wife he was needed back in town. He was seen walking up Eureka Street and over Winnebago Hill, the opposite direction of his office.

Later in the afternoon, the body of Isaac Welch was found near the spring house of the Gundy Ranch. Beside his body were the remains of crushed cyanide, a collapsed cup, and a bottle of whiskey. In his coat, there were five letters addressed to family and various friends. One letter stated "This is a plain case: cyanide. I want a plain burial. No fuss." The letter was signed.

The funeral was held at his home, with burial following in the Knights of Pythias Cemetery.

Welch's suicide remains a mystery. No discrepancies were found in the audit of the insurance books.

PROTESTANT CEMETERY

THE PROTESTANT CEMETERY IS SOUTH OF THE OTHER CEMETERIES, ON A SMALL KNOLL. IT IS THE SMALLEST CEMETERY IN THE GROUP. ENCLOSED BY BARBED WIRE, THERE ARE VERY FEW BURIALS.

CATHOLIC CEMETERY

LOCATED NORTH OF THE OTHER CEMETERIES, WHERE THE DIRT ROAD OF EUREKA STREET ENDS.

The largest of the cemeteries, it is also the best maintained. There is no distinct order. The stones are scattered from east to west and extend to the knoll at the north end. There are several trees and even more thorny bushes, that hide many stones.

Heppberger, Englebert (1851 – 1934)
Heppberger, Nora (1860 – 1941)

Immigrating from Germany, the young Heppberger couple and infant daughter arrived in America, eventually settling in Black Hawk, in 1873. A miner, Englebert worked at various mines during the boom of Colorado's gold rush years. In 1874, he bought his family a fine frame home in the heart of Black Hawk.[48]

A mining blast injured Heppberger, forcing him to end his mining career. Although he held various odd jobs, his wife Nora, took it upon herself to make ends meet, while raising their six children. Her yard contained hens, providing the eggs she sold to the merchants. She took in laundry. In time, she saved enough money to purchase six horses and enough wagons to haul ore and timber to and from the mines.

This family enterprise was carried on to the next generation, following Nora's death in 1941.

Engle and Nora are buried together in the Heppberger family plot.

NEVADAVILLE

BALD MOUNTAIN CEMETERY

THE OLD MINING TOWN OF NEVADAVILLE IS APPROXIMATELY ONE AND ONE-HALF MILES ABOVE CENTRAL CITY. FROM MAIN STREET, FOLLOW THE ROAD WEST TO NEVADAVILLE. (THERE IS A SIGN.) BALD MOUNTAIN CEMETERY IS ALMOST A MILE NORTH OF NEVADAVILLE. FOLLOW THE DIRT ROAD NORTH OUT OF NEVADAVILLE, TURN LEFT AT THE FORK IN THE ROAD JUST PAST THE OLD MILL. THE DIRT ROAD CLIMBS FOR ABOUT ONE MILE TO A FORK IN THE

ROAD. TURN RIGHT AFTER THE RANCH HOUSE. THE CEMETERY IS A SHORT DISTANCE DOWN THIS ROAD.

Perched high in the hills, far from the busy gold mining camps of yesteryear, this cemetery is removed and quaint in its setting. This remote mountain cemetery features both beauty and solitude.

The earliest burials occurred in 1865. The original cemetery, located in the middle of Nevadaville, was moved to its present location in the name of progress and practicality. Following the cemetery move, strange events occasionally occurred, creating superstitions and ghost stories. Many believed the various mishaps were caused by the spirits of those who were *not* moved to the Bald Mountain Cemetery.

Seymour, Bennett E. (1853 – 1943)

Born in Ashtabula, Ohio, Bennett Seymour was the great-grandson of Edward Seymour, Duke of Somerset. His ancestors immigrated to America in 1639. In 1868, at the age of fifteen, Bennett and his parents crossed the Great Plains by wagon train to Colorado. After a few years, Seymour settled in Nevadaville, with his family. He completed his education and worked in the mines.

In 1874, he moved to Central City, following the disastrous fire. He joined the grocery firm of Hawley and Manville. In 1885, he was elected county commissioner, serving until 1891, when he became mayor of Central City. Having a great interest in baseball, he signed a petition covering expenses for balls, bats, masks and gloves, for the Gilpin County Eagles baseball team. He was captain in the Colorado National Guard, a member and alderman of the Episcopal Church, and a member of the school board. He and his wife Mary Jane, had five children. None lived beyond infancy.

He is buried beside his wife, Mary Jane. There is a marker.

Slater, Estel (1871 – 1895)

A native of Hartford City, Indiana, he traveled west with his family, settling in Nevadaville. Following his education, he went to work in the mines of Gilpin County.

While working at the Alpes Mine on Quartz Hill, Slater, working at the 800-foot level of the mine, Slater was killed by a blasting accident.

His tombstone in the Bald Mountain Cemetery is graced with his photograph, placed by his parents.

Warren, Francis E. (1854 – 1892)

A native of Cornwall, England, Francis Warren was known as one of the many "Cousin Jacks" in the Gilpin County Mining District.

These men from England, brought with them inherited skills, having mined for tin in their homeland for centuries. Warren worked in various mines in Gilpin County.

In 1879, he married and had three children. He bought a house in Nevadaville in 1882. He belonged to the Methodist Church, of Central City, helping to build the church with the Cornish "Cousin Jacks" in their spare time.

Francis Warren died in December 1892, at the age of thirty-eight, suffering from the miner's dreaded black lung disease. There is a marker.

Williams, Elizabeth (1851 – 1949)

Of Cornish descent, Elizabeth came to the gold fields of Gilpin County with her immigrant parents, shortly after the gold strike of 1859. A widow, she had recently lost both her husband and infant daughter. While still in her teens, she married Richard "Dick" Williams of Nevadaville.

Within a year of the marriage, Elizabeth's young son from her first marriage died. She and Dick eventually had eleven children together. Of Elizabeth's thirteen children, only five lived to adulthood.

Elizabeth died on April 19, 1949, exactly fifty-three years to the day, after her husband was murdered.

Williams, Oscar (1874-1957)

The son of Elizabeth and Richard Williams, Oscar was twenty-three when his father died in the line of duty. Following his father's footsteps literally to the end, Oscar supported his mother and siblings by taking over the Williams Stables. For thirty years, he ran the family business, as well as serving the town. As his father before him, Oscar became sheriff of Gilpin County, serving from 1922 to 1946.

He followed his father to the end, dying on April 19th, the same date both his father and mother died. He is buried in the family plot. There is a marker.

Williams, Richard B. (1847 – 1896)

Born in England, Richard emigrated with his parents to America, settling in Wisconsin. His father worked in the copper mines, where Richard learned the trade. His brother John, soon followed him to America.

In 1870, young Dick left home for the mining district of Gilpin County. On Christmas Day, 1870, he married the widow of a Cornish descendent, Elizabeth Jane Bartle, known as Libbie. The couple had eleven children.

Denver Public Library
The funeral procession for Sheriff Richard Williams winds through Central City.

Dick and his brother John, operated an ore shipping business in 1877. Dick also owned a meat market, livery stable and stage line. He was popular among the miners for his wrestling and boxing abilities, winning several tournaments. Always friendly, he even treated his boxing opponent to a drink, after he knocked him out in a match.

Very active in local politics, he was elected trustee of Nevadaville, foreman of the Nevadaville Fire Department, county commissioner, and twice elected as mayor of Central City. Elected sheriff of Gilpin County in 1879, he served four terms.

In 1891, he opened a livery, known as the Williams Stables. One of five liveries in Central City, his was the largest and best equipped.[49]

On April 15, 1896, Sheriff Williams responded to a shooting on Main Street. Sam Covington, in a desperate mood, had fired at Marshal Mike Keleher. Williams confronted Covington and both men fired. Covington hit Williams in his right side. Four days later, Sheriff Dick Williams died.

Because of his popularity, the funeral was held at the Central City Opera House, the only service ever held there. Despite the large seating capacity, hundreds lined Eureka Street. Businessmen and mines shut down operations in his honor, while four clergymen delivered eulogies. The funeral procession from downtown Central City to Bald Mountain Cemetery was a long solemn journey. The entourage consisted of 116 horse-drawn vehicles, horsemen, lodge members and firemen, making the two and a half mile climb to the cemetery.

His monument reads: "Killed April 19, 1896. In the line of duty."[50]

RUSSELL GULCH

RUSSELL GULCH CEMETERY

LOCATED TWO AND ONE-HALF MILES SOUTHWEST OF CENTRAL CITY. FOLLOW THE VIRGINIA CANYON ROAD, (DIRT) ALSO KNOWN AS THE "OH MY GOD ROAD," TOWARD IDAHO SPRINGS. THE CEMETERY ENTRANCE IS ON THE RIGHT SIDE OF THE ROAD.

This almost forgotten cemetery lays near the abandoned mining town of Russell Gulch. Named for William Green Russell, who arrived in Gilpin County in 1859, Russell, along with John Gregory, prospected and located rich veins of ore in the nearby hills, causing the first Colorado gold rush.

The Russell Gulch Cemetery, established in 1878 by the I.O.O.F. #41, contains several sections, including the Welsh, Italian, Cornish, and Austrian sections. A majority of the deceased are miners or families of area miners, with a few merchants, and landowners. A Welsh chapel once stood in the cemetery, complete with a choir and Welsh minister.

The cemetery extends toward the hill, somewhat hidden by the beautiful aspen trees.

— — —

Among the burials are the Joseph Hare family. Joseph was employed at one of the local mines, where his family lived in a small mining shack. His wife, Fannie cared for the children, and helped in the mining community, often assisting with childbirth and family emergencies. Joseph and Fannie had five children, all buried in the family plot. The oldest daughter died at age twenty-one, the youngest, at age two months. Joseph died of miners consumption a few years after the children died, leaving Fannie alone. To make ends meet, Fannie moved to Central City where she opened a bakery. Joseph and Fannie are buried together, along with their children.

Ferganichich, Alois (? – 1912)
Ferganichich, Mary (? – 1908)

Alois Ferganichich was a miner living in Russell Gulch. He was heartbroken when his wife died unexpectedly in 1908. He continued to work in the mines, ending his day by visiting his wife's grave. The area miners noticed the withdrawn Alois and kept an eye on him.

Examples of early wooden grave markers.

On June 14, 1912, the miners heard a gunshot. Rushing to the cemetery, they found Alois slumped against the blood-splattered tombstone of his wife, Mary. A .38 caliber revolver was near his hand.

Mary and Alois are buried together. There is a fine dark granite tombstone. Curiously, Mary's age lists the customary months and days, however the age in years are missing.

Jones, Owen (1856 – 1894)

A Welsh miner, Jones immigrated to America first settling in Wisconsin, where he farmed for a time. Following Nathaniel Hill's successful smelting operation at Black Hawk, Jones gave up farming and came west to try his hand at mining.

As a miner in the Russell Gulch area, he had a fair amount of success before an explosion caused the loss of one hand and several fingers on the other. He died from his injuries during the cold winter of 1894.

Owen Jones received a Welsh funeral, followed by burial at the Russell Gulch Cemetery. His tombstone is one of the most unique in the cemetery. Inscribed with a Welsh tribute in poetry, it is one of only two such tombstones in the county.

Lutz Family Plot

George and Pauline Lutz are buried near their children who all died in the year 1886, three within a month. It is believed the children died of anthrax. Young Emma, eight-year-old George, four-year-old Harman, and four-year-old Pauline, are buried in the family plot.

Perry, Thomas (1840 – 1902)
Perry, Sarah (1840 – 1916)

Thomas Perry, a Welsh immigrant, came to America in 1860. First settling in Pennsylvania, he made his way west, eventually settling in Gilpin County in 1879. Superintendent of the Knickerbocker Tunnel, Perry soon gained the reputation as one of the finest miners in the gulch.[51] His reputation became stained when he was arrested and convicted of "wife abuse" in 1899. He served thirty days in jail.

Thomas Perry fell ill in January 1902 and died of pneumonia. He is buried with his wife, Sarah, who died in 1916.

— — —

Interstate 70 West
From Denver to the Utah State Line

LOOK OUT MOUNTAIN
FROM I-70, TAKE THE EXIT TO LOOK OUT MOUNTAIN, AND THE BUFFALO BILL MUSEUM. THE GRAVE OF BUFFALO BILL CODY IS LOCATED ON THE MUSEUM GROUNDS.

Cody, William Frederick (1846 – 1917)

Just west of Denver, off I-70, lies the grave William F. Cody, cowboy and famed scout extraordinaire, a self-made nineteenth century celebrity, better known as Buffalo Bill.

Cody came west from Iowa, with his family, at the age of eleven, looking for work to support his mother and family. His first job was with the newly-formed Pony Express in 1860, at the age of fifteen. Hired by famed stationer, Jack Slade, Cody carried the mail from Nebraska and the Julesburg station. He next landed a job with the Kansas Pacific Railroad. His job was to get meat for the railroad workers. He polished his shooting skills, bringing down over 4,000 head of buffalo. Hence the name, Buffalo Bill. This experience and more importantly, his new-found reputation, made him a much sought after Army scout, leading many expeditions against the Indians.

Dime novels were published all over the country that stereotyped Buffalo Bill into a wild west hero. The dime novels' most avid fan was Buffalo Bill himself! In 1883, Cody started the Buffalo Bill's Wild West Show, starring himself. The show played all over the country

Author's collection
William F. "Buffalo Bill" Cody

and eventually played in Europe before the Queen of England.

William F. Cody died at age 71, in Denver. He was buried on top of Lookout Mountain, at his request. His funeral procession took the entire afternoon, and was the largest the front range had ever witnessed.[52]

IDAHO SPRINGS

IDAHO SPRINGS CEMETERY

LOCATED SOUTH OF THE CITY OF IDAHO SPRINGS. FROM TOWN, TAKE HIGHWAY 103 SOUTH OUT OF IDAHO SPRINGS. THE CEMETERY IS ON THE LEFT, ONE MILE SOUTH ON THE DIRT ROAD.

Creek floods and rapid population growth contributed to the early history of Idaho Springs and the cemetery. An interesting story is told of the mining town's first official burial. Up the Virginia Canyon, during the winter of 1860, a body of a man who had been found shot to death was found. The miners provided a proper burial, led by one of the town fathers, Robert Griswold.[53] The day was bitter cold, the ground nearly frozen, and difficult to dig. The men kept warm and were encouraged with several swigs of whiskey. The burial ceremony ended with a rowdy song and the only prayer the men could think of; "Now I Lay Me Down To Sleep."

That first burial became the town's official cemetery, located on Colorado Boulevard, between 6th and 7th Avenues. The site proved to be low and flooded often from Chicago Creek. As the mining town grew, a new cemetery was needed.

In 1874, the Idaho Springs Cemetery was relocated one mile south of town, on higher land. Burials from the town cemetery were reinterred to the new location. The cemetery is laid out in the canyon, stretching up to the side of the mountain. This quiet setting reflects the typical hard life of nineteenth century mining. Several died of mining accidents, murder and illness. The earliest graves in the cemetery are that of J.B. and Rosamond Rowen, husband and wife, who died in 1863 and 1864, respectively. Their bodies were reinterred in this cemetery in 1874.[54]

Colorado Historical Society
Buffalo Bill Cody's funeral procession to the top of
Lookout Mountain, in 1917, took an entire afternoon.

Of particular note is the Infant Section, half-way up the hill. Row after row of weathered white marble baby stones are sad testaments to the early victims of childbirth, scarlet fever, typhoid and influenza.

While the cemetery is still in use, it is a typical mountain resting place, with nature's pine trees and sagebrush serving as the only landscape.

Dunton, Blanch (1893 – 1899)

One of the most stunning and moving tombstones in the cemetery. Little Blanch was the six-year-old daughter of William and Alice Dunton. Their love and grief is obvious in the ornate log playhouse that dominates her final resting place.

Knottege, Victor (1855 – 1902)

One of the earliest pioneers of Idaho Springs, Knottege was a pharmacist who opened the first drug store in town, at 1446 Miner Street, still standing. He was active in town affairs and community projects.

There is a granite tombstone marking his grave and that of his wife Mattie, who died in 1904.

Plummer, Henry (1836 – 1902)
Plummer, Emma (1844 – 1922)

Henry and Emma Plummer arrived at Payne's Bar, (later Idaho Springs) during the first gold rush of 1859. Mr. Plummer and his brother, Cyrus, operated the first livery stable, located at 1536 Miner Street.[55] He opened the first bank in town, with such partners as

William Doe.[56] Plummer owned and developed much of the commercial property along Miners Street.

Mrs. Emma Plummer was able to secure funds from Andrew Carnegie in 1901 and established a community library, donating a portion of her land for the site. The library still exists.

Their large tombstone is weathered and rusted, due to mineral erosion.

Roberts, John (1820 – 1896)

John Roberts arrived in Colorado Territory with his family in 1860. With his brother Henry, he started a mercantile store in Georgetown in 1861, and a second store in Silver Plume the following year.

The successful Roberts Brothers Grocery was located in Idaho Springs on Miners Street. One of the first brick buildings built, it still stands today.

He is buried with his wife. There is a marker.

Tayler, Charlie (1867 – 1939)

Tayler arrived in Clear Creek County in the 1880's, making the area near Idaho Springs his home. He was an eccentric man and soon become the talk of the town. Charlie took it upon himself to build a water mill, on a bet, by some accounts.

He built the most spectacular water mill the citizens of Idaho Springs had ever seen. Completed in 1893, it was the highlight of the year. It solved the water problems for many of the mines in the area. The wonder of Tayler's invention lasted but a few short months, due to the silver crash of 1893.

Charlie spent his remaining years watching the children play on his "great" wheel. Charlie died in 1939. But his water wheel served as his legacy. It was moved to the base of Bridal Falls after World War II, just off Interstate I-70.

There is a marker to Charlie's memory.

Wilkins, John (1844 – 1926)

This family plot next to the second diagonal road, is surrounded by pipe-like fencing.

John Wilkins arrived in Idaho Springs in the 1880s. He invested in commercial properties, contributed to the town's growth, and was a prominent member of the community.

A member of the Masons, the lodge meetings were held at his property on 7th Avenue. Upon his death, he deeded the Masonic Building to the lodge in exchange for the caring of his grave, a deed carried on today.

His tall sandstone pillar is broken at the top, yet gives testament to his pioneer stature in the community. The marker bears his name, as well as that of his wife Mary, age 39, who died in 1886.

GEORGETOWN

ALVARADO CEMETERY

LOCATED EAST OF TOWN, APPROXIMATELY THREE AND ONE-QUARTER MILES ON ALVARADO ROAD. THE CEMETERY IS ON THE RIGHT SIDE OF THE ROAD.

Legend has it that the townfolk of Georgetown felt that they should have a cemetery, like other mining towns. Due to the healthy climate, and lack of deaths a cemetery wasn't needed until March 1898 after Edward Bainbridge was lynched. Originally buried at the spot of the lynching, a place called the "Point of Rocks," his body was removed to the new Alvarado Cemetery. Bainbridge shot Jim Martin through the eye during a card game, over a can of oysters. According to legend, Bainbridge's body was exhumed and taken to Central City for exhibit.

Alvarado Cemetery has many winding and confusing dirt walkways, following the hills and many pine trees. It seems to be broken into two distinct areas. The lower end contains many graves close together, while the upper end ascends a hill toward the east, and is quite spread out.[57]

It broke our hearts to lose you
But you didn't go alone
A part of us went with you
the day God called you home
Now to your grave we travel
the flowers placed with care
But no one knows the heartache
as we turn to leave you there
Epitaph at the Alvarado Cemetery

Anderson, Emil H. (1873 – 1950)

A native of Sweden, Emil Anderson came to America with his family in the late 1880s. He settled in Georgetown in 1889. At the age of sixteen, he went to work for Henry Kneisel's hardware and grocery. Within three years, he and Kneisel were partners in the business. Anderson would operate the the successful store for nearly sixty years.

He invested in several mining enterprises. He served as a fireman with the famous Star Hook and Ladder team, that won several state championships. He was a member of the Masonic Order, the

Georgetown School Board, and an elder of the Georgetown Presbyterian Church.

He married Cora Kneisel, the daughter of his partner Henry, in 1899. Cora died in the 1918 flu epidemic.

The two are buried together in the family plot bordered with concrete and marked with impressive granite stones. A granite bench compliments the burial site.

Dupuy, Louis (? – 1900)

This small, eccentric Frenchman arrived in Georgetown in 1870. Prospecting for his fortune and future, a mining accident suddenly changed his plans. In 1875, Dupuy purchased the Delmonico Bakery on Alpine Street in Georgetown.

By 1890, he had completed the construction of the famous Hotel De Paris. Fifteen years in the making, the hotel actually was three buildings joined together with additions to the backside. It was known as one of the finest hotels and restaurants in the west, largely due to Dupuy's knowledge of French cuisine and fine wine.

Dupuy was known as a quiet, unfriendly and even cold individual. When he died of pneumonia in 1900, it was somewhat surprising that he left his hotel business to Sophie Galley, his maid of several years. Sophie died in 1901.

The two are buried together under a tall ornately engraved granite obelisk. The words inscribed in the stone marker read: "Deux Bon Amis." French for "Two Good Friends."

Ecklund, Frank (1874 – 1941)

An asthmatic, Frank Ecklund settled for the clean mountain air in Georgetown, in 1902. He worked in the mines of Georgetown and Silver Plume, yet eventually made his living as a professional carpenter and blacksmith. He was active in community affairs and stayed involved in mining, including the Pelican Dives, Waldorf and Moline mines.

He died December 7, 1941, the day Japan attacked Pearl Harbor. He is buried with his wife Emma. There is a marker.

Guanella, Joseph (1861 – 1942)

A native of Illinois, Joseph Guanella and his parents arrived in Georgetown in 1871. His father operated a bakery with his uncles, the Monti Brothers, while Joseph helped out from time to time. He married Margaret Lindstrom, daughter of a very influential family, in 1882. The young couple moved to Empire the following year, where

Joseph ran the sawmill and a brewery business owned by his wife's family.

The Guanella and Lindstrom families were also involved in ranching, their combined herds and land were one of the largest in Clear Creek County.

He and Margaret are buried together in the Guanella/Lindstrom family plot. They have separate markers.

Guanella, Thomas (1836 – 1881)

The patriarch of the pioneer Guanella family, Thomas was born in New York City. As a youth, he started a freighting business in New Orleans. There, he married Josephine Monti. In 1861, the young family set out for new fortunes in the West. Spending time in Iowa and Nevada, they finally settled in Georgetown in 1871.

He went to work for his wife's brothers at the bakery, where he managed the finances and clerked the store. Known as the Monti and Guanella Bakery, it was located in town at 6th and Rose streets. Thomas bought the business in 1876, operating it successfully until his death. His tall white marble stone is the corner piece in the Guanella/Lindstrom family plot. His wife Josephine has a very small rock stone memorial.

Kneisel, Henry (1852 – 1914)

Born in Germany, his parents migrated to America, settling in Iowa. His father, John Kneisel, was killed in the Civil War, his mother died shortly thereafter. Young Henry moved west, arriving in Georgetown in 1874.

He went to work for Thomas Guanella, in his grocery and bakery shop. He later bought the business and with his partner, Emil Anderson, the firm known as Kneisel and Anderson became the leading grocery store in the mining district.

Kneisel also owned several mining properties, including the Alto, Twin, Missouri Girl, and the Missouri Boy. He was an officer of the local I.O.O.F., county treasurer, for several years until 1896, and served as mayor of Georgetown for many years.

He is buried in the family plot with his wife Emma, who died in 1909. The small dark granite stones mark their graves, dominated by the white marble Obelisk in the center of the plot. This memorial is to their children, Lois (1879 – 1898) and Ernest (1888 – 1895).

Randall, Jesse S. (1848 – 1939)

Born in Kentucky, Randall Jesse moved with his parents to western Iowa where, at age fourteen, he was apprenticed in the printing business, in 1862.

He arrived in Georgetown in 1869 at the urging of his father Abram, a noted businessman in the mountain community. Jesse worked for the *Colorado Miner* until 1875, when he started his own newspaper, *The Georgetown Courier*. The paper was the rival of all others in the mining district, causing many to fold. Randall's editorial columns became very popular and Randall was soon the leading authority in the community.

He was active in city government, community affairs, school board decisions and the Grace Episcopal Church. There is a marker.

Spruance, William (1827 – 1889)[59]

A native of Pennsylvania, William Spruance served in the Mexican War. He fell in love with the West, eventually prospecting in Idaho Springs as early as 1860. By 1868, he was engaged in merchandising in the mining camp that would become Georgetown.

One of the earliest pioneers in the area, he was involved in the town's evolution. He was Clear Creek County Clerk for four terms, and a member of the board of Councilmen for two terms.

The largest obelisk in the cemetery, his white monument dominates near the center of the cemetery, at the side of the roadway.

Yates, Charles J. (1814 – 1888)

Born in Pennsylvania, Charles Yates left home at age twelve. At New Orleans, he found work on steamboats running the Mississippi River. He married Mary Sare in Ohio in 1842, opened a bakery and became quite successful. In 1861, he organized the 9th Illinois Volunteer Company and served in the Civil War.

He lost his wife during the war and moved West after the war ended. By 1869, he operated a bakery and small restaurant in Georgetown. He remarried in 1871 and built the Yates House, a fine hotel and restaurant.

He is buried in the Alvarado Cemetery. There is a marker.

SILVER PLUME

SILVER PLUME CEMETERY

LOCATED ON THE SOUTH SIDE OF INTERSTATE 70, ABOVE THE SILVER PLUME TRAIN STATION. TAKE PAUL STREET (A DIRT ROAD) TO THE LEFT, BEHIND THE STATION. THE ROAD IS A STEEP NARROW CLIMB, APPROXIMATELY ONE AND ONE-HALF MILES TO THE CEMETERY ON THE LEFT.

The cemetery, also known as Pine Grove Cemetery, was established in 1883.[60] The cemetery lies on a high slope, extending up the mountainside. One of the most unusual mountain cemeteries, it is easy to get confused in direction and location. While the sections are designated with wrought iron gates, the graves lay scattered in all directions. Many are hidden in the bushes and tall trees.

Blasting was necessary to prepare for burials. Two sets of pall-bearers were required to haul the casket of the dearly departed up the long hill to the burial ground. Silver Plume never owned a hearse.

The cemetery is divided into sections. The religious include the Catholic and Methodist, while organizations include the I.O.O.F., The United Order of Redmen, and Knights of Pythias. The lower end of the cemetery, to the east, (on the right side of the road) was reserved for those not belonging to any particular religion or organization. It is known as the Town Section. Located in the Town Section, is the Classon family plot. It is enclosed with a wooden fence, painted white. It contains the graves and headstone of James and Amelia Classon, marked with a large white marble stone.[61]

An epidemic of diphtheria, followed by smallpox took the lives of many young children from 1879 to 1883. There are over sixty graves of children in this small mountain community cemetery.

The most impressive monument is that of the Collins family. John Collins was the first man buried in the Catholic section. David Collins, a nephew, built a grand memorial for the the family plot at Pine Slope Cemetery. Silver Plume granite encloses the family plot, while wrought iron gates support granite angels and crosses. Toward the rear, a rock shrine holds a white marble Madonna.

Buckley, Alice Griffin (1862 – 1947)

Born in the mining camp of Nevadaville, it is believed Alice was the first white child born in the area. Her father, Daniel Griffin was a miner. He was killed on the streets of Central City by a stray bullet. Alice's mother brought her children to Silver Plume shortly after the death of her husband.

Alice married Jerry Buckley in the Catholic Church in 1885. She had thirteen children. Jerry died in 1909, leaving Alice with her large family to raise alone. She turned their small livery stable into a business of supplying wood, coal and various needs to the community.

All thirteen of her children helped in the family business and went on to businesses of their own.

Alice Griffin Buckley died in 1947, at the age of eighty-five. She is buried in the Catholic Section.

Lampshire, Samuel T. (1831 – 1891)

A native of Kerswyn, England, Sam was baptized by his father, the Reverend John Lampshire. He married Eliza Griffith. They made their home in Wales, where six children were born. They left for America, settling in Michigan in 1872.

Sam and his two older sons came to Silver Plume, where they found work, and soon sent for the remainder of the family. Sam and his wife Eliza, opened a boardinghouse at a mining camp called Brownsville, just below the 7:30 Mine, near Idaho Springs. The snow slide of 1884 almost wiped them out, but they were able to rebuild. The new boardinghouse was a popular destination for miners and travelers for years.

Both Sam and Eliza died in 1891. They are buried together in the Knights of Pythias Section.[62]

Rowe, Edward George (1891 – 1979)

The son of John and Clara Rowe, Edward Rowe was born in Silver Plume, where he spent most of his eighty-seven years. He made his living in mining and mill work, before serving his home town in public office. He and his wife Ella, had two children, both born and raised in Silver Plume.

George was very active in Silver Plume government, serving on the school board for ten years, and on the volunteer fire department for twenty years. He also held offices in the Masonic Lodge of Georgetown and the Clear Creek Metal Mining Association. He is remembered most fondly for his almost thirty years as mayor of Silver Plume, and the accomplishments of his administration. He is responsible for the cleanup of the water system, and the historical preservation program in Silver Plume.

He is buried beside his wife Ella, who died in 1938, at the age of forty-four. There is a light gray granite memorial. The Rowe family plot is located in the Knights of Pythias Section.

Rowe, John (1859 – 1923)

Born in Cornwall, England, John Rowe arrived in Silver Plume in 1882. He worked in the mines for a time. By 1884, he was practicing his carpentry trade in the mining town. He built many of the original brick structures still standing today.

John married Clara Stephens, also a native of Cornwall, England, who had arrived in Silver Plume in 1886. Clara was born in 1868. The couple had four children, including George, who would become mayor of Silver Plume.

The couple are buried together in the Knights of Pythias Section. Their granite monument is enclosed with a concrete border.

The Ten Italians Monument (February 12, 1899)

On a Sunday morning in February 1899, an avalanche struck the south side of Sherman Peak, above Silver Plume. In its path were several miner's cabins. They were instantly leveled as the snow slide swept toward town, stopping just west of the schoolhouse. The force was so strong that near the school, a mother, preparing for the church service, was tying a bow in her daughter's hair when the avalanche hit without warning. Their bodies were found in this posture.

In the recovery, ten Italian miners were found frozen to death in and near the cabins.

This tragic loss is memorialized by a tall granite marker in the Order of Redmen Section. The dead are buried together in a large rock enclosed plot, with individual tablet markers.

Vivian-Jewell Family Plot

John Henry Vivian, the patriarch of the Vivian family, came to Silver Plume from Cornwall, England, where he was born in 1841. Arriving in 1871, he built a fine house and worked in the mines, saving his money so that he could buy passage for his wife to America. In 1880, his wife Catherine and the first of their seven children sailed to America. John Vivian was very active in community affairs and played the organ at the Methodist Church every Sunday for years. He died in 1898.

John and Catherine's daughter, Mary Ann, arrived in Silver Plume with her mother in 1880. At age seventeen, Mary Ann married James Pearce Jewell, a native of Cornwall, England. Jewell also worked in the mines. The couple had five children, before Mary Ann Vivian Jewell died in 1894. She was twenty-nine. Following the death of his wife, James sent his children to England for a brief period. They returned to Silver Plume, where they were raised by John and Catherine Vivian. James left the United States for a career in South Africa.

The Vivian-Jewell plot includes two of the Vivian children, both dying in early childhood.

The family plot is located in the Knights of Pythias Section.

Williams, Kate Vivian (1864-1949)

The oldest daughter of John and Catherine Vivian, Kate Vivian arrived in America with her mother in 1880. She was sixteen years old. In 1883, she married John Williams in Silver Plume. John was a hard rock miner in the Silver Plume area. The couple had nine children. They were involved in school activities with their children and attended the Methodist Church, where Kate's parents had worshipped. In her later years, Kate traveled extensively, but always called Colorado home.

Kate Vivian Williams died at age eighty-five. She is buried in the I.O.O.F. Section.

Woodward Family Plot

James Francis Woodward was born in 1849, in Highland, Wisconsin. In 1870, he married Mary Ann Brennan of Wisconsin, born in 1845.

James brought his family to Colorado, where they settled in Silver Plume in 1874. James was a miner until he developed silicosis, forcing him to end his mining career. He became the marshal of Silver Plume. He died in Silver Plume at the age of thirty-four. Woodward Street was named in his honor. Mary Ann Woodward died in 1931.

The Woodward family plot is located in the I.O.O.F. Section.

OFF THE BEATEN PATH:

High on a mountain top above the town of Silver Plume, on the north side of I-70, are the remains and tombstone of Clifford Griffin.

Clifford Griffin followed his older brother Heneage, to America from England in the spring of 1880. Heneage had bought the Seven Thirty Mine, located above the town of Silver Plume. In short time, Clifford took over the operation of the mine. He kept the books, accounts of daily ore production, mill deliveries, ore output, inventory, and tracked the miner's pay. Under Clifford's management, the Seven Thirty became the richest mine in the Silver Plume District, and Clifford became a rich man.

With all his riches, Clifford chose to remain in his cabin on the mountain, alone, and secluded from the town. Rumor had it that he suffered from a broken heart, leaving England shortly after the death of his beloved fiancee. His only companion was his violin, the melancholy melodies drifting with the wind down to Silver Plume. Mystery surrounded the death of Clifford's betrothed, giving way to gossip. Whispers of deceit and murder floated about the town of Silver Plume.

The night of June 19, 1887, a Sunday, Griffin put a six-shot revolver to his head and pulled the trigger. He never heard the roar or felt the impact. His body was found the following morning by astonished miners. The body of Clifford Griffin lay in a crude grave he had dug for himself. A note was found nearby. Written by Clifford, it asked simply that he be buried on the mountain he so loved. Clifford Griffin was thirty-nine years old.

Clifford's brother Heneage took charge of the body and his brother's funeral arrangements. In an effort to protect his brother's memo-

Author's collection
The grave of Clifford Griffin overlooks the town of Silver Plume.

ry from the curious public, Heneage used his friendship with local editors to keep the cause of death (suicide) out of the newspapers. Therein the seed of rumor and gossip began to grow.

The miners of Silver Plume buried Griffin on the mountaintop, and under Heneage's supervision, erected a large hand-quarried marker, made of Silver Plume granite. The marker, visible under close scrutiny, is on the north side of I-70. His monument reads:

Clifford Griffin
Son of Alfred Griffin ESQ. of
Brand Hall, Shropshire, England
Born July 2, 1847
Died June 19, 1887
And in Consideration of His Own Request
Buried Near This Spot

One can hike to the grave from the base of Brown Gulch. From the top of Silver Street, at Silver Plume, it is approximately 1.5 miles to the gravesite.

Denver Public Library
John Henry "Doc" Holliday
Dentist turned gunfighter.

GLENWOOD SPRINGS

LINWOOD CEMETERY

LINWOOD CEMETERY IS LOCATED AT THE TOP OF JASPER MOUNTAIN, JUST EAST OF TOWN. THE WINDING ROAD BEGINS ON BENNETT AVENUE, BETWEEN 11TH AND 13TH STREETS. THERE ARE GREEN TOUR SIGNS POSTED THROUGHOUT TOWN WHICH DIRECT YOU TO THE CEMETERY. THE CEMETERY IS ACCESSED BY HIKING THE WINDING ROAD. NO VEHICLES ARE ALLOWED.

Businessman J.C. Schwartz saw an opportunity with the young town when he leased his land on Jasper Mountain to become the city cemetery. Schwartz also ran the hearse service. The first burial occurred in 1887. The rugged terrain and high location was soon inadequate for the growing needs of the city. The new Rosebud Cemetery became the town burial plot at the turn of the century.

Holliday, John Henry "Doc" (1851 – 1887)

Noted gunman and educated dentist, Holliday came to Colorado after the famous gunfight at the OK Corral at Tombstone, Arizona, where he backed his friend, Wyatt Earp. Stricken with tuberculosis and an alcoholic, thirty-five-year-old Holliday settled in Glenwood Springs for the hot springs and a last ditch effort at a cure. His condition was too advanced. The deadly killer lived his last months mostly in seclusion, dying in bed. His last words, as he looked at his naked feet were: "This is funny." Holliday figured he would die with his boots on.

Holliday's tombstone is located roughly in the center of the cemetery, toward the north end. Cemetery records do not record the exact spot of Holliday's burial. A marker has been placed in the general area, with a granite tombstone inside the wrought iron fencing.

ROSEBUD CEMETERY

LOCATED WEST OF THE CITY, JUST NORTH OF INTERSTATE 70. IT IS VISIBLE FROM THE HIGHWAY.

The Rosebud Cemetery was organized in 1904, located just west of town. This soon became the burial ground of choice. It is beautifully landscaped and well shaded.

Author's collection
Doc Holliday's grave.

Logan, Harvey "Kid Curry" (1865 – 1904)

A member of Butch Cassidy's Wild Bunch, Logan and his gang of outlaws held up an afternoon train near Parachute, Colorado. Little money was taken. A posse cornered the gang in a canyon, where Logan was wounded. Logan shot himself in the head. His body was buried near Doc Holliday's grave in Linwood Cemetery. Pinkerton detectives wanted to confirm Logan's identity and had the body exhumed. Positively identified, his body was reburied in the new Rosebud Cemetery.

Logan is buried in the potter's field section, his grave is unmarked.

GRAND JUNCTION

THE PIONEER CEMETERIES OF GRAND JUNCTION INCLUDE THE MUNICIPAL, ST. ANTHONY'S, VETERAN'S, I.O.O.F., ORCHARD MESA, MASONIC, AND CALVARY CEMETERIES. ALL OF THESE CEMETERIES ARE LOCATED RELATIVELY CLOSE TOGETHER, IN GRAND JUNCTION. FROM INTERSTATE 70, TAKE THE BUSINESS LOOP INTO TOWN, TO HIGHWAY 50 (5TH STREET.) GOING SOUTH ON HIGHWAY 50, TAKE THE FIRST RIGHT AT THE SIGNAL, AFTER CROSSING THE COLORADO RIVER. THE MUNICIPAL CEMETERY IS ONE-QUARTER-MILE ON THE RIGHT. THE OTHER CEMETERIES ARE ONE-QUARTER-MILE FARTHER, ON 26 1/4 ROAD.

MUNICIPAL CEMETERY

The Palmer family originally donated the land to the city of Grand Junction for the purpose of a park, in 1911. It became designated as a cemetery in 1922. The large acreage is dotted with over 2,700 graves, and is still in use.

McClintock, Merle M. (1879 – 1942)

An Iowa native, Merle McClintock came to Grand Junction with her parents at age two, in 1881.[63] Personal friends with town promoter, George A. Crawford, the McClintock's settled here at Crawford's invitation.

Miss McClintock grew up in Grand Junction, graduating from the local school system and attended Colorado College at Colorado Springs. She returned to her hometown of Grand Junction, where she was hired as a reporter with the *Grand Junction Daily Sentinel*. She soon became a regular columnist for the paper, writing for twenty-five years. Focusing on the area's history, her writing is now prized by Mesa County historians.

She took an active interest in her town, being associated with the women's division of the Democratic Party. She was a lifelong member of the Baptist church, a regent in the local DAR organization, and a member of the National Press Women.

Miss McClintock fell ill in the summer of 1942. Seeking treatment at the Mayo clinic in Minnesota, she was diagnosed with incurable cancer. Her only wish was to return to her beloved Grand Junction. Merle McClintock died in August 1942, on a train, near Denver, on her way home.

She is buried in Block 6, Lot 47. There is a marker.

Spencer, John F. (1848 – 1938)

A native of Wisconsin, John Spencer was raised on the family farm. He learned first-hand of the virtues of farming and rarely attended school. He settled near Grand Junction in 1882, where he served two years as sheriff.

In 1884, he bought 160 acres of prime land in the Grand Valley. He planted fruit orchards and perfected the growing process for seedless apple. His pear and peach orchards yielded the largest crops in the county, and the quality was known statewide.

He is buried next to his wife Ida, in Lot 57, Block 7.

MASONIC CEMETERY

This fraternal organization established their cemetery in 1898. It was acquired by the city in 1966. The landscaping is ideal to the area, and complimentary to the cemetery grounds.

Bucklin, James W. (1856 – 1919)

Born in Illinois, the family lineage of James Bucklin includes soldiers of the American Revolutionary War. He spent his youth in Illinois, where he attended the Wheaton College. In 1875, he entered the State University of Michigan, graduating with a law degree in 1877.

Bucklin practiced law in Denver at age twenty-one. Three years later, he located in Mesa County. Bucklin, along with a party of men, including George C. Crawford, organized the town of Grand Junction in 1882. The land was once part of the Ute Reservation, recently removed to Utah.

In February 1882, he opened the first law office in Grand Junction. His first case before a circuit judge was defending an Indian accused of stealing a blanket. A leader of the community, he was elected in 1884 to the Legislature, serving Mesa, Gunnison, Montrose, Delta, and Pitkin counties. He became mayor of Grand Junction in 1886. He established a city code, a park system, and repealed the poll tax. In 1899, he authored the public utility law, spearheading the drive for municipal ownership of community water rights. Opposed by founding father George Crawford, community water ownership eventually became a reality, largely due to Bucklin, following a long and bitter feud.

Bucklin was mayor of Grand Junction for one term in 1886, and went on to serve as state senator in 1900. He later led the law firm of Bucklin, Stanley & Safley, the leading attorneys in Grand Junction.

Married in 1884 to Margie Champion, she died in childbirth in 1895. The twin sons died a few weeks later. He later married Mary Lapham, with whom he had two children. He and Mary were instrumental in the building of the Church of Grand Junction, serving at Sunday School services and funeral services.

They are buried together in Lot 25, Gravesite C.

Moyer, William J. (1859 – 1943)

Born in Reading, Pennsylvania, Moyer received a limited education before going to work in a country store at age ten. He worked his way through Indiana, Minnesota, and Kansas, before arriving in Colorado in 1888.

He settled in Grand Junction in 1890, where he started the Fair Store, a mercantile that became very successful.

Active in Grand Junction business affairs, he was an organizer of the Grand Valley National Bank, becoming vice president. He and his wife, Ida, were involved in Grand Junction business and society.

Mr. Moyer died in 1943, his ashes were buried beside his wife, Ida, in Lot 147, Gravesite B. There is a marker.

Rice, William A. (1846 – 1901)

A native of Dade County, Missouri, William Rice received his basic education and taught school for three years. He married Mary Elizabeth Gover of Kentucky, in 1871. The young couple first settled in Canon City, Colorado, in 1881. Rice operated a lumberyard and became quite successful.

In 1883, he and his brother, P.A. Rice, started a lumberyard in Grand Junction. While running the business, William expanded his horizons to include farming and livestock.

Rice served on various community projects, and had many social obligations. He was a member of the Cumberland Presbyterian Church, serving as an officer for many years.

He is buried in Lot 27, Gravesite C. There is a marker.

ORCHARD MESA CEMETERY

Established in 1887, and owned by a private mortuary, it is presently owned by the city of Grand Junction. There are over 7,000 burials in this beautifully landscaped resting spot.

Armstrong, William J. (1855 – 1905)

A native of Ontario, Canada, William Armstrong arrived in Colorado in 1880. By 1901, he had settled in Mesa County. A foreman on the Wellington Ranch, in 1902 he married the widow of John A. Wellington. Armstrong ran the Wellington Ranch, improving the livestock and the land. Pioneers of the Mesa area, they were instrumental in the founding of the community and active in many of the church and social functions.

He is buried in Block A, Row 7B, Lot 15B. There is a marker.

Carnahan, James S. (1859 – 1910)

Born and raised in Pennsylvania, James Carnahan headed for adventure in the West at the age of twenty. He located in Georgetown, where he mined until 1884. He earned his law degree in York, Nebraska, where his brother was a successful attorney. Returning to Colorado 1889, he first practiced law in Julesburg, where he became a county judge. In 1892, he was elected to the Colorado state Legislature, serving two terms as the Republican representative for Sedgwick, Logan, and Phillips counties.

Following his term in the Legislature, he moved to Grand Junction, where he renewed his law practice, serving as city attorney for several years. He later formed the law partnership of Carnahan & Van Hoerebeke, a leading law firm in Mesa county.

He is buried in Block A, Row 38, Lot 8. There is a marker.

Sweney, Joseph P. (1846 – 1914)

A native of Pennsylvania, where he spent his youth, Joseph Sweney followed his education with employment in the Pennsylvania coal mines, working as a bookkeeper and paymaster. He arrived in

Grand Junction in 1886, where he opened a hardware store. Within a year, he was elected mayor. In 1893, he became justice of the peace, a position he held until his death. He also served as police magistrate in his later years.

He is buried in Block A, Row 40, Lot 17. There is a marker.

Crawford, George Addison (1827 – 1891)

The grave of George A. Crawford is located on the hill overlooking the cemeteries. Follow 26 1/4 Road south around the bend, to the hill on your left.

Crawford is known as the "Father of Grand Junction," a town builder and president of the Grand Junction Town Company.

Born and raised in Pennsylvania, he completed his education at Jefferson College. He taught school in Salem, Kentucky. In 1850, he returned to Pennsylvania and began the study of law. He became the editor of the *Clinton Democrat*, and soon entered politics.

He later drifted toward Fort Scott, Kansas, where he and a group of men established the township of Lawrence, in 1857. He served as president of the town company for twenty years. He was appointed to the Centennial Exposition in 1871, by President Grant.

Crawford arrived in Colorado in 1871, staying for awhile in Gunnison. Surveying the land of the Western Slope, he saw promise at the junction of the Gunnison and Grand rivers, on the Ute Reservation. When the Utes were moved from the land in 1881, Crawford rushed to stake a land claim. Within a month, he plotted the townsite of future Grand Junction and applied for incorporation. He founded the Grand Junction Town Company, with a group that included fellow pioneer James Bucklin. Crawford promoted town growth and was a major factor in the Denver & Rio Grande Railroad decision to build a line through Grand Junction. Because of Crawford's efforts, by 1882, one year after the town was founded, Grand Junction became the principal rail center between Pueblo and Salt Lake City.

Crawford built the first hotel, promoted ecology by planting trees on the main streets and organized a brick company. He helped to build the first school, the first church, and was instrumental in bringing the first newspaper to Grand Junction.

A grand pioneer and father of Grand Junction, George A. Crawford is buried in an elaborate sandstone mausoleum, high above the city he created.

— — —

North/South Highways
Interstate Highway I-25 South

FORT COLLINS
GRANDVIEW CEMETERY
1900 WEST MOUNTAINVIEW AVENUE.

The military post of Fort Collins, established in 1864, provided protection for the travelers along the Overland Trail. Although the post served for a short three years, the military cemetery became a necessity. The burial ground was located on high ground just southwest of the fort.[64] Approximately twelve soldiers were buried in the cemetery.

In 1873, a new cemetery was established at Fort Collins, following the demise of the old fort. Mountain Home Cemetery was located at the present site of Eastdale Drive, southeast of town. Six of the graves from the post cemetery were found and reburied at the new cemetery.

One of the caskets contained a small bottle with a note identifying the remains and cause of death–W.W. Westfall of Company J, 13th Missouri Volunteers. He died in November 1865. According to the note, cause of death was "typhogastro-interic disease." He is buried south of the Soldier's Monument, in Section S of the Grandview Cemetery. There is a small memorial marker.

As the new cemetery grew, burials from rural sites were also moved to this location. Unprecedented in Colorado history, the cemetery was moved in its entirety to a third and final location. Land was acquired a mile and a half west of the city for a new community cemetery in 1887.

The Grandview Cemetery is laid out and landscaped in a forty-acre tract. The formation is a circular landscape, with newer sections surrounding the original tract. Section S contains the reinterred burials of the post cemetery, and is dedicated to the early military burials. Dominating this section is a life-size statue of a Civil War soldier, erected in 1905.

The first official burial was three-month-old Felix Scoville. Buried in 1877, the tiny infant lies in an unmarked grave, located in Section K. The state wide flu epidemic of 1918 reduced the available space at the cemetery. An additional ten acres were needed and eventually acquired.

One of the most beautiful cemeteries in Northern Colorado, Grandview Cemetery is rich in pioneer heritage.

Anderson, Peter (1845 – 1927)

A native of Norway, Peter Anderson arrived in America at age five, with his widowed mother and four siblings. The family settled in Wisconsin, where Peter was forced to hire out for work at age nine. In 1864, he ventured west, where he worked in the saddler's trade in Denver. During the gold rush of 1859, he freighted for the travelers between Denver and Missouri.

In 1865, he bought a homestead near Fort Collins, and started his own a cattle ranch. By 1887, his ranch was one of the largest in the county, despite a loss of 3,000 head of cattle in the winter of 1887 – 1888. The following year, he broadened his empire by opening a mercantile store in town. He served as the county alderman, as well as three terms on the board of education, and vice president of the First National Bank.

He is buried in Section E, Lot 9. There is a marker.

Avery, Franklin C. (1849 – 1923)

One of the founding fathers of the town of Fort Collins, no one did more for the promotion and leadership than Franklin Avery.

Born in New York, Avery earned a degree in civil engineering. He came to the Colorado Territory in 1870, where he surveyed and platted the town of Greeley. In 1871, he located near Laporte in Larimer County, where he operated a cattle ranch. The following year he was appointed as engineer to plat the town of Fort Collins. Later elected county commissioner, he served two terms. He organized the Larimer County Ditch Company, and engineered the water project that brings water from the Larimer River across the mountains to the Poudre Valley.

In 1880, he founded the Larimer County Bank, which became the First National Bank in 1882. The bank, located in the Avery business block, also included a real estate office, founded by Avery, still operating today. A wealthy landowner, his property covered a large portion of both Larimer and Weld counties. His Fort Collins home stands today.

He is buried in Section E, Lot 13, next to his wife, Sarah, who died in 1884, and their two infant children. Sarah's parents are also buried in the Avery family plot.

Franklin's brother, William H., is buried in Section C, Lot 5. William was murdered in 1890. His widow and her subsequent new husband were tried for the murder, but were acquitted. Franklin never agreed with the verdict.[65]

Howe, James Henry (1849 – 1888)

It is believed James H. Howe arrived in the community in 1880, where he found employment at Hottel's mill. Also known as a fine mechanic, James, and his wife, Eva, were highly regarded throughout the community. In 1888, the couple and their five-year-old daughter were living in a small frame house on Walnut Street.

In the early afternoon of April 4, 1888, James Howe brutally stabbed his wife to death with his pocket knife. Neighbors saw Mrs. Howe struggle to the front gate of the yard, where she fell into the ravine and died. Several men gathered at the Howe home, arrested a drunken James Howe and escorted him to the jail. Howe had berated his wife on several occasions and often stayed at the saloon well into the morning hours.

News of such a brutal murder spread through the town quickly. People gathered together as events of the tragedy unfolded by word of mouth. By early evening, the group had turned into an angry mob.

Shortly after dark, the electricity was mysteriously shut off to the entire town. A group of masked men stormed the jail, overpowered the sheriff, and dragged Howe from his cell. Howe was hanged from a rope tied to a construction beam near the new courthouse. Immediately following the hanging, the lights were suddenly restored.

The Howe's daughter was sent east, where she was raised by Eva's parents. Eva's obituary states her body was sent east as well, however, cemetery records list her as buried in Section K, Lot 93, along with James Howe.

There is no marker to either of the Howes.

Lory, Dr. Charles A. (1872 – 1970)

Born in Sardi, Ohio, Lory went to work in a sawmill at age nine. He came to Colorado with his parents in 1888, where he worked as a ditch digger in Weld County. He worked his way through college, graduating in 1898, and received his masters degree from the University of Colorado in 1902.

Following his education, he worked as an assistant in the physics department at the University of Colorado for one year. He was principal of Cripple Creek High School for two years, and professor of physics at the Colorado Agricultural College at Fort Collins, in 1907.[66] He became president of the college in 1909, a position he held for thirty-one years. He was known as a fair and just educator, and directed the college to today's university status.

He is buried in Section G, Lot 116, next to his wife Carrie, who proceeded him in death in 1948. There is a marker.

Mason, Joseph (1840 – 1881)

A French Canadian by the name of Messieve, he changed his name to Mason. He is the first recorded settler in the area, arriving in 1862. An opportunist, he raised cattle and horses, which he sold to the military at Ft. Collins. When the original camp was flooded, he found higher ground, offering drainage, and good visibility, not to mention the close proximately to his own ranch.[67] He became the sutler of Fort Collins, where he gained a monopoly in merchandising, profiting quite handsomely.

When the fort closed in 1866, Mason stood to lose his entire enterprise. To protect his interests, he persuaded the Territorial Legislature to move the Larimer county seat from Laporte to Fort Collins. By 1868, the transaction was complete. All county business was conducted in Mason's store.

In 1873, he purchased the grain mill built by Auntie Stone. With his improvements, the mill became the largest in the county. In 1879, he donated land for the agriculture college, and was one of the promoters of what would become Colorado State University.

The founder of Fort Collins, he died in an accident in 1881. He is buried in the north end of Section E, Lot 37. There is a marker.

Nugent, James (? – 1874)

Known in Colorado legend as "Mountain Jim," James Nugent was the scout and guide for Isabella Bird on her famous climb to the summit of Long's Peak. The group of four climbers ascended the mountain in September 1873.

Mountain Jim was a strange figure to the refined Englishwoman. A hunter, a trapper, and a mountain man, Jim dressed in custom leather and buckskin clothing. He wore his hair long, capped by a beaver skin hat. He had only one eye, a result of an old injury. His prized Arabian mare carried a saddle covered in beaver skin, complete with claws. His loyal dog, Ring, watched and followed his every move.

According to Isabella's account, Jim was strong willed, harsh and keenly aware of his surroundings, yet a perfect gentleman toward Ms. Bird, the first woman to ascend the mountain. During the journey to the top of Long's Peak, the weather turned bad. It was Jim who assured Miss Bird she would reach the top, even if he had to carry her. Cold and near frostbite, she did indeed reach the top of the mountain, with his help.

During the decent, Miss Bird slipped on the rocks twice. Jim saved her life on both accounts and saw the party safely down the mountain.

On June 19, 1874, Jim was shot in the head at his cabin near Estes Park. He lingered for several months before his death in September

1874. The shooting was result of a dispute with a neighbor named Griffith J. Evans.

"Mountain Jim" Nugent was buried in the Mountain Home Cemetery. His remains were later moved to the undeveloped north end of the new Grandview Cemetery.

He is buried in an unmarked grave.

Sherwood, Frederick W. (1831 – 1906)

Frederick Sherwood migrated west from his native home of New York in 1858. In Wisconsin, he worked in the lumber business with his brother, Jesse. In 1860, he and his brother left for Colorado Territory by covered wagon.

Mining for a time at Russell Gulch, the brothers eventually settled on the river bottom of the Cache' la Poudre River, about four and one-half miles south of the Fort Collins military camp. There, they raised horses and cattle and became very successful. In 1864, Sherwood Ranch was an Overland Trail stage stop and was known across the country. Chief Friday and his band of Arapaho Indians camped at the ranch during the winter of 1865. Sherwood was commissioned in 1865 by President Lincoln as Indian agent to the Arapaho in Colorado Territory.

One of the earliest pioneers of Fort Collins, he served as a county commissioner for three terms. A community leader, he was on several town boards and was an active member of the school board.

Frederick Sherwood is buried in the center of Section E. There is a marker.

Stone, Elizabeth Hickock (1801 – 1895)

Known as the first woman settler in camp Fort Collins, Elizabeth Stone arrived with her husband in 1864. Staying at the fort, she influenced the soldiers, creating a sense of community and caring which carried over to the founding of the town. It was during those years that she became known as "Auntie Stone."

Born in Connecticut, she was raised in New York, where she received her education and married Ezekiel W. Robbins in 1824. This union produced eight children. The family lived in Missouri and Illinois, where Mr. Robbins died unexpectedly in 1852. Elizabeth, forced to make her way alone with the children, went to Minnesota, where she married Lewis Stone in 1857.

In 1862, the Stone family crossed the Plains by covered wagon, arriving in Denver. They purchased land where Union Station now stands. Leaving the property in the care of Mr. Stone's son, the family went on to the camp of Fort Collins. In 1864, the Stones built the first house at the camp. Mrs. Stone ran a mess hall for the soldiers and travelers from this log home.[68] Mr. Stone died in 1866 and was buried in the Post Cemetery.

Shortly after the death of her husband, Auntie Elizabeth Stone entered into business with H.C. Peterson. They built the first flour mill in Larimer County, the second in the state, completed in 1868. The operation was very successful despite two fires. In 1871, Auntie Stone founded the first brick kiln in northern Colorado. The first firing provided enough bricks for the first two brick homes in Fort Collins, one of which was her own.

Because of her strong business acumen, she was the only woman included in the founding of Fort Collins. Her ideas were unique, a quality inherited in the town today.

Ever mindful of the community, she contributed to all church causes, regardless of denomination. She was a leader in the Woman's Christian Temperance Union.

When she died in 1895, her funeral was conducted by the ministers of the Presbyterian, Methodist, Christian, Episcopalian, and Baptist churches. Bells tolled throughout the city in solemn remembrance, with business suspended for the day.

"Auntie" Elizabeth Stone is buried in the south end of Section E, Lot 22. There is a granite marker.

Stover, William C. (1841 – 1907)

A native of Bottletourt County, Virginia, William Stover came west with a wagon train in 1860. He hired on at a hay farm near Fort Collins and spent some time in Wyoming. By 1862, he had his own ranch in the Big Thompson Valley.

In 1870, he opened a grocery and supply store in the town of Fort Collins, in the old Grout building.[69] In 1878, Stover and partner Charles H. Sheldon, established the Poudre Valley National Bank, where Stover served as president until 1893.

He was elected to the Territorial Council in 1873 and represented Larimer County at the Constitutional Convention in 1875. He was responsible for a clause in the state constitution designating Fort Collins as the location for the state agricultural college.

Following Colorado statehood in 1876, Stover held several public offices and was once nominated to the Senate, being narrowly defeated in 1876.

He is buried in the north end of Section E, in Lot 2, next to his wife Sarah.

Whedbee, Benjamin T. (1812 – 1910)

Born in Orange County, North Carolina, Benjamin Whedbee first settled in Missouri in 1832. He was a carpenter and owned a mercantile establishment for a time. He came to Colorado Territory in 1863, where he established a farm in the area of Pleasant Valley, a name he gave to the luscious green meadow.

In the spring of 1871, he moved to Fort Collins, where he opened the first drug store. Later, he owned a successful mercantile operation at the corner of Mountain and College Avenues. He erected the first jail in the community.

With the organization of Larimer County as one of the original counties of the Colorado Territory, Whedbee was appointed county treasurer in 1864. Because there was no post office, Mr. Whedbee conducted his governmental duties on the street. The county tax records and money were carried in his pocket, collecting the taxes due when he met people. He paid county warrants in the same fashion. He later became the first mayor of Fort Collins.

He was buried in the Grandview Cemetery in October 1910 with full Masonic honors. Buried beside his wife, Susan, his grave is located in the southeast quarter of Section L, Lot 43.

OFF THE BEATEN PATH:

BINGHAM HILL CEMETERY

LOCATED SOUTHWEST OF LA PORTE, JUST OFF HIGHWAY 287. FOLLOW THE OVERLAND TRAIL ROAD SOUTH ONE-HALF-MILE. AT THE FORK, GO WEST (LEFT) ONE-QUARTER-MILE TO THE CEMETERY.

One of the oldest cemeteries in Larimer County, Bingham Hill Cemetery sits just off the historic Overland Trail. Also known as the La Porte Cemetery, it is a very small, rural graveyard. The oldest marker is dated 1862. It was abandoned in the 1940s, with many burials removed to the Grandview Cemetery at Fort Collins.

Among those buried in this small pioneer cemetery is Alphonse Larocque, one of the earliest pioneers of Larimer County. A farmer in the Pleasant Valley area, he died in 1877. There is a marker.

Barbara Bingham, a member of the family for whom the cemetery is named, died in 1876, at the age of nineteen, just days before her wedding to George Sterling.

LOVELAND

LAKESIDE CEMETERY

LOCATED A ONE-HALF-MILE NORTH OF LOVELAND. FROM INTERSTATE 25, TAKE THE LOVELAND EXIT TO THE INTERSECTION OF HIGHWAY 34 AND

LINCOLN AVE. (US 287). THE CEMETERY IS ON THE EAST SIDE OF LINCOLN AVENUE.

The Lakeside Cemetery was incorporated in 1880. The first recorded burial is that of Mrs. Matthew Burnett, in February 1880. Cemetery records reveal previous burials, all unmarked. The name of Mrs. Moses (Emily) Markley is listed as the first white woman to die in Larimer County. Her death occurred sometime around 1860. H.L.W. Peterson and Mexican Joe were later interred from the Namaqua Trail area. Approximately fifty bodies were moved here in 1884 from the Old Saint Louis Cemetery, which was located at the corner of St. Louis Avenue and 1st Street in Loveland.

Duffield, Anna V. (1865 – 1947)

From her native state of Ohio, Anna came west with her parents, J.W. and Avis Vinacke, in the late 1890s. The family settled in Loveland where Mr. Vinacke opened a hardware store.

Anna married Charles William Duffield in Loveland. Four sons were born to this union. The marriage was short, ending with the death of Charles in 1899. Tragedy struck again when two of Anna's sons died from typhoid and diphtheria in 1901.

It was about this time that Anna started a small community library with a few books available from the parlour of her home. Through her efforts, a $10,000 grant from the Andrew Carnegie Foundation, led to the establishment of the Loveland Library. She served two terms as president of the Colorado Library Association. A memorial stands in her honor.

Anna Duffield is buried in Block G, Lot 7.

Milner-Smith, Sarah (1844 – 1939)

The Milner family traveled to America from Canada, first settling in the Chicago area. Young Sarah attended school and gained her first teaching position some years later.

The family left Chicago in 1864, during the height of the Colorado gold rush. They lived in several mining camps before finally settling in Old Burlington.[70] Sarah came to the Big Thompson Valley in 1866. She was hired to teach at the first public school at Old St. Louis, southeast of Loveland. She taught for four years, graduating the first high school students in the county. In her memoirs, she writes: "I wasted one year by a spell of brain fever, which came near ending my life, and began teaching the Big Thompson School in September 1866 in a log house with homemade furniture. I spent here the happiest years of my life."

In 1870, she married Edward Smith and moved to the Arkansas Valley. Financial hardships brought them back to the Big Thompson Valley in 1878, settling in the young town of Loveland. Here, Sarah ran a boardinghouse for a time. She was asked to teach again at Loveland's new brick schoolhouse, the old Washington school. She taught for several years, before spending her final years at her ranch.

She is buried in Block C, Lot 19.

Osborn, William B. (1824 – 1916)

A native of New York, William Osborn left for Ohio at age twenty-one. He taught school for three years and spent his free time studying medicine until he met and married Margaret C. Castetter.

In 1860, after contracting tuberculosis, he and his wife joined one of the many wagon trains headed west. He prospected in the hills near Central City, during the gold rush days. He served as judge of the miner's court in Gilpin County's boom years.

At the suggestion of a friend, he bought land in the rich Big Thompson Valley. He paid for the 160 acres with gold. He built a log home for his family, the first in Larimer County with a wooden floor and shingle roof. He grew hay and raised cattle, while his wife raised the finest vegetable garden around.

This pioneer of Larimer County had many firsts associated with his name. He was the first judge and performed the first marriage in the county. He also performed the first funeral, (Mrs. Markley). Church meetings were held in the Osborn home, the beginnings of the First Methodist Church later formed in the community.

Family values and tradition taught in the Osborn home stand today. The Osborn farm is the oldest farm in the state of Colorado to remain in the same family.

Mr. and Mrs. William Osborn are buried in the family plot in Block C, Lot 30.

Sprague, Abner E. (1850 – 1943)

A native of Dundee, Illinois, Abner Sprague came to the Big Thompson Valley in 1864. He was a student in the first school in Loveland, taught by Sarah Smith. He became a surveyor in the Estes Park area, and worked in that capacity for the Missouri Pacific Railroad. He served as Larimer County surveyor for three terms.

In 1875, he started the Sprague Resort Ranch near Estes Park. He married Alberta Morrison in 1888. The couple had no children.

Abner and Alberta moved to the suites of the Brown Palace Hotel in Denver, in 1943. In December of that year, Abner died of heart failure.

Services were held at the Olinger Funeral Home in Denver. His ashes were interred in the Loveland Cemetery.

FORT NAMAQUA PARK
LOCATED AT COUNTY ROAD 19E AND THE BIG THOMPSON RIVER, JUST WEST OF LOVELAND.

This area was the site of a stage station operated by Mariana Modena, who came to the area in 1858. It is one of the earliest and most historic sites in Colorado.

Born in Taos, New Mexico in 1812, Modena joined a group of beaver trappers as a teenager. His adventures took him north into Colorado, where he struck out on his own. He was a valued scout, a government guide, an Indian fighter, and finally a rancher. Known as one of the most notable frontiersmen, he kept company with Jim Bridger, Mountain Jim, and Jim Baker.

He and his Indian wife took a claim near the St. Vrain River in 1858, where they built a large building, fortified with stone. More buildings followed when Modena opened a trading post. His stone building offered refuge during the Indian scares.

Beginning with the gold rush of 1859, and through the westward migration, the area was known as Modena's Crossing, or Namaqua Station. It was the crossing of several trails. The Texas and Overland Trails crossed here, as well as the Denver/Laramie Trail. Offshoots of the Platte River Trail and the Oregon Trail also passed through Modena's land.

Mariana Modena died in 1878. He was buried in the small family cemetery on his farm.

In 1960, the farm became a victim of progress, and the five graves were moved to the Fort Namaqua Park. An impressive stone marker with a plaque was erected at the approximate site of the historic stage station.

* **Of Note**

The town of Estes Park does not have a cemetery. Early pioneers are scattered among many cemeteries and ranches in the area. Early planners of Estes Park "did not wish to bring even a shadow of sorrow or grief into their beautiful park so a cemetery was never planned."[71] Several residents of Estes Park are buried in the Loveland Burial Park. Established in 1912, the cemetery is across the road from the Lakeside Cemetery and contains a separate section for Estes Park residents.

LONGMONT

BURLINGTON CEMETERY

FROM INTERSTATE 25, TAKE THE LONGMONT EXIT WEST. LOCATED TWO AND ONE-HALF MILES SOUTHWEST OF LONGMONT, AT 1400 S. SUNSET STREET, NEAR THE JUNIOR HIGH SCHOOL.

Burlington Cemetery is on a hill overlooking the town of Longmont to the north, and the Rocky Mountains to the west. The oldest cemetery in the area, the pioneers of the St. Vrain Valley rest here, in a community called Old Burlington. The oldest graves date to 1864, those of five-year-old Sarah Greenly and her two-year-old brother, Elmer. Records reveal they died of an unknown ailment. The records of the cemetery are incomplete and block and plots are inconsistent. Nevertheless, the old historic cemetery has a majestical presence in our pioneer heritage.

Allen, Alonzo N. (1820 – 1894)

Traveling west from St. Joseph, Missouri, Alonzo Allen mined in the Boulder Canyon area. His cabin is known as the first built in the Longmont area. Allenspark was named for him.

By 1863, he built a stopover stage house, known as Allen House. Stages, freight wagons, mule trains and soldiers traveled to the Allen House. In 1871, he moved his hotel to the new Chicago-Colorado colony, later known as Longmont. While he continued his prospecting, the duties of running the hotel fell to his wife, the former Mary Ann Dickens, of Wisconsin. She served meals twice a day to as many as twenty-five people per sitting. Her most famous meal was served to Colonel Chivington and his men on January 2, 1865. The occasion was the celebration of the 100-Day Volunteers, following the Sand Creek Massacre.

One of the earliest pioneer families involved in the prosperity of the St. Vrain Valley, Alonzo is buried in the older section of the cemetery, with a marker.

Beasley Family Plot
Beasley, James Jackson (1831 – 1907)

Raised in Schuler County, Maryland, where he was educated, James Beasley married Eliza Jones at age twenty-one. Because of the Pike's Peak gold rush, or to escape the threat of war in the East, Beasley brought his wife and family to Colorado in 1860. For the next six years, he sold livestock and moved from Missouri to Colorado.

In 1871, he bought 240 acres on Boulder Creek, where he started his farm and ranch. He led the movement for irrigation projects along

Left Hand and Boulder Creeks. He was instrumental in a number of community projects, including the school system and the Burlington Cemetery Association. Beasley School District Number 42 is named for him, as well as the Beasley Ditch Company.

His is buried in the family plot, in Block 6, Lot 3.

Beasley, Thomas Newman Jones (1870 – 1960)

The son of James J. Beasley, Thomas was born in Jefferson County, Colorado in 1870. He graduated from the Longmont High School his father helped to build. In 1894, he married Grace Reliance Miller. He built a farmhouse for his wife in 1907, complete with a commemorate brick cornerstone containing the history of his family back to 1779. Mrs. Beasley died in 1909 and Thomas raised the three children.

He served as the director of the White Rock Ditch Company for many years, the director of the Burlington Cemetery Association, and became involved in the Farmer's Mill and Elevator for a number of years. He collected fine artifacts of geology, Indian and pioneer memorabilia, later donated to the museums of Boulder and Longmont.

He is buried in the Beasley family plot, in Block 6, Lot 3.

Franklin, R. I. (? – ?)

Mr. and Mrs. Franklin arrived in the St. Vrain Valley in 1865. The pioneers homesteaded east of Burlington. In 1867, Franklin bought the Red Barn Livery from the Allen brothers. The Franklins were the center of the early community, in both social and business development. Among their achievements was the establishment of the Burlington school.

The Franklins are buried in the family plot. The tall obelisk marks the gravesite of R.I. Franklin, although weathered, and hard to read. The granite markers in the plot are those of W.J. and Emma Franklin, Emma J, and Lela J.

Zweck, George (1829 – 1902)
Zweck, Mary Louise (1848 – 1934)

Born in Rhine Province, Prussia, George Zweck came to America as a teenager, working as a farmhand in Iowa and later, in Omaha, Nebraska. He arrived in Colorado Territory with the gold rush of 1859. A wandering gypsy told Zweck his wealth would come from the ground. (Not so amazing, given the frantic gold fever atmosphere of 1859.) In any case, Zweck headed for Colorado, staking such claims as the Gray Eagle, Elkhorn, and Greeley mines. By 1879, Zweck, along with partners, had developed the Prussian Mine on Left Hand Creek. The yield per month was $4,000.

Suddenly a wealthy man, Zweck bought land and established a farm three miles west of Longmont, on the St. Vrain River. He planted crops and raised Hereford cattle , including a prize bull bought in Chicago. Running his ranch and raising a family, he managed time to prospect for gold in the summer.

The mines poured more wealth into the Zweck accounts. He invested in Longmont real estate, including the Groom Hotel, later called the Zweck Hotel. Built in 1881, it was lavishly furnished with European furniture, glass, mirrors, carpet and floors.

Before the winter of 1881 ended, Zweck was broke. Several of his mines played out, the hotel failed, and a northern blizzard killed his cattle. The farm and real estate were taken by creditors.

Mrs. Zweck rebounded by selling produce, dairy, and feed supplies, she managed to save a piece of the land, where her eight children were born.

George and Mary Zweck are buried in Block 7, Lot 4. There is a marker.

MOUNTAIN VIEW CEMETERY
LOCATED ON MAIN STREET, BETWEEN 11TH AVENUE AND MOUNTAIN VIEW AVENUE, IN LONGMONT.

The cemetery was formed shortly after the founding of the Chicago Colony (later to become Longmont). Among the original organizers was J. J. Beasley, who had previously formed the Old Burlington Cemetery. The southwest corner is the original land laid out for the cemetery in 1876. The first known grave is that of John Owen, born in 1822 and died in 1876. His sons dug the post holes for the fence surrounding his gravesite.

During the late nineteenth century, many fund raisers were held to aid the cemetery and improve the grounds. One event pitted the Main Street merchants against each other in a baseball game. Because of such events, the cemetery is well maintained.

Boynton, Charles W. (1853 – 1926)
Born in Buffalo, New York, in his youth Charles Boynton spent three years in the shipping industry on the Erie Canal. He moved west in 1877, eventually locating in the Longmont area. He operated a farm east of town for three years.

Boynton, along with a few local men, established the Ledger Publishing Company, where he became editor in 1897. He held the position until his death in 1926. In community affairs, he was instrumental in securing the Carnegie Library for Longmont. He was elected twice to the city council. He was a member of the local fire department, and helped secure the electric light plant.

A passionate photographer, many of his photos rivaled those of Jackson, the noted photographer of the area. Boynton's glass slides are part of the local museum exhibit.

His tombstone is in the older section of the cemetery.

Coffin, George W. (1838 – 1905)

A native of Roxbury, New York, George Coffin settled in Colorado Territory in 1860. He homesteaded land some six miles east of Longmont where he farmed and had a ranching partnership with his brother. He was a member of the initial drive for statehood in 1864, the State Constitution Convention, formed to lobby Washington D.C. for Colorado statehood. He later served as Weld County treasurer, Longmont city councilman and mayor.

On January 20, 1905, Coffin was fatally injured. His assailant and the question of why, remain a mystery today. He was found in his farm house lying on his bed in a pool of blood. His jaw was dislocated and his skull crushed. He was taken by an ambulance to Longmont, where he died five days later. He regained consciousness long enough to tell his brother the assailant went through the fence and down the road.

Because Coffin's family was out of town, they were eliminated as suspects. Further investigation revealed blood on the door handle to the farmhouse. It was surmised that Coffin was accosted in the field and somehow made his way to the house.

He is buried in Block 11, Lot 8. There is a marker.

Dickens, William H. (1843 – 1915)

Dickens was born aboard a ship sailing from England to North America. His parents settled in Canada, later moving to Wisconsin, where his father and two of his sisters died. In 1848, his mother Mary married Alonzo N. Allen. In 1859, following years of crop failures, Alonzo joined the great gold rush of Colorado. Seventeen-year-old William Dickens joined his stepfather the following spring.

Dickens filed on a quarter section of land next to Allen's land, built the first log cabin in the valley, and helped establish the Allen Stage House, operated by his mother. He served with the Third Colorado Cavalry in 1861.

Following the war, he farmed his land, adding 400 acres over the years. A portion of the land is now the site of the Longmont Community Hospital.

Dickens became marshal of the young community of Burlington. In this capacity, he was responsible for the arrest of the murderer,

William Dubois.[72] In 1881, he built the Dickens Opera House. The first floor contained the Farmers National Bank, which he founded. He organized the Farmers Mill and Elevator Company, one of the largest in the state.

He was fatally shot at his home on November 30, 1915. His murderer was never identified.

He is buried in Block 31, Lot 23.

Goodwin, Harrison (1827 – 1885)

A graduate of Rush Medical College in Chicago, Harrison Goodwin migrated west during the great gold rush of 1859. With his wife and young son, he walked with his oxen and covered wagon to Fort Leavenworth, Kansas. Following the Smoky Hill Trail, he arrived in Colorado Territory, and eventually the early tent city of Denver.

In June 1859, the Goodwin family settled at the booming gold camp of Central City. Mrs. Goodwin was said to be the first white woman in the mining camp. Unsuccessful at mining, Goodwin brought his family to the St. Vrain Valley where he filed a land claim two miles west of Burlington.

Being the first educated doctor in the area, he traveled between Central City, Burlington and Denver, serving patients for two years. By 1863, he was raising crops, and buying livestock. He continued seeing patients in the Longmont and Estes Park area on a limited basis, for some twenty years. The doctor, who weighed more than 200 pounds, would travel the countryside by horseback with a special saddle to carry his weight.

As the first member of the local Masonic Lodge, he was given an honorable Masonic funeral with burial rites performed at the Mountainview Cemetery.

He is buried in Block 1, Lot 26. There is a marker.

Johnson, Charles A. (1869 – 1955)
Miller, Charles A. (1870 – 1955)

Known throughout the area as the "Two Charleys," they were partners in business until their deaths. Both were from the same area of Smaland, Sweden, yet did not know each other in those days. Both crossed the Atlantic Ocean for new beginnings in America. The two eventually settled in the Longmont area, where they met.

In 1892, the two formed a partnership, and did custom threshing and general farm work. Later, they purchased the Hills Land and Cattle Company, forming the Golden West Milling Company and several other interests.

Miller married Johnson's cousin, Anna Nelson in 1899 and began a family. Johnson married Amanda Johnson in 1906 and started his own family. The two families lived on the farm near Rinn, and later moved to Bowen Street, a few houses apart from one another.

Miller and Johnson's lives were intertwined. Their children were raised together, and their wives used the same bank account.

Charles Miller died in the early hours of April 14, 1955. At two o'clock the same day, his friend, Charles Johnson also died.

The joint funeral service was held at the First Lutheran Church. The life-long friends were buried in adjoining plots in Block 44, Lots 56 and 57. There are markers to their memory.

McKeirnan, Jennie (1851 – 1928)

Jennie and her husband, John, left their home in Summerside, Prince Edward Island, in November 1877. Due to John's poor health, the couple traveled to the arid climate of the western United States. By 1878, they had settled in Longmont, where they opened a grocery store on the corner of Fourth and Main streets. Jennie helped in the store, while raising her three children. When John died in 1885, Jennie took oover the family business. She became the first female merchant in Longmont.

For the next twenty years, Jennie made a success of the store, and became well respected in the community. She sold the business in 1905, and spent the rest of her days serving the local church board and various clubs, as well as the Longmont Welfare Board.

She is buried in Block 2, Lot 5.

Nethaway, Bessie (1871 – 1955)

Bessie Nethaway came to Colorado with her parents, James and Permelia Weese, from Missouri, in 1876. The family homesteaded between present day Lyons and Hygiene, where Bessie was married to William H. Nethaway in 1891. Their first son died at birth in 1893. A second son, David Harvey, was born in 1894.

Shortly after the birth of David, Bessie began her long nursing career by assisting Doctor C.F. Andrews in births across the county. During a typhoid epidemic, she left her family for nearly a month, while nursing the sick. By the turn of the century, she founded Longmont's first hospital above Gunning's drug store at Fourth and Main. In 1908, she began taking patients into her home at 410 Baker Street. For the next fifty years, Bessie kept the door to her home open twenty-four hours a day, to nurse the sick.

A true pioneer, both to her time and her gender, she was buried in her nurse uniform, at her request. She is buried in Block 1, Lot 12. There is a marker.

Sullivan, Neil C. Sr. (1848 – 1931)

A native of Iowa, Neil Sullivan came to Colorado in 1891, settling in Longmont with his wife Annie and their three children. He bought into George Dell's hardware store, later named Sullivan and Rowen Mercantile. He became city treasurer in 1899 and was elected to the city council in 1903.

Sullivan did more than any other man in lobbying for and securing the Longmont sugar beet factory. Knowing the economic growth that the factory would bring to the community, he drove his horse and buggy to every farm in the area, a one-man crusade to convince the farmers to back his cause.

Once the sugar beet factory became a reality, Sullivan went on to serve the community as director of the school district and water commissioner. He was a member of the volunteer fire department, and led the movement for a local sewer system.

He is buried in Block 20, Lot 1.

Tobin, Thomas P. Jr. (? – 1928)

The son of famous scout Tom Tobin, Tom, Jr. lived in the St. Vrain area with his mother and step-father, George Lopez.[73] He lived in Canon City for a time, where he worked at the Colorado State Penitentiary. He was shot and wounded while on guard duty.

He died in 1928, in a car accident along with Lopez and a cousin, Herman Martinez. He is buried in Block 32, Lot 116. There is a marker.[74]

RYSSBY CEMETERY
LOCATED WEST OF LONGMONT ON 63RD STREET, SOUTH OF NELSON ROAD.

This quaint, remote cemetery lies behind the historic Ryssby Church. The church was the center of the Ryssby community, the first Swedish settlement in Colorado, established in 1869. The cemetery was laid out in 1880, with the first known burial in the same year. Cemetery records are not complete. In time, loved ones previously buried on nearby farms were reburied at the church. The church was built in 1881, on land donated by Hugo Anderson. The stone was quarried and hauled by the congregation. Funeral services for many of the burials were held in this church. The church became a State Historical Site in 1931.

Today, the cemetery is well maintained by members of the First Lutheran Church. Many of their ancestors are buried here, pioneers of a proud community.

Among those buried at the Ryssby Cemetery are the Nelson Brothers. The Nelson boys were born and raised near Holmstad,

Sweden. John (1837 – 1909), August (1841 – 1915), and Louis (1845 – 1931), all migrated to the United States on a steamship, after the Civil War. Settling in Chicago, August found work at the nearby quarries. John and Louis soon followed suit.

By 1870, the brothers had traveled farther west, working in the smelters of Black Hawk until they saved enough money to buy farmland near the Swedish settlement of Ryssby.

August was the first to arrive in the area on June 2, 1873. Driving his livery rig toward Ryssby, he came upon a group of men in the act of hanging a boy. The boy allegedly burned down the nearby Pella schoolhouse. August Nelson had saved $1,000 in gold, and offered the gold to the boy's father, Mr. Hoover, in an effort to save the youth's life. Mr. Hoover turned over his homestead to Nelson that very day, taking his son and family toward the Oregon Trail.

By 1878, the three Nelson brothers had built one of the finest ranches in the county. Their draft horses were legendary and purchased by the Denver and Boulder fire and police departments.

The section of land at the Boulder-Hygiene Road is the location of the Nelson ranch. The Nelson Road is named for the pioneer brothers, as well as the Nelson School in Longmont.

— — —

Colorado Highway 131 South

OAK CREEK

OAK CREEK CEMETERY

LOCATED ONE-QUARTER-MILE EAST OF HIGHWAY 131, AT THE SOUTH END OF TOWN, NEAR THE HIGH SCHOOL.

Also known as the Crown Hill or WOW Cemetery, the first recorded burial was that of Era B. Johnson in 1900. Real estate records show the land passed through many hands, including Albert Shempp in 1909, a funeral director. In 1929, the land was sold to the Neighbors of the Woodcraft #803. In 1962, the town of Oak Creek deeded the land to the Oak Creek Cemetery Association. The cemetery is in good condition, and is surrounded by a metal fence.

Bell, Samuel (? – 1922)

Samuel Bell lived and prospered in Cripple Creek during that town's boom years. He came to Routt County in 1903, where he opened the Bell Mercantile Company. He was instrumental in the founding of the town of Yampa.

He purchased the Bingham G. Shuster Ranch, where he and his brother Soward laid out the town, originally called Belltown. The town of Yampa prospered with the area coal mines and later the railroad.

Bell went on to become one of the largest property owners in the county, and was elected mayor of Oak Creek at the time of his death in 1922. He died of appendicitis.

He is buried in Section 1, Block E, Lot 10. There is no marker.

Hamidy, Edward (1899 – 1921)

Edward Hamidy arrived in the United States with his parents as an infant, settling in Oak Creek in 1909. Here he was raised and lived his life as a lonely rancher. He never married.

He is buried in Section 1, Block D, Lot 14.

Hubbard, Frank A. (1874 – 1955)

A native of Ohio, Frank Hubbard and his wife Elizabeth, moved to Oak Creek in 1925. He was a carpenter and interior decorator by trade, yet he also did quite a bit of mining. He was active in politics and social activities. He was a member of the Knights of Pythias for over forty years.

He is buried in Section 2, Block C, Lot 15.

Mudra, Kathryn (1878 – 1921)

Of Czecho-Slovack decent, Kathryn married Frank Mudra in the old country in 1899. The young couple settled with their children in the Yampa area in 1910. They homesteaded and built a ranch about fourteen miles from Oak Creek, known as Twentymile Park. Kathryn ran the ranch and raised the children, while Frank worked for the Moffat Coal Company, keeping him away from home for weeks at a time.

In January 1921, Kathryn was shot to death in her bed by her fifteen-year-old daughter, Annie. Katheryn's body was hidden on the ranch in a manure pile. It was discovered nearly three weeks later, when Frank returned home.

Annie was convicted of the murder, and sent to a female reform school. Her reason for the murder was she was not allowed to associate with a local boy of German-Slovack decent.

Kathryn is buried in Section 1, Block U, Lot 5.

Perry Mine Explosion (1921)

Oak Creek, being primarily a coal mining community, was not exempt from mining disasters. A terrible explosion occurred at the Perry Mine in February 1921. Five men died in the blast.

Mining communities typically buried the victims of such disasters in mass graves. This was not the case at Oak Creek. Samuel Patrick was buried in Bruseville, Indiana, while the other four victims were buried separately at the Oak Creek Cemetery.

Testas, Celestin J.B. (1890 – 1921)

A native of France, Testas came to Oak Creek in 1919, with his wife Amelia. They later had two children.

He is buried in Section 1, Block 1, Lot 14.

Wagner, Henry (1857 – 1921)

Born in Allentown, Pennsylvania, he served in the Spanish American War in 1898.

His grave is unmarked.

YAMPA

YAMPA CEMETERY

LOCATED TWO MILES NORTH OF TOWN FROM THE YAMPA RIVER BRIDGE ON HIGHWAY 131. TURN WEST ON THE GRAVEL COUNTY ROAD 21. THE CEMETERY IS LOCATED ONE-HALF-MILE DOWN THE ROAD.

The first recorded burial occurred in 1884. A beautiful cemetery, enclosed by a metal fence, it is still well maintained and sees occasional use. Cemetery records do not contain a complete list of the earliest burial records.

Bird Family Plot

The Bird family located at the Egeria Park (later known as Yampa,) in 1882, filing on a homestead. As one of the earliest pioneer families in the area, they were active in town affairs and well respected.

Several members of the family are buried in the plot, including William Bird, who died in 1918.

Hoage, Elmer (1855 – 1898)

Elmer Hoage was one of the first pioneers to settle in the area in 1882. He homesteaded and lived with his mother, who was affectionately known as "Aunty Hoage."

Elmer died at age forty three.

Neiman, Charles W. (1861 – 1947)

At age eighteen, Charles Neiman left his native Pennsylvania for the West. He spent a few years as a range rider north of Denver and in Wyoming, before coming to Routt County in 1884.

A cowboy turned lawman, he was Routt County's sheriff from 1895 to 1899. He was elected again in 1918 and served until 1924. He married Ruby Carle and had seven children.

He was responsible for the capture of the notorious outlaws Harry Tracy and David Lant. The outlaws escaped from the Hahn's Peak jail and Neiman led the posse in frigid conditions, capturing the pair the next day. They escaped again, but not under Neiman's protection.

He died in Steamboat Springs in 1947, and was buried in the Yampa Cemetery. His grave is located near the right side of the drive at the branch in the driveway. There is a large pink marble headstone.

Simon, Peter (1852 – 1933)

Peter Simon arrived in the Yampa area in 1881. He filed a homestead a mile and a half above the present site of Yampa, where he lived until his death.

OFF THE BEATEN PATH:

PAGODA CEMETERY

LOCATED IN SOUTHWESTERN ROUTT COUNTY AT THE JUNCTION OF HIGHWAY 317 AND ROUTT COUNTY ROAD 29. THE CEMETERY IS JUST NORTH OF THE NEARLY ABANDONED TOWN.

The Pagoda Cemetery was established shortly after the town was founded in 1890. Many of the graves date back to this period, but are unmarked. The first death in the community was that of Mrs. Henry Davis in 1888. She was a freed slave who homesteaded in the area with her husband, following the Civil War.

The oldest marked grave is dated 1900. James Bennett officially deeded the land to the Pagoda Cemetery Association in 1922. The West Routt County Cemetery Board bears the responsibility today. The cemetery is somewhat cared for, with occasional use.

Bennett, James A. (1857 – 1930)

A native of Pennsylvania, James Bennett spent his youth in several areas, including Wisconsin. At age twenty, he came to Colorado, working in various ore mines and prospecting at Georgetown, Breckenridge, and Leadville.

He homesteaded on the Williams Fork River in Routt County in 1887. He was one of the leading businessman of Pagoda. He started a general store and post office in 1890, and served as postmaster for several years. In 1922, he deeded a portion of his land which had been used as the Pagoda Cemetery.

He is buried in Lot E, 231.

Butler, Jones, Elsie G. (1856 – 1911)

Elsie Butler was born and raised in Berkshire County Massachusetts. On April 11, 1885, she married Frank Jones near her birthplace.

The couple homesteaded on the Williams Fork River in 1900. They were devoted to the community. Mrs. Jones contributed to many social and church causes.

They are buried in Lot W 232. An interesting note, Mrs. Jones obituary lists her as Elsie G. Butler, rather than Mrs. Frank Jones. Her tombstone reads Elsie G. Jones.[75]

Dunstan, Josephine Hauck (1853 – 1943)

Born in New York, Josephine married John Hauck in Illinois in 1871. The couple had two children, Mary and John. John Hauck left his wife and children in 1878. He never returned.

Josephine made quilts and sold them to the community, saving the money for the railroad fare for herself and children to Denver. In Denver, she worked for Mr. and Mrs. Bennett at the D&RG Boardinghouse. She married Mrs. Bennett's son from a previous marriage, Dick Dunstan, in 1884.

The couple, along with their infant daughter Maud, and Josephine's two children, arrived at Williams Fork in 1886. Together they built a ranch and a grand home, complete with a shingle roof.

The couple later moved to California, but were laid to rest in the Pagoda Cemetery. They are buried in Lot N 77.

— — —

Highway 13 South

MEEKER

MEEKER CEMETERY

LOCATED ONE-HALF-MILE SOUTH OF TOWN. FROM 10TH STREET, TURN WEST, CROSS THE BRIDGE, AND TURN LEFT TO THE CEMETERY.

The first cemetery for the Meeker community, located at the north end of town, (now the site of the hospital,) was abandoned in 1888, to make way for the new Highland Cemetery, also known as the Meeker Cemetery. Many graves were moved to the new cemetery. Victims of the Meeker Massacre were moved to the cemetery in 1898. Cemetery records are somewhat confusing. They are listed by owner of the block, thereby not necessarily the occupant of the gravesite. Among the many graves in this quiet resting spot, is that of Homer James (1884 – 1918). His stone reads: "Grandson of Jesse James."

A large plaque toward the top of the hill relates the story of the infamous bank robbery at Meeker, of which the victims are buried in this graveyard.

Bain, George (? – 1896)

On October 13, 1896, Bain along with Jim Shirley and a man called "The Kid," attempted to rob the Bank of Meeker. Bain was a large man with red hair and mustache and apparently the leader of the trio.

Bain reached for the cashier when his gun went off twice. While Shirley grabbed the sack full of money, Bain and The Kid each grabbed a hostage. Once outside, Shirley shot at a man and the hostages ran. The townfolk of Meeker opened fire on the trio. Bain took a bullet in the back and never recovered.

George Bain, alias George Low, or George Harvies, is buried with a marker in the southeast portion of the Meeker Cemetery.[76]

Pearce, "The Kid" (? – 1896)

His real name is unknown. He was called "The Kid" by some. Local newspaper media called him Pearce. He was with George Bain and Jim Shirley during the attempted holdup of the Bank of Meeker. When the robbery turned into a bungled affair, The Kid grabbed a hostage and headed out the door. Meeker's townfolk were waiting for the trio, rifles in hand. His hostage bolted and The Kid fell in the dirt hit by five bullets.

He is buried in the southeast corner of the Meeker Cemetery with Bain and Shirley.

Sanderson, Edward S. A. (1854 – 1917)
Sanderson, Amy (1867 – 1943)

Born in England to a noble parentage, Edward Sanderson enjoyed a fine childhood, including horse racing. He became an expert rider and horse trainer. Following school, he traveled the world, working for a time at the family tea plantation in India. From Canada, he made his way to Colorado during the Leadville silver boom.

Following the Meeker Massacre and the removal of the Ute Indians, the White River Country was opened for settlement. Sanderson found prime ranch land in the river bottom country. Sanderson explored the area in 1883. He spent that winter with a partner, hunting deer and tanning the hides. The following spring, he had hides to sell in England for a premium price. With the money, he was able to get financial backing and organized his cattle company.

"Sandy," as he was fondly known, drove 3,000-head of cattle to the White River, headquarters for his English Cattle Company.

As the company progressed, land as well as stock increased, and smaller ranches were bought out. In 1896, at the peak of success, Sanderson sold his great cattle empire.

Earlier in the year, Sanderson had married an English nurse named Amy Charlotte Johnston. The couple moved to Meeker, where Sandy built a fine home on Main Street for his bride.

Amy was very accomplished in her own right. While she continued her nursing profession, she also sang in the Episcopal choir and performed at the Sanderson Opera House in five languages.

Sandy continued his business in Meeker, buying and selling houses. He built the Opera House, the Antlers Hotel and organized the construction of the North Fork Ditch.

Edward Stanhope Sanderson, "Meeker Millionaire," is buried beside his wife Amy, in Block 98, Lot 2.

Shirley, James (? – 1896)

James Shirley, the third member of the bank robber trio, made history not as successful holdup man, but as one of the participants in the most bungled bank robbery in all of Colorado.

As the trio made their way to the street with the hostages, the sack full of money somehow was left in the doorway. In the street, Shirley fired at an armed man. Pandemonium broke out. Hostages fled, bullets flew and glass shattered. Shirley was the first to go down when a bullet pierced his lung.

He is buried in the Meeker Cemetery with his companions in the southeast corner of the cemetery. There is a marker.

MEEKER MASSACRE TRAGEDY (SEPTEMBER 29, 1879)

LOCATED TWELVE MILES SOUTHEAST OF MILK CREEK CROSSING , JUST OFF US HIGHWAY 13.

Nathan C. Meeker was agent of the White River Agency near present day Meeker, Colorado. Well-meaning, yet over-zealous, Meeker believed in stern leadership, forcing the Ute Indians to live in houses, fence and farm the land. A peaceful nomadic people, the Utes resisted and eventually reacted violently.

Food rations were limited to once a week and the government constantly delayed shipments of clothing, provisions and assigned annuities.

Tension mounted in March 1879, when Meeker reported to Washington that the Utes were buying ammunition at renegade stores. In balance, the Utes sent Captain Jack to Denver to complain of Meeker's leadership. He warned Governor Pitkin of the trouble to come if there was no change in leadership.

Major Thomas T. Thornburgh and his command were dispatched by the government to the White Indian Agency in early 1879. To the Utes, this was a sign of war. Yet Captain Jack met the army on behalf of the Utes, at Williams Fork, asking for a meeting with Meeker. Thornburgh refused. The soldiers pushed on to Milk Creek, where they split into separate divisions, flanking the Indian Agency.

Shots were fired by both sides. The battle raged for two days. When it was over, the dead included Agent Meeker, Major Thornburgh, nine US. soldiers and thirty-seven Indians.[77]

Meeker's wife and daughter were taken hostage by the Indians. Chief Douglas forced Josephine Meeker to watch as her father was stripped, gutted and scalped. A rescue party later rescued the women.

The Meeker massacre was the last major Indian war in the western United States. The Indians gained some satisfaction from the government, receiving a monetary award for peacefully ending the situation.

The Meeker Tragedy is commemorated by a large marker at the site, and a wooden sign telling of the tragedy.

— — —

Ghost Notes, Mysteries, & Other Related Findings

William Tull was a twenty-six-year-old hired hand working on a farm east of Boulder. One day in 1867, he left with two horses, heading north of Boulder to visit his Cheyenne Indian wife camped near Fort Collins. Because he was a hired hand, he was apprehended and questioned about the ownership of the horses. Deputy Sheriff Anderson arrested Tull and brought him back to Boulder. According to an interview from an eye-witness in the *Boulder Daily Camera* of March 28, 1908, the sheriff told young Tull, "This will not cost the county anything."

Shortly thereafter, a mob appeared, taking the prisoner with little effort. Tull was taken to a grove of trees along the Boulder Creek and lynched. The tree was a short one, causing Tull to strangle to death. It was later learned Tull held full title to the horses.

Following the lynching, local newspapers occasionally reported the sighting of the ghost of William Tull, a piece of rope dangling from his blood soaked neck.

* * *

William Harvey Doe and his young bride, Elizabeth Bonduel McCourt Doe, arrived in Black Hawk in July 1877. Harvey Doe, as he was known, came to take over management of his father's Fourth of July mine on Quartz Hill, above Central City. Harvey did not relish mine work and soon found the saloons more to his liking. His wife, Lizzie took up Harvey's duties at the mine and was admired by the miners who dubbed her "Baby Doe."

When the Fourth of July Mine was shut down in 1878, Baby Doe turned to her friend Jacob Sandelowsky for help. The two soon became lovers. When Baby Doe became pregnant in the winter 1878, Harvey left his wife and Central City. Sandelowsky stood beside Baby Doe until Harvey's father forced him back to Central City and his wife. The Doe reconciliation seemed a happy one.

On July 13, 1879, Baby Doe gave birth to a stillborn son. Harvey was nowhere to be found. Jake Sandelowsky cared for Baby Doe until her father-in-law arrived. The senior Mr. Doe took care of the burial arrangements for the infant and quietly left town. Baby Doe and Harvey eventually divorced and Baby Doe left for the silver mines of Leadville.

Central City cemetery records do not record the location of the infant Doe burial. Given the time and circumstance, the City Cemetery seems to be the logical place of interment.

* * *

Following the burial of John Cameron in Central City's Masonic Cemetery, a young woman lingered at the grave. People said she was there every day for hours. She brought flowers. But by summer, she stopped coming to the Cameron grave. On November 1, the anniversary of Cameron's death, she appeared again. The cemetery sexton said she appeared every November 1 for years, yet no one spoke to her. Rumors suggested she was a scorned lover. Others said she denied Cameron, and visited his grave out of guilt. Whoever the mysterious woman was, witnesses claimed she did exist and rebuked the town's "ghost" theories.

* * *

The ghost of Clifford Griffin seems to be a source of curiosity. Death cast its gloomy pall high on a mountain top above the town of Silver Plume on the night of June 19, 1887. With the daylight of the next morning, the gloom settled into a fog of rumor and gossip, hugging the mountainside and floating down to the mining town below. For on that particular night, the sweet sound of a violin gave way to a crisp report of a single gunshot.

Although ghost tales of Clifford Griffin began shortly after his death, the stories faded midway into the twentieth century, only to be resurrected in the 1960s.

Described as quite dashing, visitors say Griffin appears near his monument, dressed in black and smoking a cigar. Others have claimed he can been seen near the edge of the cliff, pulling his bow across the strings of his violin. A punctual ghost, he seems to make his appearance on the anniversary of his death.

It is said on nights when the wind is just right, his sad violin music can be heard below in the old mining town of Silver Plume.

At the top of the mountain, lingering at the tombstone, in the wind and the mountain serenity, perhaps one can sense the love Clifford Griffin had for these mountains. With a moments reflection, we might realize the true mystery and wonder of those we never knew.

The true ghosts, indeed.

* * *

William Dubois, an early pioneer of the Burlington settlement near Longmont, never revealed his past. Known as a troublemaker since his arrival in the area, he was arrested in 1867 for larceny. There is no clear explanation for the actions of Dubois on February 22, 1870.

Ed Kinney and John Wells were returning from the Big Thompson River, when they were confronted by Dubois. According to Wells, Dubois demanded $300 from him, for reasons unknown. Dubois then drew his pistol and shot twice at Kinney. The horses bolted and Wells fought for control as Dubois turned and emptied his gun into Kinney. Dubois then rode up to Wells and very calmly stated "I have been abused like a dog by you and Kinney . . . Damn you, I'll have you all yet."[78]

A posse was formed in Burlington by Marshal Dickens. The hunt lasted two days. Dubois, confronted, refused surrender and was killed in a shoot-out he instigated. The body was taken to the town of Burlington, where a coffin was made by Charles Baker. The Dubois family took the body home for a private burial.

William Dubois is buried somewhere on the family Ranch Road toward Lyons. The exact location is unknown.

* * *

Tabernash (? – 1878)

The Indian troubles of Grand County climaxed in 1878. Increased white settlement brought on Indian hostility which led to bloodshed.

Tabernash, a Ute brave was known throughout the area as the most incorrigible among the Utes. Eye witnesses including Frank

Addison attested to several murderous acts committed by the young brave.

On a warm August day in 1878, a band of Utes, including Tabernash and led by Uncompahgre chiefs, Piah and Washington, attempted to take over the William Cozen Ranch. They backed away at the sight of Cozen's aimed rifle. Five miles below the Cozen Ranch, the Utes tore down fences and scattered horses at a place called Junction Ranch.[79] They camped at the site for several days, roaming the area on horseback until the settlers were in a panic.

A posse was summoned and rode to the area from Hot Sulphur Springs on September 1, 1878. Tabernash attempted to pull his rifle on posse member Frank Addison. Addison reacted and fired his weapon. Tabernash slumped as his horse ran toward the meadow. The explosive incident ended as the stunned Utes retrieved the body of Tabernash.

Tabernash was buried approximately one mile north of present day Highway 40, at the site of Tabernash. The burial spot is not marked.

* * *

Wilson, Charles W. (1865 – 1884)

Wilson arrived in Grand County in the spring of 1883. It is said he came from New Mexico or the Panhandle of Texas. He settled in the Hot Sulphur Springs area and did occasional ranch work. He roamed the town streets, dressed in a sombrero, carrying two revolvers and various hidden weapons. Generally looking for trouble, he frequented the saloons, usually ending the night by a round of shooting at the feet of the patrons, and using full liquor bottles for target practice. Known as "Texas Charlie", his reputation grew worse when he was suspected of cattle rustling and rumored to have murdered a few men.

Texas Charlie sealed his fate on a cold December night in 1884. Entering the billiard hall of William (Ute Bill) Thompson, he demanded Thompson's rifle, then proceeded to beat one of the patrons over the head with his revolver. A warrant was issued for the arrest of Texas Charlie, whereupon the young tyrant threatened to kill any and all who dared to arrest him.

The citizens of Hot Sulphur Springs took the law into their own hands. On the morning of December 9, 1884, Texas Charlie and a couple of his cronies rode into town on a buckboard, stopping at Frank Byers' general store.[80]

Gunfire erupted from the Bock Building across the street. Texas Charlie and his pals darted into the alley next to the Byers building. A bullet hit Wilson's hand, while another volley dropped him to the ground. Over a dozen prominent men of the community emerged from the Bock Building. They were never identified.

Texas Charlie Wilson lay dead with a bullet in his chest and a shattered skull. His own revolver had not been fired. The coroners inquest concluded death by gunshot by persons unknown.

Charles W. Wilson was dead at the age of nineteen. He was denied interment in the Hot Sulphur Springs Cemetery. His body was buried on a hill south of town and unmarked. The exact location is lost to history.

* * *

A half mile south of Pagoda is the remains of the schoolhouse built in 1891. Two lonely graves are near the building. They are the resting place of Sally Buckner and Lydia Ann Hart. For many years, the students kept fresh flowers on the graves during the summer months. They are believed to have been early teachers at the school.

— — —

Additional Cemeteries Listed by County

Boulder County

Cemetery	1st Burial
Altona Cemetery	1864 – plowed over
Old Boulder Cemetery	1859
Caribou Cemetery	1870
Eldorado Springs Cemetery	1875
Gold Hill Cemetery	1859
Hygiene Cemetery #1& #2	1861
Jamestown Cemetery	1875
Kossler Cemetery	1870
Lafayette Cemetery	1888
Louisville Cemetery	1878
Lyons Cemetery	1890
Marshall Cemetery	1876
Niwot Cemetery	1874
Riverside Cemetery	?
Salina Cemetery	1882
S. Boulder CatholicCemetery	1873
Sugarloaf Cemetery	1867
Sunset Cemetery	1883
Sunshine Cemetery	1875
Superior Cemetery	1873
Valmont Cemetery	1863

Ward Cemetery   ?
Wiesner Cemetery   ?

Clear Creek County

Cemetery	1st Burial
Dumont Cemetery	1864
Evans Ranch	?
Miners' Cemetery	1859
Shank-Kennedy Cemetery	1859
Silverdale Lower Cemetery	1877 – Abandoned
Silver Dale Cemetery	Abandoned – covered by PSC dam

Eagle County

Cemetery	1st Burial
Cedar Hill Cemetery	1890
Dotsero Cemetery #1& #2	1890
Edwards Cemetery	1890
Fulford Cemetery	?
Gold Park Cemetery	1878
Greenwood Cemetery	1880
Gypsum Cemetery	?
McCoy Cemetery	1893
Riverview Cemetery	1889
Sheephorn Cemetery	?
Sunset View Cemetery	1885
Valley View Cemetery	?

Gilpin County

Cemetery	1st Burial
Lake View Cemetery	?
Missouri Cemetery	1863

Grand County

Cemetery	1st Burial
Arrow Cemetery	1904
Granby Cemetery	1905
Troublesome Cemetery	1873

Jackson County

Cemetery	1st Burial
Helena Old Cemetery	1906
Pinkhampton Cemetery	? – Abandoned

Teller City Cemetery	?
Walden Cemetery	1886

Jefferson County

Cemetery	1st Burial
Ault Cemetery	1889
Bergen Park Cemetery	1862
Buffalo Creek Cemetery	1902
Creswell Cemetery No. 2	1888
Foxton Cemetery	1879
Miners' Cemetery	1859
Mount Vernon Cemetery	1860
Old Golden Cemetery	1860
Pine Cemetery	1889
Silver Springs/Pine Grove Cemetery	1879
South Platte Cemetery	?
St. Anne's Camp Cemetery	1933
St. Joseph's Catholic Cemetery	1876
Wambles Valley French Canadian Cemetery	1879

Larimer County

Cemetery	1st Burial
Adams Cemetery	1880
Boyd Ranch Cemetery	?
Craddock Ranch Cemetery	?
Estes Park Cemetery	1912
Grange Ranch Cemetery	?
Greenlawn Cemetery	1884
Harmony Cemetery	1880
Highland Cemetery	1905
Livermore Cemetery	1891
Manhattan Cemetery	1892
Patterson Cemetery	?
Pittington Cemetery	?
Stoney Park Cemetery	1886
Timnath Cemetery	1886
Virginia Dale Cemetery	1885
Wooster Cemetery	?

Moffat County

Cemetery	1st Burial
Fairview Cemetery	?
Great Divide Cemetery	?
Lily Park Cemetery	?
Slater Cemetery	?

Rio Blanco County

Cemetery	1st Burial
Black Sulphur Cemetery	1896
Miller Hill Cemetery	1896
Pyramid Cemetery	1896
Rangely Cemetery	1886
Strawberry Cemetery	1918
White River Cemetery	?

Routt County

Cemetery	1st Burial
Bugtown Cemetery	1874
Dead Mexican Park Cemetery	1906 – Abandoned
Deep Creek Cemetery	1906 – Abandoned
Elk Mountain Cemetery	1888
Trull Cemetery	?

— — —

Sources

Clear Creek County Records – Georgetown
Clear Creek Funeral Records 1885 – 1913
Colorado Genealogical Society
Colorado Historical Society
Columbia Cemetery Records – Boulder Carnegie Library
Cusick, Roger – National Association for Cemetery Preservation
Denver Public Library Western History Department
Ellis, Susan – Grand County Historical Association
Frontier Historical Society, Glenwood Springs
Gilpin County Museum
Historical Society of Idaho Springs
Home and Community Service – Public Service of Colorado
Publication – 1967
John Tomay Memorial Library – Georgetown
Lakeside Cemetery, Cemeteries of Larimer County Vol. IV
Loveland Public Library Archives
Museum of Idaho Springs

Newspapers

Avalanche Echo
Boulder Daily Camera
Denver Post
Denver Republican
Denver Tribune
Fort Collins Courier
Georgetown Colorado Miner
Georgetown Courier
Gilpin County Observer
Grand County Community Record
Longmont Times Call
Loveland Reporter Herald
North Park Miner
Register Call
Rocky Mountain News
The Miner
The Ute Press

Interviews and Correspondence

Bradley, Christine – Clear Creek County Archivist
Jones, Linda – Gilpin County
Luton, Susan – Grand Lake
Mayor Gene Stover – Grand Lake
Prochaska, James – Gilpin County Historical Society
Thompson, K. Don, President, Mesa County Historical Society
Wilson, Glenn – Fraser Cemetery-including family histories from Lucille Morrow, Florence Petersen, Ruth Newman, and Elsie Clayton
Zobel, William and Yvonna – Meeker

— — —

Chapter Four Notes

[1] Records are maintained by the Grand Lake Historical Society, and do not list block and plot.

[2] Records, courtesy of Gene Stover, Mayor of Grand Lake.

[3] Mississippi State Archive records.

[4] Mills was backed by the editorials of the North Park Miner.

[5] Weber died the next day, while Dean lingered for thirteen days, before he died.

[6] Some newspaper accounts reported Day was the first to fire. This is doubtful, given the obvious element of surprise, the ambush and the masked men. The newspapers took sides in the political turmoil, slanting the details toward their own agendas.

[7] See Ghost Notes at the end of this chapter.

[8] Josie's mother's name by a second husband.

[9] A bronze plaque on the university campus honors Arnett, among others for "beginning the dream of CU in 1872."

[10] Horn's tombstone incorrectly gives DOB as 1861.

[11] See Brown's Park.

[12] In his biography, Horn states he was set up by the cattlemen who employed him, fearing the law was closing in on their murderous scheme.

[13] There are two separate cemetery inventories of Columbia Cemetery. Neither list Thomas Horn. There is a marker in the cemetery, and the Boulder County archives have a letter from Charles Horn to a sister, describing the funeral and the burial of their brother, Tom Horn in the Columbia Cemetery.

[14] See Sand Creek battle site, Chapter 4.

[15] The dwelling still stands in Dutch Park, although in disrepair.

[16] This house is located at 1019 Spruce Street.

[17] This fort was later named Fort Morgan. See Chapter 1.

[18] See Fairmount Cemetery, Chapter 2.

[19] See Sand Creek Battle Site, Chapter 4.

[20] At the time, the store was known as Bradley & McClure.

[21] Clear Creek County records, held at Georgetown, are incomplete and next to impossible to verify block and plot information. Tombstone dates are verified if possible and differences are noted.

[22] Huet's painting of the Taylor Lake now hangs in the Idaho Springs Library. It was purchased second hand by author Lafayette Hanchett and donated by Hanchett's daughter.

[23] Harrison is the author of Empire and the Berthoud Pass.

[24] See Central City.

[25] See "Ghosts" this chapter.

[26] The marriage certificate is on display at the Colorado Historical Society in Denver.

[27] Another infant Alexis Cozens, is buried in the Masonic Cemetery at Central City. See Central City.

[28] Grand County Commission records.

[29] See Weber, at the end of this chapter.

[30] Now known as the Diamond-Bar-T Ranch.

[31] David's great-grandfather, Joseph Gardner, married Aneke Crockett, sister of David (Davy) Crockett, in 1820.

[32] See "Ghosts" at the end of this chapter.

[33] See Chapter One.

[34] The dripping blood from Dean's bedside remained on Mrs. Young's wooden floors, until the building was razed in 1936.

[35] He was the brother of Chipeta, wife of Chief Ouray.

[36] The area was renamed Tabernash when the Moffat Railroad reached this site. See "Ghosts" this chapter.

[37] This area is now a historical site.

[38] Rosella Teagarden Breeze is the niece of town founder William Tucker.

[39] Renamed "Brown's Park by Ann Bassett.

[40] See Logan, Harvey.

[41] Herbert Bassett is buried in Quincey, Illinois.

[42] The land where Dart's cabin was, belonged to MacKnight.

[43] See Horn, Tom.

[44] The spot is accessible by four-wheel-drive. There is no marker, however, the gravesite is crudely fenced.

[45] See Mount Olivet Cemetery.

[46] The spelling of Hinrich and Heinrich appears on the stone. Possibly, the mistake of the stone cutter.

[47] Register Call Vol. XXXIV. Following his death it was learned the name Covington was most likely an alias.

[48] The original structure now houses the Wild Card Saloon.

[49] This building still stands in Central City.

[50] The tombstone is a bit misleading. Williams was shot on April 15, and died on April 19, 1896.

[51] The twenty-two-foot Knickerbocker Tunnel still exists just south of the gulch.

[52] Following the death of Cody, the townsfolk of Cody, Wyoming petitioned to have him buried in their town. A feud continued for a few years. Fearing removal of Cody's body, his remains were covered by six feet of concrete.

[53] Griswold's grave is located in the Idaho Springs Cemetery.

[54] Burials are not recorded by block and plot numbers.

[55] Still standing, it is the oldest structure on Miner Street.

[56] William Doe was the father-in-law of "Baby Doe" Tabor, before she divorced Harvey Doe.

[57] Clear Creek County records, held at Georgetown, are incomplete and next to impossible to verify block and plot information. Tombstone dates are verified if possible and differences are noted.

[58] His real name was Adolphe Francois Gerald. His name was changed for reasons not substantiated. Louis Dupuy is listed on the marker.

[59] Family records list date of birth as 1828, while Clear Creek County History lists 1986.

[60] Clear Creek County records, held in Georgetown are incomplete and next to impossible to verify block and plot information. Tombstone dates are verified if possible and differences are noted.

[61] When the author last visited in the summer of 1996, the paint was fairly fresh. Unfortunately, no information regarding the family could be obtained.

[62] Henry F. (1825 – 1896) and Mary L. (1835 – 1909). Lampshire are buried nearby. It is known Samuel came to America with a brother. This may be his brother. Records do not indicate.

[63] Her obituary in the Grand Junction Daily Sentinel of 8/30/1942, incorrectly listed her date of birth as 1881.

[64] The location is approximately the site of the intersection of Oak Street and College Avenue.

[65] A son-in-law, Newton Cross was murdered in his law office in 1914.

[66] Now known as Colorado State University at Fort Collins.

[67] The original location of the camp was near present day Laporte.

[68] The cabin was moved twice and now sits at the Fort Collins Pioneer Museum.

[69] Joseph Mason built and owned this building.

[70] This settlement later became the town of Longmont.

[71] Corothers, June E., Estes Park Past and Present.

[72] See Ghost Notes.

[73] Tom Tobin is responsible for hunting down and killing members of the Espinosa gang.

[74] His mother, Maria, is buried beside her first husband, Tom Tobin. See Chapter 5.

[75] Routt County Republican November 3, 1911.

[76] Some historians identify Bain as George Law, an outlaw from Browns Park. George Law lived to a ripe old age, and is buried at the Hot Sulphur Springs Cemetery.

[77] Meeker, and fellow men who also died in the tragedy, originally from Greeley, are buried in Linn Grove Cemetery; See Greeley, CO.

[78] Rocky Mountain News, 2/23/1870.

[79] Today, the small community is known as Tabernash, in honor of the Indian brave.

[80] Frank Byers, the son of William Byers, lived and prospered in the town his father founded and promoted in his paper, The Rocky Mountain News.

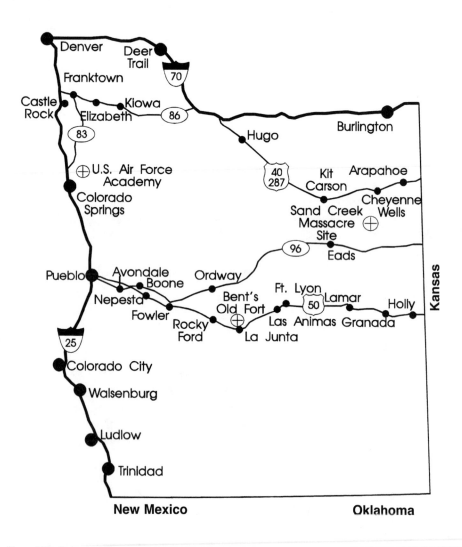

Chapter Five

Southeastern Colorado
The Grasslands

ncient arrowheads, stone implements, and broken pottery are
among the articles found in the rocky soil of southeastern
Colorado, evidence of early inhabitants of the area. Indian pic-
tographs are carved in the canyon walls, and crumbled remains of
stone houses, once the homes of pioneer families, dot the landscape.

Colorado's oldest history is found here, southeast of the historic
Overland Trail (today's Interstate 25), south of the historic Smoky Hill
Trail (today's Interstate 70), and in the midst of the legendary Santa
Fe Trail (Highway 50). This is the Comanche National Grasslands.[1]

Across this vast prairie, often called the cradle of the Great
American Desert, Indians hunted buffalo and roamed free. The Indian
history is known through Spanish accounts, as the Indians left no
early records. The Spanish who first met them, gave them the name
"Apache." Spanish explorers traveled the Grasslands to the north and
to the west. Coronado's 1540 expedition is known to have traveled
along the Arkansas River, and possibly a portion of what is now
known as the Santa Fe Trail. This was the land Mexico hoped to colo-
nize. For most of the eighteenth century, the grasslands were popu-
lated by the occasional band of Indians and the ever present buffalo.

The Arkansas River is the single dominant force of this area. It has
been claimed by the Indians, the Spanish, the Mexicans and the
Americans. It served as an international border, and separated Texas
from the United States prior to Texas statehood. This great river provided guidance to the Indians and trappers, and later the traders and
travelers. Wagon trains followed the river and forts were built along
its banks. Today, railroads and highways follow the river's flow from
west to east.

The beginnings of the Santa Fe Trail were laid out as early as the
1740s. French explorers established the road. Deep ruts still exist in
the soil, cut by caravans of wagons during the westward expansion of

the 1850s. By the 1870s, forts dominated the area, protecting the settlers and serving the armies on the march.

Following the Louisiana Purchase of 1803, the United States government sent explorers west. Men such as John C. Fremont, and Lieutenant Zebulon Montgomery Pike, were among the first to explore the area now known as Southern Colorado. Indian scouts, trappers and traders were the first white man to inhabit the area. The land became the domain of such historic figures as Charles Autobees, William Bent, Kit Carson, Tom Tobin, Richens L. "Uncle Dick" Wooton, and the Baca family. These men opened the area for permanent settlement.

The Santa Fe Trail enters Colorado at Holly and crosses the state in a southwest direction, where it exits the state at Raton Pass. In between lie some of the most colorful miles and names in the history of the West. The Bent brothers opened their famous trading post and tried to keep the peace with the Indians, while Kit Carson negotiated on behalf of the government. The Indians were losing their land, and war was inevitable. The Indian wars of the 1860s, largely fought in this area of the state, shed more than blood. Life seemed to change overnight, yet the Westward Migration pushed on.

Westward trails became embedded in the soil with such names as Smoky Hill, Sante Fe, the Goodnight/Loving Trail, and Cimarron. Wagon trains over a mile long crossed these paths during the spring and summer months, when travel was easiest. The travelers included displaced Confederates, impoverished Northerners, Prussians, Swedes, Canadians, Scotsmen, Russian and English immigrants. Over a quarter of a million pioneers traveled these trails between 1849 and 1880.

The Homestead Act of 1862, passed by Congress in an effort to populate the West, caused a massive westward movement. No other event, with the exception of the Civil War, changed America in the nineteenth century, as did this migration. Southeastern Colorado experienced three great homestead booms. Dry land agriculture seemed to rise and fall as much as foothill coal mining, another attraction to the area.

The typical settler claimed 160 acres of land for $16 dollars. The homesteader agreed to live on the property five years, and improve on the land.[2] The settler then purchased the land from the government for $1.25 an acre. Thousands came west to stake their claims. These rugged pioneers found ways to farm the land, graze their cattle and breed their horses.

Great herds of cattle were driven north, supplying a land frenzied with gold fever. The cattle trails of the nineteenth century led to the rich cattle country of today's Grasslands. It is here that men such as John Prowers, Joe Doyle, Casimero Barela, and Thomas Boggs built great ranching enterprises, and George Swink capitalized on the agriculture aspects, making melons and Rocky Ford famous.

Industry has played its part as well in Southeastern Colorado. The sugar beet industry of Holly, and Pueblo's Colorado Fuel & Iron Company offered hope, work and boosted the economy. Southwestern Colorado suffered tragedy as well. From the Indian massacre at Sand Creek to the miner's strike at Ludlow, all contributed to the history of the area.

From the Indians, to the trappers, traders, frontiersmen, homesteaders, ranchers, town fathers, merchants, and manufacturers, all are a part of the pioneer heritage of Southern Colorado.

Tom Grill photo

Kiowa Courthouse monument to pioneers killed in Indian wars.

— — —

US Highway 86 West

KIOWA

PIONEER MEMORIAL

LOCATED ON THE FRONT LAWN OF THE ELBERT COUNTY COURT HOUSE IN KIOWA.

The memorial reads:[3]

> *Erected by Pioneer Women of Colorado*
> *1939 A.D.*
> *In memory of Pioneers massacred by Indians.*
> *1864 A.D. Nathan W. and Ellen Hungate*
> *and children Laura V. and Florence V.*
> *1868 A.D. Dietemann, Henrietta and son John*

Louis Alama
Joseph Bledsoe

OLD KIOWA CEMETERY

*LOCATED SOUTHWEST OF THE TOWN OF KIOWA. FROM TOWN, TAKE HIGHWAY
86 WEST ONE-HALF-MILE TO COUNTY ROAD 157. GO SOUTH ON 157
APPROXIMATELY FOUR MILES. THE CEMETERY SITS ON THE TOP OF THE HILL
ON THE WEST SIDE OF THE ROAD.*

The prairie town of Kiowa, established in 1859, was originally a
stage stop on the historic Smoky Hill Trail. The abandoned cemetery
contains the graves of early Kiowa residents and of people from the
surrounding area. There are several unmarked graves and many broken and vandalized tombstones. The oldest marked grave is that of
Norris West, dated 1879. There are a total of five small rows containing such names as Diedrick, Hoffman, Folster and Ehrler. The cemetery appears to have been abandoned in the early 1890s, as there are
no stones dated after 1891. It is curious that a new cemetery was
never established for the residents of Kiowa.

OFF THE BEATEN PATH:

WEIDEMEYER-BROCKMAN CEMETERY

*THE WIEDEMEYER-BROCKMAN CEMETERY IS EIGHT MILES EAST OF KIOWA,
AND THREE MILES NORTH OF HIGHWAY 86. THIS CEMETERY, LOCATED ON
PRIVATE LAND, IS THE FAMILY RESTING SPOT OF THE WIEDEMEYER AND
BROCKMAN PIONEER FAMILIES, AS WELL AS LOCAL AREA PIONEERS.*

The oldest marked grave is that of Henry Brockman, who died in
1879. It is assumed by the cemetery name, that members of the
Wiedemeyer family are buried here. No tombstones bear the
Wiedemeyer name, however there are several unmarked graves.

The graves of Henry P. Brockman (1867 – 1879) and his mother,
Catherine (1830 – 1889) are located here. Henry's father Hans,
brought his young family west from Iowa. Their small wagon train
arrived in Denver City in the summer of 1860, and soon moved on to
Breckenridge, Leadville, and finally Central City.

By 1874, the Brockman family homesteaded at Bijou Basin, ten
miles east of Kiowa. A two-story home and large barn were constructed, where Henry's father often held barn dances.

Henry worked on the farm, helping his father. In July 1879, Henry
and a friend were sent to retrieve a team of horses. The early morning air was dim and foggy, soon giving way to a heavy downpour. The
two sought shelter under a high bank in the river gulch. The bank
caved in, killing young Henry. His friend escaped uninjured. A search

party found Henry's body three days later. Henry Brockman was twenty years old, and recently married when he died.

He is buried next to his mother, Catherine, who died in 1889.

ELBERT

ELBERT CEMETERY
LOCATED NORTH OF THE TOWN OF ELBERT. FROM KIOWA, TAKE THE ELBERT ROAD APPROXIMATELY NINE MILES SOUTH TOWARD THE TOWN OF ELBERT. THE CEMETERY IS ON THE HILL JUST NORTH OF TOWN.

This pristine cemetery overlooks the eastern prairie and the town of Elbert. Established in 1876, it is well maintained and still in use. The original section is on the west side and contains the older graves.

McFarlin, Joseph Jacob, Sr. (1861 – 1917)

Joseph McFarlin brought his wife Lucy Lucinda, and five children to Colorado by covered wagon in 1899. Joseph filed on a homestead near Fondis, ten miles east of Elbert, in 1900. He bought a herd of cattle and raised dairy cows. The family first lived in a dugout until Joseph was able to make a profit from his land and cattle. Joseph later became the notary public for the town of Fondis, and ran the local brick factory. He built a home for his family in town, which still stands today.

Lucy Lucinda died in childbirth in 1908. Many of the McFarlin children were adopted by local families after the death of their mother. Joseph married Myrtle Adeline Woods in 1911. Two children were born to this marriage, which ended in divorce in 1914. Later that year, Joseph married Anna Hunyadi.

Joseph J. McFarlin died in 1917, and is buried in the Elbert Cemetery. He is buried with his first wife, Lucy, in Lot 20 of the West Section. There is a marker for both Lucy and Joseph.

Rinnert, Adam (1851 – 1918)

Born in New York, Adam Rinnert was the son of German immigrants. He came west after his schooling, settling in Elbert County in 1870.[4] Taking on various ranch jobs, Rinnert eventually filed for a homestead. He built upon his land, adding over 1,700 acres near Elbert.

A prosperous landowner, Rinnert married twice. His second wife, the former Edith Caswell, also owned a large piece of land. Rinnert became a charter member of the local I.O.O.F. Lodge and also served as Elbert County sheriff.

He is buried in Lot 64 of the West Section.

Elbert County has extensive records on several rural cemeteries. While rural graveyards are common across eastern Colorado and listed in public records, Elbert County has done an excellent job of preserving the history of these cemeteries. The following pioneer cemeteries are on privately owned land. Permission to visit is recommended.

BIJOU BASIC CEMETERY

LOCATED SOUTHEAST OF ELBERT. FROM THE TOWN OF ELBERT, TAKE ELBERT ROAD SOUTH TO THE AIRPORT, TURN EAST. GO APPROXIMATELY ONE AND ONE-HALF MILES. TURN SOUTH AT THE INTERSECTION ON COUNTY ROAD 37. FOLLOW THIS ROAD FOUR MILES SOUTH TO THE CEMETERY.

This lonely abandoned cemetery contains five rows of forgotten pioneers. An old graveyard indeed, the tombstones date to 1868, that of twenty-seven-year-old William Matthews. The Matthews family plot is the most prominent in the graveyard. Other names include Hayden, Sides, Boyd and Mobley.

The Matthews family plot includes the graves of Henry and Louisa Matthews, early Colorado pioneers. Henry, born in 1812, emigrated to America in 1856. He settled his family in Indiana and later Illinois, where his son Charles was born. In 1874, he came to Colorado by railroad, where the family took a homestead near Elbert. He worked as a ranch hand to make ends meet for the family, but died suddenly that year. His wife Louisa died in 1882. A single stone marker bears their names.

Charles Matthews, born in 1857, came to Colorado with his parents. Charles worked for the town of Bijou Basin, hauling timber for construction.[5] In 1879, he purchased land seven miles from the town of Elbert for $1.50 an acre. He married Mary Schillinger at Kiowa, in 1884. Nine children were born to this union, two dying in infancy.

Charles farmed and hauled ties for the railroad. Later, he studied engineering and surveyed for the Union Pacific railroad. Charles died in 1957, at the age 100, and is buried in a fenced plot next to his infant daughters, Lynn and Caroline.

ELIZABETH

ELIZABETH CEMETERY

LOCATED ON THE WEST END OF THE TOWN OF ELIZABETH.

The Elizabeth Cemetery, established in 1883, is maintained by the city of Elizabeth and still in use. The wide rows of burial plots are graced with flowers, bushes, and trees, all in a serene setting. The

Fairview Section, located at the north entrance, is the original land donated for the cemetery.

Vicky Phillips
John Dietemann grave.

Dietemann, John W. (1829 – 1899)

One of the earliest homesteaders in what would become Elbert County, John Dietemann homesteaded land on Comanche Creek, in 1862, near the future site of the town of Elbert. He made a home for his wife, Henrietta, and his family, raised livestock, and planted crops.

In 1868, John's wife, Henrietta, and their five-year-old son Johnny, were found murdered at their ranch in Elbert County. Their bodies were riddled with Indian arrows, and their scalps removed. Seeing a band of Indians taking horses out of the corral, Henrietta, her sister, and hired hands took as many possessions as they could carry and with her son and daughter, the group began to walk to the stage line, some two miles away. The Indians rode toward the group, and they scattered. Henrietta, heavy with child and pulling her young son, did not get away. Henrietta and young Johnny were shot full of arrows and scalped.

John W. Dietemann died at the age of sixty-nine, in 1899. He is buried in Lot 258 of the Mountview Addition.

Killin, Bernard C. (1845 – 1911)

Following the Civil War, Bernard Killin joined a wagon train from Omaha, heading to the "Wild West." Attacked by Indians, the wagon train was forced to stop in Denver in 1866. Killin chose to file on a homestead and make Colorado Territory his home. The homestead, located in Elbert County, proved to be a prime piece of land. Killin eventually owned over 3,500 acres.

Killin served as county sheriff in 1873, as well as superintendent of schools, justice of the peace, and was a charter member of the state Board of Stock Inspectors. When the issue of equal suffrage for women was put to the Colorado voters, in 1879, it is said that Killin cast the only "yes" vote in Elbert County. Killin married Olive Grigg in 1891. Two sons were born to this marriage.

Bernard Chester Killin is buried in Block 2, Lot 53 of the Fairview Addition. There is a marker.

Kusma, Michael (1871 – 1941)

A native of Austria, Michael boarded a ship bound for America at age fourteen. Arriving in Michigan in 1885, he stayed with an uncle before making his way west to Denver. Kusma found work in the steel foundries of Globeville in north Denver, where he met Barbara Oster. The couple were married in April 1895.

Mike Kusma continued his work at the foundry until 1900, when he filed on a homestead two miles northeast of Kiowa. Moving his young family to the country, he built a house and raised livestock. The Kusma family became intertwined in Elbert County, with two of the children marrying into the pioneer Wood family.

Mike and Barbara Kusma are buried together in Lot 341 of the Mountview Addition.

Mauldin, James A. (1846 – 1908)

The son of Terrill and Sarah Mauldin, James left his native Georgia following the death of his father in 1862. He brought his mother and three sisters west by covered wagon, arriving in Elbert County in 1867.

One of the earliest pioneers in the area, Mauldin increased his land to over 1,600 acres in a few short years. He served as county commissioner, being elected for three consecutive terms and contributed to the town board during his forty years in Elizabeth.

Mauldin's first wife, Caroline died in 1890. In 1892, he married Frances Emiley Tee of Illinois. The couple had five children.[6]

James Absalom and Frances Emiley Mauldin are buried in Lot 260 in the Mountview Addition.

Nelson, Nels (1864 – 1941)

Born Nils Nelson in Sweden, he changed the spelling of his name when he arrived in America in 1887. Twenty-three-year-old Nels Nelson, a cabinet maker by trade, came to Denver in 1888, where he met and married Kristina Bostrom. In 1896, Nels brought his growing family to Elbert County, filing on a homestead northeast of Elizabeth. He improved on the land, built a large two-story house, and raised livestock. Kristina died in 1905, with burial in the Elizabeth Cemetery. Shortly after the death of Kristina, Nels married Betty Brown, who died a few years later.

Nels continued his carpenter trade, building several houses and barns still standing in the Elizabeth area. Nels Nelson is buried near his first wife, Kristina, in Block 2, Lot 6, of the Fairview Addition.

Weidner, Mary Noon (1871 – 1954)

As a child, Mary traveled by covered wagon to Colorado with her parents. She grew up in Leadville during that town's silver boom, and later became a teacher.

Mary Noon married Phillip A. Weidner in Denver, in 1893. While living in Denver, Mary had three children. The Weidner family moved to Elizabeth in 1904.

Phillip died in the fall of 1913, leaving Mary with a financial burden. With her children in school, Mary secured employment as postmistress of Elizabeth. She was allowed to serve the rural routes, thus increasing her salary. In 1915, Mary's three-year-old daughter, Ruthie died of accidental poisoning.

Through Mary's hard work and determination, she saved enough money for two of her children to continue their education beyond high school.

Mary Weidner is buried beside her husband, Phillip, in Block 5, Lot 3 of the Fairview Addition. There is one stone marking the graves of Mary, Phillip, and their daughter, Ruthie.

BOOT RANCH CEMETERY

LOCATED APPROXIMATELY SIX MILES SOUTH OF ELIZABETH. TAKE COUNTY ROAD 17, FIVE AND ONE-HALF MILES SOUTH TO THE FIRST INTERSECTION IN THE ROAD. GO WEST ONE-QUARTER-MILE. THE CEMETERY IS ON THE TOP OF THE HILL, ON THE SOUTH SIDE OF THE ROAD.

This rural pioneer cemetery contains several unmarked graves, as well as many infant graves. There are several family names among the tombstones, leading one to believe this was a community cemetery at one time.

The Mauldin family plot includes the garves of Caroline A. Mauldin (1853 – 1890) and Sarah Mauldin (1812 – 1884).

Sarah Mauldin, a native of Hall County, Georgia, and the mother of six children, lost her husband in 1862. Following the Civil War, she came west with her youngest son, James, and her three daughters. Settling in Elbert County, James filed on a homestead a few miles southeast of what would become the town of Elizabeth. He built a home for his mother and sisters and cultivated the land. Sarah ran the household and raised her three daughters, all of whom married into the community.

Sarah died at the age of seventy-two, in 1884. There is a marker and foot stone.

Caroline A. McCurry was the first wife of James Mauldin, Sarah's son. She died on New Year's Eve 1890, at age thirty-seven. There is a marker.

Rachel C. Baldwin (1852 – 1877), was the daughter of Sarah Mauldin, and the sister to James Mauldin. She married J.G. Baldwin. Rachel died at age twenty-five. There is a small unmarked grave next to her burial spot, leading one to wonder if she died in childbirth?

FRANKTOWN

FRANKTOWN CEMETERY

LOCATED AT THE NORTHEAST CORNER OF THE INTERSECTION OF HIGHWAYS 86 AND 83.

The tall iron gate greets the visitor entering this small graveyard. Passing through the arch, the dirt road winds around the hill to the prairie cemetery. Only a few tombstones are visible at first glance. The pioneer cemetery slopes into a ravine beyond the knoll. It is here that the majority of the early pioneers are buried, in the natural setting of wild flowers, overgrown natural grasses, bushes and amazingly large pine trees.

Many of the pioneers buried in this cemetery are early residents of the first gold camp in Colorado Territory. Russellville, now a prairie ghost town was located five miles southeast of Franktown. It was named for Green Russell in 1858. It was here, at the east branch of the Cherry Creek, that Russell and his party first discovered gold.[7] The site is on the old Santa Fe Trail from Denver to Pueblo, and Santa Fe. There were no great gold discoveries, but it generated enough interest for permanent settlement. Russellville faded away in the 1890s.

The land for the cemetery was donated by James Kelley in 1870, following the death of his wife. Today the Franktown Cemetery, as do many of the cemeteries, stands as a legacy to the pioneers who broke the land, built the settlements and called the prairie their home.

Binkley, Emma N. (1868 – 1887)

Emma Binkley died at age nineteen. There is very little recorded history of Emma's life. She was the wife of Henry M. Binkley, an early pioneer in the Russellville area. Henry Binkley hauled lumber from the forests to Denver, owned a livery stable at Franktown, and hauled flour and grains from the railroad station at Parker.

There is a white sandstone marker on Emma Binkley's grave, in the north section of the cemetery.[8]

Campbell, John R. (1848 – 1941)

John Campbell arrived in the area in 1872. He operated a stage-coach station at Russellville, a stop-over along the Santa Fe Trail. He married Elizabeth Jennings in 1874. Elizabeth died a year later.

Following the founding of Frankstown by James Frank Gardner, Campbell went into partnership with Gardner, in the grocery business. He married Rosa Bella Schutz, daughter of pioneer Jacob Schutz, in 1886. The Schutz-Campbell holdings, over 5,000 acres, became one of the largest family ranches in the county.

Campbell became known as one of the best cattle judges in the state, and was instrumental in organizing the Denver Western Stock Show.

John R. Campbell is buried on the south knoll of the cemetery, in a section that includes members of the Campbell and Schutz families. John's wife, Rosa Bella Schutz Campbell, who died in 1918, is buried nearby. Her white marble tombstone includes the name of Caroline Jones. John and Rosa's children, John Jr, Dora and Bessie are also buried in this section.

Gardner, James Frank (1834 – 1904)

James F. Gardner, along with George Chilcott, drove their oxen from Omaha to Colorado Territory in 1859. They spent the summer prospecting for gold on Clear Creek. Giving up on gold, Gardner followed Cherry Creek south to the settlement at California Gulch where he worked at a sawmill. By June 1860, he became an independent operator, hauling lumber from the sawmills to Denver.

In late November 1860, Gardner took up a squatters claim four miles south of California Ranch, on Cherry Creek. As more settlers moved into the area, Gardner organized a legal settlement and called it "Franks Town." He formed a partnership with his longtime friend, George Chilcott. The two operated a shingle mill at Franks Town, hauling hewed shingles to Denver. Chilcott sold his interest to Gardner the following year, when he went on to Pueblo, where he was elected to the First Territorial Legislature, in 1861.[9]

One of the responsibilities of this first legislative body, was to divide the territory into counties, and choose a county seat for each. Gardner's old partner, Chilcott, as a member of this historical body, did not forget his friend. When Douglas County became one of the original counties, Chilcott introduced and helped pass a bill designating Frankstown as the county seat, in 1862.[10] County business was conducted at Gardner's cabin, until county buildings were erected. Fire destroyed the town on December 31, 1863. In less than a month, sawmills were once again producing lumber, and Franktown, as it came to be known, was rebuilt.

In June 1864, members of the Hungate family were found murdered by Indians in western Douglas County. Outrage seethed throughout Colorado, while fear gripped Douglas County. A stockade was built at California Ranch, with water supplied from nearby Cherry Creek. More than forty families came to the fort for protection against Indian violence. James Gardner, commander of the military force at the fort, later became the Indian agent at the Ouray Agency, serving from 1883 to 1886.

Following the Indian wars, Gardner bought the California Ranch and the surrounding 150 acres. He married Helen S. Knox in 1867. The couple turned the acreage into one of the finest farms in the county.

James Gardner continued to serve the people of Douglas County, serving in the state Legislature in the 1890s, and organized the Douglas County school system.

James Frank Gardner, the father of Franktown, is buried in the north section. There is a white marble tombstone engraved with the word "Pioneer." His wife Helen, is buried next to him, with an identical marker.

Kelty, Andrew (1867 – 1941)

An early pioneer of Franktown, Andrew Kelty helped build the town, and served the community as one of the first schoolteachers, as well as postmaster. He owned a creamery, just outside of town.

Andrew Kelty is buried in the north section. There is a red granite stone to his memory.

Metzler, August (1864 – 1896)

August Metzler and his brothers, Milton and Herman farmed near Russellville. August operated sawmills in various locations, supplying much of the lumber that built early Denver.

The Metzler brothers were favorites of the surrounding communities, often providing the music for dances and area socials.

August Metzler is buried in the north section. There is a marker.

Schutz, Jacob (1836 – 1907)

Born in Germany, Jacob and his brother, Benedict, immigrated to America as teenagers. They arrived in Colorado in 1859, where they signed on with a cattle drover to guide a herd of cattle to California. The brothers parted with the cattle drive at Russellville, where they worked in the sawmills.

Within a year, Jacob and Benedict each took squatter's claims near what would become Frankstown. Continuing to haul lumber to Denver and other surrounding settlements, the Schutz brothers built their holdings to over 2,500 acres.

Jacob added Shorthorn cattle to his homestead, which were bred and sold throughout the valley. He married Caroline Schumaker and built the first stone house in the area. Jacob was the first to success-fully grow fruit in the valley. His apple orchards were praised throughout the Pikes Peak region. Jacob became county commission-er in 1868, following the establishment of Douglas County.

One of the first pioneers to toil the soil of Douglas County, Jacob Schutz died in 1907. He is buried on the south knoll, in the section that includes the Schutz and Campbell families. There is a granite marker. His brother Benedict is buried next to him.[11]

Welty, Lawrence (1832 – 1913)

An early pioneer of Frankstown, Lawrence Welty enlisted with James Frank Gardner in Governor Evans' 100-Day Volunteers, in June 1864. Welty served in Company M of the Third Colorado Cavalry, with men from the California Ranch area. Following the bru-tal murders of the Hungate family, in western Douglas County, Indian warfare raged in the area, and swept across all of eastern Colorado during the next four years. At the close of 1864, Welty moved his wife and children into the stockade at California Ranch. In 1865, Welty, with a detail of men, left the stockade to bring a valuable herd of Shorthorn cattle back to the stockade. The men were attacked by a band of Cheyenne Indians. The men scattered. Two men arrived back at the stockade that evening. Welty hid under the brush throughout the night, making his way back the following morning. The fourth member of the party, Conrad Moschel, was found dead six days later. He had been shot in the head, an Indian arrow pierced his back, and he had been scalped. Moschel was buried at the spot.

Following his military service, Welty returned to civilian life in Franktown, where he operated a general store and shoe shop.

Lawrence Welty is buried in the north section, with an unusual granite obelisk.

Wheeler, Francis E. (1839 – 1913)

A veteran of the Civil War, Francis Wheeler served with the Union Army in Company D of the First Minnesota Infantry. He came west by covered wagon, with his wife Ella and children, in 1870. The fam-ily settled in Franktown, Douglas County. Wheeler's first occupation was sign painting, providing most of the signs for Franktown businesses. Wheeler later purchased land outside of town, where he raised horses.

A white marble military tombstone marks the grave of Francis Wheeler, in the north section. His wife, Ella, is buried next to him, with a granite stone marker.

— — —

US Highway 40 West

ARAPAHOE

ARAPAHOE CEMETERY

LOCATED ONE-QUARTER-MILE NORTHWEST OF THE TOWN OF ARAPAHOE.

The Arapahoe Cemetery District was formed in 1911. Two acres of land were purchased for thirty dollars from A.B. Kibbee. The oldest stone in the cemetery is dated 1912, that of William T. Williams. There are several infant burials and many victims of the flu epidemic of 1918.

Howard, George C. (1843 – 1923)

A veteran of the Civil War, Howard served under General Rosecrans in the Union Army. He was wounded in the Battle of Stone River, in January 1863. Howard served the remainder of the war as a clerk for General McClellan.

He married Permelia Crane in Illinois, in 1865. The couple had seven children. He brought his family to Colorado in 1906, where he had a small farm. Involved in the small community of Arapahoe, he was the leader in the formation of the First Presbyterian Church.

George and Permelia are buried toward the center of the cemetery. There is a granite marker very close to a large shrub.

CHEYENNE WELLS

FAIRVIEW CEMETERY

LOCATED ONE-HALF-MILE SOUTH OF CHEYENNE WELLS. FOLLOW COUNTY ROAD 44 TO THE CEMETERY.

Originally named Cheyenne Wells Cemetery, the land was platted and designated as a cemetery in February 1893. The land changed ownership over the next few years, finally being sold to the Cheyenne Wells Cemetery Association in 1892. The cemetery name was changed to Fairview by the county commissioners in 1952. The oldest known grave is the infant daughter of Claus Beeks, buried in 1892. There are several unmarked graves, while many graves are marked with only the funeral home metal plates.

A tall granite obelisk marks the grave of Frederick Johnston. He and his brother were swimming in a pond north of town, when Frederick suffered cramps and drowned, in 1904. He was twenty-three years old.

Neatly laid out, the cemetery includes a section reserved for the Civil War members of the Grand Army of the Republic. The oldest section of the cemetery is in the middle, just east of the office. The following pioneers are located in this section.

Beek, Claus (1846 – 1919)

Born in Germany, Claus Beck was orphaned at an early age. To avoid service in the harsh German military, he stowed away on a ship bound for America. Nineteen-year-old Claus spoke no English, but managed to work at various odd jobs on the busy streets of New York City. Later, Claus applied for citizenship. He discovered his papers had his name misspelled as "Beek." He decided to keep the name.

In 1880, Claus bought land in Iowa, where he had a small farm. He later worked for the B & M Railroad. In an arrangement similar to the mail order bride system of the time, Claus paid for passage of a young German woman to America. Othelia Opolius arrived in Iowa in 1882. The couple were married a year later. In 1883, Claus heard of additional government land opened to settlement in Colorado. He secured two separate sections of land, one south and the other east of Cheyenne Wells. He built a home for his wife and family, and raised fruits and vegetables, which he sold throughout the surrounding area.

Claus and Othelia Beek are buried in Block 1, Lot 41. There is a large, uniquely carved granite marker.

Clossen, George (1856 –1946)

Born in Iowa, his parents both died before George was a teenager. He was sent west to Texas, where he lived with an uncle. He worked on his uncle's farm, until his marriage to Maggie May Hammes in 1883. Eight children born to this marriage. George went to work for the Union Pacific Railroad, and did bridge work for several railroads, including the Rock Island.

In 1888, George moved his family to the new town of Cheyenne Wells. He homesteaded land a mile north of Arena, and continued working for the railroad. He later acquired additional land from the railroad.

In 1911, he went into partnership with Henry Van Lorn. The two purchased cattle and several head of registered Hereford bulls. This partnership ended with the deaths of the three Van Lorn brothers, who were killed in a cave-in. Clossen expanded his cattle ranch and became a major stockman in the area. He was active in local politics, running for office on two occasions.

In March 1931, he lost several head of cattle in a blizzard. Shortly thereafter, the Depression hit. He lost his ranch in 1935. He lived with the Fick family for several years.

George Clossen died in 1946, and was buried next to his wife Maggie, who proceeded him in death in 1907.

He is buried in Block 1, Lot 30. There is a marker.

Hamilton, Harvey S. (1841 – 1912)

A native of Indiana, Harvey Hamilton moved to Iowa with his parents as a child. He traveled to Kansas and on to California before settling in Cheyenne Wells in 1887. He built a wood frame house on Main Street, and later purchased the W. I. Ray & Company general store. At the same time, a young woman from Ohio came to Cheyenne Wells. Miss Maggie Woodrow built a small soddy just outside of town, and found work as a waitress at the U.P. eating house. Harvey Hamilton married Maggie Woodrow in May 1889.

When the town of Cheyenne Wells incorporated in 1890, Hamilton served on the first board. Now a wealthy man, Hamilton built a new home for his wife. It was the largest home in Cheyenne Wells. He became involved with the first bank in town, serving as president of the board of the State Bank until his death in 1912. During the Depression in the 1930s, Maggie let the home go for taxes, and moved to Florida.

Harvey Hamilton is buried in Block 1, Lot 36. There is a large gray headstone, with a lovely floral carving.

Mitchek, Charles T. (1848 – 1916)

Born Charles Thomas Mitschek, a native of Czechoslovakia, he came to America in 1872. Mitchek spoke several languages. Living in New York, he gained his citizenship in 1884, and changed his name to Mitchek. In 1886, he traveled back to his homeland, and brought his childhood sweetheart, Frances, to the states. Frances and Charles were later married in New York. The couple had two children, the first born out of wedlock.

Charles brought his family to Cheyenne Wells in 1888, where he homesteaded. he raised cattle, which he butchered and sold throughout the community. He also worked for the railroad, at the round house located at Cheyenne Wells.

Charles promoted the town, was involved in politics, and was a member of the Cattleman's Association. In later years, he was rumored to be a member of the KKK, an association active with the cattleman of eastern Colorado at the time.

His funeral service in 1916 was the largest ever held in Cheyenne Wells. Twenty automobiles drove slowly through the cemetery.

There is a small granite obelisk marking his grave, located in Block 1, Plot 32.

Homer, Herman C., M. D. (1869 – 1934)

A native of Black Hawk, Iowa, Herman Homer became a physician and worked as a surgeon for the Union Pacific Railroad for seventeen years. He brought his family to Cheyenne Wells, in 1911, where he set up a family medical practice. For many years, he was the town and county health officer, and a member of the state medical board.

During the widespread flu epidemic of 1918 – 1919, Dr. Homer treated over 160 flu patients. In a time of sickness and high panic, Dr. Homer lost only one patient, a testament to his pioneer medical knowledge.

There is a small stone marker at his gravesite, located in Block 2, Lot 82.

Wells, Willoughby (1832 – 1907)

A native of Vermont, Wells served in the Union Army during the Civil War, reaching the rank of sergeant. Remaining with the U.S. Army, he was sent west to Montana, where the army presence protected the gold seekers from the Indians. Sergeant Wells distinguished himself in several Indian fights.

In 1906, at the age of seventy-four, he made his last westward journey, settling in Cheyenne Wells. He died in April 1907.

In 1911, a group of Civil War veterans, including J. H. Thompson, E. C. Wilson, W. L. DeMunbrum, and Carl Shy, organized a local chapter of the national GAR. In honor of Wells, the branch was called the Willoughby Wells Post 11.

Civil War veteran and Colorado pioneer Willoughby Wells is buried in Block 1, Lot 34. His grave is marked by the standard military white marble tombstone.

KIT CARSON

KIT CARSON CEMETERY

LOCATED JUST NORTH OF THE TOWN OF KIT CARSON.

Situated near the junction of the old Chisholm Trail and the Kansas Pacific Railroad, this pioneer cemetery was established at the close of the nineteenth century. The original cemetery, located a mile northwest of town, is on private property, and was plowed over years ago. The new cemetery was officially deeded to the town of Kit Carson in 1916. The oldest marked tombstone is dated 1901. Several of the unmarked graves recently received stones, made by Roy Wombles. Mr. and Mrs. Cecil Brown planted evergreen trees, hauling water for years, during the 1920s, in an effort to beautify the cemetery. Today, the cemetery is a quiet, peaceful spot for many Colorado pioneers.

Henderson, Thomas (1832 – 1919)

A native of Scotland, Thomas Henderson arrived in America in 1847, at the age of fifteen. He lived in Iowa for several years before coming to Kansas, and eventually Colorado, where he homesteaded north of Kit Carson, in 1890. He soon became known as a great horseman. His livestock included wild horses he broke himself. Tommy, as he was known, prided himself in his fine horses. He never went unnoticed when he came to town, driving his shiny buggy, pulled by two jet black glossy horses.

Thomas Henderson died at the home of his son, William, in 1919. He is buried in the Kit Carson Cemetery. There is a marker.

Henderson, William H. (1868 – 1938)

The son of Thomas Henderson, William settled with his father in Colorado in 1890. His father started a horse ranch north of Kit Carson, where William herded horses and roped cattle. "Pinky" as he was known, purchased land next to the town of Kit Carson, where he operated his own ranch.[12] He added a herd of buffalo, moving them to a corral in town during the winter.

In 1906, "Pinky" Henderson became the state brand inspector for Cheyenne County, a position he held until his death. He played the violin at many of the square dances held at Kit Carson. Pinky never married. Very involved in the community, he ran for county commissioner twice, being defeated in both elections.

In an effort to preserve the history of the county, Pinky erected a marker near the cemetery, designating the junction of the old Chisholm Trail in Cheyenne County.[13]

In December 1938, William "Pinky" Henderson died of an apparent heart attack in his doctor's office. He is buried next to his father. There is a marker.

Meier, Paul (1872 – 1949)

Born in Rochester, New York, Paul Meier began his journey west at the age of fourteen. In 1887, he got a job on the "17 Ranch" on Sand Creek, southeast of Kit Carson. He eventually bought a portion of that ranch, as well as a few head of cattle. Within ten years, he added horses and built his cattle herd into one of the best in the area. Paul married Alena Rhodes of Cheyenne County, in 1897.

Paul served as county commissioner in 1896, and served on the school board.

Paul Meier is buried next to his wife, Alena. There is a marker.

Rhoades, Sarah I. (1876 – 1936)

A native of Sullivan, Indiana, Sarah came west with her parents as a child. The family settled at Elbert, Colorado, where her father had previously visited on a recruiting mission for the Army. The family later moved to Hugo, where Sarah's father practiced law and Sarah received her education.

Sarah became a teacher, a profession she would follow until her death. She married William Rhoades in 1897. They made their home in Kit Carson, where five children were born. Three sons lived to adulthood. Sarah continued her teaching career, teaching in many rural communities. An event that shook Sarah very deeply, was the murder of one of her female students in 1900. A black man was suspected of the murder and subsequently lynched.[14]

Sarah became the county superintendent of schools in 1926, serving two terms. She returned to teaching at Smoky Angle School north of Kit Carson and later at the Wild Horse School.

In her third term at Wild Horse, Sarah suddenly took ill, dying five days later, on February 12, 1936. There is a marker at the gravesite of Sarah Rhoades, in the Kit Carson Cemetery.

Weisbrod, Henry (1859 – 1942)

Born to German immigrants, Henry Weisbrod came to Colorado in the winter of 1870. At the age of fourteen, he hunted wild game for the soldier camp of Aroya, later a part of Cheyenne County.[15] He received a dollar for each antelope he shot. The carcasses were shipped east by train.

Henry filed on a homestead, and eventually increased his holdings to over 200 acres. He later married, bringing his wife Winifred, to his homestead.

A family by the name of Oswald, purchased land next to Weisbrod's land in 1909. A lawsuit was soon filed by Henry and Winifred, concerning the water rights of the irrigation ditch on Rush Creek. The situation escalated to a mini range war, with Oswald fencing off his property, denying the Weisbrod cattle access to water. The case was tried in court, with a lease option to the water rights given to the Weisbrods.

The Weisbrods later divorced, with Winifred receiving the land in the settlement. Henry Weisbrod went to live with his daughter, Josephine.

Henry Weisbrod died in 1942. His funeral, held on a cold February day, took place at the Kit Carson Methodist Church. He was laid to rest in the Kit Carson Cemetery. There is a marker.

Wild Horse

WILD HORSE CEMETERY

LOCATED ONE-HALF-MILE NORTHWEST OF THE TOWN OF WILD HORSE.

Also known as the McIntyre Cemetery, the land for the cemetery was donated by John McIntyre in 1904. The oldest tombstone is dated 1884. Daughters of pioneer Alexander Hinkley, Lydia and Fredericka are among the earliest interments. Both died of diphtheria in 1887.

Fox, Charles (1880 – 1972)

"Charlie," as he was known spent his early years working as a ranch hand in the area of Cheyenne County. In 1905, he married Alice Hinkley, daughter of pioneer Alexander Hinkley.[16] On land he and his wife homesteaded, Charlie raised cattle. He served as one of the first county commissioners.

In 1903, Charlie was among the group of men who hosted a western chuck wagon dinner for President Theodore Roosevelt.

There is a granite marker for the grave of Charles Fox.

McIntyre, John (? – 1931)

In 1876, John McIntyre arrived in Deadwood, South Dakota, where he prospected for gold. He was in Deadwood the day Wild Bill Hickok was murdered, and in Lead, South Dakota, where the first word of General Custer's death at the Little Big Horn was received.

In the fall of 1876, McIntyre traveled to Wild Horse, where he became section foreman for the new Kansas Pacific Railroad. In 1885, he started a sheep ranch with his brother, Jim. He lost half of his flock in the flood of 1905, and was forced to sell the operation. He later served as county commissioner, and formed the Cheyenne County Land Company with Judge Hedlund.

John McIntyre died in 1931 and is buried in the cemetery he founded.

HUGO

EVERGREEN CEMETERY

LOCATED NORTHWEST OF THE TOWN OF HUGO. FROM TOWN, TAKE COUNTY ROAD 31 NORTH, APPROXIMATELY ONE-QUARTER-MILE. THERE ARE TWO CEMETERIES, THE CATHOLIC CEMETERY IS ON THE LEFT. EVERGREEN CEMETERY IS ON THE RIGHT SIDE OF THE ROAD.

This small prairie cemetery began in 1885. The Old Hugo Cemetery was abandoned, with the establishment of the Evergreen Cemetery. Many graves moved to the new cemetery, however, a few remain.[17] There are several victims of the diphtheria epidemic of 1895, including many children.

The Evergreen Cemetery is well maintained and burials are recorded.

Brockway, Daniel B. (1854 – 1942)

Born and educated in Hancock, Massachusetts, Daniel Brockway married Eleanor A. McClere in 1886. The couple eventually settled in Colorado, where Brockway filed on a preemption claim. He and his brother owned a blacksmith shop for a time, near present-day Hugo.

In 1890, he filed on a homestead west of Hugo and operated a profitable sheep ranch. Later, he expanded his ranch to include cattle and horses, which were sold in the eastern markets.

Brockway was elected sheriff in 1901, succeeding John Freeman. He served as Lincoln County Sheriff from 1901 to 1910.

For many years, he served as sexton of the Evergreen Cemetery, which he helped form, and was the first president of the cemetery association in 1908.

Daniel Brockway is buried in Block 8, Row 1, Lot 8. There is a marker.

Echternacht, Carrie B. Kunkle (1872 –1940)

A native of Ohio, Carrie came west to Nebraska with her parents, in 1881. At Gibbon, Nebraska, she married William H. Echternacht, in 1892. The following year, the young couple moved to Colorado, where they would live out their lives together. They settled near Bovina and later moved to Genoa.

Mr. Echternacht is known as the founder of Genoa, having established the townsite, taking a keen interest in the growth of the community.

Carrie Echternacht, while busy with her home and six children, ran the boardinghouse adjacent to the Rock Island Railroad Depot. She became postmistress at Genoa, a capacity she held from 1903 to 1915. Active in community and school activities, she always found time to volunteer for the Evangelical church functions.

She is buried next to her husband, William, in Block 13, Row 1, Lot 5. There is a marker.

Fletcher, George L. "Kid" (1914 –1957)

Born in Missouri, George Fletcher came to Colorado with his parents, in 1922. The family settled at Hugo, where George was educated. In his youth, George developed a keen interest in riding bareback broncos. At age twenty-three, he competed nationally. In New York he won a saddle, and continued to win trophies and championships from Massachusetts to California. He won the title of World Champion Bull Rider in 1938, and All-Around Champion Cowboy in 1945. He was recognized by Ripley in his *"Believe It or Not"* feature. Ripley noted that Fletcher had broken nearly every bone in his body, yet remained active on the pro rodeo circuit for seventeen years.

George "Kid" Fletcher retired in 1954 and died in an accident near Enid, Oklahoma, in 1957.

Posthumously, Fletcher was admitted to the National Rodeo Hall of Fame. A wing of the museum in Oklahoma City is named in his honor.

He is buried next to his wife Frances. There is a marker.

Freeman, John W. (1859 – 1923)[18]

Born in Sweden, Freeman emigrated to the United States with his family, at age ten. The family lived in Illinois and Nebraska for many years. In Nebraska, in 1884, he married Hester M. Jackson, a descendant of President Andrew Jackson. In 1889, he and Hester traveled by covered wagon to Lincoln County, where they homesteaded.

Popular and active in the community and politics, he became sheriff of Lincoln County in 1897, and moved his family to the town of Hugo. He also operated a blacksmith shop in town and worked as a carpenter.

In 1900, Sheriff Freeman, while transporting a black prisoner named John Porter, accused of the rape and murder of a young white girl near Limon, was overpowered by a mob between Hugo and Limon. The mob burned Porter at the stake.[19]

In his later years, Freeman started a broom factory at Bovina and was instrumental in building the Bovina School in 1904.

He is buried in Block 11, Row 1, Lot 3. There is a marker.

Hill, William A. (1835 – 1917)

The first pioneer to settle near what is now the town of Hugo, Hill homesteaded in 1870. A native of Massachusetts, he served in the Union Army during the Civil War. He participated in several battles, receiving a life-long facial injury during a skirmish in Virginia. He achieved the rank of first lieutenant.

In July 1870, Hill opened the first business in Hugo. Through his promoting and encouragement, the town eventually grew. It is said he was the founding father of Hugo, and his original homestead is now the main business section of town.

The first cemetery at Hugo, now known as the Old Hugo Cemetery, is on land once owned by Mr. Hill. He agreed to a cemetery on his property sometime prior to 1880.

William Hill arrived in Lincoln County before the settlement of many towns, and before the railroad, believing in the area and the opportunity.

He is buried in Block 11, Row 1, Lot 9. There is a marker.

Will, David (1835 – 1891)

A native of Lochlee, Scotland, David Will emigrated to America in 1871. He spent time mining in Black Hawk, during the gold rush of 1859, and lived in New Mexico Territory for a time, before making Lincoln County his home, in 1882. He married Elizabeth Cameron in 1880. There were four children born to this union.

He homesteaded near Hugo, where he operated a cattle and sheep ranch, with over 6,000 head. Respected for his business ethics, he was quite popular in the county.

David Will died in September 1891, following an accident near Arriba, where he was thrown from his spring wagon.

Originally buried in Hugo's Old Cemetery, David Will's remains were removed to the new Evergreen Cemetery. He is buried in Block 5, Row 1, Lot 3.

— — —

US Highway 96 West

EADS

EADS CEMETERY

LOCATED APPROXIMATELY THREE-QUARTERS-MILE NORTH OF EADS, ON HIGHWAY 287.

The cemetery, well maintained by the town of Eads, began in 1887. There are several sections, including the Potter's Field. Of particular interest are the following American veterans buried in the Eads Cemetery.

Coast, Reuben A. (1842 – 1915)

Reuben Coast enlisted in the 1st Wisconsin Artillery in June 1861. He served in the Union Army during the Civil War and was mustered out as a private, in July 1865.

Dillman, Jeremiah (1840 –1913)

Dillman joined Company A of the 7th Maine Infantry in 1861. He served in the Union Army until his discharge in September 1864.

Drais, Rutherford Buchard (1876 – 1923)

A native of Ohio, Rutherford Drais enlisted in the 157th Indiana Infantry in April 1898, and served in the Spanish American War. He died in Cripple Creek, in 1923, and was buried in the Eads Cemetery.

Hickman, Byard (1841 – 1918)

Born in West Virginia, Hickman joined the Illinois Volunteers in February 1865, near the end of the Civil War. He fought for the Union cause until the war ended in April 1865.

Johnson, William C. (1846 –1930)

William Johnson enlisted with the 15th Regiment of the Ohio Infantry in March 1864. He served the Union until the close of the Civil War in 1865.

Low, Edward M. (1873 – 1924)

Edward Low was a private in the 111th Coast Artillery. He served in the Philippine Insurrection from 1901 until his discharge in 1924.

ORDWAY
VALLEY VIEW CEMETERY
LOCATED TWO MILES NORTH OF ORDWAY, ON COLORADO HIGHWAY 71.

This cemetery lies in the center of Crowley County farmland. Originally established in 1897, the cemetery was on land owned by William F. Boyd, who donated the land to the town of Ordway.

Boyd, William F. (? – 1897)
One of Ordway's earliest pioneers, William Boyd came to the area from Kansas. He filed on a homestead, and helped found the town of Ordway. He later donated a portion of his land for the cemetery, and became one of the first interments.

William Boyd was fishing on Lake Henry, northeast of Ordway, when his small boat was caught in a storm. His body was found three days later, and buried that afternoon in the new Valley View Cemetery. His tombstone is located in Section A–11, Lot 10.

Lundahl, Olaf (1869 – 1912)
Born Olaf Peterson in Sweden, Olaf came to the United States as a stowaway on a ship to avoid service in the Swedish Army. In America, he changed his name to Lundahl, so he would not be caught. Traveling through the West, Lundahl worked as a barber before settling in near Ordway in 1894. Filing on a homestead some six miles north of town, Lundahl built a small house for his wife, Josephine, where six of their eight children were born.

Lundahl cultivated large orchards, a vineyard, and potatoes, lettuce, and onions. By the turn of the century, he had built a two-story home complete with surrounding veranda, which was the showplace of the county.

In 1912, Lundahl lost his home and land in a real estate deal. Stricken with uremic poisoning, He died later that year. He is buried next to his wife, Josephine, in Section A-7, Lot 10. There is a marker.

Trainor, James (1842 – 1919)
Born in Canada, Trainor became a blacksmith, following his education. He eventually returned to his father's farm, where he improved the family holdings. In 1871, he married Catherine Jordan.

The newlyweds entered the United States in 1872, first locating in Nebraska. For the next seventeen years, Trainor operated a successful farm, and held several political offices. In 1888, Trainor moved his family further west, homesteading near Ordway. He served as postmaster, deputy sheriff, and deputy assessor. When Crowley County was created in 1911, Trainor became the first county commissioner.

James Trainor is buried next to his wife, Catherine, who preceded him in death, in 1910. The Trainor monument is located in Section A-10, Lot 6.

Weimer, Jacob (1875 – 1911)

A native of Germany, Weimer sailed aboard the ship *Olympus* to America, eventually settling in Ordway in 1906. Jacob found work in town, where he and his wife, Fredrica first lived. In October 1906, they welcomed their first child, Wesley.

Jacob homesteaded land two and one-half miles northwest of Ordway in 1907. He built a home for his family, and raised produce for sale in the growing community of Ordway.

Jacob Weimer died of typhoid fever, in 1911 at the age of thirty-six. He is buried in Section A-6, Lot 6. There is a marker.

— — —

US Highway 50 West

HOLLY

Holly Cemetery

LOCATED NORTH OF HOLLY. AT THE JUNCTION OF US HIGHWAY 50 AND STATE HIGHWAY 89, TURN NORTH ON HIGHWAY 89. TURN RIGHT AFTER CROSSING A SMALL BRIDGE. THE CEMETERY ROAD IS APPROXIMATELY THREE-QUARTERS OF A MILE LONG AND WINDS TO THE TOP OF THE HILL.

The cemetery was originally part of the homestead of R. Millinger. Holly town records reveal the incorporation date as 1903, although the cemetery was in existence prior to that date. The oldest known grave is that of William Stecher, who died in 1898.

The cemetery is well maintained and still in use. It is enclosed by an iron fence, erected in 1901.

Bryce, Anna E. (1893 – 1982)

A 1910 graduate of Holly Union High School, Anna Bryce attended the University of Boulder. She was one of the first women to graduate from the institution.

Anna returned to her hometown of Holly, where she taught for several years.[20] She maintained a challenging atmosphere for her students. She was admired and respected. The administration building in Holly, built in the 1960s was named in her honor.

A legend persists that she lost the love of her life to her sister. Anna never married. She is buried in Block 1, 1st Addition, Plot 263.

Duncan, John (1869 – 1940)

John Duncan arrived in Holly in 1896, as an engineer for the Amity Canal.

He stayed in the Amity area, going into the real estate business. He founded the firm of Lancaster-Hartman, and was involved in the community affairs and county improvements.

His cremated remains are in Block 2, 1st Addition, Plot 479.

Dupree, Edward (1885 – 1954)

Dupree married Ella May Jones Christmas Day 1908, in Balko, Oklahoma. They arrived by covered wagon in Prowers County in 1909, homesteading about twenty miles south of Holly. Ed worked for an irrigation company to make ends meet until 1932, when he farmed full time. The drought and the Great Depression of the 1930s caused him to loose almost everything he had. For the next twenty years, he carried the mail from the Plains Post Office to Holly, a distance of twenty miles. He personally informed everyone on his mail route the day World War II ended.

He is buried beside his wife Ella, in Block 1, 2nd Addition, Plot 50.

Gores, John (1837 – 1911)

A veteran of the Union Army, John Gores and his family settled near Granada in 1873. He worked for the large SS Holly Ranch as a carpenter and blacksmith. He and his family lived in one of the many red ranch hand homes, located about one-quarter-mile east of the main house.

Later, he built the only blacksmith shop in town, a brilliant idea, considering the wagon train traffic through the area. Gore's operation was considered the most profitable business in town.

He was known as the town diplomat, befriending both soldiers and Indians. He was involved in several Indian negotiations, but was unable to prevent the final wars in the early 1870s.

He is buried in Block 2, Original Section, Plot 167.

House, Elisha (1866 – 1928)

Among the first cowboys to work at the SS Holly Ranch, Elisha House proved himself as a strong and loyal hand. The youngest cowboy, he worked for several years on the ranch, earning the trust and respect of his older companions.

In 1905, when the local sugar beet factory faced violent labor opposition, it was House who was called upon by the town administration to oversee the situation. He would continue in law enforcement for the remainder of his life. He faced danger several times, including a face off with a knife-wielding opponent. House was stabbed in the chest, the blade breaking at the bone. He recovered, but the blade point remained in his chest. He later became a special agent for the Santa Fe railroad, a position he held until his death.

He is buried in Block 2, Original Section, Plot 85.

Pettee, Harry A. (1854 – 1925)

A hired cowboy for the SS Holly Ranch, Harry Pettee soon gained the reputation of a tough and spirited individual. He was promoted to foreman of the ranch in 1884. His reputation earned him the respect of the cowboys he supervised. He worked for the ranch until 1902, when he opened a meat market in the town of Holly. He moved to Denver in 1912 to take a position with the state water commission.

Pettee's sons, Ed and Hiram, both served as marshals of Holly, in the early 1900s.

He is buried in Block 1, 1st Addition, Plot 337.

Romer Family Plot

The family of Colorado Governor Roy Romer is buried in Block 1, 1st Addition.

Romer was born and raised near Holly, where his parents made their home. Roy became involved with the family business at an early age, and later cultivated agricultural enterprises in Holly, before seeking public office. He is still very much involved in the John Deere business in Holly, and Lamar.

In the family plot are Romer's grandparents, Rudolph and Mattie Romer, their son Irvine R. and wife Bessie Romer, the parents of Roy Romer, and Roy's brothers, Rodger Irvine (1937) and Robert (1933.)

Rudolph Romer started a machinery business in Holly in the early 1920s. His sons, Irvine and Rodger later joined the business, with grandson Roy eventually taking over.

Towner Bus Tragedy (March 26, 1931)

A storm was predicted the morning of March 26, 1931. Light rain fell, followed by a strong wind. Then the snow hit. About fourteen miles south of the town of Towner, the school bus arrived at the school with some twenty children. The storm was already strengthening, so the teacher asked the bus driver to return the students to their homes.

On the return trip, the storm turned in a blizzard. Suddenly, the bus driver, Carl E. Miller, could no longer see the road. The bus slid into a barrow pit and became stuck. Leaving the children in the bus, the driver set off on foot for help.

Searchers found the bus the following day. Three of the children, Mary Louise Miller, the daughter of the bus driver, Kenneth E. Johnson, and Robert Brown, were dead. The remaining children were taken to a nearby farm house where two more died–Arlo D. Untiedt, and Mary Louise Stonebaker.

The following day, the bus driver, Miller, was found frozen to death in a field a few miles from the bus. His hands, arms and legs were cut from the barbed wire fencing he followed for direction.

The tragedy brought national attention to the small community. The brick monument in the Holly Cemetery reads:

> *In Memory of those children and the bus driver of the Pleasant Hill School District No. 17 of Kiowa County, Colorado who gave their lives during the Blizzard of March 27, 1931.*
> *Mary Louise Stonebaker*
> *Kenneth E. Johnson*
> *Robert C. Brown*
> *Arlo D. Untiedt*
> *Mary Louise Miller*
> *Carl E. Miller*[21]

The Towner Tragedy plot is located in Block 2, 1st Addition, Plots 449, and 450.

OFF THE BEATEN PATH:
AMITY

LOCATED FIVE MILES WEST OF HOLLY ON HIGHWAY 50. TURN NORTH ON HIGHWAY 169 (HARTMAN HIGHWAY). THE CEMETERY IS TWO AND ONE-HALF MILES NORTH, ON THE RIGHT SIDE OF THE ROAD.

The Amity Colony was a remarkable experiment in humanity and self-preservation. A Utopian haven for the poor, it became a idealistic venture that eventually failed.

The Salvation Army was founded in England in 1865, by minister William Booth. The purpose was to provide help for the needy and impoverished. By the 1880s, farm colonies were organized and proved beneficial. The colonies spread to the United States within ten years.

One of the selected sites in the United States was a spot along the Arkansas River, in eastern Colorado, known as Amity. Booth's daughter, Emma Booth-Tucker and her husband Frederick St. George Tucker, headed the Amity project in 1898.

A model farm community was laid out with the first thirty families coming to Amity in April 1898. Each family was given ten acres of land, tools, seeds and equipment for farming. This was not charity. The loans were noted and payment was due in ten to fourteen years. The settlers built their own homes, primarily out of the stone they quarried themselves from the nearby hill, now the cemetery.

Much of the community was devastated by the flood of 1908. The bank of Amity was robbed in the same year, by Kid Wilson and Henry Starr, husband of Belle Starr. It seems the town never fully recovered from the financial setbacks of 1908. The colony slowly died, and the settlers moved on.

The tiny Amity Cemetery, also known as Mount Hope Cemetery, bares witness to a strong, yet struggling community. It lies as forlorn as the colony itself. The land was donated by stone mason, T. Frank McAbee and his wife, Julia. There are no records of those who rest here. The few headstones give us pause and lead us to wonder. Several gravestones date to 1902. Many are the victims of the horrible typhoid epidemic of that year. There are several gravestones of small children; victims of scarlet fever that ravaged through the community. Crude coffins were hastily fashioned during the weeks of continuous death.

Joe H. Hargreaves is buried here with his wife, Alice. Hargreaves was born in 1862 in England, where he married and had a son. His wife died in childbirth. Shortly after this tragedy, he came to America with his infant son. Settling in New York, he remarried, but found little work.

Hargreaves applied for the Amity Colony in Colorado in 1898. Diagnosed with tuberculosis, he was accepted to the colony within two years.

A staff captain, Hargreaves had many duties at Amity. He was in charge of the farming operations and various organizations. When the sanitarium was built, he was the supervisor.

The Amity Project began to die in 1908 and barely existed through the Depression. Yet Joe Hargreaves managed to hang on. His wife died in childbirth in 1920. Joe stayed in Amity until his death in 1934.

GRANADA

HILLSIDE CEMETERY

LOCATED ONE-HALF-MILE SOUTH OF THE TOWN OF GRANADA.

This old nostalgic cemetery is a testament to a bygone era. A wire fence and worn wooden posts border the crumbling and weathered tombstones, monuments to the rugged pioneers. Cemetery records are scarce and incomplete.

The first death in Granada occurred in 1886, a few months after the town sprang up. A team wagon crashed through a bridge railing, causing the driver to be thrown and crushed to death. There was no undertaker, or minister. The town carpenter built a pine coffin and offered to read a verse from his bible. A grave was hastily dug at the edge of the sand hills. Thus the Hillside Cemetery, was created. In the first six months of Granada's history, twelve men died on the rough and lawless streets.

Dodge, Arthur (1843 – 1937)

A native of Nova Scotia, Arthur Dodge ran away from home at age fourteen. He worked for his passage on a ship bound for Texas, where he found employment with a Texas rancher, riding herd on the Goodnight Trail into Colorado. At age twenty, he was trail boss. Three years later, Arthur moved on to the Oklahoma Indian Territory, where, in 1883, he married a Cherokee wife, Nancy Jane Punkin, who owned seventy-five mares. This was beginning of his famous XXU horse breeding ranch. Following the death of Nancy in 1893, Arthur married Ella, a widowed half Cherokee with three children. An additional five children were added to Arthur's four children and Ella's three. Because of Ella's Indian ancestry, Arthur was able to acquire a large piece of Oklahoma land and enlarged his horse ranch.

In 1898, he sold his land and moved his family and horses to the vast grassland near Granada. His horses became known throughout the area. The Dodge horses were distinguished on the open ranch by their bobbed tails.

One of the most prominent ranchers of Prowers County, Dodge was known as "Pappy." A colorful character, he did not fit the normal rancher mode. As the grass around his cattle land grew out of control, he bought some sheep to solve the problem.

In 1915, Pappy Dodge bought the Dripping Springs Ranch in the Oklahoma Panhandle, but soon lost it and the cattle in the postwar depression. He held onto his Granada holdings, one of the few able to do so during the Depression.

Pappy Dodge died in 1937. There is a marker to his memory.

Karn, Alzada Lotz (1870 – 1935)

The daughter of a wealthy farmer in Carrolton, Ohio, Alzada was diagnosed with tuberculosis as a young adult. On the advice of her doctor, she packed a trunk full of her prized possessions and boarded the Santa Fe Railroad bound for Colorado. A brave woman facing the unknown, she chose to travel alone, leaving behind her fiancé, George Karn.

Alzada settled in Granada, in 1887, where she soon found employment. Not the traditional woman of the Victorian age, Alzada went to work for the freighting company, hauling mail by horseback or wagon, some sixty miles daily, between Albany and Granada.

The outdoor activity and exercise so improved her health, she decided to make Granada her home. When she turned twenty-one, she picked out a homestead near an abundant water supply. She built a small house into the hillside, and worked the land. She later returned to the East for a visit in 1893. She and George Karn were later married in Florida, where a son Lewis was born in 1896.

Alzada brought her family to Granada in 1898. George was quite reluctant, but eventually found the climate suitable. Together, Alzada and George were able to improve their land and raise cattle. Alzada, still good with a horse, rode the range daily. The couple built a large home on their land, where two more children were born. The daughter, Mary, died in infancy, in 1903. Following the death of George in 1931, Alzada's health slowly deteriorated.

On July 12, 1935, Alzada and her youngest son, twenty-nine-year-old Leo, were returning to the ranch, when a flash flood of the Granada Creek overtook their buckboard. Both were drowned.

Alzada was buried next to her husband, along with Leo, in the Karn family plot.

Karn, George (1866 – 1931)

Born into an influential Ohio family, George Karn grew up in Carrolton, Ohio. He became engaged to Miss Alzada Lotz, but she left Ohio for a better climate.

George attended the Protestant Methodist College in Adrien, Michigan. He returned to Ohio when the family farm fell into financial trouble. He later worked in the orchards of Dade County, Florida, where he and Alzada were married. While in Florida, he entered the political arena. Early in 1897, George contracted malaria, a sickness from which he never fully recovered. His heart had suffered and his legs were permanently damaged from the infected flea bites.

In 1898, George agreed to move west to Granada and the land his wife had homesteaded some years previously. In 1899, George and Alzada took up additional land known as the Rocking 7K Ranch.

Alzada and oldest son Lewis worked the ranch, while George, due to his health, held a variety of odd jobs. He worked as a carpenter, a tax assessor and as a dray man. His greatest talent proved to be in public speaking. He was often asked to address public gatherings, lodge organizations and political fund raisers. He became a promoter and leader of Granada.

He died in 1931, and was buried in the Karn family plot at Hillside Cemetery. There is a marker.

AMACHE

AMACHE CEMETERY
LOCATED ONE MILE WEST OF GRANADA, AND ONE MILE SOUTH ON COUNTY ROAD 23.5.

A World War II Japanese internment camp, it was named for Amache Ochinee Prowers, the Indian wife of John Prowers. Following the Japanese bombing of Pearl Harbor on December 7, 1941, hysteria gripped America. Thousands of Japanese-Americans were herded to camps. Between 1942 and 1945, 7,657 Japanese-Americans were illegally imprisoned at Amache.

The first arrivals came by train in August 1942. They were provided with tools and wood to build their own furniture. The camp was enclosed with tiers of barbed wire. A school was built for the children, while the men and women worked in the fields, raising the crops for the war effort. Meals were taken in groups at the community mess hall. During the height of the war, thirty-one men from this camp volunteered to serve in the Japanese-American 442nd Regimental Combat Team. All died serving America.

Amache was abandoned in 1945.

The cemetery is the resting ground for 120 members of the Japanese-American community. In 1983, a memorial was placed at the site honoring their sacrifice.

LAMAR

RIVERSIDE CEMETERY
LOCATED EAST OF LAMAR, JUST OFF HIGHWAY 50. FOLLOW MAPLE STREET EAST FROM TOWN, THE CEMETERY IS ON THE LEFT SIDE OF THE ROAD.

> *To whom it may concern: All parties are forbidden from digging a grave or graves on my land from this date. Any violation of this notice will be prosecuted to the extent of the law.*

This notice, posted by Mrs. T.J. Burnes, appeared in the February 22, 1890 edition of the *Lamar Register*, to which the editor replied: "We have to have a cemetery."[22]

The young community of Lamar had struggled with the cemetery land issue for nearly four years. A small spot at the edge of Lamar proper was used for informal burials. By 1887, the town had grown so rapidly that the bodies were removed and the site became known as Block 13 of the platted township.

By 1895, the cemetery issue was resolved. The Riverside Cemetery was established on the northeast side of town. In March 1895, Arbor Day was spent planting cottonwood trees at the new graveyard. Old, yet majestic, the cemetery is well cared for to this day. Cemetery records are well kept, yet burials are not recorded by block and plot.

Frisbie, James H. (1857 – 1906)

Frisbie was under sheriff of Lamar, involved in the apprehension of Cherokee Bill, who led a robbing spree in Granada on Thanksgiving Day, 1902. Frisbie and Sheriff Frank Tate followed the trail from nearby Clay Creek, finding Cherokee Bill and two accomplices hiding out at the stage line south of Lamar. A gun battle erupted, injuring Tate. The outlaws escaped. With a posse, Frisbie eventually captured the outlaws some three weeks later.

In 1906, Under Sheriff Frisbie, on a routine town walk, questioned two suspicious characters in front of the Lamar Union Hotel. One of the men, Andrew Johnson, pulled a gun and fired, killing Frisbie instantly. Johnson was sentenced to death. The sentence was commuted to life in prison at the request of Mrs. Frisbie.

James H. Frisbie was laid to rest in the Riverside Cemetery. His wife, Nora, joined him in 1928.

Goodale, Charles C. (1844 – 1925)

A Union veteran of the Civil War, Charles Goodale saw three days of action before being captured by the Confederates. He spent the remainder of the war as a prisoner at Andersonville, in Georgia.

In 1878, he became part owner of a newspaper in Iowa and by 1882, he passed the bar and became a lawyer. He married Sarah Jane McManus in 1870 and arrived in Lamar in 1887. He filed a homestead at the edge of the young town, and began practicing law. He was involved in the bitter fight to divide Bent County, which resulted in Lamar becoming the county seat of the newly created Prowers County. He held the title of Land Office Receiver in 1889. He was instrumental in water and ditch developments and promoted the town of Lamar.

Hottell, Andrew J. (1852 – 1899)

Hottell came to Colorado in 1876, where he first settled in Fort Collins. He worked at the first flour mill in northern Colorado. He relocated to Lamar, following the construction of J.K. Mullen's flour mill in 1892. A cornerstone of early Lamar business, Hottell ran the mill until his untimely death in 1899.

Strain, Morton (1860 – 1913)

Born in Lawrence County, Indiana, Morton Strain grew up on his father's farm, which included a sawmill and a flour mill. It was here he got his early training in milling and farming. He left Indiana in 1881, and headed west for a better opportunity. He homesteaded at Meade County, Kansas, selling within two years and moved on to Colorado.

At Lamar, he operated an ice business in 1883. By 1889, he had invested in a coal business, alfalfa seed and other agriculture ventures. Already a wealthy man, he bought the Lamar Union Hotel in 1898, which became one of the best hotels in all of southern Colorado.

Strain was responsible for building the first electric light plant and Lamar's first telephone system. Many of the brick buildings in the Lamar business section are attributed to Strain's business acumen. In 1900, he organized the Lamar State Bank, became the town alder, and expanded his real estate ventures. He served the town of Lamar for several years as councilman and two terms as mayor.

FAIRMOUNT CEMETERY

LOCATED AT THE SOUTHERN EDGE OF LAMAR. FROM MAIN STREET, GO SOUTH TO COLLEGE ROAD. TURN EAST ON MEMORIAL DRIVE. FOLLOW MEMORIAL DRIVE SOUTH TO THE CEMETERY ON THE EAST SIDE OF THE ROAD.

Doughty, James K. (1853 – 1927)

A native of Cincinnati, Ohio, Doughty earned his law degree in Larned, Kansas, where he also married Minnie Brott. He brought his family to Colorado, where he settled in Lamar in 1886.

An early prominent resident, Doughty was elected in the first town election in November 1886 to serve as the first city attorney and clerk. He became county judge in 1889, following the creation of Prowers County. He had a long career in Lamar politics, while remaining socially active in church and community affairs.

James Doughty is buried with his wife Minnie, who died in 1946. There is a marker in Row 18, Plot 3.

Markham, Lincoln Wirt (1861 – 1929)

An early pioneer of Lamar, Lincoln Markham first homesteaded near the town of Wiley. By 1893, he had proved up on the land, selling it at a profit. He then moved to Lamar.

Markham operated the Lamar Union Hotel, a partnership he formed with Morton Strain in 1898. Involved in the early development of Lamar, and active in many community projects, he was well respected in the community.

He is buried in Plot 3. There is a marker.

Maxwell, Charles (1864 – 1938)

Orphaned as a teen, Charles Maxwell left his native Tennessee seeking adventure in the West. He arrived in Golden, Colorado in 1872, where he became a barber. He married Mary F. Hayes in 1889.

He worked at J.K. Mullen's mill in Lamar in 1889, following the death of manager Andrew Hottell.[23]

Maxwell increased productivity and profit at the Lamar flour mill. He furthered his interests by purchasing land and becoming involved in local affairs.

One of Lamar's most prominent businessmen, he owned the Maxwell Implement Company, Maxwell Furniture, and the Maxwell Investment Company. He bought the Ben-Mar Hotel, which was demolished and built the Maxwell House Hotel, still standing today.

He organized and was president of the Valley State Bank in 1920, housed in his hotel.

In 1920, taxpayers defeated a ballot to finance the building of a hospital. Charlie Maxwell stated to the press he would build the hospital himself. The Maxwell Hospital had forty rooms.[24]

He also served Lamar mayor for twelve years, and headed the Prowers County Fair for fifteen years.

There is a marker in Plot 1.

McMillin, Marsena (1863 – 1931)

The McMillin Ranch, established in 1878, is the oldest ranch in Prowers County, still operated by the McMillin family. The ranch is located near the town of Granada.

Marsena McMillin was sixteen when his family moved from Pennsylvania to Colorado.

Working on the family ranch, Marsena filed a preemption claim and added to the ranch holdings. He added two tree claims to the property, being one of only four in Prowers County able to make such a claim profitable, as it was a "pay per acre" agreement. He operated the ranch successfully following the death of his father, James.

Through Marsena's work and dedication, the ranch became one of the most successful in the county and survived the Great Depression, when many rural farms and ranches collapsed.

In his later years, he became heavily involved in community and social affairs. His name is often linked with the annual rodeo, being a great promoter as well as participating in roping and riding events.

He is buried with his wife Margarita, in Row 5, Plot 5.

Simpson, John A. (1875 – 1928)

The son of pioneer homesteaders Colin and Catherine Munro Simpson, the family came to America from England in 1872. John grew up on the family homestead a few miles northeast of Coolidge, Kansas, just east of the Colorado state line. He later married Alma Walker of Granada, Colorado, where he made his home and raised his family.

While working a small homestead, John also worked as a ranchhand for the famous Holly SS Ranch, operated the Apex Bar in Granada, and was sheriff of Prowers County.

As sheriff, Simpson roamed the county on horseback. In the twentieth century, he tracked criminals by automobile. In 1908, the State Bank of Amity was robbed by Kid Wilson and the notorious Henry Starr. A posse was formed, but the two escaped. Simpson followed the trail of the outlaw Starr for a year, finally apprehending him in Arizona. Simpson brought him back to Lamar, where Starr was tried and convicted of robbery.

John Simpson is buried in Row 20, Plot 3.

OFF THE BEATEN PATH:
SAND CREEK BATTLE SITE (NOVEMBER 29, 1864)

ONE OF COLORADO'S BLOODIEST BATTLES, THE SAND CREEK MEMORIAL SITE IS APPROXIMATELY FORTY MILES NORTH OF LAMAR, ON THE BIG SANDY CREEK. FROM LAMAR, TAKE COUNTY ROAD 49 NORTH TO ROAD T, CROSSING THE SAND CREEK. THERE IS A SIGN POINTING TO THE SAND CREEK MASSACRE SITE.[25]

The Indian War of 1864 escalated after the Hungate family was murdered by Indians earlier that spring.[26] Territory citizens demanded protection and revenge.

On November 29, 1864, Colonel John M. Chivington deployed his Colorado Volunteers at Sand Creek.[27] The purpose was to kill as many Indians as possible. The result was a bloody massacre, led by citizens and troops, yet "unofficially" sanctioned by the government, according to records. The controversy concerning the event continues today, and probably will never be resolved.

Chief Black Kettle, in an effort to keep his people out of trouble, made winter camp at Sand Creek, along the stream's westward bend with the Big Sandy, north of present day Lamar.

On November 29 the camp was shrouded in fog when the soldiers attacked. Although the troops claimed a major victory against the hostile Indian warriors, the truth of the horrifying incident was soon known. It was a peaceful camp of about six hundred people, the majority of whom were elderly men, women and children. Counts vary, but it is safe to say at least 150 Native Americans died on that fateful day. Two-thirds of them were women and children. The bodies were mutilated, scalped and burned in a most brutal manner. The dead lay for days before burial.

The massacre at Sand Creek, more than any other Indian conflict, set the stage for the bloody conflict on the American Plains, which lasted for years. In history, it would remain to the Indians the most decisive symbol of white-man betrayal.

The memorial at Sand Creek briefly tells the story of this American atrocity.

FORT LYON NATIONAL VETERAN CEMETERY
LOCATED SIX MILES EAST OF LAS ANIMAS, ON THE SOUTH SIDE OF HIGHWAY 50. THE SIGN DIRECTS YOU SOUTH ON COLORADO HIGHWAY 183, COLORADO'S SHORTEST HIGHWAY, (ONE MILE.)

The original fort, named Fort Wise, was located forty miles west of Lamar. The fort was renamed Fort Lyon in 1862.[28]

The Colorado Volunteers were stationed at Fort Lyon during the Battle of Glorietta Pass, the only Civil War battle fought in the American West. In 1864, Colonel John M. Chivington used Fort Lyon during his infamous attack of Sand Creek. Buffalo Bill Cody was chief scout under General Sheridan at the fort in 1869.[29]

Heavy flooding of the Arkansas River in 1867, caused Fort Lyon to be moved twenty miles upstream, just below the mouth of the Purgatoire River. The new location was the site of William Bent's second fort, purchased by the government. The new vantage point provided protection for the travelers on the Santa Fe Trail. A detachment of soldiers was sent there in 1876. The soldiers spent two weeks in the rain and mud, removing the bodies of the dead soldiers buried in the fort's cemetery near Graveyard Creek. The bodies were hauled by wagon to Fort Leavenworth for reburial.

The cemetery is located on the northern edge of the military post. Officially designated in 1914, there are earlier burials. Enclosed by a

Steve Bollig

Entrance to the historic Fort Lyon Cemetery.

beautiful wrought iron fence, the entrance is graced with tall natural stone posts, and an impressive iron gate. It is well maintained and landscaped. The various sections contain the graves of soldiers from the Civil War, Spanish American War, World Wars I and II, and the Korean War. The newest section is located along the fence toward the entrance. The eastern edge of the cemetery contains a small section of civilian graves, including several women and children. Many were the victims of the flu epidemic of 1918. Civilian burials were discontinued in 1930. The fort's cemetery was given national historic status following World War II and designated Fort Lyon National Cemetery.

The memorial flag, located in the center of the cemetery is flanked with bronze plaques commemorating the interred soldiers and their dedication to our country.

On fames camping ground
Their silent tents are spread and
Glory guards with solemn Round the Bivouac of the dead.

It was here that famed scout and mountain man, Kit Carson died at the Fort Lyon Hospital in 1868. Born in 1809, Christopher (Kit) Carson moved with his parents from Kentucky to Missouri, where he grew up.

In 1826, he joined a group of hunters en route to Santa Fe, New Mexico. He learned the Spanish language which would later serve him well in his career. By 1832, he had located to the Colorado Territory, where he worked as a hunter for William Bent. His reputation as an Indian fighter and scout so impressed John C. Fremont, that he was hired as a guide on Fremont's famous government expeditions in 1842, 1843, and 1844. The two became life-long friends.

In 1843, Carson married fifteen-year-old Josepha Jaramillo at Taos, New Mexico, where he started a ranch and a family, before Fremont reenlisted him in the California expedition of 1846. It was Carson who reported the findings of the expedition to the government in Washington in 1847.

In 1854, he became the Indian agent at Taos, New Mexico, having settled the Indian uprising of 1850. During the Civil War, he served the federal government in New Mexico, Colorado and Texas, primarily calming the Indians. He was commander of Fort Union in New Mexico in 1864. He became Brevet Brigadier General in 1865, and commanded Fort Garland, Colorado Territory, during 1865 and 1866.

In late 1867, Kit brought his pregnant wife, Josepha, and his six children to Boggsville, south of Las Animas. The Carson family lived in a small dwelling on the property of his good friend, John Prowers.

Josepha died following childbirth in April 1868. She was buried in the "Gardens" of the Prowers estate. Two weeks later, Kit, in ill health, was taken to the hospital as Fort Lyon. Under the care of friend and Doctor H. W. Tilton, he was treated for complications suffered during his winter trip to Washington D.C.

Christopher "Kit" Carson died at Fort Lyon on May 23, 1868 of a ruptured aneurysm near his heart. His body was laid to rest next to his wife at the Prowers estate in Boggsville. Thomas Boggs, a dear friend of Kit's was executor of the will. According to his wishes, both Kit and Josepha were reinterred in Taos, New Mexico. Thomas Boggs, and his wife, a niece of Carson's, raised the Carson children as their own, while the oldest son attended Notre Dame University, paid for by Civil War General William Tecumsah Sherman.

A true American legend, Kit Carson was a rare combination of courage, nobility and pride. A frontiersman with a keen instinct for land and development, he forged the American frontier for progress, and searched for peace with the Native American.

The building where Kit Carson died at Fort Lyon has been restored as the Kit Carson Memorial Chapel. It is listed on the National Register of Historic buildings along the Santa Fe Trail. It is built of thick native stone and contains many stained glass windows. Through its restoration, it is a finer building than the original. It is a remarkable tribute to the great pioneer who served our country.

From a memorial plaque at Fort Lyon
National Cemetery:

Your own proud Land's Heroic Sisters
Must be your fitter grave,
She claims from was
His richest soil
The ashes of the brave

LAS ANIMAS

LAS ANIMAS CEMETERY

LOCATED SOUTH OF HIGHWAY 50. TURN OFF
THE HIGHWAY, SOUTH ONTO COUNTY ROAD
10.1. GO SOUTH APPROXIMATELY ONE MILE.
THE CEMETERY IS JUST OFF THE NEXT DIRT
ROAD, ON THE EAST SIDE. THERE ARE SEVERAL TREES, AND A TALL WATER
TANK NEAR THE CEMETERY.

Author's collection
William Bent

Bent, William (1809 – 1869)

Of French Canadian descent, and a fur trapper by trade, William Bent came west in the 1820s. He opened the territory's first trading post on the Arkansas River, fourteen miles west of present day Las Animas, along with his partners, brother Charles and Ceran St. Vrain. Bent's Old Fort was constructed in early 1826. Famous traders and scouts such as Kit Carson, Jim Bridger, Charles Autobees, Jim Baker, and Cheyenne Chief Black Kettle, all passed through this historic post. Following the Mexican War, the government offered to buy the fort. When negotiations broke down in 1849, William Bent blew up the fort. Bent built a second fort of adobe, downstream on the Arkansas River, along the Santa Fe Trail, in the Big Timbers area.

The new fort, built in 1853, was originally called Fort William. Still standing, it is now known as Fort Lyon.[30] Despite ever-present Indian opposition, the fort was a major supply service for the trappers, and Mexican trade, along the Santa Fe Trail.[31] Bent operated his fort for some seventeen years.

A friend to the Indians, Bent married Owl Woman, daughter of Indian Chief Gray Thunder. Upon her death, he married her sister, Yellow Woman, as was the Indian custom. Bent encouraged rival tribes to make peace and work together for peace with the white man. However, his son George, visiting his Cheyenne mother's people at Sand Creek, became an innocent bystander to the slaughter at that site in 1864.[32]

Denver Public Library
John Powers

Denver Public Library
Amache Powers

George Bent, wounded in the battle, recovered at the Fort Lyon hospital, where is father William watched over him. George later returned to the Cheyenne people, and fought furiously against the white man, participating in raids and causing terror across the Eastern Plains. William disowned his son who later attempted to murder his father.[33]

Bent continued to negotiate for peace between the white man and the Indian, testifying before congressmen assembled at Fort Lyon in August 1865, against the actions of Colonel Chivington at the Sand Creek Battle.

William Bent died of pneumonia in 1869 and was buried in the Las Animas Cemetery. In the southern portion of the cemetery is a large monument marking his grave.

Faber, Charlie (? – 1876)

A deputy sheriff of Las Animas, Faber was called to the Olympic Hall on a disturbance involving famed gunslinger Clay Allison and his brother John. Faber asked for the Allison's guns. Gunfire rang out. Faber countered by shooting John Allison. An enraged Clay Allison shot Faber, ripping a hole through his chest. He died instantly. No witnesses were willing to testify, and Allison was cleared of all charges.

Prowers, John (1839 – 1884)

Southern Colorado's most prominent rancher, John Prowers was the first to winter his cattle in the Arkansas Valley and became a leader in cattle breeding. He left his home in Westport, Missouri at age eighteen. Uneducated, he worked for an Indian agent along the Santa Fe Trail. He arrived in the Colorado Territory in 1856, where he went to work for William Bent at his fort. For the next seven years, he freighted for Bent, making some twenty trips along the Santa Fe Trail.

He later worked for the influential landowner, Thomas Boggs, where he introduced several farming innovations. By 1861, he had his own land. He was the first in Colorado to bring Hereford cattle to his land and crossbreed the stock. His beef was considered the best in Colorado. He furnished beef for the Army at Fort Wise and elsewhere.

Prowers spoke several Indian languages and was often in demand as an interpreter. In 1861, he married a fifteen-year-old Indian princess, Amache. She was the daughter of Chief One Eye, who lived on the Sand Creek. During the massacre at Sand Creek, Prowers was held under guard by the Army, to avoid any possible warning to the Indians. Hundreds of Indians were killed, including Amache's father, Chief One Eye.[34] Prowers protested against the murders and testified against the Army in Washington.

The Indians were given land in reparation, but were nomads and sold the land to their good friend, Prowers. He became the largest landowner in the Big Timbers of southern Colorado, with nearly 50,000 head of cattle.

In 1868, he built a large ranch house for his wife and family, near Boggsville, the small settlement started by his friend Thomas Boggs and the home of retired frontiersman, Kit Carson. The large two-story adobe home served as a hotel, post office, school and county office. The beautiful gardens in 1868 became the initial burial site of Carson and his wife.[35]

When the Kansas Pacific Railroad built a few miles north of Boggsville, Prowers moved to the new site of Las Animas in 1873. He established a freight station near the railroad. He operated a large retail store and organized the Bent County Bank in 1875. He represented Bent County in the 1873 Territorial Legislature and was elected to the General Assembly in 1876.

John's wife, Amache Prowers, stands out as one of our unique pioneers. Born into an American Indian lifestyle, she graced both cultures. Active in community service, church affiliations and the local school, she also maintained Indian customs in her home.

The marriage and life of John and Amache Prowers involved personal tragedy, hard work, and personel triumph over both land and culture. In the end, their lives shaped southern Colorado values.

They are buried together with a granite monument to their memory.

LA JUNTA

FAIRVIEW CEMETERY

LOCATED ON THE NORTHERN EDGE OF TOWN. THE CEMETERY SITS ON A HILL VISIBLE JUST OFF HIGHWAY 50, ON THE SOUTH SIDE OF THE ROAD.

This beautiful cemetery, landscaped with lush green lawn, foliage, flowers, and large shade trees, sits high on a hill overlooking the city to the south. The busy highway to the north is the only flaw in this resting spot of Colorado pioneers.

The first cemetery was hastily established in 1876, across from the main road in town, part of the historic Santa Fe Trail. Today, the area is known as Cemetery Hill on Kansas Street. The few known bodies were moved to Fairview Cemetery by 1890.[36]

Chambers, John B. (? – 1876)

His death created La Junta's first cemetery. John Chambers was a fiddler player at the Bronco Dance Hall. It is said he died on the floor of the hall, the result of consumption.

He was buried without ceremony across the road from the dance hall, in an empty lot. His body was later removed to Fairview Cemetery, where a marble stone was erected by the city in 1931, designating his grave as the first burial in La Junta.

May, John (1836 – 1886)

A German immigrant, John May served in the Sixth U.S. Cavalry. Achieving the rank of sergeant colonel, he fought with Company L in the Indian Wars. In August 1870, he was awarded the Medal of Honor, for battles he fought in Texas.

The standard white marble military headstone replaced the original marker years ago.

Shay, Tim (? – 1876)[37]
Harrington, George (? – 1876)

Tim Shay was a gambler from Dodge City, arriving in La Junta in early 1876. One evening during a poker game, he stole a stack of chips from another player. An argument ensued, and Shay was thrown out of the saloon. The following day, Shay went gunning for his accuser. Rufe Edwards shot Shay, and he died instantly. Shay became the first murder victim in La Junta.

These facts are undisputed in history, however his actual burial site is somewhat mysterious.

A grave was dug for Shay, next to Chambers' grave in the new cemetery. However, a woman claimed the body before burial, taking the body with her.

While the location of Shay's remains is unknown, his grave does not lie empty. A few weeks after Shay's murder, another murder occurred.

George Harrington, a bartender at Patterson's Saloon, refused a drink to a minor. The boy shot him in cold blood. Harrington was buried in the grave dug for Tim Shay.

His grave is unmarked.

Rocky Ford High School history class
Abraham Hamm grave

ROCKY FORD

VALLEY VIEW CEMETERY

LOCATED SOUTHEAST OF THE TOWN OF ROCKY FORD. FROM HIGHWAY 50, TURN SOUTH ON MAIN STREET AT THE ONLY STOP LIGHT. TURN EAST ON WASHINGTON AVENUE (WASHINGTON AVE. TURNS INTO HOPKINS AVENUE). FOLLOW THIS TO 17TH STREET. TURN SOUTH. THE CEMETERY IS ONE-HALF-MILE DOWN THE ROAD.

Rocky Ford's first cemetery was near the Arkansas River, the result of a tragic death. In 1877, Ben Vroman was taking his neighbor's twelve-year-old daughter to school on horseback, when a thunder storm developed. A bolt of lightening struck, killing the two instantly. They were buried near the new Liberty School. For the next ten years, families often buried their loved ones at this tiny cemetery.

In 1887, the town commissioners voted to build a new cemetery. The land was purchased from Carl Ustick, and joined the original site. The Hillcrest Cemetery is located at the main gate, while the Valley View addition is east of the flag pole.

There are over 150 unmarked graves in the cemetery. There are several victims of the 1918 influenza epidemic. While the oldest tombstone is dated 1877, there is also a Civil War veteran who died in 1946. He was 102 years old.

There are several sections, including many fraternal orders, as well as the Potter's Field, used for county burials. Today, the Valley View Cemetery is still used by the community. It is well maintained

Denver Public Library
George Swink
His melons put Rocky Ford on the map.

and managed by the city. Records are documented by the name of the purchaser, rather than burial name.

Frazier, Enoch M. (1868 – 1941)

A native of Missouri, Enoch Frazier was a trapper and trader. He came west in 1888, trading furs with the Indians. In Oklahoma, he fell in love with a Cherokee Indian maiden named Ruth. Eventually, Enoch was adopted into the tribe and allowed to marry Ruth. The couple lived on the Oklahoma reservation for several years, where all six of their children were born in a tepee.

Enoch brought his family to Colorado for health reasons. He was told the cool climate of the area would be good for his oldest son's tuberculosis. He homesteaded land near Rocky Ford, where he raised corn, onions, and later the famous Rocky Ford melons.

Enoch Frazier is buried next to his wife, Ruth, in Block 2, Lot 27. There is a marker.

Hamm, Abraham (1844 – 1901)

Abraham and his wife Sarah, came to Rocky Ford with their eight children in 1905. Abraham, a stone carver, cut several of the tombstones in the Valley View Cemetery. He worked at a sawmill, and later at the brickyard.

The Hamm family plot is one of the most impressive in the cemetery. Abraham and Sarah are buried together, among several of their children and their families.

Lance, Henry W. (1864 – 1944)

Henry operated a dry goods store in partnership with his neighbor, Joseph Price. The building, located at 304 Main Street burned in 1898. Following the fire, Lance became postmaster for Rocky Ford, a position he held for nine years. In 1914, he opened a second dry goods store, called the Rocky Ford Trading Company, which he operated for several years, prior to his death in 1944.

Henry Lance is buried next to his wife, Addie, in Block 8A, Plot 20. There is a flat marker.

Pollock, Robert M.
(1858 – 1921)

A doctor and pharmacist, he was an early pioneer in Rocky Ford. He was instrumental in establishing the first hospital, and served as mayor from 1903 to 1909.

Rocky Ford High School
George Swink's grave.

He is buried next to his wife, Jane, in Block BA, Plot 21.

Potter, James W. (1833 – 1900)

One of the earliest pioneers of Rocky Ford, James Potter homesteaded just northeast of the town in 1870. With help from his three grown sons, he built a fine ranch, known throughout the county. His daughter, and his wife, Eliza, served the young community in various organizations.

Potter was a freighter by trade, having carried merchandise by oxen to the Rocky Mountains. He later expanded as far as Ogden City, Utah, and Santa Fe, New Mexico, hauling freight for the railroad. When the railroad was completed, Potter retired from freighting, and turned to the cattle business at Rocky Ford.

His death in 1900, caused the entire town of Rocky Ford to suspend business. His funeral was the largest in the town's history to that date. The procession through town and to the cemetery, was lined with county dignitaries, paying their respects. Masonic services were held during the burial.

He is buried in Block 2, Lot 44 of the adjoining Hill Crest Cemetery. There is a marker.

Swink, George W. (1836 – 1910)

Born near Hardenburg, Kentucky, George Swink moved to Illinois with his family, at the age of four. Working on the family farm, he had limited education. He married at the age of twenty, and rented his first home for his bride.

Following the Santa Fe Trail, he ventured west in 1871, eventually settling in the Arkansas Valley. He filed for the first timber claim in the state, near present day Rocky Ford.[38] He sent for his family, after he built a home on his land.

In 1876, he purchased the old Russell General Store at the trading post. He later moved the store near the railroad, where business was good. With the arrival of the railroad, Swink envisioned a growing community. He and Levi Beghtol, laid out the new town of Rocky Ford, where he became mayor, and postmaster, in 1887. A leading businessman, he invested in many of the town's growing businesses.

Intrigued with the rich soil in the area, Swink devised a unique method of irrigation. He collected rainwater in barrels and pulled the bung, or plug, when the water was needed. With this invention, he planted melon seeds, the results of which are now Colorado pride and legend. Jubilant over his agricultural triumph, he put a hundred melons aboard a passenger train passing through Rocky Ford. Word-of-mouth was the best advertising for his delicious melons. By 1881, he was shipping up to 400 tons of melons in a single season.

Known as the "Father of the Melon," and the "Father of Rocky Ford," Swink became the first mayor, serving two terms. With his melon industry, primarily the cantaloupe, Swink single-handedly put Rocky Ford in the national limelight. Rocky Ford melons are shipped all over the United States. Annual melon festivals are a tradition today, as they were 100 years ago.

Swink furthered the interest of Colorado agriculture when he was elected to the Senate in 1893, serving several terms. One of his greatest accomplishments as a Senator, was the bill to test soil in eastern Colorado. The results of the testing, brought the sugar beet industry to Colorado.

George W. Swink, credited with one of Colorado's finest agricultural industries, died in 1910. His funeral was a grand one, as all of eastern Colorado mourned his loss.

He is buried in Block 12, Lot 24 of the adjoining Hill Crest Cemetery. There is a marker.

FOWLER

FOWLER CEMETERY

LOCATED ON HIGHWAY 50, ONE-HALF-MILE EAST OF TOWN, JUST NORTH OF THE RAILROAD TRACK. THE CEMETERY IS VISIBLE FROM THE HIGHWAY.

The cemetery wasn't established until 1897, several years after the founding of Fowler. The Cemetery Association, with Henry M. Fosdick as president, purchased several acres north of the Atchison, Topeka & Santa Fe railroad track. Prior to its establishment, residents buried their loved ones at Rocky Ford to the east, or the Nepesta Cemetery, to the west of Fowler. After the cemetery was opened, many burials from the Nepesta Cemetery were reinterred here. The oldest burial is dated 1869, obviously, a reinterment. The town of Fowler has owned the property since 1920.

The cemetery, unusually close to the railroad tracks, is laid out in neat rows, and well sectioned. Few trees grace the area, however it is well maintained with flowers, shrubs, grass and irrigation.

Burbridge, Albert J. (1840 – 1920)

A native of Wisconsin, Albert James Burbridge joined the Union Army in 1861. He served in Company A5 of the Wisconsin Infantry, and was present at the battles of Williamsburg, Antietam, and Fredericksburg. At the battle of Rappahanock, on November 7, 1863, he was wounded and soon mustered out of service. He came to the Colorado Territory sometime thereafter, homesteading south of present-day Fowler.

He is buried in the southwest corner of the cemetery, with a government issue military stone.

Fosdick, Henry M. (1849 – 1927)

One of the earliest of eastern Colorado's pioneers, Henry Fosdick arrived in the Colorado Territory in 1861. He acquired land near present day Fowler, where he slowly put together a cattle ranch that would eventually become one of the largest in Bent County.[39] Following the arrival of the railroad, the first post office for the area was located on his ranch.

When the town of Fowler was planned, Fosdick donated a portion of his land for the site. Known as the "Founding father" of Fowler, Fosdick became the first justice of the peace, and later served as county commissioner.

He is buried in the Original Section, in Block 6, Lot 3. There is a marker.

Murphy, Lodessa Ellen Evans (1871 – 1962)

As a child, Lodessa Evans, came west with her parents in a covered wagon. As a young woman, she married a man named Murphy, who died early in their marriage. She came to Colorado, again by covered wagon, with her parents and brothers, in 1892. Her parents died during the journey.

"Dessie" as she was known, along with her brothers, Elijah and Thomas, decided to build a home of natural rock by the side of the trail they were traveling. Dessie spent the rest of her life making a home for her brothers, and became active in the new community that eventually grew, called Fowler. The rock house still stands today.

Colorado Historical Society
Charles Autobees
Fur trapper and Indian fighter.

Lodessa Evans Murphy is buried in the Original Section, in Block 7, Lot 28. There is a marker.

NEPESTA

NEPESTA CEMETERY

LOCATED FIVE MILES WEST OF FOWLER, JUST OFF HIGHWAY 50. THE CEMETERY IS ON THE SOUTH SIDE OF THE HIGHWAY, ON A SMALL HILL, NEAR MILE MARKER 344, AND CAN BE SEEN FROM THE HIGHWAY.

This tiny prairie cemetery is all that remains of the long-ago stage stop of Nepesta. Years of neglect show in the broken tombstones, weathered wooden markers, and broken fencing. The new wrought iron fence was a gift of Mr. Byron Griffy, in 1996. The oldest known burials date to 1879, that of the Erdman children, however, the area was settled years earlier, and doubtless has older unmarked graves.

There are five family plots, one is particularly sad. The rectangular-shaped marble headstone with the name Erdman, marks the gravesite of Charles and Christina's six young children. Tragically, all six died from diphtheria, in March 1879. The victims were Charles age fourteen, Theodor age twelve, Albert age nine, six-year-old Flora, four-year-old Ellen, and nine-month-old Minna. History does not record what became of the heartbroken parents.

Moore, Jack S. (1835 – 1927)

John "Jackie" Steuben Moore came west for the adventure, early in 1860. He found it with the famed Pony Express. He rode from St. Joseph, Missouri, and stayed with the Pony Express during it's short history. He later settled in the Arkansas Valley area of Colorado. It is said he was the first white settler in this area. He drove a stage and ran a small cattle ranch, located a mile north of Fowler. He remained in the area until his death, in 1927, at age ninety-two.

He is buried in an unmarked grave.

Poteet, William M. (1844 – 1933)

William Poteet came to the settlement of Nepesta with the railroad, where he worked as a pumping station attendant. He homesteaded land near the site of Nepesta, which is still in the family. His memoirs recall many early-day encounters with the Indians.

He is buried with his wife, Fannie Ann. There is a marker.

True, A.E. "Kip" (1844 – 1940)

A veteran of the Civil War, and one of the first pioneers of the Nepesta area, A.E. True arrived ahead of the railroad, in 1872. He homesteaded land near the "Rio Nepesta" River.[40] He married Eliza C. Aldred in 1880.

Indians were a common sight along the river bottom, and were often camped on True's land. True stated in his memoirs, he once witnessed an Indian scalp dance, watching from a treetop.[41]

He and his wife, Eliza are buried together. There is a marker.

AVONDALE

ST. VRAIN CEMETERY

LOCATED SOUTHEAST OF HIGHWAY 50. FROM AVONDALE BLVD., THE CEMETERY IS THREE MILES EAST, JUST OFF 56TH LANE, A DIRT ROAD.

Autobees, Charles (1812 – 1882)

A fur trapper and mountain man, Charles Autobees fought under Ceran St. Vrain during the Mexican uprising of 1847. In 1853 Autobees started a small settlement at the confluence of the Arkansas and Huerfano Rivers, just east of present day Pueblo. There, he and his wife Sycamore, built a trading post. Guests included Kit Carson, John C. Fremont, and Autobees' famous step-brother, Tom Tobin.[42]

Autobees fought and eventually made peace with the Indians of the area. He is largely responsible for the agricultural development of southern Colorado.

He died in 1882 and was buried in the St. Vrain Cemetery, later washed away by floods. There is a monument at the north end of the cemetery, although his actual burial site is unknown. Several descendants are also buried there.

CHICO CEMETERY

THIS OLD PIONEER CEMETERY IS LOCATED EAST OF PUEBLO'S AIRPORT. FOLLOW HIGHWAY 50 WEST TOWARD PUEBLO. APPROXIMATELY EIGHT MILES EAST OF PUEBLO, TURN NORTH ON CHICO ROAD. THE CEMETERY IS LESS THAN A HALF-MILE DOWN THE CHICO ROAD. THE CEMETERY GATE CAN BE SEEN FROM THE HIGHWAY.

The cemetery is enclosed by a chain link fence and is well maintained in its natural prairie setting. Two gates greet the visitor, both at the southern edge of the property. A map of the cemetery grounds, including burial names, is displayed in a metal pedestal near the gate.

The oldest known burials date to the 1860s, making this one of the oldest cemeteries in Pueblo County.

Among those buried in this pioneer cemetery are the Johnson brothers. The two men arrived in Pueblo County in 1881. Both were veterans of the Civil War. Alfred fought for the Union, Isaac fought for the Confederacy. They rest side-by-side.

Family plots include the names of Nesslages, Yarberrys, and Calhouns. There are several children buried here, including the Middlecamp child, who was run over by a wagon. The Young family plot includes three infants, Rosa, Susan and Willis. Their father, Willis H. M. Young, died in 1898, the year his son was born.

The pioneers of Chico rest in a lonely spot, while the Wet Mountains in the distance provide a natural comfort.

— — —

North / South Highways
Interstate Highway I-25 South

CASTLE ROCK

CEDAR HILL CEMETERY

LOCATED ONE-HALF-MILE WEST OF TOWN. FROM THE I-25 EXIT, GO WEST ON WOLFENSBURGER ROAD, PASSING THE FAST FOOD RESTAURANTS. THE CEMETERY IS ON THE LEFT SIDE OF THE ROAD.

This picturesque resting spot, nestled against the foothills, began in 1875. There are several older graves throughout the cemetery. The section known as Potter's Field, located in the southeast portion, is marked with metal plates, indicating the various unnamed graves. The cemetery was fenced and stone pillars were added in 1883. The original gate was at the south end. By 1899, the Castle Rock Cemetery Association had formed and received donations to dig a well, add a windmill and build a new gate at the north end.

The newest addition to the grounds is a beautiful memorial to all veterans. Dedicated in 1992, the black polished granite four-part monument is engraved with the names of all interred veterans. Located at the west edge of the grounds, the impressive structure shouldn't be missed.

Briscoe, Cole (1849 – 1937)

Born in Illinois, Cole migrated west, settling in Colorado Territory. He eventually located on land south of present-day Castle Rock, where he started a ranch, producing some of the finest stock in the area. He entered politics in the 1880s. As a member of the House of Representatives in 1897, Briscoe introduced a bill providing for a four-year county high school in Douglas County. Through his efforts, the county high school, the first in the state, became a reality in 1899. Briscoe's initiative became a model act, leading to eventual state law.

He is buried in Block 97.

Cantril, John R. (1842 – 1931)

An early pioneer of Douglas County, John Cantril operated a sawmill in the valley of Upper West Plum Creek. Prominent in the area, he was the son-in-law of well-known pioneer Benjamin Quick. The first school in the area, a one-room schoolhouse was built on Cantril's land by Quick. The school became the community meeting center and the small town of Glen Grove was established. Mrs. Clara Quick Cantril taught Sunday School until her untimely death in 1887. Her funeral was held in the schoolhouse, with burial in the nearby Quick Cemetery.[43]

The Cantril family members were gracious and supportive to the community. In 1887, Mrs. Baby Doe Tabor, wife of the legendary mining king, passed through the Glen Grove area in her carriage. She stopped at the Cantril Ranch for the night. In appreciation of the hospitality, she sent a hundred roses to grace the Cantril garden.

The Cantril family plot is located in Block 1, Lot 8.

Craig, John H. (1827 – 1892)

An elite member of Colorado's 59ers, John Craig staked a land claim at the junction of the East and West Plum Creeks. Craig's Round Corral became the central meeting point for travelers to rest and feed their animals along this first Territorial road.[44] Despite the constant threat of Indians, in 1869, the site had developed into the little community of Plum Town, or Town of Plum. In 1868, Craig led a group of twenty-five men in pursuit of marauding Indians who had killed and scalped a settler named O'Comb. Capturing the Indians, Craig turned them over to friend and Indian agent, Major D.C. Oakes.

With the arrival of the Denver & Rio Grande Railroad in 1871, the Round Corral became the main shipping point and the town of Sedalia sprang up. Craig built the first brick house in the new town, considered the finest in the region.

Craig was a founding father of the new town of Castle Rock in 1874. He built the Craig & Gould addition, located on the eastern edge of town. He sold residential lots to promote the growth of Castle Rock.

Craig served an unprecedented five terms as mayor from 1887 to 1891. He was the Democratic party chairman for Douglas County for several years and was a member of the state Legislature.

His tall, elaborate obelisk stands just inside the main gateway, in Block 128.

Dillon, William (1850 – 1935)

One of the early Douglas County pioneers, William Dillon arrived in Sedalia in 1883, where he opened a law office. He later moved to Castle Rock, where he was appointed county attorney. He owned a cattle ranch and was one of the first to organize a committee of stockholders among the many dairy farmers. Under his leadership, Douglas County became the "dairy county" of the state by 1889.

In 1885, he married Elizabeth Ratcliff, daughter of Charles Ratcliff, pioneer and county commissioner. The Dillon and Ratcliff Meat Market and Dillon Building were a major part of Castle Rock's business district. Through Dillon's efforts, the beautiful native stone Saint Francis of Assisi Catholic Church became a reality in 1888.

He is buried beside his wife Elizabeth, who preceded him in death, in Block 70, Lot 2.

Dyer Family Plot

Perhaps the most famous of all interments in the Cedar Hill Cemetery, is that of Father John L. Dyer. The Dyer family plot began in 1878 with the burials of Father John Dyers' father, Samuel, and John's son Elias. Dyer sent his son Samuel, and son-in-law Charles C. Streeter, to Granite to remove the body of his son Elias, who was murdered in 1875. On the return trip, they stopped the wagon at Bailey and removed the body of Dyer's father, Sam, who had died in 1871. They were buried side-by-side in a prominent section of the cemetery. A third monument was placed in memory of Dyer's third son, Joshua.

Dyer, Elias Foster (1836 – 1875)

The second son of John and Harriet, Elias became probate judge of Lake County during the infamous county war of 1874–1875.[45] Originating as a feud between two individuals, the quarrel escalated to a bloody county war, leading to the breakdown of the local legal machinery. As probate judge, Dyer was caught in the middle of the

Author's collection

The magnificent Veteran's Memorial at Cedar Hill Cemetery.

war. Because of his efforts to uphold the law, he became the target of the powerful vigilante committee.

In February 1875, Dyer was ordered before the committee to answer trumped up charges. Taking the law into their own hands, the committee held Dyer and some thirty citizens in a schoolhouse for three days. Upon his release, Dyer was ordered to leave the county and his life was threatened. His father, the noted Methodist minister, pleaded with the governor to declare martial law, but to no avail.

Elias Dyer remained in Lake County, sworn to his duty. From his office in Granite, he issued sixteen warrants against members of the vigilante committee ranging from harassment to murder. Sheriff Dobbins refused to serve the warrants. Again, Dyer was threatened by a mob that held him hostage in his office near the courtroom.

On July 2, 1875, members of the vigilante committee entered the courtroom, refusing to lay down their guns. Judge Dyer dismissed court for the day. The next morning, Elias wrote a letter to his father, not knowing if he would live another day. He didn't.

The following morning, at about 8 a.m., five men mounted the stairs to Dyer's quarters next to the courtroom. Three shots rang out The assassins were unmolested by the crowd. Judge Elias Dyer was dead at the age of thirty-nine.

He was buried in the Granite Cemetery. His father, the Reverend John Dyer, was unable to attend the funeral due to the hasty arrangements. No murder charges were ever filed.

Elias Dyer's body was brought to Cedar Hill Cemetery by family members, in 1878. A large native stone obelisk marks his grave.

Inscribed on the monument is a portion of his last words in a letter to his father. "A victim of the murderous mob ruling in Lake County. I trust in God and His mercy. At 8 o'clock I sit in court. The mob have me under guard, I die for law, order and principle."

Dyer, John L. (1812 – 1901)

The Methodist Church circuit riders organized the first religious movements in the Pikes Peak region, following the gold rush of 1859. The most famous and devoted of all the ministers was Father John L. Dyer.

Dyer entered the ministry in Wisconsin in 1851, when early tragedy struck his life. He lost his wife Harriet, and newborn daughter in childbirth. A second marriage ended in divorce, and the subsequent suicide of his ex-wife.

The ministry sent him to the Colorado Territory, where he arrived in Denver in 1861. He traveled by foot to the South Park area, arriving in Buckskin Joe in July. Although he faithfully served the early mining camps of the Fairplay and Alma districts, his family and religious commitment would take a real hold at his final home in Douglas County.

For twelve years, he preached the word of God at the mining camps dotting the Continental Divide. He paid his own way, supplementing his income by carrying the mail over the many high mountain passes. It was in this way he earned the famous title "Snow-Shoe Itinerant." During the winter, he resorted to a pair of skies, hand fashioned to an ideal length for the rugged mountain terrain. Over Mosquito Pass, he would haul the mail, gold dust and provisions, such as sugar and flour. The snow varied from three feet to as much as twenty feet.

By 1866, Dyer settled in the booming town of Fairplay. He moved an empty building from Montgomery in 1867, where he established his first permanent church.[46] During his time in Fairplay, the Espinosa Gang terrorized the residents of Park County. Not knowing the identity of the killers at the time, the posse chased a stranger on foot from Leadville. Father Dyer recognized the man and saved his life.

In 1870, the ministry assigned Dyer to the Divide circuit, which included Douglas County. This move proved to be his toughest challenge. The ranchers had their own ways, based on a reality of land and logic. The move was a slow adjustment for Dyer and one of learning and eventual respect.

In 1870, he married Lucinda Rankin of Cherry Creek and built a permanent home north of present-day Franktown. He continued to travel Douglas County, preaching in the many churches and visiting Castle Rock often.

He is buried in the Dyer Family Plot, next to his wife Lucinda, who proceeded him in death in 1888. His memorial is the tall sandstone obelisk facing the road with his son Joshua's name. Father Dyer's inscription is on the south side of the monument.

Dyer, Joshua (1834 – 1865)

The first-born son of Reverend John L. and Harriet Dyer. Joshua served in the Union Army during the Civil War. A soldier in the 1st Regiment of the Minnesota Volunteers, he was captured and held prisoner at Andersonville for the duration of the war. Among a group of sick and starving prisoners, he was placed aboard a steamship bound for the North in 1865. The steamship, *General Lyon* was sabotaged and all lives were lost at sea.

The memorial to his memory was placed in the family plot in 1878. It is a tall native stone obelisk with the name of his father, Reverend John L. Dyer carved on the south side of the monument.

The Dyer family plot is located in Block 15, Lots 3, 4, and 5.

Triplett, George A. (1852 – 1918)
Triplett, Hattie L. (1860 – 1925)

An early pioneer of Castle Rock, Triplett served as the first town clerk and recorder in 1881, an office he held for eight years. He was mayor for one term and was county judge for several years.

He owned a mercantile store, and stock in the Canon City coal operations. He owned a ranch outside of town, where he raised pedigree horses. He established the Douglas County Horse Show in 1890. He and his wife Hattie Streeter, the granddaughter of Father John Dyer, were active members of the Methodist Church.

The dark granite monument to George and Hattie Triplett is just south of the Dyer family plot, in Block 6, Lot 4.

Woodhouse, Charles (1833 – 1913)

A native of Sheffield England, in his youth, Charles and his brother James, learned the iron and brickmaking trade. He and his wife Amelia, emigrated to America, settling in Douglas County in 1871. He joined his brother James in a small brickmaking business. The Woodhouse Brickmakers soon turned into a very profitable business.

Using clay deposits on James' ranch, a mill was constructed, and a horse-powered mixing device added to turn the clay into bricks. The bricks, baked in home-made kilns, were used in the construction of many Castle Rock homes that still stand today.

With a highly successful company, Charles acquired a 1,000-acre ranch northwest of Castle Rock, the present site of Cedar Hill Cemetery. In 1883, he built a beautiful two-story home, the showpiece of the valley.

The Woodhouse brothers contributed to the beauty of Castle Rock with many brick buildings in the business district. In 1889, they built brick chimneys for each of the rooms in the newly-constructed court-house. In 1911, in partnership with F. Fetherhoff, he started the Castle Rock Brick Factory. Located east of town, the factory utilized the great clay deposits in the area. It became the largest brick company in the state, producing 250,000 bricks a day. A spur of the Denver & Rio Grande ran directly to the plant for shipments north and south.

His red sandstone monument is located in Block 196, Lot 4.

SEDALIA

BEAR CANON CEMETERY

LOCATED WEST OF THE CEDAR HILL CEMETERY AT CASTLE ROCK, AND SOUTHWEST OF SEDALIA. FROM CASTLE ROCK, FOLLOW WOLFENSBURGER ROAD WEST SEVEN MILES TO THE INTERSECTION OF HIGHWAY 105 (ALSO KNOWN AS PERRY PARK ROAD.) THE CEMETERY IS ACROSS THE ROAD DIAGONALLY, TO THE WEST. THERE IS A SIGN ON THE SIDE OF HIGHWAY 105 WHICH READS: "ST. PHILIP CHURCH AND BEAR CANON CEMETERY."

In February 1872, the Bear Canon Methodist Church was founded. It was the first church in Douglas County. Built by Newton S. Grout, the church served the early community of Plum Town and later, Sedalia. The following year, David T. Wolf deeded three acres of land adjoining the church for a burial ground. In his deed, Wolf stipulated that the graveyard be free to all settlers. The women of the community planted shrubs and wild roses, complimenting the natural landscape.

Over 100 years of family burials are evident in this rural cemetery. Marking the centennial anniversary, Robert Hier wrote:

"St. Philip-in-the-Field Church and Bear Canon Cemetery represent in the relatively new section of our country a sense of continuity with the past and hope for the future without which, human beings would not be human. St. Philip is an emblem of the best of their old life to a new and difficult one. The basic purpose of all monuments is to link the past, the present and the future-to make manifest the usually forgotten bonds between our ancestors and ourselves."[47]

Curtis, Henry Harper (1830 – 1911)

A native of Wales, Henry Curtis brought his wife Julia, and nine children to America, where he settled in Douglas County, Colorado, in 1871. He homesteaded some three and one-half miles south of Sedalia. He called it Oaklands for the trees covering the hillside. A wealthy man by pioneer standards, he built his home, bought livestock and purchased additional land within the year. He later rebuilt his house, still standing today and remaining in the Curtis family.

The road along Plum Creek, the main route between Colorado City and Denver, was also used by the Indians. The Indians often camped on the Curtis land. Chief Ouray once made an unannounced visit to the Curtis home. Following the removal of the Indians to the reservations, many of then wandered back to the Curtis land, begging for food.

Appointed Justice of the Peace in 1871, Curtis was a strong supporter of the newly organized church at Bear Canon. He took an active part in the construction, while his family participated in the activities of the church. All nine of his children are buried in the Bear Canon Cemetery.

Henry H. Curtis is buried near the church. There is a marker.

Grout, Newton S. (1842 – 1901)

Grout arrived in Colorado Territory in 1869, along with Guy and Upton Smith, the earliest pioneer families in the area.[48] He settled in the upper West Plum Creek area, where he used his carpenter skills to make his living.

Newton built the Lone Tree School in 1872, the second school in the Plum District. He built many of the ranch homes in the area, including the Perry and Ratcliff homes. Following the commission of the Methodist church in 1872, Newton Grout built the lovely church at the crossroads. He built the St. Philip-in-the-Field Church, modeled after New England churches. The church, refurbished, still stands. A prosperous individual and very involved in community affairs, he contributed many landmark structures that survive today.

He is buried in the Grout family plot, enclosed by an iron fence. The large dark granite monument marks the plot. At the edge of the plot is a second monument to Newton S. Grout. A military marker, it is inscribed with his service in Company E1, Maine, Civil War.

Grout, Robert (1815 – 1899)

The father of Newton and Sarah "Lizzie" Grout Smith, Robert came to the Plum Creek Valley from Maine, where he lived with Lizzie and her family. A skilled craftsman in wood and metal, he built many

Author's collection
Albert Carlton
He made a fortune at Cripple Creek.

of the homes and barns in the area. He designed and built a microscope and telescope, which were sold to the Colorado A & M College, and are still in use.

He is buried near the Upton Treat Smith family plot. There is a granite stone to his memory.

**Smith, Upton Treat
(1843 – 1925)
Smith, Sarah "Lizzie"
(1849 – 1939)**

Upton Smith arrived in Colorado Territory in 1869, where he worked in the mines of the Central City district. Desiring a more permanent lifestyle, he and brother Guy, along with Newton Grout, located in Douglas County, on West Plum Creek. He filed on a homestead and proved up on his land. He built a three-room house furnished with handmade furniture.

He returned to Maine, married his sweetheart, Sarah Elizabeth Grout, sister of Newton, and brought her west to his new home. One of the first pioneer families in the valley, the Smith's built their homestead into one of the finest ranches in the area. They raised cattle, poultry, and sold butter and timber from their land.

Upton and Lizzie were both involved and committed in the ranch community of West Plum Creek. They participated in the activities and social events of the St. Philip-in-the-Field church and left a pioneer heritage unmatched.

They are buried together in the Bear Canon Cemetery, near the church in a family plot. There is a dark granite marker to both Upton and Lizzie. A second marker, a military stone is dedicated to Upton's service in the Civil War.

UNITED STATES AIR FORCE ACADEMY

CAPPS CEMETERY

LOCATED WEST OF INTERSTATE 25. TAKE EXIT 156B TO THE NORTH ENTRANCE OF THE ACADEMY. TURN WEST AT THE INTERSECTION OF STADIUM BOULEVARD AND COMMUNITY CENTER DRIVE. FOLLOW COMMUNITY CENTER DRIVE TO THE CAPPS ROAD, TURNING RIGHT. THE

Colorado Springs Parks and Recreation
The original stone entrance to Evergreen Cemetery is gone.
But the church in the background has been restored.

*DIRT ROAD WINDS INTO THE FOREST. THE CEMETERY IS AT THE END OF THE
ROAD. A MAP OF THE GROUNDS IS AVAILABLE AT THE VISITORS CENTER.* [49]

The oldest building on the grounds of the Air Force Academy today
is the Burgess Ranch Cabin. The cabin was built in 1870 by William
A. Burgess. It was moved to its' present site during the construction of
the Academy.

Near the cabin is the original burial spot of five members of the
Capps family; George Capps (1885 – 1885), Bettie Capps (1881 –
1884), Clarence Capps (1887 – 1890), and parents, Leonard Capps
(1816 – 1898), and Sarah Capps (1818 – 1896). The Leonard Capps
family were friends and neighbors to the Burgess family. The cemetery and cabin are now on the National Register of Historic places.

COLORADO SPRINGS

EVERGREEN CEMETERY

1005 S. HANNOCK AVENUE, IN COLORADO SPRINGS.

Evergreen Cemetery lies in the shadow of Colorado's most famous
mountain, Pikes Peak. The original cemetery, called Mesa, or Pioneer,
is now Pioneer Park, established in 1903. The bodies were removed to
Evergreen Cemetery.

The land for the new cemetery was deeded by city founder General
William Jackson Palmer in 1876.[50] Land was cleared amidst groves of
Ponderosa pine and cottonwood trees. Additional landscaping includes

Winfield Scott Stratton
Cripple Creek's first millionaire.

beautiful rock gardens, flowers and bushes. Tall rose trellises dot a majority of the cemetery, a tradition since the early 1900s, when local residents donned their loved one's burial site in sweet natural fragrance. The roses were so plentiful that at one time Evergreen Cemetery was listed in *Ripley's Believe It Or Not* as "the largest rose garden in the world."

A prominent feature is the historic chapel, built in 1909. Recently restored, it features a manually-operated cork-screw casket lift, bringing the casket up from the cold basement storage. The original tract of land is known as the Pioneer Section, with the El Paso County Pioneers' Association Monument nearby, honoring all pioneers buried therein. The Evergreen Cemetery has recently been listed on the National Register of Historic Places.

Carlton, Albert E. (1866 – 1931)

Albert Carlton arrived in Cripple Creek with his brother, during the gold rush. Suffering from tuberculosis, he came west for a cure and stayed, becoming a very successful entrepreneur. He was the first to start a wagon freight hauling service. His Colorado Trading and Transfer Company building now holds a portion of the District's museum.

He went on to secure freight contracts with the railroads, holding a monopoly. He brought banking to the heart of Cripple Creek, acting as first president and owner. His biggest accomplishment, although completed after his death, was the Roosevelt Tunnel, which brought a drainage system to the mines of the Cripple Creek District.

He is buried in Block 68, Lot 17.

Howbert, Irving (1846 – 1934)

He and his father arrived by covered wagon at Colorado City in 1860. At the age of twenty-three, Irving Howbert was elected as the first clerk of newly-formed El Paso County. He went on to serve in the Colorado State Senate, after statehood. He was instrumental in

founding the town of Colorado
Springs, with General Palmer in
1871.

He organized The First
National Bank of Colorado
Springs in 1880, serving as pres-
ident for eight years and again
from 1919 to 1923. He was
involved in the Colorado
Midland Railway and became
president of the great Portland
Gold Mining Company at
Cripple Creek.

He is buried in Block 58, Lot
95.

Jackson, Helen Hunt (1831 – 1885)

Denver Public Library
Robert Miller Womack
He found gold at Cripple Creek
but died broke.

Ill health and family tragedy
brought this talented woman to
the famed health resort of Colorado Springs in 1873. Helen Hunt married prominent businessman William S. Jackson two years later. She
is the author of *A Century of Dishonor* and *Ramona*, bringing new
interest nationwide to Indian policy, as well as an appointment by the
government as an Indian commissioner.

She died in San Francisco in 1885. At her request, her body was
brought back to Colorado Springs for burial on Cheyenne Mountain,
near today's Seven Fall's attraction. Flocks of tourists vandalized the
gravesite, and Mr. Jackson had her body exhumed and reinterred in
the Jackson family plot in the Evergreen Cemetery.

There are four prominent dark granite ledger memorials in the
Jackson plot. The one on the end is Helen Hunt Jackson, next to her
husband. On the other side of William is the second Mrs. Helen
Jackson, Helen Hunt Jackson's niece who married Mr. Jackson at the
first Helen's request. The offspring of this union are also buried in the
family plot located in Block 17, Lot 52.

Kelly, Rankin S. (1826 – 1913)

From Maine, Kelly settled in Old Colorado City in 1860. He was
the first sheriff of El Paso County.

Shortly before his death, it was revealed he had come west to
escape a murder charge. In fact, the man he fought defending his sis-

ter's honor, was actually alive. When Kelly died, he was eulogized as the finest lawman of El Paso County.

He is buried in Block 57, Lot 84.

Palmer, William Jackson (1836 – 1909)

William Palmer was a Union General in the Civil War. Following the war, he was in charge of bringing the Kansas Pacific Railroad to Denver from St. Louis. While surveying for the railroad, he discovered the beautiful area now known as Colorado Springs. Unable to convince the railroad company to build an extension south from Denver, he built his own railroad. The Denver & Rio Grande Railroad rolled into Colorado Springs in 1871.

Palmer built the prestigious Glen Erie Castle, where he died following a fall from one of his prized horses. There is a natural stone monument in his memory, marking a 12x12-foot plot under which lies a brick vault containing his cremated remains. The site is located near the chapel in Block 74, Lot 82.

Stratton, Winfield Scott (1848 – 1902)

A carpenter from Indiana, Stratton left his family and settled in Colorado Springs in 1872.

As a carpenter, he did very well in the young community, building several homes, including the home of Helen Hunt Jackson. In his spare time, he prospected for gold in the Cripple Creek mining district. He staked a claim on a hill near Victor on July 4, 1891, calling it The Independence. His discovery was a mother lode of some twenty-seven million dollars. He became the Cripple Creek District's first millionaire.

He gave freely to the communities of Victor, Cripple Creek and Colorado Springs, dealing with electricity needs, transportation improvements and establishing a trust fund to build a home for the poor, in his name.

He is buried in Block 72, Lot 65, near the cemetery chapel. A large granite boulder serves as his simple marker.

Womack, Robert Miller "Bob" (1844 – 1909)

The first to discover gold in a cow pasture at the south side of Pikes Peak, in 1891, he was called "Crazy Bob" and at first, no one believed his claim. When Bob's cow pasture developed into the Cripple Creek mining district, thousands of men trudged over the pass, seeking gold. Bob sold his claim for a mere $500. Within a year, Cripple Creek was known as "The World's Greatest Gold Camp."

Pueblo Library District

A Pueblo funeral.

He was honored in Cripple Creek's Founder's Day Parade in 1902 and dubbed the "Father of Cripple Creek."

Bob Womack died penniless and lonely in Colorado Springs.[51] He is buried in the family plot in the older section of the cemetery, in Block 39, Lot 2.

FORT CARSON MILITARY RESERVATION

FORT CARSON MILITARY CEMETERY

LOCATED SOUTH OF COLORADO SPRINGS. FROM INTERSTATE 25, TAKE HIGHWAY 115 TO THE ENTRANCE OF FORT CARSON.

Established in 1942, this Army training center is named for the famous frontiersman, Kit Carson. During World War II, movie star Lt. Clark Gable was stationed here.

Harkens, Henry (? – 1863)

He was one of the victims of the Espinosa gang's bloody rampage.[52] His grave lies five miles south of Gate #1 at the military post.

World War II Burial Section

Near Gate #3 of Fort Carson, lies burial sites of America's prisoners of war during World War II.

Pueblo Library District
Alva Adams
He served two terms as governor.

PUEBLO

PUEBLO PIONEER CEMETERY

LOCATED ON THE NORTHERN EDGE OF PUEBLO. FROM THE 29TH AVENUE EXIT, TURN SOUTH ON ELIZABETH STREET. FOLLOW ELIZABETH ST. TO 22ND AVENUE. THE CEMETERY IS ON THE RIGHT, COVERING THE ENTIRE BLOCK.

This cemetery is actually four separate sections. The I.O.O.F. Cemetery is across the street, and was established in 1871. The Jewish Cemetery was established in 1885, The Pioneer in 1885, and the Masonic in 1870.

The grounds are well maintained by the city, and are very attractive. Cemetery records are kept at the office of the Mountain View Cemetery.

Among the burials in this pioneer resting spot, is that of George M. Chilcott (1828 – 1891). An early pioneer of Pueblo, Chilcott was involved in Pueblo politics from the start. As a U.S. land officer, he participated in both the local and statewide campaigns for Colorado statehood, as early as 1861. He represented Colorado in the Territorial Congress from 1861 to 1868.

In 1868, he expanded his personal holdings with a partnership with pioneer Thomas O. Boggs. The two formed a sheep business which was quite successful until 1883, when the operation was sold.

Chilcott was appointed Colorado Senator in 1882. He fulfilled Senator Henry Teller's term, and was succeeded in the same term by H. A. W. Tabor.[53] He went on to serve in the Colorado Legislature.

He is buried in the Masonic cemetery, in Block 5M, Lot 10W, grave 1. There is a marker.

ROSELAWN CEMETERY

LOCATED ON THE EASTERN EDGE OF THE TOWN OF PUEBLO. FROM I-25, TAKE HIGHWAY 50 EAST (EXIT 98A.) TURN RIGHT ON ASPEN ST. THE CEMETERY IS ABOUT TWO BLOCKS ON THE LEFT.

Among the earliest cemeteries now lost to history, are the Pest House cemetery, and the Colorado State Hospital Cemetery. Both contained graves of disease victims and the mentally ill. The cemeteries were condemned in the late nineteenth century.[54]

The Roselawn Cemetery was established in 1890 by the Pueblo Cemetery Association. Three hundred and fifty acres of land was acquired from the Colorado Coal & Iron Company in 1891. Originally known as Riverview, this genteel resting spot became a modern-day state-of-the-art cemetery, proudly serving the community into the dawn of a new century.[55]

Burial lots were sold at five dollars for adults, four dollars for children, and three dollars for children under the age of three. The cemetery is laid out in several sections, including the religious and fraternal organizations. There is a Civil War section just to the left of the entrance. Dedicated in 1902, it includes the burials of two Congressional Medal of Honor recipients. Adjacent to this section, is the Veteran Section. The beautiful landscape adds a grace and dignity to our Arkansas Valley pioneers.

The silver panic of 1893 caused financial reassessment of the cemetery association. Unable to make the land payments to the Coal & Iron Company, the cemetery land was reduced to 131 acres, and officially renamed Roselawn Cemetery in 1905. The association also purchased a wagonette and hired a driver to provide transportation from the city to the cemetery. The transportation service operated on weekends and included a picnic at the cemetery for fifteen cents.[56]

Among the some 50,000 interments, is one mass grave in Section K, known as the Historic Section. The victims of the Eden Train wreck are buried here. Noted as one of the worst train wrecks in history, the accident occurred five and one-half miles north of Pueblo, in August 1904. A severe rainstorm washed out a railroad bridge on the Missouri Pacific line. The train plunged into the river and many cars were lost in the rain formed quicksand. Ninety-six bodies were recovered, fourteen others were never found. The remains of these victims were buried in one mass grave in Section K. There is a memorial.

Adams, Alva (1850 – 1922)

A native of Wisconsin, Alva Adams came west with his family in 1871. Colorado's climate offered relief for Alva's brother Billy, who suffered from asthma.[57] Alva and Billy first hauled ties for the Denver Rio Grande Railroad. Moving on to Alamosa, Alva and Billy operated a hardware store. By 1873, Alva had expanded his business to Colorado Springs and Pueblo.

He made Pueblo his home, where he was active in business and politics. In 1876, he was elected to the first state Legislature. Alva Adams became governor of Colorado in 1887, and served again from

1897 to 1899. In 1905, he ran for a third term as governor, in one of the most bizarre events in Colorado's political history. Running against James Peabody, the campaign turned ugly. Each party accused the other of bribing and contriving votes. The final vote put Adams in office, but only for sixty days. The Legislature declared the election void, with both parties being fraudulent. Jesse McDonald of Leadville was named governor in the aftermath of the investigation.

In private activities, Adams served as president of the Pueblo Savings and Trust Company, vice president of the Western National Bank of Pueblo, and director of the Standard Brick Company. He was one of the principle forces behind the growth of Pueblo and all of Colorado.

Alva Adams died in 1922. He is buried in the family plot next to his wife Ella, in Block 13, Lots 270-300. There is a large memorial to their memory. Note the horse hitching post nearby.

Blake, Annie (1838 – 1927)

Annie and her husband George, lived in Rye, Colorado, where he was engaged in the real estate business. George suffered from asthma and by 1869 he could no longer conduct business. Annie took over the business, her first transaction being the purchase of the forty-eight plus acres of the Nolan Land Grant for $10,000. Making a handsome profit, she sold one third of the land to Peter and Jacob Dotson for $5,000 and another one third to Charles Goodnight for the same amount. Retaining a third of the land for herself, it eventually became the community of South Pueblo. The original acreage covered all of Pueblo south of the Arkansas River, and the land between the Greenhorn Mountains and the St. Charles River.

Annie made several investments in Pueblo, including the Roselawn Cemetery. The census for Pueblo County in 1870, listed only eight employed women. Annie Blake led that group of pioneer women.

She is buried next to George in Block 13, Lot 343. There is a marker.

Barry, Mary (1845 – 1914)

An early Pueblo pioneer, Mary Barry was the first female physician in the county in 1896. Committed to humanity, she gave freely of her time to aid others. Ambitious and quite accomplished, she went on to serve in the Colorado State Legislature, one of the first women of Colorado to do so.

She is buried in Block 29, Lot 109. There is a marker.

Black, Louise (1867 – 1935)

One of Pueblo's early pioneers, Louise Black was among the first female doctors in the area. In 1905, she was the physician of the Clark Spring Water treatment facility. A fifty-seven room sanitarium housed patients at the artesian water complex. She contributed to the health and betterment of Pueblo.

She is buried in Block 28, Lot 4A. There is a marker.

Bowen, Thomas M. (1835 – 1906)

A veteran of the Civil War, Thomas Bowen became Brevet Brigadier General before the conflict ended in 1865. Following the war, he traveled west, eventually settling in Pueblo. A successful attorney and active in town politics, he went on to become county judge and was elected to the state Legislature. In 1883, he became a U.S. Senator, defeating H.A.W. Tabor by one vote. His residence at 325 W. 15th Street is on the National Register of Historic Places.

He is buried in the Civil War Section A. There is a military memorial.

Gallup, Samuel C. (1837 – 1904)

An early pioneer of Pueblo, Gallup brought his saddle trade to the area in the late 1870s. In partnership with Robert Frasier in 1880, his saddle shop grew to be the largest in the West.[58] Frasier advertised the business nationally and Gallup's business became known as "The World's largest manufacturer of cowboy saddles." The partnership dissolved after ten years. Gallup continued his saddle craft until his death in 1904, at which time his sons took over the business.

He is buried in Block 13, Lot 630.

Lambert, John J. (1837 – 1916)

A native of Ireland, John Lambert immigrated to America in his youth. Following service in the Civil War, he came west, where he was an officer at Fort Reynolds, Colorado Territory, in 1867. Captain John J. Lambert held the post of quartermaster and commissary for the five years of the fort's existence.

During his time at the fort, he purchased the *Colorado Chieftain*, a Pueblo newspaper, started by Michael Beshoer, in 1868.[59] Following the abandonment of the fort in 1872, Captain Lambert resigned his commission and moved to Pueblo. He took over the management of the paper, converting it from a weekly publication to a daily paper, and changed the name to the *Pueblo Chieftain*.

In 1873, he married Susan Lorimier. Through the financial success of his paper, Lambert and his wife, contributed to many charities, including funding to build the Sacred Heart Orphanage.

Mrs. Lambert died in 1891, and was buried at Roselawn Cemetery. When Captain John J. Lambert died in 1916, he was buried next to his wife. In 1919, the remains of the couple were disinterred and reburied in a small plot on the eastern edge of the Sacred Heart orphanage property. When the orphanage closed, John and Susan were moved for a third and final time, back to Roselawn.[60]

John and Susan Lambert are buried in Block 149, Lot 103. There is a marker.

Orman, James (1849 – 1919)

Born in Muscatine, Iowa, James Orman came to Colorado by mule train in 1868. From Denver, he moved to Pueblo, where he settled, becoming one of the most prominent railroad contractors in Colorado.

He and his brother, W. A. Orman, contracted with the Kansas Pacific Railroad to build the road west for the company. Their first enterprise in 1869, succeeded at an astonishing pace. Orman went on to construct many railroads in Colorado and the West, including the Colorado Midland to Cripple Creek, the Denver & Rio Grande to Colorado Springs, and the Canadian Pacific. He was responsible for building Pueblo's street railway system in 1879.

Orman later acquired a large real estate interest and became a leader in the business community. He built several of Pueblo's buildings, became president of the Bessemer Ditch Company, built and operated the Pueblo Opera House, and held mining interests in Ouray, Leadville and Ashcroft.

In public life, he served several terms on the city council. He was elected to the Colorado General Assembly in 1880, and served in the Senate from 1881 to 1885. He became mayor of Pueblo in 1897. The Democratic candidate for state governor in 1900, he won the endorsement of the Silver Republicans and the People's Party. He was governor from 1901 to 1903. During his governorship, he entertained President Theodore Roosevelt on his famous Colorado hunting trips.

His home in Pueblo, at 102 West Orman, was built in 1890. He and his wife Nellie, occupied the home until 1918. It was sold to his good friend Alva Adams, during the financial panic. The Orman's, stripped of their fortune, remained in Pueblo until their deaths.

James and Nellie Orman are buried together in Block 13, Lot 243. There is a handsome marker.

Thatcher Family Monument

John A. Thatcher, one of Pueblo's earliest pioneers, arrived in 1862. He opened one of the first stores in the small settlement. By 1867, in partnership with his brother Mahlon, his store had expanded and included a warehouse. The following year, the brothers opened the First National Bank. The Baxter and Thatcher grist mill opened in 1864, the first major industry in Pueblo. In 1870, he joined the legendary Charles Goodnight in a large cattle operation located five miles from Pueblo.

A self-made millionaire, John Thatcher built an elaborate mansion in 1891. Two years in the making, the Victorian home of pink lava consists of three floors and thirty-seven rooms. Known as Rosemount, it is now a museum, located at 14th and Grand.

John A. Thatcher died in 1913.

— — —

Mahlon Thatcher arrived in Pueblo in 1865, joining his brother, John in business. He became the first president of the chamber of commerce, known as the Board of Trade of Southern Colorado. Under Thatcher's leadership, the board was successful in persuading the Santa Fe Railroad to extend its rails to Pueblo.

Along with his brother John, Mahlon established the First National Bank in 1868. With the success of his bank, he went on to own some thirty-two banks in Colorado by the time of his death in 1916, including the local Minnequa Bank, incorporated in 1902. Involved in community affairs, he became mayor of Pueblo in 1877.

— — —

Henry C. Thatcher, the youngest of the Thatcher brothers, joined his brothers in Pueblo in 1862. With Charles Gast, he opened one of the first law practices in Pueblo. When the town of Pueblo became incorporated in 1870, Henry became a town trustee. A successful attorney, businessman, and politician, he became a member of the Constitutional Convention, and upon Colorado statehood, went on to become the first Colorado Supreme Court Justice, in 1876.

Judge Henry C. Thatcher died in March 1884, while on a family pleasure trip in San Francisco, he was forty-one years old. His body was brought back to Pueblo for burial, originally in the Pioneer Cemetery. A special memorial service was also held in Denver in the Supreme Court chambers. On the occasion, Judge Samuel Elbert said: "He was a most excellent judge, pure, conscientious, and clear. His statements and arguments were always clear, logical, and accurate."

In 1900, Judge Thatcher's remains, as well as those of his wife Ella, and daughters Minnie and Flora, were removed to the Roselawn Cemetery and the Thatcher family plot.

The elaborately carved Thatcher monument is located in Section F, Block 15, Lots 1 and 2.

Thombs, Pembroke R. Dr. (1840 – 1902)

A native of Maine, Pembroke went to Chicago in 1859 at the age of nineteen, where he entered the Rush Medical College. Receiving his degree in 1862, he joined the Union Army, serving as assistant surgeon of the 89th Illinois Infantry. Two years later, he was promoted to chief surgeon. Following the war, he settled in Pueblo. Dr. Thombs was one of the first physicians in Pueblo. He became the first superintendent of the Colorado Insane Asylum at Pueblo, appointed by Governor Pitkin in 1879. he later became president of the Pueblo County Medical Society, formed in 1881. In this capacity, he spearheaded treatment for diphtheria, typhoid fever and small pox.

He is buried next to his wife, Louisa, in Block 13, Lot 240. There is a marker.

Zupan, Father Cyril (1862 – 1951)

Of Slovenian heritage, Cyril Zupan became the second pastor at St. Mary's Church in Pueblo, serving from 1894 to 1939. He understood and related to his congregation, a trait which endeared him to the community. In 1917, Father Cyril Zupan campaigned to organize a Holy Rosary parish in Denver. Bishop Tihen of Denver granted the petition in 1918. Father Zupan commuted by train from Pueblo to Denver, serving as the first pastor from 1918 to 1921.

He is buried in Block 21, Lot 153.

MOUNTAIN VIEW CEMETERY

LOCATED ON THE SOUTH SIDE OF PUEBLO BETWEEN BEULAH AND PRAIRIE AVENUES, AT 1315 ACERO STREET.

This cemetery was established in 1881. Early burials date to 1870, when the locals buried their loved ones on the vacant land. One of the older cemeteries in Pueblo, it is carefully maintained and includes the St. Peter's, St. Joseph's, and GAR sections.

Taylor, Cyrus F. Dr. (1858 – 1940)

Cyrus Taylor became one of the leading pioneers of the third Pueblo community now known as Central Pueblo. Dr. Taylor became the second mayor of the community in 1884. While the town only existed for four years, Dr. Taylor became a leading physician and resident of Pueblo.

He is buried Block G, Plot 22, grave 4. There is a marker.

Martin, John A. (1868 – 1939)

A native of Ohio, John Martin came west to Pueblo. He had a distinguished career in politics, serving the state of Colorado as a member of the House of Representatives. John Martin Reservoir is named in his honor.

He is buried in Block 2, Lot 160, grave 5. There is a marker.

COLORADO CITY[61]

COLORADO CITY CEMETERY

LOCATED THREE AND ONE-HALF MILES WEST OF I-25 ON HIGHWAY 165.

Denver Public Library
Joseph Doyle

Hicklin, Alexander "Zin" (? – 1874)

This glorified mountain man married the daughter of New Mexico's governor, thereby gaining a large land grant. Hicklin established a trading post on the Greenhorn River.

A Southern sympathizer, he trained rebel soldiers for the cause. When Fort Garland troops investigated, Hicklin denied involvement.

By 1860, a key stage station was built near Hicklin's homestead, where the town of Greenhorn was established. Hicklin became very active in the community. Known for his kindness and sense of humor, his dying wish in 1874, was to be buried with a bottle of whiskey so he could serve his friends in the "here after."

Nearly 100 years later, his grave was removed to the city cemetery, when construction began on his former land.

Off The Beaten Path:

SOUTH OF PUEBLO ON LANE 36, THE DIRT ROAD TURNS INTO DOYLE'S ROAD. APPROXIMATELY FIFTEEN MILES DOWN THE ROAD LIES CEMETERY HILL OR DOYLE'S CEMETERY, ONE-HALF-MILE WEST OF HUERFANO ROAD.

Joseph Brainbridge Doyle signed with William Bent at St. Joseph in 1839 and headed or Bent's Fort. He worked as a freighter at the fort until 1844. He helped Charles Autobees establish a settlement along the Huerfano River. He became a partner of George Simpson and William Kroenig at the Hardscrabble Trading Post up the Arkansas River, doing business with trappers, Indians and frontiersmen such as R. L. Wooton. There, he married Marie de le Cruz Suaso.

He began farming along the Arkansas River, just east of present day Pueblo. He built a large ranch home called Casa Blanca.

With the gold rush of 1859, Doyle turned his interests to freighting once again. Wagons of food, clothing and supplies were hauled to Denver City. The J. B. Doyle Company was an instant money making venture. Within a year, Doyle was a millionaire.

Doyle's wealth allowed him to enlarge his farm to a 600-acre ranch, with cattle, and horses. A flour mill was also constructed. A community of Doyle's workers soon grew into a small settlement. He established a school where the worker's children attended classes, with his own children. It is said the first teacher was O. J. Goldrick, who went on to be Denver City's first teacher.

He was elected to the Territory Council, in 1864, working toward statehood. Forty-six-year-old Joseph B. Doyle, died of a heart attack, while serving his term in Denver. Governor John Evans lead the party of dignitaries escorting Doyle's wagon hearse out of Denver. At the time of his death, Doyle was considered the richest man in Colorado Territory.

He was buried on a small hill, overlooking his empire along the Huerfano River. His wife died a year later and is buried beside him. Their weathered, broken stones stand just above the ruins of the Doyle School.

WALSENBURG

WALSENBURG MASONIC CEMETERY
LOCATED SOUTH OF TOWN, BEHIND THE HIGH SCHOOL. THE CEMETERY IS VISIBLE FROM THE HIGHWAY.

Farr, Edward J. (1867 – 1899)
He was a sheriff of Huerfano County. Sheriff Ed Farr lead a posse to catch the Black Jack Ketchum gang. At Turkey Creek Canyon near Cimarron, New Mexico, Farr's posse ambushed the gang.

Following an all-day shoot out, Farr was killed in the gunfire. The Ketchum gang escaped.

Farr is buried in the Masonic Cemetery, north of Walsenburg.

LUDLOW

LUDLOW MASSACRE SITE
LOCATED ONE MILE WEST OF EXIT 27, OFF INTERSTATE 25. THERE IS A SIGN.

Mining was the backbone of Colorado's economy, yet labor conditions were a constant source of contention. By the turn of the centu-

ry, reform was in vogue. In 1903, an
eight-hour workday law was passed
for miners and other occupations.

However, miners still maintained
their grievances, while the owners
fought union control. By 1913, a
series of strikes broke out throughout the northern portion of the state
and ended tragically at Ludlow.

The feud had been building for
months, if not years, since the strike
of 1903. The participates were the
owners of the Colorado Fuel & Iron
Company, a coal company under the
control of John D. Rockefeller, Jr.,
and the United Miners Workers
Union, led by Frank J. Hayes and an
elderly spokeswoman for Mother
Jones.

Colorado Historical Society
Monument to those killed
in Ludlow mining strike.

The miners went on strike on September 6, 1913, demanding better working conditions, wage increases, (based on national averages,)
the right to trade at any store and choose their boarding condition,
among others. The company countered by evicting families from the
company housing projects.

Hostilities mounted and martial law was invoked. The strike continued through the winter. Mother Jones was arrested for picketing
and hospitalized as a result.

On April 20, 1914, a detachment of the National Guard attempted
to arrest Louis Tikas, one of the strike leaders. Faced with opposition,
the National Guard opened fire with machine guns onto the tent city
of the evicted miners, killing Tikas and several others.[62] Fire broke
out and many women and children died as the tent camp burned.[63]

Federal troops restored order and the strike eventually ended, the
worst in Colorado history. But no one won.

The monument to the Ludlow Massacre was dedicated on
Memorial Day, 1918. It is said that the monument stands over the
"Black Hole" where two men and nine children died.

OFF THE BEATEN PATH:

Three miles northeast of Aguilar (off I-25) is the cemetery known
as Foster's Stage Stop. The site is located near the remains of the
townsite of Apishapa, on the banks of the Apishapa River.

Denver Public Library
Casimario Barela
Helped write the state Constitution.

Originally a stage stop established in 1862–1863, Ex-Confederate Colonel James Allen Foster took over operation in 1868. He built a two-story hotel of adobe, while his wife brought in the guests with her good cooking.

Foster's Place was the most popular stop along the stage line. Indian scares were frequent, but Foster's was never attacked.

When the Denver & Rio Grande Railroad built a track through the area, Foster's Place became a railroad stop. Foster built a station and hotel down the line, called "Augusta." In later years the buildings were used as a sanitarium for the tubercular patients.

Mrs. Susan Foster died in 1889. James Foster left Colorado for a time, only to return with a new bride, a southern belle named Margaret.

When James Foster died in 1895, the second Mrs. Foster buried him next to the first wife. Margaret (the second wife) died in 1908. A large stone marker was erected with her name on one side, and Susan's, (the first wife) name on the other side. James Foster's monument stood next to the memorial of the two wives, until it was vandalized in the 1970s.

TRINIDAD

TRINIDAD CATHOLIC CEMETERY

LOCATED NORTHEAST OF TOWN, ON US HIGHWAY 350 (MAIN STREET).

The cemetery was established in 1874. Still operating today, it is well maintained and the landscaping is beautiful.

Baca, Don Filipe (1828 – 1874)[64]

He was the man responsible for the founding of Trinidad. Baca first camped on the Purgatoire River in 1860, while on his way to sell goods at the new Cherry Creek settlement.

By 1861, Baca had settled his family in the Trinidad area and filed on land near the river. The fertile soil produced the best crops the Bacas had ever seen. In addition to farming, Baca raised cattle and sheep.

He donated land so that a Catholic Convent could be built. He was very prominent in political and social events that shaped the community of Trinidad. The stately Baca mansion, is now a museum.

He is buried in the Old Section.[65]

Barela, Casimario (1847 – 1920)

Casimario Barela came to Colorado in 1867. He settled southeast of Trinidad with his bride, childhood sweetheart, Josefita Ortiz. By 1871, his farm and ranch were among the largest in southern Colorado Territory.

He was elected to the Territorial Assembly in 1874 and was among the political leaders who wrote the State Constitution. Following statehood in 1876, Barela was elected state Senator, a position he held for forty years.

The Barela empire grew to include race horses and breeding stock, as well as first class cattle. A small town grew around his "castle-like" mansion. The residents were the families of Barela's employees.

In 1884, following the death of his wife, Barela started a second ranch six miles northeast of Trinidad.[66] Here, he brought his second wife, Damiana Rivera.

Barela served the public interests until 1916, when at age seventy, he was defeated at the polls. He was a spokesman for minorities and agriculture. He was selected as one of the sixteen original Colorado pioneers included in stained glass portraits in the Colorado capitol building.

He is buried in Lot 75, Old Section 4, with his second wife, Damiana. The large granite stone is inscribed in Spanish.

Tafoya, Juan C. (1820 – 1872)

Juan Tafoya was a deputy sheriff in January 1868, when the infamous Trinidad War broke out. Following the murder of one John Dunn, Frank Blue was arrested and placed in jail. A group of Blue's friends stormed the jail, apprehended deputy Tafoya and released Blue. Tafoya rounded up a posse and cornered the Blue group in a hotel on Main Street. The siege went on for two days. The military was finally called in to end the stand off.

Tafoya was elected sheriff in 1870, only to be removed in December 1870. In the election of 1871, he was appointed sheriff, after the removal of the elected sheriff, W. G. Rifenburg. Tafoya was re-elected, but was murdered in January 1872.

He is buried in the Old Section.

Kreeger, Louis Michael (1848 – 1913)

A Colorado lawman, Kreeger devoted more than thirty years of service to Las Animas County and the city of Trinidad. The office of city marshal had changed from appointive to elective in 1882. It was during this time that famed gunfighter Bat Masterson was appointed city marshal in an attempt to stop the murderous gunfights in Trinidad. However, Bat's appointment had no effect on the shoot-outs. In 1883, Bat ran for reelection, rather than gain reappointment and lost in a landslide to Lou Kreeger. Kreeger's long years of service are an obvious testament to his ability and a peace officer.

He is buried in Lot 117, Section 4.

Wooton, Richens Lacy "Uncle Dick" (1816 – 1893)

Richens L. Wooton came west from Virginia in the 1830s, serving in the Mexican War. He settled in what is now the area of the Colorado/New Mexico border. He was a mountain man, buffalo hunter and entrepreneur.

He was responsible for building the toll road over Raton Pass. He owned a buffalo ranch near present day Pueblo and is credited with the first cross-breeding of buffalo and cattle, and herding sheep over the Continental Divide to California. He is best known for providing food and "Taos Lightning" to the early settlers of Denver on the occasion of that city's first Christmas, in 1858.

A real opportunist, Wooton's generosity was calculated. He was the hero of Denver and dubbed "Uncle Dick." He opened a merchandise store the next day and became the leading merchant of the city. He retired to his Colorado beginnings near Trinidad. He opened a toll road over Raton Pass, along the Santa Fe Trail.

He is buried in Trinidad Catholic Cemetery in Lot 29, next to his fourth wife. There is a marker.

TRINIDAD MASONIC CEMETERY
LOCATED NORTHWEST OF TOWN.

One of the oldest cemeteries in Las Animas County still in operation, the Trinidad Masonic Cemetery was established in 1867. Several burials occurred on the grounds prior to official establishment, most of which are unmarked.

Beshoar, Michael M.D. (1858 – 1907)

Born in Pennsylvania, Michael Beshoar was living in Arkansas when the Civil War broke out. He was chief surgeon of the Arkansas Infantry when he was captured by Union forces. For the remainder of the war, he cared for the wounded on both sides of the conflict.

Following the war, Beshoar made his way west, arriving in the young town of Trinidad in 1867. Operating the first one-horse buggy in town, he traveled throughout the mostly unsettled territory, helping the sick, delivering babies, performing operations, and was one of the first to help the Indians and Hispanics with vaccinations against smallpox.

He opened the first drug store between Denver and Santa Fe, founded the first city newspaper, *The Advertiser,* as well as the *Pueblo Chieftain.* He was the first president of the Rocky Mountain Medical Association, organized in 1874.

He was a member of the Masonic Lodge, a founder of the Trinidad Chamber of Commerce and held such public offices as county coroner, clerk, judge, school superintendent, and was a state legislator.

He is buried in the family mausoleum high on the hill, over looking the Masonic cemetery.

Bloom, Frank G. (1843 – 1931)

Bloom arrived in Trinidad in 1867. He was the store manager for the prosperous Thatcher Brothers & Company. He later started the first bank of Trinidad, and became the director of the Bloom Cattle Company. He was one of the most respected and influential businessmen of Trinidad. He married Sarah Thatcher in 1869.

He is buried in Block 80, Lot W2.

Rice, Elial J. (1822 – 1872)

The young reverend is credited with organizing and preaching the town's first protestant sermon in 1868, at the newly-built Methodist Church. While many preachers served from town-to-town, Rice stayed in Trinidad. His church affiliation served many social functions and laid a moral foundation for the young community. Upon his death, Rice High School, the E. J. Rice Hose Company, and other landmarks were named in his honor.

He is buried in Block 66, Lot E2.

SIMPSON'S REST

Simpson, George S. (1818 – 1885)

A tall cliff on Trinidad's north side is the final resting place for George Semmes Simpson. Born in St. Louis, he left for the opportuni-

Denver Public Library
Preston Porter was burned to death by a mob in 1900, without benefit of a trial.

ties in the west, at age twenty. He joined a group of fur trappers, trapping on Colorado's rivers, until he reached Bent's Fort. There, he traded with the Indians, finally opening his own fort called El Pueblo (Fort Pueblo.)

By 1866, Simpson and his young family owned a small spread along the Purgatoire River at Trinidad. He was involved in the community, serving on various town commissions, including the school board. In later years, he wrote articles and poetry, published locally, and in the East.

In 1866, the Trinidad area was under constant threat from the Utes Indians. Simpson and his daughter Jennie, were chased by a band of Indians, yet managed to hide in a cave on a slope overlooking the small town. The incident was so profound, Simpson expressed a desire to be buried on the slope that saved his life and his daughter's.

When George S. Simpson died in 1885, a crew of men hauled his coffin to the top of the rocky ridge, a day-long ordeal. A monument was erected of granite and a bronze plaque was placed at the base.

Due to vandalism, the monument was restored in 1970, although not to the original height. The original plaque is now at the Trinidad History Museum.

Simpson's daughter, Jennie died in 1887, and is also buried atop the hill.

— — —

Ghost Notes, Mysteries,
& Other Related Findings

Evan Hall, a gambler and saloon keeper, had a bad reputation in Elbert County. Hall lived in a cabin near Bijou Creek with his four-teen-year-old wife. A man with deep set eyes, which never wavered, he was quick on the draw. He had a number of killings to his credit or discredit. Often the target of a disgruntled gun-toting gambler, Hall returned the fire, and rarely missed.

The law finally caught up with Hall. Hastily leaving the scene of his latest shooting, he tossed his gun aside, and fled on horseback. The posse caught up with Hall, made the arrest, and took the prison-er to Denver. Hall later escaped and returned to Elbert County, where he hid in a sawmill. A posse followed his trail, surrounding him at the mill. Hall eventually surrendered to the posse. A deputy, whose father was a victim of Hall, started toward Denver with his prisoner. As soon as the pair were out of sight, the deputy shot and killed Hall. He returned to the posse, stating Hall had tried to escape. The deputy was never questioned.

Hall's final burial spot, if there is one, is unknown.

* * *

On November 8, 1900, the body of thirteen-year-old Louise Frost was found in a prairie slough near her farm home south of Limon and north of Hugo. She had been raped, beaten, and stabbed fourteen times. There were heel marks on her forehead.

Mob mania seethed in the town of Limon. Denver newspaper reporters, encouraged the vigilante behavior. Two days later, a six-teen-year-old black youth named Preston Charles Porter confessed to the crime in Denver.[67] Lincoln County Sheriff John W. Freeman escorted young Porter by train to Limon for trial.[68] The Denver reporters alerted the citizens of Limon that the murderer was on his way and which train he would be on.

A mob of Limon men confronted Sheriff Freeman and pulled Porter off the train. He was dragged behind a buckboard to a spot south of Limon, near the site of the murder. He was chained to a wooden stake. The father of young Louise lit a match to the oil soaked timber at the feet of the accused. Porter screamed for over twelve minutes. As his cries died away, the crackling timber was the only sound in the dark night.

Although the ringleaders were all well-known, an inquest conclud-ed the incident was the work of parties unknown.

Preston Porter's charred remains were left on the open, windy prairie.

* * *

The site of Edgerton is near the south entrance to the Air Force Academy, north of Colorado Springs. Established in the 1860s, it is best remembered for one of the most brutal, unsolved murders in Colorado history. In 1886, neighbors found an older woman by the name of Kearney, in the barn of her ranch with her head split open by an ax. The horribly mutilated body of her six year-old grandson was found in a nearby grain bin. The kitchen table was set for three, the third person is unknown. A $500 reward was posted for information leading to the murderer, but the case has never been solved. Unfortunately, history does not record the burial site of Kearney and her grandson.

* * *

Colorado Springs' Pauper Cemetery was located at 21st Street and Lower Gold Camp Road. In 1960, the remains of the County Poor Farm burials were removed to Evergreen and Fairview Cemeteries.

* * *

Fort Pueblo, a very strategic military post was first documented by the Spanish explorers in 1673. Zebulon Pike used the fort in 1806 as did John C. Fremont during his explorations of the 1840s.

On Christmas Day, 1854, a band of Utes led by Chief Tierra Blanco, stormed the fort, killing most of the inhabitants. The fort was eventually abandoned. Mountain men and traders believed the fort was haunted.

It is unknown where the dead are buried, if they were buried. There are no records.

* * *

One of the oldest and largest cottonwood trees in Colorado once stood in the middle of Pueblo's South Union Avenue. The tree was eighty feet tall and twenty-six feet in circumference at its base. Known as "Old Monarch," it was more often called the "hangman's tree." Legend has it that fourteen men were hanged from the tree and one woman died beneath it. However, early Pueblo history records many hangings among the trees at the Fountain River.

The tree was cut down in June 1883, despite citizen protest. It seems the tree interfered with the heavy horse and wagon traffic. A new city council was elected shortly thereafter. A cross section of the tree is on display at the El Pueblo Museum in Pueblo.

* * *

William "Bill" Coe, and his band of outlaws roamed southern Colorado Territory during the 1860s. They robbed and terrorized travelers and homesteaders. The band boldly robbed wagon trains, merchants and stole horses from the Army in broad daylight. Coe publicly bragged in saloons of the Army's inability to catch him.

Finally captured at North Ranch, Coe was taken to Fort Lyon, where he managed to escape.

Recaptured and taken to the Pueblo jail, a lynch mob stormed through the town, intent on hanging Coe. At daybreak, Coe's body was discovered dangling from a tree in the nearby meadow.

Years ago, during an excavation project near Pueblo, a skeleton with leg irons was unearthed, and tentatively identified as the remains of William Coe.

— — —

Additional Cemeteries Listed by County

Baca County

Cemetery	1st Burial
Atlanta Cemetery	?
Boston Cemetery	?
Campo Cemetery	?
Carrizo Cemetery	?
Chapel Hill Cemetery	?
Dunkard Cemetery	1913
Konantz Cemetery	1891
Lone Star Cemetery	?
Lyons Camp Cemetery	?
Maxey Cemetery	?
Minneapolis Cemetery	?
Mount Carmel Cemetery	?
Prairie Queen Cemetery	?
Pritchett Cemetery	1927
Rodley Cemetery	?
Springfield Cemetery	?
Stonington Cemetery	?
Two Buttes Cemetery	?

Bent County

Cemetery	1st Burial
Bethel Cemetery	?
Caddoa Old Cemetery	?
Fort Bent Cemetery	? – Abandoned
Hasty Cemetery	?

Hight Cemetery	1918
Indian Rock Cemetery	?
Little Kansas Cemetery	? – Abandoned
McClave Cemetery	?
Pruett Cemetery	?
Wiley Cemetery	?

Cheyenne County

Cemetery	1st Burial
Aaby Cemetery	?
Aroya Cemetery	1911
Badito Cemetery	?
Indian Cemetery	?
Kennedy Cemetery	? – Abandoned
Mennonite Cemetery	?
Waterville Cemetery	1909
Weber Cemetery	?

Crowley County

Cemetery	1st Burial
Harrington Cemetery	?
Wagon Train Family	? – Abandoned
Ingram Cemetery	?
Lakeview Cemetery	?
Olney Springs Cemetery	1905
Parker-White Cemetery	?
Sand Arroya Cemetery	1914
Stradder Cemetery	?

Douglas County

Cemetery	1st Burial
Blight Cemetery	1880
Quick Cemetery	1866
Greenland Cemetery	1875
J. S. Parker Cemetery	1916
Jarre Canyon Cemetery	1884
Lake Gulch Cemetery	1865
McMurdo Cemetery	1871
Newlin Cemetery	1896
Palmer Lake Cemetery	1889
Rock Ridge Cemetery	1870
Russellville Cemetery	?
Spring Valley Cemetery	1870

Stone Canyon Cemetery	1906
Westcreek Cemetery	1896

Elbert County

Cemetery	1st Burial
Catholic Cemetery	? – Abandoned
Dunkers Cemetery	1916
Ebenezer Cemetery	1915
Gair Cemetery	1889
James Cemetery	1879
Kanza Cemetery	1907
Miller Cemetery	1876
Mountain View Cemetery	1907
Norton Cemetery	1908
Pleasant Plains Cemetery	1915
Sakala Cemetery	1906
Simla Cemetery	1915
Sproch Cemetery	1917

El Paso County

Cemetery	1st Burial
Antioch Cemetery	1913
Calhan Cemetery	1893
Crescent Cemetery	1910
Falcon Cemetery	?
Flynn Cemetery	1899
Forest View Cemetery	1892
Hanover Cemetery	1912
Lenardt Cemetery	1880
Monument Cemetery	1871
Myers Cemetery	1894
Peyton Cemetery	1891
Ramah Cemetery	1867
Shadeland Cemetery	1865
St. Mary's Cemetery	1905
Table Rock Cemetery	1872
Will Rogers Shrine Memorial	1935

Kiowa County

Cemetery	1st Burial
Arlington Cemetery	1891
Chivington Cemetery	1887
Eads Old Cemetery	? – Abandoned

France Cemetery	?
Galatea Cemetery	?
Hainer Cemetery	?
Haswell Cemetery	?
Jones Cemetery	?
Plainview Cemetery	?
Sheridan Lake Cemetery	?
Towner Cemetery	?
Wagoners Cemetery	?
Wargo Cemetery	?
Water Valley Cemetery	?

Las Animas County

Cemetery	1st Burial
Abeyta Cemetery	?
Aguilar Cemetery	?
Albertson Cemetery	?
Burro Canyon Cemetery	?
Carpio Cemetery	?
Cedar Hill Cemetery	?
Cejita Cemetery	?
Chicosa Cemetery	?
Cordova Cemetery	?
Crane Cemetery	1892
Earl Cemetery	1916
Edenview Cemetery	1919
Engleville Cemetery	?
Gulnare Cemetery	1904
Hicks Cemetery	?
Jansen Cemetery	1901
Kim Cemetery	?
Long Canyon Cemetery	1908
Maxwell Grant Cemetery	?
Medina Cemetery	1901
Mountain View Cemetery	1916
Reilly Canyon Cemetery	1908
San Juan Plaza Cemetery	1896
San Pedro Cemetery	1900
Sopris Cemetery	1876
Starkville Cemetery	1910
Stonewall Cemetery	1888
Temple Aaron Cemetery	1878
Tercio Cemetery	1905

Trujillo Cemetery   1887

Lincoln County

Cemetery	1st Burial
Boyero Cemetery	1915
Bucklin Cemetery	1927
Clifford Cemetery	1893
Liberty Bell Cemetery	1908
Mount Calvary Cemetery	1929
Ruby Cemetery	1913
Spring Hill Cemetery	1912
Walks Camp Cemetery	1918

Otero County

Cemetery	1st Burial
Bent's Old Fort Cemetery	1865 – Abandoned
East Holbrook Cemetery	?
Higbee Cemetery	1898
Mount View Cemetery	?

Prowers County

Cemetery	1st Burial
Amerine Cemetery	?
Bethel Cemetery	?
Butte Cemetery	1889
Crawford Cemetery	1888
Fort Holly Cemetery	?
Garber Cemetery	?
Hartman Cemetery	?
South Side Cemetery	1889
Sunnyslope Cemetery	?

Pueblo County

Cemetery	1st Burial
Beulah Cemetery	1869
Brookside/Riverside Cemetery	1865
Bucciarellis Cemetery	?
Colorado State Hospital Cemetery	?
Dog Town Cemetery	?
Finn Cemetery	?
Fisher Cemetery	1885 – Under I-25
Hicklin Cemetery	? – Under I-25
Highland Cemetery	?

Indian Burial Ground	?
Lime Cemetery	1898
Cedarville Cemetery	?
Mt. Olivet Cemetery	?
Overton Cemetery	1891
Peck Cemetery	?
Pinon Cemetery	?
Pueblo Pest Cemetery	?
Robinson Cemetery	?
San Jose Cemetery	?
St. Charles Cemetery	?
Tacony Cemetery	?
Turkey Creek Cemetery	1875
Verde Cemetery	?

— — —

Sources

Bent's Fort Museum, Las Animas
Big Timbers Museum, Lamar
Blevin, Terry – Lincoln County Historical Society
Carnegie Public Library, Trinidad
Carroll, Joan – Eastern Colorado Historical Society
Cedar Hill Cemetery Records
Colorado Historical Society, Denver
Elbert County Clerk and Recorder's Office
Jensen, Kay – Fowler Historical Society

Contributors

Air Academy High School History Class – 1997
Cheyenne Wells High School History Class – 1997
Crowley County High School History Class – 1997
McKean, Karlene – Cheyenne County
Phillips, Vicki – Elbert County
Rocky Ford High School American History Class – 1997

Newspapers

Castle Rock Journal
Castle Rock Independent
Denver Republican
Douglas County News
Gazette Telegraph

Fowler News
Fowler Tribune
Holly Chieftain
Las Animas Leader
La Junta Tribune
Lamar Daily News
Lincoln County Democrat
Lincoln County Ledger
Pueblo Chieftain
Rocky Ford Enterprise
Rocky Mountain News
The Holly Chieftain
The Parker Press Centennial Edition

Interviews

Dupree, Cliff, Historian, Holly, Colorado
Graff, Darla, Roselawn Cemetery, Pueblo
Griffy, Byron, Griffy Funeral Home, Fowler
McCarthy, Tim, McCarthy Funeral Home, Pueblo
Medrano, Steve, Valley View Cemetery Sexton, Rocky Ford
Murphy, Sara, Carnegie Public Library, Trinida

— — —

Chapter Five Notes

[1] While this area is commonly known as the Comanche National Grasslands, there are only a few areas designated as such.

[2] The term "proved up" on the land was common terminology.

[3] The Hungate family are buried in Denver. See Chapter 2.

[4] Elbert County was originally part of Douglas County.

[5] The site of Bijou Basin is now a ghost town on the Plains.

[6] Caroline and James mother, Sarah, are buried in the Boot Ranch Cemetery.

[7] It was later in the year that Russell moved his party upstream toward the future site of Denver, where his famous gold strike sparked the Colorado Gold Rush of 1859.

[8] Some historians spell the name as Binckley. Binkley is on the tombstone.

[9] Chilcott is buried in the Pueblo Pioneer Cemetery.

[10] The spelling of Gardner's town changed over the years, finally becoming Franktown.

[11] Jacob's seven-year-old daughter, Emma, is buried in the north section of the cemetery.

[12] Henderson's land is located at the south end of the Kit Carson Museum.

[13] Following the death of William Henderson, the marker was moved to the museum park in Kit Carson.

[14] See "Ghosts."

[15] A corrupted spelling of the Spanish word Arroyo, meaning "deep gulch."

[16] Not to be confused with the famous pioneer, Alexander Hicklin.

[17] This cemetery still exists, the oldest marked burial being 1880. However, there are many unmarked graves, while many graves were moved to the Evergreen Cemetery.

[18] His obituary lists his date of birth as 1861, however, research, and family reference give it as 1859.

[19] See Ghost Notes at the end of the chapter.

[20] One of her students was Cliff DuPree, who has graciously provided much of the information on the Holly Cemetery.

[21] The monument was erected by friends and sympathizers, sponsored by the I.O.O.F. The blizzard hit on March 26, 1931.

[22] Lamar Register, and Prowers County History.

[23] See Lamar's Riverside Cemetery.

[24] A new facility was built in the 1870s, with an annex called Maxwell.

[25] As of this writing, the land is on private property, and the owner is not known for his hospitality to visitors. Caution is advised. The land is reportedly under sale negotiations with the U.S government, although the exact site of the massacre is in some dispute.

[26] See Hungate Murders.

[27] See Chivington, John M.

[28] The name Wise, for Governor Wise of Virginia, was changed when that state left the Union in 1861. Officer Lyon was the first Union officer killed in battle in 1862, thus the name change.

[29] See Cody, William F.

[30] See Fort Lyon Cemetery.

[31] Bent's Old Fort is now a National Historic Site, located fifteen miles west of Las Animas on CO 194.

[32] See Sand Creek Battle Site. Secondly, historians differ with regard to the mother of George. Owl Woman died in childbirth in 1847. Yellow Woman gave birth to a child in late 1848. Both dates coincide with the reported age of George.

[33] Lueber, "William Bent's Family," Colorado Magazine, January 1936.

[34] See Sand Creek Massacre Site.

[35] The small community of Boggsville is now a National Historic Site. Kit Carson and his wife were reinterred in Taos, New Mexico.

[36] Few cemetery records exist prior to 1890.

[37] The surname is sometimes spelled Shea.

[38] The timber claim, on file at the Rocky Ford museum, is signed by President Grover Cleveland.

[39] One of the original counties of Colorado, Bent County was later divided. Fowler became a part of Otero County.

[40] Later named the Arkansas River.

[41] Manzanola Sun newspaper article, 1910.

[42] See Off The Beaten Path, Chapter 5.

[43] See appendix.

[44] The main road ran along the foothills, following Plum Creek from Denver to Colorado City.

[45] See Lake County, Chapter 5.

[46] This building is now a part of the South Park City Museum in Fairplay.

[47] Letter on file at the Colorado Historical Society.

[48] Grout's sister was Mrs. Upton Treat Smith.

[49] The United States Air Force Academy Cemetery used today was established in the 1960s.

[50] See Palmer, William J.

[51] The author is a distant relative to Womack.

[52] See Tobin, Thomas T.

[53] See Tabor, Mount Olivet Cemetery, Chapter 2.

[54] Recently, several graves were found on the grounds of the Pueblo State Hospital.

[55] Some sources claim the original name as Riverside, however, early cemetery records and mortician listings give the name as Riverview.

[56] A walking tour brochure is available at the cemetery office.

[57] "Billy" Adams is buried in the Alamosa Cemetery, Chapter 5.

[58] Robert Frasier is buried in Block 15, Lot 12.

[59] Michael Beshoar is buried in Trinidad's Masonic Cemetery.

[60] Other members of the Orphanage Cemetery were also moved at the same time in 1978, including six nuns, five orphans and one priest.

[61] Not to be confused with Old Colorado City, on Highway 24.

[62] Reports reveal some fifty bullets in the body of Louis Tikas.

[63] In research, it seems historians can not agree on the number of deaths, figures range from 13 to 50.

[64] His ornate tombstone incorrectly gives the date of death as 1875.

[65] There is no record of block or plot.

[66] Josefita Barela and other family members are buried at the original homestead, one-half-mile south of Barela. There is also a cemetery at Rivera.

[67] Many historians believe Porter's confession was forced. Because he never stood trial, the truth will never be known.

[68] John W. Freeman is buried in the Evergreen Cemetery, Hugo.

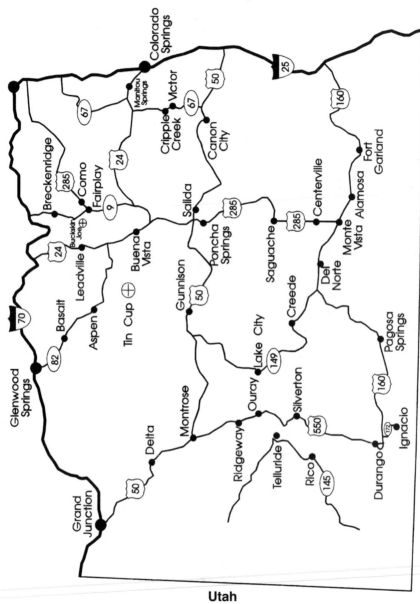

Chapter Six

The Great Divide

C olorado, west of the Continental Divide, belonged to Mexico until 1848, when it was ceded to the United States, following the Mexican War. The Divide is a jagged ridge, some 7,500 feet above sea level, running southwest through the state. It is high in these Rocky Mountains that the many rivers of Colorado are born. From peaks over 14,000 feet, flow the waters of the Platte, the San Juan, the Rio Grande, and the great rapids of the Arkansas and Colorado rivers.

The rugged Rocky Mountains are rich with minerals, ores, granite, and marble. Mineral veins of untold value run through the rock formations. They also produced hopes and dreams of thousands of early pioneers.

The first inhabitants of the land, the Anasazi, and Ute Indians, were forced off their homeland, and onto reservations. The white men moved in and claimed the land, in the name of Manifest Destiny.

The San Juan area grew slowly, but steadily. The 1870s became Colorado's Silver Era, with mining camps springing up across the mountain range. Legendary places like Ouray and Silverton made millions and millionaires. The Rockies seemed to open up and pour forth their riches.

These isolated mining camps, with their rich ore, needed roads. The adventurous and ingenious pioneer, Otto Mears, built that system. Mountain toll roads, and later, railroads, connected the mountain communities, allowing transportation of ore, and supplies. Smelters, factories, and a host of businesses supplied the western slope. The railroad expansion created several towns, such as Durango, Salida, and Buena Vista.

The repeal of the Sherman Silver Purchase Act, in 1893, came close to crippling the state of Colorado. The Sherman Act, passed in 1890, doubled the amount of silver backing for United States currency. Silver prices were at a premium, with Colorado mines producing sixty percent of the nation's reserve. With the repeal of the Sherman Act by the Senate in 1893, the price of silver plummeted to less than sixty cents an ounce. Mines closed overnight. Thousands went into bankruptcy. The period was known as the "Silver Panic of 1893."

Colorado's saving grace was the new discovery of gold in 1890. An unsuspected area at the base of Pike's Peak, where cattle lazily grazed, produced the largest gold strike in the United States. A curious cowpoke named Bob Womack, discovered gold in the volcanic rock structure at an area known as Cripple Creek. By 1893, more than two million dollars worth of gold had been extracted from the hills of Cripple Creek and Victor. Colorado's statewide depression got a short-lived reprieve.

— — —

US Highway 24 West

OLD COLORADO CITY

FAIRVIEW CEMETERY

SOUTH 26TH STREET, COLORADO SPRINGS

Colorado City, the busy supply town to the rich mining camps, was founded in 1859. The city had three cemeteries at one time, all of which have succumbed to progress.

Fairview Cemetery was officially established in 1895 on land donated by Anthony Butt, in exchange for water rights. Located just west of Colorado Springs, the city annexed the cemetery in 1917.[1] The beautiful grounds are maintained by purchaser endowments.

Burton, Blanche (1859 – 1909)

She is thought to be the first madam of the Cripple Creek gold camp. By the turn of the century, Blanche Burton had made Colorado City her home. She was known in the community for her charitable donations and volunteer work for the poor.

Her life came to a tragic and mysterious end in 1909. According to newspaper accounts, she was in her home on Colorado Avenue when a curtain caught fire from a knocked over oil lamp. With her clothing burning, Blanche ran from the house. Two policemen met her, throwing coats and snow on her. Hours later she was dead.

According to witnesses, a man was seen running from the scene. The police were unable to link the man to the crime.

Blanche had spent her only money the day before her death on a ton of coal, much of which she gave away.

She was buried on Christmas Eve with the services paid for by a fellow madam. Her grave was unmarked.

In 1983, a local club raised money to erect a marker. The granite stone memorializing Blanche says, "Pioneer Madam."

Blanche is buried in Block 12, Lot 28.

Gayer, Garland (1885 – 1971)

Garland Gayer was born in the Cherokee Nation, and raised by the Quip Indians. He later married, and with his wife, Stellar, and baby daughter Irene, Gayer journeyed to Colorado in 1908. He homesteaded land near Woodland Park. He built a frame cabin for his family, and raised potatoes, barley and oat hay, which he delivered to the Colorado Springs market, a two-day trip.

Later, he moved to Green Mountain Falls, where his children were nearer to schools. There he established a thriving livery business. He was an El Paso County deputy sheriff for eight years and town marshal of Green Mountain Falls for several years.

He is buried beside his wife Stellar, in Block 17, Lot 63.

Lamont, Duncan (1865 – 1940)

A native of Scotland, Duncan Lamont came to America at the turn of the century. He settled in Colorado City in 1902.

He became the pastor of the First Baptist Church, at a salary of fifty dollars for the first six months. While a pastor, he became a leader of the opposition to saloons and brothels. His wife Katherine was the president of the Women's Christian Temperance Union.

In his later years, he was a member of the town school board. In 1916, President Woodrow Wilson appointed him postmaster of Colorado City. In 1936, he was elected to the Colorado Senate.

He is buried beside his wife in Block 1, Lot 8.

McDaniel, Laura Bell (1861 – 1918)

At age twenty-one, Laura Bell McDaniel left her native Missouri for Colorado, eventually settling in Colorado City a few years later.

She opened her business of pleasure one block south of Colorado Avenue, in Colorado City. The Tribly House, as it was known, became so popular for the politicos, that tunnels were built under Colorado Avenue, connecting to the Red Light District, including a direct tunnel to Laura Bell's place. The favoritism of politicians toward Laura Bell was short-lived. By 1917, the Conformist Movement succeeded in closing down the Red Light District.

On a January day in 1918, Laura Bell took a blind miner to Denver for an appointment. They were traveling in her 1910 Mitchell sedan, when a serious accident occurred. Laura died of internal injuries.

She is buried in the family plot, beside her mother and stepfather, in Block 2, Lot 8.

Robinson, Amanda (? – 1914)

A runaway slave, Amanda fled west, leaving her mother behind. She rode to freedom with a family bound by wagon train to New Mexico. By 1866, she had married Charles Robinson at Fort Union.

Eventually, the couple brought their family to Colorado Springs. Charles hired out as a cook, and soon became employed at General Palmer's Glen Eyrie estate.[2] The family moved to a home close to the Eyrie estate. Charles eventually opened his own bakery, while Amanda raised their seven children. Years later, Amanda finally located her mother, living in Illinois.

She is buried in Block 8, Lot 18.

Winternitz, Isaac A. (1862 – 1908)

A native of Pennsylvania, Isaac Winternitz received his medical degrees in Ohio, before traveling west. He first settled in Hoxie, Kansas, where he practiced his profession and married Nellie Huff in 1889. Years later, he brought his family to Colorado City, where he set up his medical practice.

Serving three terms as city physician, he remained in this capacity for fifteen years. While city physician, a disgruntled citizen once shot the good doctor. Public health laws caused him to deny a burial permit for a young girl who had died from diphtheria. The grieving father of the young woman confronted Winternitz, shooting him in the abdomen. The doctor survived.

In 1908, while treating a patient for blood poisoning, the doctor became infected. Within a week, a finger, then an arm were surgically removed to stop the spread of the disease. Winternitz died of blood poisoning in July 1908.

A Master Mason, the local lodge headed his funeral procession down Colorado Avenue, the largest funeral ceremony in their history.

The granite tombstone bears his name and his wife, Nellie. There are several headstones in the family plot in Block 9, Lot 27.

MANITOU SPRINGS

CRYSTAL VALLEY CEMETERY

LOCATED WEST OF TOWN. FROM MANITOU AVENUE, GO WEST TO THE STOP LIGHT, THEN TURN LEFT ON CRYSTAL PARK ROAD TO PLAINVIEW. TURN RIGHT ON PLAINVIEW TO THE CEMETERY.

The original cemetery was located in town, on Pawnee Avenue. Doctor Isaac Davis owned the land, and donated a portion of it to the cemetery in the late 1880s. The Crystal Valley Cemetery was established in 1890. The majority of the graves from the original location were moved at that time. The cemetery is beautifully landscaped and well maintained by the city. Among the ornate monuments is that of Mabel Jane Willie, the first female mayor of Manitou Springs.

A small stone building remaining on the original property, contained a few of the deceased inhabitants of the former cemetery. One was Tom O'Neal. He was killed in a saloon brawl in nearby Colorado City. Dr. Davis was the county coroner holding the inquest. While an attempt was made to locate relatives of the deceased, O'Neal's body was placed in the stone lodge.

Dr. Davis relied on his druggist knowledge to devise an embalming process for O'Neal. He used chemicals, salt, and the sun for drying purposes. After two years of post death care, Tom O'Neal was decidedly the nearest specimen of a perfect mummy Colorado and perhaps all of America had ever seen. Following the death of Dr. Davis, the contents of the stone building, including O'Neal's mummified remains, were removed.

Tom O'Neal was buried in a loose gravel grave. Shortly after the burial, a couple of thieves dug him up, hoping to showcase him. Eventually, O'Neal's body did go on tour, last seen at a county fair in Seattle, Washington.

Adams, Charles (1840 – 1895)

Born Charles Adams Schwanbeck in Prussia, in 1840, he dropped the last name when he migrated to the United States. In 1861, he enlisted in the Union Army and served in the Civil War, where he achieved the rank of General. By 1869, he was in Colorado Territory, serving as secretary under General Edward McCook, whom he knew during the War. McCook had been appointed Territorial Governor of Colorado at the time. Adams later married McCook's sister, Margaret.

Adams became the Indian agent for the White River Utes, following the tragedy at Meeker, in 1879. He was instrumental in arranging the release of the Meeker women, who had been taken hostage by the Indians during the Meeker Massacre.[3] He also served as minister to

Bolivia under President Hayes, where he administered the negotiation for peace between Bolivia and Chile.

He retired to the Manitou area in the 1870s, where he organized the Manitou Water Company and the Glass Works at Colorado City. He remained a friend to the Ute Indians, often receiving Chief Ouray and his wife Chipeta, in his home in Manitou.

He died in the gruesome Gummery Hotel fire in Denver, which claimed twenty-two lives, in 1895. He is buried in Section 17, Lot 3.

Crawford, Emma (1863 – 1891)

Like several of Manitou Springs' early settlers, Emma came west in 1889, with the hope of regaining her health. Her fiancé, William Hildebrand, followed her to the area. Emma loved to gaze at the mountain scenery and take walks in the hills around Manitou, as her health improved. One particular evening, she returned quite late, explaining she had climbed Red Mountain and tied a kerchief on a tree, expressing her desire to be buried at that spot.

Plans were underway for her wedding, when she suffered a relapse and died. Her wish for burial on Red Mountain was carried out. Working two shifts, twelve pallbearers carried her casket to the mountain top.

With time, weather and erosion, the casket eventually washed down the canyon. Emma's remains were gathered and reinterred in the Crystal Valley Cemetery. The exact location is unknown.

Davis, Isaac, Doctor (1836 – 1891)

Dr. Davis, the town's first physician, was also the first druggist, undertaker and county coroner for six years. He served as mayor for one term, justice of the peace for five years and town trustee for several terms. He organized the community school district, and served as president of the school board for several years.

He was involved in commercial property development, including land deals which resulted in the new Crystal Valley Cemetery.

Dr. Davis is buried in Section 12, Lot 4.

Duclo, George E. (1893 – 1918)

An early pioneer of Manitou Springs, George Duclo, served in World War I. He died in France during the war, the only causality from the city of Manitou Springs. Memorial Park was dedicated in his honor, following his death. Duclo Avenue is named for him.

He is buried in Section 4, Lot 8.

Grafton, Homer H.
(1852 – 1921)

Homer Grafton came west from Ohio, eventually settling in Manitou Springs. He was postmaster in 1893, serving twenty-six years. He was a school principal and member of the state Legislature.

He is buried in Section 4, Lot 6.

Kenny, Theresa M.
(1859 – 1943)

The story of Theresa Kenny centers around her unusual mausoleum at Crystal Valley Cemetery. Constructed in the late 1930s, Kenny built it herself, with the exception of the roof. The wall texturing was done with a kitchen spoon.

Author's collection
Mt. Olivet Cemetery, Buena Vista

She was known as a hard-working, self-reliant woman of Austrian descent. She built and made improvements on her home at 364 Ruxton Avenue.

Upon completion of her mausoleum, her greatest joy was to rock in her chair, placed on the porch of her "little house," as she called it. Her funeral plans and payments for the cemetery site were completed fourteen years prior to her death.

The Kenny mausoleum is located in Section 2, Lot 7.

BUENA VISTA

MT. OLIVET CEMETERY

LOCATED JUST SOUTHWEST OF THE TOWN OF BUENA VISTA. FROM THE ONLY LIGHT ON MAIN STREET, GO WEST TO TIN CUP ROAD. THE CEMETERY IS LESS THAN ONE-QUARTER-MILE, ON THE LEFT SIDE OF THE ROAD.

Organized in 1875, this cemetery lays in the shadow of Mt. Princeton. It is well planned with sections thoughtfully laid out, maintained roadways, including street signs, and nice landscaping.

Mt. Olivet claims a celebrity of some fame–Elaine Perry Frehauff. Born in 1921, Elaine was the daughter of Antoinette Perry and Frank Frehauff. Elaine's mother was involved in many Broadway productions, including directing the long running play, *Harvey*, by Denver author Mary Chase.[4] The Tony Awards were named in honor of Antoinette Perry. Elaine followed in her mother's footsteps, as a producer and director on Broadway. Her credits included the famed play *Guys and Dolls*. Her ashes are located in Tier 4. There is a marker.

At the eastern edge of the cemetery, toward the center, is the Children's Section. Several of the tiny graves lining the fenced boundary, are unmarked.[5] To the north of this plot, is the section reserved for the unclaimed inmates of the Buena Vista Reformatory. Wooden crosses painted white are the only markers. [6]

Leadville Hill is located at the extreme north end of the cemetery. Thirty-three bodies were discovered in a land excavation north of Buena Vista in the 1930s. The bodies were moved in three boxes to their present resting spot in the cemetery.

Bonney, Josiah M. (1851 – 1925)[7]

Josiah Bonney was one of the founders of the First National Bank, established in 1900. He served as president for several years, as well as county commissioner.When the bank failed during the Depression, Bonney's First National Bank was one of only two banks in the country to pay off all depositors before closing. His ornate Victorian frame home still stands on San Juan Avenue.

His family plot is located in Old Block 4, Lots 41 and 42.

Cogan, Jeremiah (1838 – 1904)

Jeremiah Cogan arrived in Buena Vista in 1880. It is said he escaped Ireland to avoid prison. By 1889, he owned a cattle ranch. His ranch was self-sufficient, his electricity provided a generator in a creek running through his property. One of the largest ranches in the county, it is still family-owned and still self-sufficient.

He is buried in the north end of the cemetery, in Tier 4.

Condrall, Waible Milam Hewitt, Colorado Debera (1870 – 1955)

Colorado Debera, (her real first name) was born aboard the *U.S.S. Colorado*, sailing from England to America, in 1870. Her mother died during childbirth. The captain of the ship christened her "Colorado," and cared for her until the ship docked at New York.

In 1880, at age ten, she was a nurse at Fort Fetterman, Wyoming.[8]

At age twelve, she was listed in Leadville as a laundress. She worked as a laundress in Buena Vista, marrying several times, including a marriage to the town marshal, and lost two husbands to illness.[9]

She is buried in Old Block 3, Lot 21.

Enderlin, Alphonse A. (1862 – 1932)
Enderlin, Elizabeth (1857 – 1929)

Alphonse Enderlin, a native of France, arrived in Buena Vista in the early 1890s, earning his living as a plumber. It was at Buena Vista, that he earned the nickname "Foozy."

A respectable businessman in the community, he became captain of the Buena Vista Hose Cart Team. [10]

Elizabeth arrived in Buena Vista in 1886. Her fancy dress and painted face told the town her trade. In no time at all, she had acquired a lot on the north side of Main Street, where she built a brick house. She has been described as fairly tall, over five feet seven inches, dark brown hair and blue eyes, fair skinned and beautiful. Some historians believe her real name was Elizabeth Marshall.[11]

"Cock-Eyed Liz," as she was known, opened the finest parlor house within a hundred miles of Buena Vista. She acquired the name "Cock-Eyed Liz" after drunken men caused a fight at her parlor on behalf of a rival madam. She received a blow to the right eye, causing blindness and loss of eye muscle control.

Alphonse "Foozy" Enderlin was a frequent visitor to the "House of Joy," as Cock-Eyed Liz called it. In time, Liz let him make wine in her kitchen. The relationship grew into marriage in 1897.

Liz became a respectable wife, and "Foozy," a doting husband. They lived in a small quarter of the parlor house, renting out the rest. The marriage lasted thirty-one years until Elizabeth died in 1929. Her husband "Foozy," followed five years later.

They are buried together in Block A, Lot 12. There is a large granite marker at the edge of the cemetery, enclosed with plumber's pipe fencing.

Wahl, Charles F. (1853 – 1930)

Charles Wahl owned several mines, including the Anna Derika Mine at Tin Cup. He shot Clanson Gregg in 1886, at the town store in Tin Cup. He later was exonerated of all charges. He was a member of the Mason's Lodge.

He is buried in Old Block 6, Lot 30.

Wright, Dr. Abner E. (1816 – 1907)

Born and educated in New York, he brought his medical degree with him, when he arrived in Buena Vista. One of the earliest pioneers, Dr. Wright later served as Lake County coroner. He invested in mining, selling his Mary Murphy mine at Tin Cup, for $72,000. He was known to have been involved in the Lake County War.[12]

He is buried in Old Block 7, Lot 130.

Author's collection

Lewis Lamb was murdered on the streets of Leadville by Martin Duggan in 1880. Mrs. Lamb danced on the killer's grave when he died seven years later.

LEADVILLE

EVERGREEN CEMETERY

LOCATED WEST OF THE TOWN OF LEADVILLE. TAKE 8TH STREET WEST TO JAMES STREET, TURN RIGHT. THE CEMETERY IS APPROXIMATELY ONE-QUARTER-MILE ON THE LEFT. ENTER THROUGH THE STONE GATE ON THE EAST SIDE.

Leadville's first burial occurred in 1879, at the west end of Chestnut Street. In November of the same year, the city bought 160 acres northwest of the city for a proper burial site. The land was located on one of the many mineral deposits of the area. The enormous mountain timber gave way to the name of Evergreen. Evergreen Cemetery has been the scene of many of Leadville's events. The first legal hanging in the area occurred at the cemetery. Convenient, to say the least! Most of the town turned out to witness the event. During the nineteenth century, Decoration Day celebrations were held at the cemetery.[13] Full of color, picnic lunches, bands and speeches, it was an annual event all looked forward to.

> *Hereafter, when the excursionist and the visitor come to look upon our city and its vast carbonate fields, the Leadvillian may with pride, carry him over Capitol Hill to look upon Evergreen Cemetery, the city of the dead.*[14]

The cemetery is laid out in twelve sections, the Catholic, Catholic Free, Elks, G.A.R., Jewish, Knights of Pythias, A.O.U.W., I.O.O.F., Masonic, P.O.S.A., Protestant, and Protestant Free. Landscaping is purely natural, with many pine trees, and shrubs. There are few wild flowers, as the cemetery is so shaded by abundant trees.

The oldest part of the cemetery, reserved for burials of the less affluent is in very sad condition. The massive old pine trees have grown through the coffins, bringing some of them to the surface, where many are visible. The cemetery's expansion during the silver boom years was mainly due to the pneumonia, typhoid fever and diphtheria epidemics which swept the mining camp.

Lamb, Lewis (? – 1880)
Lamb, Mindy (? – 1888)

An early pioneer of Leadville, Lewis Lamb became the victim of random murder in Leadville. Eye witness accounts say retired Marshal Martin Duggan, driving a sleigh, rounded the corner of Pine and 5th streets, almost knocking down Lewis Lamb. Words were exchanged, and Duggan turned the sleigh around, speeding down the street. Lamb pulled his gun, while Duggan jumped from the sleigh and fired at Lamb, killing him instantly. Duggan was not

Author's collection
Buffalo Bill Cody placed this marker on the grave of his close friend, "Texas Jack."

charged. The widow, Mrs. Mindy Lamb hated Duggan and wore "widows weeds" until Duggan's death. She further swore to dance on Duggan's grave and deliver her widows weeds to Duggan's wife. Seven years later Duggan was killed and Widow Lamb danced on his grave in Denver and delivered her widows weeds.

The Lamb graves are located in Block 15, lot 3 at the west end of the road.

Mickey, Maggie (Molly May) (? – 1887)

Molly May, as she was known, was one of Leadville's most famous madams. Generous in her contributions to the town's welfare, including large sums of money to both churches and hospitals, socially, Molly was an outcast. Involved in a deadly rivalry with fellow madam, Sally Purple, insults turned into gunfire between the two bordellos, owned by Molly and Sally. Amazingly, there were no injuries.

In business, Molly's was very successful. In 1882, she broke into the headlines by adopting a destitute child. Some of the townsfolk saw it as sinister, while others praised her. Molly died in 1887, leaving a considerable fortune to the child. Her funeral was one of the largest in Leadville.

Her grave is located in Block 25, lot 8.

Omohundro, John Baker (Texas Jack) (1846 – 1880)

A noted scout, "Texas Jack," as he was known, became a showman in Buffalo Bill Cody's Wild West Show, and was a great friend to Wild Bill Hickok.[15] He retired to Leadville, where he died of pneumonia. Several years after his death, Cody personally placed the headstone standing today.

The grave is located on the second road left from the entrance about 150 yards west. The grave is behind the George Stuart marker on the right.

CAMP HALE

At the foot of Tennessee Pass, atop the Continental Divide, stands the large granite monument dedicated to the loss of nearly a thousand members of the 10th Mountain Division during World War II.

A few short miles below the monument is Camp Hale, where the 10th Mountain Division trained from 1942 to 1944. The rugged mountain terrain of the Colorado Rockies proved good training for mountain troops.

Members of the National Ski Patrol filled the first ranks, followed by ski instructors and qualified skiers. Training included mountain climbing, back packing and war maneuvers in sub zero weather.

Entering the European war theater, the 10th Mountain Division performed admirably. The enemy blocked mountain passes that were overcome by the men of the 10th.

While all of America's soldiers served bravely in war, a tribute stands to the 10th Mountain Division, our Colorado boys.

— — —

US Highway 82 West

ASPEN

ASPEN/RED BUTTE CEMETERY

LOCATED WEST OF ASPEN. FROM MAIN STREET (HIGHWAY 82,) GO WEST, CROSSING THE CASTLE CREEK BRIDGE. TURN RIGHT ON CEMETERY LANE. THE CEMETERY IS ON THE RIGHT SIDE OF THE ROAD, APPROXIMATELY ONE-QUARTER-MILE.

Officially established in 1879, there is a marker dated 1874. The cemetery is well maintained, with many looming trees.

Bowman, John L. (1845 – 1924)

Arriving in Aspen in 1888, John Bowman operated the Schiller Mine. An amateur photographer, he later opened a bar and museum, known as Bowman's Musee.

Heavily involved in politics, he supported the Populist Party which won the election of fellow townsman Davis Waite to the office of Colorado governor. So confident in the party, he stated he would never cut his beard if the party lost the presidential election of 1892. The Populists lost, and Bowman kept his word.

He is buried in Block 7.

Elrod, George (1844 – 1914)[16]

George Elrod arrived in Aspen from his native South Carolina in 1890. He owned a contracting business. Involved in community affairs, he was elected town trustee in 1891, serving four consecutive terms.

He is buried in Block 4. There is a marker.

Koch, Harry G. (1862 – 1936)

Harry Koch came to Aspen in 1885. He found work as a ditch digger at ten cents a foot. Aspen was booming and growing rapidly. Four days into his employment, Koch became foreman for the company.

He started the Koch Lumber Company, a pioneer business of the community, and went on to be one of the most respected citizens in Aspen.

Harry Koch is buried in Block 7.

Waite, Davis H. (1825 – 1901)
Waite, Celia O. (1844 – 1937)

A pioneer of Aspen's early mining beginnings, Davis Waite was the editor of the *Aspen Union Era*. The uncertainty of silver prices during the Sherman Silver Purchase Act years, beginning in 1890, allowed for the Populist Party to emerge and take a stronghold in Colorado. Believing in the Silver Trade issue, Colorado's backbone industry, Waite rallied to the cause, while the Democrats and Republicans differed and dallied over the issue. Amidst the political upheaval, Waite was elected governor of Colorado on the Populist ticket in 1893.

Strong in his opinions, he attempted an iron rule approach to the state leadership. With this philosophy, Waite became known as "Bloody Bridles" Waite. The famous Denver City Hall War was waged against Waite. He had appointed and then fired two entire city fire and police boards. The two refused to resign, barricading themselves in City Hall with reinforcements. Governor Waite called in the State

Militia as thousands jammed the building. The matter was settled in court.

Waite's leadership had no chance against the repeal of the Sherman Silver Purchase Act of 1893. Mines closed, thousands were out of work and economic upheaval became rampant. Mining camps still in operation suffered strikes across the state. Waite called in the Militia at Cripple Creek and El Paso County, under great criticism.

To his credit, he signed legislation in 1893, granting women the right to vote in Colorado. After his term as governor, he returned to Aspen where he lived out his days.

Mrs. Waite came to Aspen with her second husband, Davis, and three children from her first marriage, in 1885. The new family arrived by a horse-drawn sled in the dead of winter. While her husband served the young town as legal adviser, Mrs. Waite was involved in social causes. One of her closest friends was Mrs. Baby Doe Tabor.

The Davis H. Waites are buried side by side in Block 1.

ASPEN GROVE CEMETERY
LOCATED EAST ON MAIN STREET (HIGHWAY 82) TOWARD INDEPENDENCE PASS. TURN LEFT ON MCSKIMMING ROAD, AND CROSS THE ROARING FORK BRIDGE. THERE IS A DRIVEWAY AT THE ENTRANCE TO THE CEMETERY. FROM THERE THE WALK IS ABOUT ONE-HALF-MILE.

This quiet, forlorn mountain cemetery was established in 1889. It is overgrown, yet that lends a beauty all its own. Among the burials are two of Aspen's more notable pioneers.[17]

Cowenhoven, Henry P. (1814 – 1896)
Cowenhoven arrived in the young town of Aspen in 1880, with his wife and young daughter. He opened the first grocery store on the corner of Cooper and Galena. He had many investments in the area, including large mining claims. A $250 grubstake led him to a partnership in the Aspen Mine, the richest in the world.

His fire and hose company was the first to serve the community. He was involved in community affairs and politics. One of the wealthiest pioneers of the area, his brick and stone mansion on Hallam Street was the talk of the town. His daughter married his long- time business partner, D. C. R. Brown.

King, J. H. (1856 – 1895)
A native of Athens, Georgia, King earned his law degree at the University of Virginia. He settled in Aspen in 1880, where he served his community in legal affairs. Instrumental in the town's founda-

tions, he became the first city attorney upon Aspen's incorporation in 1881. He served the town in a legal capacity until his death.

UTE CEMETERY
LOCATED EAST ON MAIN STREET (HIGHWAY 82) TOWARD INDEPENDENCE PASS WHERE THE ROAD TURNS INTO SPRING STREET. CONTINUE ON SPRING STREET PAST THE FOUR-WAY STOP SIGN TO UTE AVENUE. TURN LEFT, FOLLOWING THE ROAD TO THE UNPAVED PARKING LOTS. THE CEMETERY IS BEYOND THE FENCE TO THE WEST.

This rustic cemetery, established in 1879, sits at the foot of Independence Pass. No longer maintained, the scattered monuments stand among overgrown brush and trees that whisper sad tales with the mountain wind.[18]

A tale of mystery and sadness marks the grave of Ida Chatfield. Very little is known of her life prior to arriving in Aspen. She was a clerk at H. W. Pierson's store in Aspen, when she suddenly disappeared in July 1886. A few days later, a ransom of $500 was demanded for the return of Miss Chatfield.

The sheriff's office raised the ransom and accompanied a Mr. Osgood to the ranch of John T. Peck, two miles north of Aspen. A partner of Mr. Osgood's stated he had seen Miss Chatfield through the window of the cabin on the previous Sunday. Mr. Peck allowed the sheriff's party to search his cabin, but stated he had not seen Miss Chatfield. The search party revealed nothing.

The ransom money was returned, but the investigation did not end. A few of the men in the search party decided it was all a hoax, perpetrated by the concerned citizen, Mr. Osgood. There, the matter was dropped.

Ida Chatfield's body was found in the Roaring Fork River on August 6, 1886.[19]

The coroner listed the cause of death as drowning. She was buried at the Ute Cemetery.

BASALT

BASALT CEMETERY
LOCATED JUST SOUTH OF THE TOWN OF BASALT. FROM BASALT, GO SOUTH ON THE TWO RIVERS ROAD (OLD HIGHWAY 82.) TURN LEFT ON ELK RUN DRIVE. FOLLOW CEMETERY LANE TO THE CEMETERY.

The Fairview Cemetery Association was organized in June 1898. Records indicate that the land was given to the town of Basalt by Sam Cramer. The oldest recorded burial is that of Sarah Alice Willis, who died in 1895 at the age of twenty-five. Prior to the establishment of the cemetery, a small burial site existed on the north branch of the Frying Pan River, across from the present Ranger Station. Burials consisted primarily of those killed during construction of the Colorado Midland Railroad. It was known as Graveyard Hill. The present cemetery is maintained and includes a memorial to the GAR.

Danielson, Albert (1861 – 1897)

Albert Danielson was the lead engineer of the Colorado Midland Railroad, driving the train a mile above Lime Creek, when tragedy struck. Leaning out the gangway to check for water or steam from the exit pipes, the train was so close to the road cliff that his head hit a protruding rock. His body was ejected from the train, due to the force. It was several miles later when Danielson was discovered missing from the train.

He is buried in the south section of Block 18, Lot 3.

Hyrup, Jens P. (1857 – 1899)

A horrific train accident occurred on November 24, 1899. The coal branch out of Cardiff was a treacherous mountain route, at times exceeding a four percent grade.

Jens "Peter" Hyrup was an experienced engineer on the route, having worked for the Colorado Midland Railroad for a number of years. He arrived in America in 1885, and later married and settled with his family in 1891, in the Basalt area.

On this particular trip, while Hyrup was familiar with the route, his crew was not. After a stop at the Spring Gulch tank, Hyrup whistled off, and the train resumed its trip down the mountain. In the meantime, the brakeman released the hand brakes and retainers. Engine thirty-two was instantly out of control, hitting a bank causing the boiler to blow. The brakemen managed to jump off the train, but Hyrup died in the explosion.

He is buried in Block 20, Lot 1, with his wife Anna, who died in 1921.

Lupton, Daniel W. (1855 – 1930)

An early pioneer of Basalt, Daniel and his wife Nancy, arrived in 1891 from Leadville. Very active in business and industrial enterprises, they were instrumental in the town's foundation. Lupton served on the first town council, holding an office for several years.

The couple owned a saloon, a meat market, a fruit farm, and eventually an entire block in Basalt's business district. Investing interests included mining and the railroad. Nancy Lupton was an active leader in the Methodist church until her death in 1935.

They are buried together in Block 82, Lot 3.

Olson, Anna (1872 – 1960)

Born Christmas Day in Switzerland, Alma arrived in the United States at the age of seventeen. She worked at the cheese factory in Carbondale and later married Charles Peterson. By 1902, they owned a ranch two miles north of Basalt. Eight children were born to this union.

Following the death of Mr. Peterson, Anna married Enoch Olson around 1905. Born in 1874, he too was a native of Switzerland. They had four children.

Anna Olson was a prominent figure in Basalt. Caring for her large family as well as working the family ranch, she was very active in community life. She was involved in school functions, church affiliations and recorded much of the history of Basalt.

She is buried in a small plot, close to her son Fred, in Block 12, Lot 3.

Tierney, William (1849 – 1897)
Tierney, Ella (1858 – 1924)

William Tierney was born in New York. His father died when he was six years old, his mother died when he was twelve. Passed off to various family members, he managed to get an education. He traveled the world as a merchant seaman, mined and prospected in the United States and Alaska before settling in the Basalt area.

He owned a large ranch on Woody Creek between Aspen and Basalt. The T-W Bar brand became the most acclaimed in horse breeding in western Colorado. In 1887, he leased the ranch and moved to Aspen Junction. A pioneer merchant of the town, he operated the first general store.

William Tierney died on Easter Sunday, April 18, 1897, of pneumonia. The new bell installed in the Methodist Church rang for the first time at Mr. Tierney's funeral.

Following the death of Mr. Tierney, his widow Ella continued the local business. She oversaw the completion of the brick church structure, begun by her husband, It stands in the business district of downtown Basalt.

William and Ella are buried together in Block 18. Lot 2.

— — —

Highway 50 West

CANON CITY
GREENWOOD CEMETERY

LOCATED SOUTH OF CANON CITY. FROM FIRST STREET TURN SOUTH. FOLLOW THE ROAD SOUTH THAT BECOMES TEMPLE CANYON ROAD. THE CEMETERY IS APPROXIMATELY SIX BLOCKS SOUTH OF TOWN.

In 1865, a man by the name of William M. Davis was buried in the field of the W. C. Catlin homestead, southwest of Canon City. It was the first recorded burial of the area. Sometime in the 1870s, the Catlin family donated part of their land, including the burial site, to the city as a cemetery.[20]

The Greenwood Cemetery was laid out in sections including the Catholic, Masonic, Odd Fellows, Soldiers of War, Confederate Veterans, and GAR Union sections. Somewhat ironic, and a little confusing, the Confederate Veterans Section is located in the northern part of the cemetery, while the GAR Union Section is located in the southern end of the cemetery. The Confederate Section is marked with a granite marker, while the GAR Union Section is marked with a mound of rocks which once held a flag pole. The last interment in the GAR Section was in 1940–that of ninety-ninety-year-old John Weed, a Union Veteran of the Civil War. The location is Block GAR, Plot N.

The section dedicated to the veterans of the Spanish American War includes the steel government marker dedicated to Eliphalet Comer Baldwin. The plate says:

> *1898–1902 Spanish War Veteran–Philipines, Cuba,*
> *U.S.A., Puertico Rica.*

He was buried in 1912.

The pauper section was a project of the WPA in the 1930s. The wooden crosses erected at that time have long since deteriorated. A separate section was laid out for the inmates of the Colorado State Penitentiary.

Official records of the cemetery burials began in 1876. Trees were planted in the 1930s and evidence of landscaping is visible. Natural grasses and wild flowers abound throughout the cemetery. Large family plots are prevalent, the Davis and Griffin plots being the largest.

Blancett, Truman (1839 – 1945)

The oldest pioneer buried in Greenwood Cemetery, Truman Blancett, a famed scout and mountain man, was 106 years old at his death.

He is buried in Block 14, Plot 79.

Cameron, Robert A. (1828 – 1894)

A native of New York, Robert Cameron served in the Union Army during the Civil War. He was involved in several battles, including the siege at Vicksburg. He ended his military career as Brevet Major General of the 34th Indiana Volunteers.

Following the war, Cameron settled in the Colorado Territory. He was an aide on William Palmer's railroad projects, establishing townsites along the railroads. He was instrumental in the founding of town colonies such as Colorado Springs, Greeley and Fort Collins. He served as warden of the Colorado State Penitentiary at Canon City from 1885 to 1887.

His granite tombstone is ornately carved with a Civil War sword. He is buried in Block AF, AM, Plot 81.

Catlin, W. C. (1825 – 1896)

Born in England, Catlin migrated to America eventually settling near Canon City. He was one of the first pioneers of the community, arriving in the early 1860s. He homesteaded land southwest of what would become Canon City.

He was very prominent and a vital part of the town's early foundation. He owned the first brick factory, which employed inmates from the state penitentiary. In the 1870s the need arose for a town cemetery. Catlin donated ten acres of his land to the city, which included the burial site of W.M. Davis, the first recorded burial in the area.

The Catlin family plot is one of the largest in the cemetery, located in Block 2, Plot 26.

Griffin Family Plot

This is the largest family plot in the cemetery. The Benjamin Griffin family homesteaded land across the river from today's Canon City in 1860. They were one of the earliest pioneer families to the area. It is said Griffin was a respected friend of both Chiefs Ouray and Colorow.

The large granite tombstone dominates the family plot in Block 1, Plot 25.

Hardy, Guy U. (1872 – 1947)

An early pioneer of the Canon City area, Guy Hardy, like many others, came to Colorado in search of a cure for his tuberculosis. He arrived in Canon City in 1893, working for the local newspaper. Within two years, he became the owner of the *Canon City Record*. This would be his life long interest and a business he held until his death. In 1899, he married Jessie Mack, the daughter of early Canon City pioneers.

Instrumental in business and community affairs, he was responsible for securing the grant which resulted in the Royal Gorge Park, in 1903. Very successful in Canon City, he went on to become a U.S. Congressman, a position he held for fourteen years.

He is buried in Block 1, Plot 129.

Massaro, Father John (1844 – 1889)

Father Massaro was one of the first priests to the area. Loved and respected in the community, he performed many ceremonial duties for the people of Canon City.

He is buried in the Catholic Row, Plot 4.

Peabody, James H. (1852 – 1917)

A prominent member of early Canon City, James Peabody was a town leader. A bank owner, he was active in the social events of the town, including functions of the Episcopal Church. He organized the town's volunteer fire department, and was mayor for a time.

He served two terms as governor of Colorado, being re-elected in the most bizarre election in state history, in 1905. Fraud and corruption were a few of the allegations against Peabody. He served his term during the turmoil of statewide mining strikes. He was considered a very controversial governor.

His tall obelisk monument is surrounded by a low rock border in the family plot, in Block AF,AM, Plot 44.

Rockafellow, George (1805 – 1880)

George Rockafellow, a native of New York, worked his way west by mining and prospecting. As one of the original pioneers to the area, he was instrumental in business development and town leadership, as well as agriculture. He became the first mayor of Canon City in 1872.

He is buried in the Little-Rockafellow family plot, in Block Af, AM, Plot 40.

Ulrich, John J. (1833 – 1907)

John Ulrich settled in the Canon City area in 1880, eventually homesteading land just southwest of the present cemetery. An early pioneer, he made Canon City his home and raised his family.

His son Isaac served as Greenwood Cemetery's sexton from 1907 to 1916. Isaac's son John, carried the tradition as caretaker of the cemetery for many years, retiring just a few years ago.

According to John, his grandfather, John Jefferson Ulrich is the only person known to be buried in the new Lakeside Cemetery and reinterred in the pioneer Greenwood Cemetery.

The Ulrich plot is in Block 1, Plot 130.

WOODPECKER HILL CEMETERY
LOCATED IN THE SOUTHWEST PORTION OF GREENWOOD CEMETERY.

This is a desolated piece of ground unto itself. An addition to the original cemetery, it was added when the original plot at the northwest corner of the cemetery filled faster than anticipated. This area became the final resting place for the deceased inmates of the Colorado State Penitentiary. Unclaimed in life, they lie unclaimed in death.

The forlorn ground is overgrown with wild grass. It has very few trees. The rows of graves are not laid out in any order and very few records exist to indicate a block of burial. The first burials were marked with simple wooden crosses, which the woodpeckers eventually destroyed. Thus, the name Woodpecker Hill. One of the very few tombstones in the section is dated 1880. This is the oldest marked penitentiary burial.

Prisoners dug the graves and served as pallbearers on the rare occasions when a service actually occurred. The simple pine boxes were lowered into the ground by hand-held rope.

Metal tags were used as markers. A majority of these markers have long since weathered away and are unreadable. The inscription "CSP Inmate" can be read on some markers and the few markers containing names of the interred record a history of crime. The last man executed by hanging lies here, as well as the first and last to die in the gas chamber.

This cemetery has not been used since the mid 1970s. Modern practice dictates that unclaimed bodies be cremated when every effort to involve the family fails, including monetary allowances.

Bizup, John Jr. (? – 1964)
John Bizup was a thirty-year-old painter in Pueblo County, convicted of murdering a cab driver and was sentenced to death at the Colorado State Penitentiary. He was one of the last to die in the gas chamber in 1964.

Brophy, Harry (? – 1910)
Harry Brophy was a highway robber committed to the penitentiary in 1907, serving a sentence of nine to fourteen years. On April 25, 1910, Brophy, along with inmate Andrew Johnson, made a daring

escape attempt from the prison. Alarms were sounded immediately. Brophy wounded several guards and was shot to death.

Daniels, Danny (? – 1929)
Davis, A. H. (? – 1929)

A riot erupted at the penitentiary in 1929, led by Danny Daniels, A.H. Davis, and "Red" Reiley. The inmates held eleven officers hostage in Cell No. 3. Eight correctional officers were killed in the riot. Albert Mogareidge, an inmate, described as a "snitch," was murdered by Daniels. Daniels and Davis were killed in the violence. In all, thirteen men died.

The two convicts were buried in the same plot.

Ives, Edward (? – 1930)

Edward Ives was convicted of killing a Denver police officer, and sentenced to death by hanging in 1929. On January 10, 1930, his sentence was carried out. The noose was placed around his neck. As the rope was lifted, Ives jumped down. The rope broke against the force, and Ives claimed he should be freed because he survived his execution. A new rope was promptly placed around his neck, and Ives died. He was the last prisoner to die by hanging.

His grave is marked by one of the few stone markers in the Woodpecker section. It is said fellow inmates pooled their resources to purchase the stone.

Johnson, Andrew (? – 1910)

Convicted of murder, Johnson's sentence was reduced to life in prison by acting Governor Harper in 1907. Johnson and fellow inmate Harry Brophy attempted a daring escape on April 25, 1910. Johnson was killed by guards in the attempt.

Kelly, William Cody (1901 – 1934)

Close to the grave of Edward Ives, lies William C. Kelly, the first man executed in Colorado by the gas chamber.

Mercer, Ida (? – 1925)

Ida Mercer was approximately sixty years old when she was convicted of murdering her son-in-law. She was an inmate at the penitentiary for eleven years, where she was known as a good prisoner. She died peacefully in the prison hospital in 1925.

Mogareidge, Albert (? – 1929)
Reiley, "Red" (? – 1929)

Reiley was one of the ring leaders in the prison riot of 1929, resulting in the murder of Mogareidge. Mogareidge was considered a "snitch" by fellow inmates. Reiley was shot by prison guards. Thirteen men died in the riot.

The two are buried together in the same plot, not an uncommon practice.

Monge, Luis J. (? – 1967)

Convicted on several murder charges, Luis Monge was sentenced to death row. He had sexually assaulted his daughter, than murdered his wife and three children. On June 2, 1967, he was the last man in the state to be executed.[21]

His grave lies a few feet from John Bizup, Jr. The metal marker is marred with bullet holes.

Noakes, Raymond (1904 – 1928)
Osborn, Arthur (1903 – 1928)

Sentenced to death, they were barely teenagers. The two were found guilty of one of the most horrific murders in Colorado at the time. They beat and murdered an innocent homeless man near Grand Lake, Colorado.

They were both executed by hanging on March 30, 1928. Noakes was twenty-two, Osborn was twenty-three years of age.

They are buried side by side, with two wooden markers.

SALIDA

FAIRVIEW CEMETERY

LOCATED NORTHWEST OF TOWN. FROM SALIDA, TAKE COUNTY ROAD 144 NORTH. TURN WEST ON COUNTY ROAD 142 TO THE CEMETERY.

Established in 1891, the cemetery is very well organized. The lanes are wide and very well marked. The landscape is carefully pruned for the most part. Tall, majestic trees line the lanes.

Near the entrance of the cemetery is the section devoted to the Grand Army of the Republic. Standard white military stones grace the area. As with most cemeteries, the pauper section is separated. At Fairview, it is located at the extreme west end, overgrown with weeds, and facing a dirt alley way. [22]

Author's collection

This monument to two brothers
is a wonderful example of
Colorado cemetery art.

Bartlo, A. N.
(1861 – 1906)

He owned a candy store in Salida, was a prominent member of the community and a family man. He and his daughter, sixteen-year-old Grace, were traveling on the Denver & Rio Grande Western when the train wrecked at Adobe Switch, three miles west of Florence. The two died in the tragedy.

They are buried in the family plot, along with Sadie, wife and mother, in Section G, Block 18, Lot 10.

Evans, Laura
(1874 – 1953)[23]

Very secretive about her upbringing, we do know she was from the South. Laura Evans married at age seventeen, left her husband and headed west for a new life as a prostitute. She was in her late twenties when she came to Denver, working on Market Street (Holliday Street). By the 1890s, she had left Denver for Leadville's silver boom.

Laura's boisterous personality and flamboyant characteristics soon became legend. She was arrested for horse racing on Leadville's Harrison Street, and crashed a high social event by dressing as a nun. Another time, she hid a $27,000 payroll beneath her skirts while riding horseback to deliver the cash for the mine owners, during the Leadville mining strike. Her brass check from Leadville reads: "Eat, drink, dance, go to bed, or get out."[24]

In 1896, she had settled in Salida, near the railroad station, a perfect location to set up her business. By 1906, she not only had her own parlor house on Front Street, but a row of cribs across the street as well. As her business flourished, she gave back to the community. During the flu epidemic of 1918, she closed her business, while she and her girls nursed the sick.

For the most part, the town of Salida accepted and even appreciated Laura. As times changed, Laura's house was forced to close down by the town council in 1951.

She died uncharacteristically in 1953. She went quietly and perhaps even peacefully. Her well-attended funeral took place on a cold snowy April day.

Her flat granite marker is located in Section K, Block 13, Lot 4.

Harrington, Owen (1831 – 1916)[25]

One of the earliest pioneers in the area, Owen Harrington arrived in 1865 and filed on a homestead. He owned the town water rights, and became active in community and social affairs, and helped develop the town of Salida.

Author's collection
The ornate headstone of William Roller.

He is buried in Circle Section H, where his beautiful handtooled monument stands. Made of blue granite, it is adorned with elaborate roses.

Roller, William W. (1841 – 1916)

This is perhaps the most interesting and certainly the most intricate monument in the cemetery. The beautiful folds of the American flag are neatly carved in stone, draping the blue granite marker, all marvelously hand tooled.

Roller was a captain in the New York Infantry during the Civil War. In Salida, he had a furniture store and was engaged in the real estate business. He was involved in the early Salida land deals which led to the platting of the town. He was instrumental in the Salida Electric Light Company and the Opera House Company.

William Roller is buried in Section I, Block 5, Lot 1. There is a marker.

Watkins, Lauren E. (1841 – 1916)

Suspected of cattle rustling, Lauren Watkins was hanged in Canon City. Originally buried in Poncha Springs, following the death of his father in Salida, his body was moved to the family plot at Fairview.

He is buried in Section G, Block 8, Lot 8.

Author's collection
Boon family plot at the Poncha Springs Cemetery.

WOODLAWN CEMETERY

LOCATED ONE MILE SOUTH OF SALIDA ON COUNTY ROAD 107.

Also known as Woodland Cemetery, it was incorporated in 1889. The first known burial was that of Clara Clossen in 1881. Several of the graves were washed out in a flood sometime after 1887, and were never recovered.

Unique to this cemetery is the number of small wooden crosses, which are the dominant markers throughout the cemetery. The brush weeds have taken over the cemetery and many graves are unmarked.

Among those buried in this forgotten cemetery are Oliver Briley and Pat Sullivan. Briley was lynched for killing Sullivan, a railroad man.

Mrs. Nancy Warman is buried here. She died at the age of seventy-two, in 1890. She is the mother of famed writer and poet Cy Warman.[26] It is also believed the first wife and two children of Cy Warman are buried in this cemetery, although available records do not record the burial.[27]

PONCHA SPRINGS

PONCHA SPRINGS CEMETERY

LOCATED ONE-HALF-MILE SOUTH OF TOWN, JUST OFF HIGHWAY 285. TAKE COUNTY ROAD 206 TO THE WEST. THE ROAD IS A STEEP HILLSIDE CLIMB TO THE CEMETERY ON THE BLUFF.

This cemetery was established in 1882. Few cemetery records exist. William H. Champ, Jr. is believed to be the first burial, an infant who died in 1882. The cemetery is laid out in two sections, appropri-

ately called the Upper and Lower
Sections. The Lower Section is
the oldest part of the cemetery,
containing the graves of those
reinterred from older rural cemeteries such as Droney Pasture
and Centerville. Because there
are so many unmarked graves in
the Lower Section and lack of
records, burials are no longer
allowed. The Upper Section, high
on the bluff, contains burials
after 1966.

Denver Public Library
Laura Evans, one of Colorado's most
colorful madams, lived a full life, when
many in her profession died young.

Boon Family Plot

David C. Boon, born in 1843,
served in the Ohio Infantry during the Civil War. He came west,
where he made his home, ranching in Lake County, Colorado.

During the violent Lake County War, Boon joined forces with the
"Committee of Safety." Water and land rights seemed to be the central
issue of the war, launched in 1872. Shortly after the murder of George
Harrington of Centerville, the safety committee formed, beginning a
reign of terror over Lake County that lasted over a year.

In retaliation for the murder of Harrison, (the accused, Elijah
Gibbs, was acquitted), the vigilante committee set fire to Gibbs' home.
Gibbs opened fire on the group. The men returned the fire and in the
melee, David Boon was killed by one of his own men. He died the next
day.

— — —

Samuel Boon, born in 1844, served the Union Army in Company H
of the Ohio Infantry. He was also a member of the "Committee of
Safety" vigilante group. He took part in the raid of Gibbs home, in
January 1875, along with his brother, David. It was Sam Boon who
attempted to light the fire to burn Gibbs out of his home. Gibbs shot
at Boon, hitting him in the chest. Sam Boon died two days later.

The two Boons, originally buried in the Droney Pasture Cemetery,
were reinterred at the Poncha Springs Cemetery in 1882.

Their white sandstone markers are lined with the Boon family
members, including Civil War Corporal Hugh C. Boon. The Boon family plot is located in Section F of the Lower Cemetery.

Jackson, Harvey A. (? – 1883)

One of the early pioneers of Poncha Springs, Harvey Jackson became the first mayor of the new town. He opened the Jackson Hotel in 1878.

The thirty-one-room hotel was renowned for miles. The register included such notables as Frank and Jesse James, Billy the Kid, and William Jackson Palmer. The hotel stands today.

H.A. Jackson is buried in Section F. of the Lower Cemetery. The tombstone is enclosed with a wire fence. There are no dates on the marker.

Kane, Finlay B. (? – 1875)

A veteran of the Civil War, he served with the 39th Ohio Infantry. He was a victim of the notorious Lake County War. Originally buried in the Droney Pasture Cemetery, he was reinterred at the Poncha Springs Cemetery in 1882.

The uncle of David and Samuel Boon, also victims, he is buried in the Boon family plot, in Section F of the Lower Cemetery. His military issued stone marks his burial spot.

GUNNISON

GUNNISON CEMETERY

LOCATED ONE MILE EAST OF TOWN ON THE NORTH SIDE OF HIGHWAY 50. THE CEMETERY IS VISIBLE FROM THE HIGHWAY.

The original Gunnison Cemetery, established in 1880, is now the airport. The new cemetery, established in 1900, offers a beautiful landscaped setting. Many burials were removed from the old Gunnison Cemetery to the southeast corner of the new cemetery. Wide gravel roads wind around the carefully-pruned grounds. At the east end of the cemetery, a very moving monument bears mentioning. It is that of the Gunnison High School football coach and members of the football team of 1971. They were killed in a bus crash on Monument hill enroute to a game.

Gillaspey, William A. (1850 – 1935)

William Gillaspey was one of the first pioneers of the Gunnison County. He is fondly known in history as the father of Gunnison's cattle industry. One of the original members of the Stock Growers Association, and president from 1900 to 1907, his hat hangs in the Gunnison Pioneer Museum.

It was Gillaspey who brought the first pure blood bull to the area for breeding. His cattle ranch was among the finest from miles around.

Gillaspey and the Stock Growers Association were adamantly opposed to the area sheep herders and the closing of the open range. The contention grew to a long six-year war between cattlemen and sheepherders. The dispute was finally settled on the eve of World War I.

William Gillaspey is buried in Block 39, Lot 8.

Hurley, Thomas J. (1856 – 1886)

Thomas Hurley was a member of the "Molly Maguire" faction of miners in Pennsylvania. He settled in Gunnison after the Pennsylvania labor wars erupted.

He was arrested for killing Luke Curran with a knife. Awaiting trial in the Gunnison County jail, he slit his throat with a razor reportedly belonging to Alfred Packer, who had been released that day.[28]

Hurley is buried in Block 6 at the southern edge of Gunnison Cemetery.

Outcalt, John B. (1845 – 1927)

A native of Brunswick, New Jersey, John Outcalt served his apprenticeship as a carpenter and shipbuilder. He journeyed west in 1870, arriving on the second train to pull into the "Queen City" of Denver. He carried with him his tool chest and twenty-seven cents. He worked as a carpenter in Denver for four years, before joining the Richardson Colony headed for the Gunnison country in 1874. Along with Sylvester Richardson, he would become one of the first pioneers of the Gunnison area.

He worked as a carpenter at the Los Pinos Indian Agency, becoming the most trusted white man with the Indians, earning the name "Tongue of the Great White Father."

He and his brother William, homesteaded three miles north of Gunnison, along the Gunnison River. Rich crops of hay and grain were raised and the brothers expanded their land. In 1881, he persuaded the Denver & Rio Grande Railroad to build a spur through his property. This allowed local farmers to ship their produce at a fair market value. In 1905, he was instrumental in the building of the Paragon School.[29] He is also noted for building the grand spiral staircase at the Brown Palace Hotel in Denver.

One of the three original Gunnison pioneers, he is buried in Block 74, Lot 32.

Parent, Alex (1859 – 1930)

An immigrant from Canada, Alex Parent arrived in Colorado in 1880. He mined in the Gunnison and Tin Cup areas until he was injured in an explosion. He handled a series of odd jobs for a time, before operating the livery stable in Tin Cup. He was best known as pioneering the mail carrier service on the Tin Cup-St. Elmo route. He served two terms as mayor at the turn of the century. He was elected mayor of Tin Cup again in the final mayoral election.

His wife Mary, had died in 1901, just four months after their marriage.[30] Parent raised Mary's son from a previous marriage, as his own.

After the decline of Tin Cup, Parent moved on, making his final home in Gunnison. His wish was to be buried next to his wife Mary, in the Tin Cup Cemetery. However, due to the inclement weather, he was buried in Gunnison in Block 66, Lot 26. There is a small ground level marker.

Shores, Cyrus W. (1844 – 1934)

Born in Michigan, Cyrus Shores hauled ties for the Union Pacific Railroad. He settled in Gunnison, in 1880, running a freighting operation to the mining camps.

One of the most famous lawmen in Colorado history, his name dots the pages of history books. In 1884, he was elected sheriff, serving eight years. He was appointed deputy U.S. marshal in 1892. He had run-ins with the likes of Wild Bill Hickock, Jim Clark, and Tom Horn.[31] He was responsible for the security of the notorious Alfred Packer.[32]

In April 1883, he was charged with the duty of moving the convicted cannibal, Alfred Packer from Lake City to the Gunnison Jail for sentencing. Packer spent the next three years in Shores' jail. Under a change of venue, Packer was retried in Gunnison, found guilty and sentenced to life in prison. Shores escorted Packer under tight security to the Colorado State Penitentiary.

During the height of the 1891 coal strike at Crested Butte, Sheriff "Doc" Shores, as he came to be known, was called in from Gunnison. Arriving with twenty-four deputies on the Rio Grande train, he was met by an angry mob of armed miners. A fight erupted between the miners and the sheriff's posse. Thirty-six miners were wounded before Shores gained control of the situation. All miners were released by the sheriff. Shores said, "No one was killed and anybody ought to be excused for losing his head once in awhile."

He worked as a railroad detective and as a criminal investigator for the Wells Fargo Express. In 1915, he was appointed chief of police in Salt Lake City, Utah. He returned to Gunnison where he died in 1934 at age eighty-nine.

He is buried beside his first wife Agnes, who died in 1908. His son Cyrus Jr. who died in the flu epidemic of 1918, and other family members are also buried in the family plot. There is a large dark granite stone in Block 46, Lot 1.

Vidal, Regis (1839 – 1901)

Regis Vidal arrived in 1875, with his brother Philip. They were French immigrants who homesteaded on the land near the juncture of the Ohio Creek and Gunnison River.

Ten years later, the Denver South Park Railroad ran its tracks through their land. The Vidal brothers had the "Number One" water right to the Ohio Creek. The land was split between the two brothers with a handsome bonus, courtesy of the railroad, while each retained a portion of the land. A spur on Regis' land was known as Vidals, where a small hub developed for the loading of cattle and hay.

Regis died suddenly in 1901, leaving his widow, Albine and nine children. The 700-acre Vidal ranch was heavily in debt. The eight daughters of Regis and Albine worked the ranch day and night. They paid off the $15,000 debt and turned a profit in succeeding years. By 1907, the sisters, along with their younger brother, were producing 400 tons of hay a year, as well as produce and poultry. In 1907, one of the sisters, Dollie, and her husband Gad Jones, bought the family ranch. It remained in the family for many years.

The Vidal family plot is located in Block 51, Lot 2. The plot includes Regis, his wife Albine, their only son Robert, and daughters Josephine and Pearl.

OFF THE BEATEN PATH:

From Gunnison, north on Highway 135, just past the town of Almont, is the site of Jack's Cabin Cemetery. The area was named for Jack Howe who built a cabin at the junction of the old Gunnison Road and the Crested Butte Road. The site later became a stage stop with two hotels, two restaurants, two saloons and two stores. All that remains today is the forlorn cemetery. The inhabitants are lost to history.

MONTROSE

CEDAR CEMETERY

LOCATED EAST OF MONTROSE. FROM MAIN STREET (HIGHWAY 50) GO TO HILLCREST DRIVE. TURN RIGHT ON MIAMI STREET, THEN LEFT TO THE CEMETERY.

The land for Cedar Cemetery was purchased by the city of Montrose in 1883. The city has continued the operation and provides maintenance for the well-groomed landscape, including trees and shrubbery.

Bell, John Calhoun (1851 – 1933)

A native of Tennessee, John Bell was raised on the family farm and later attended Winchester University, earning a law degree in 1874.

He moved to Colorado, where he practiced law at Saguache. He became county attorney, a position he held until 1876. That year, he moved to Lake City, again practicing law. In 1878, he was elected county clerk, and mayor in 1885, serving two terms.

In 1887, he located to Montrose, where he opened a law office, and became district judge in 1888. Appointed to the United States Congress in 1892, he served four terms. During his tenure in Congress, he secured federal appropriations for a state building in Colorado Springs, and opened the Ute Indian Reservation for settlement. His greatest accomplishment was the Gunnison Tunnel and water irrigation.

He is buried next to his wife Susie. There is a marker.

Buddecke, Adolph E. (1840 – 1925)

Adolph Buddecke arrived in Montrose in 1882. In partnership with Richard Diehl, they opened one of the first mercantile stores, including deliveries to the mining towns. In 1883 he was appointed chairman of the first Board of County Commissioners by Governor Grant.

By 1885, Buddecke and Diehl had built the Montrose Opera House. He died in Denver in 1925.

His body is buried in Montrose's Cedar Cemetery in Section F, Block 32, Lot 8.

Devore, James W. (1849 – 1928)

James Devore came to Montrose from Illinois in 1889, where he established the Devore Cider Mill. The mill was a great success and an asset to the town of Montrose. Devore operated the mill for thirty-eight years, before turning it over to his daughter shortly before his death.

He is buried with his wife, Rose in Section F, Block 33, Lots A and E.

Diehl, Richard C. (1850 – 1910)

At Hays, Kansas, Diehl formed a partnership with Adolph Buddecke. Together, they established a mercantile business in

Montrose in 1882. Following the building of the Opera House, Diehl moved to Alaska in 1893. He and his family eventually returned to the Montrose area in 1908.

He is buried in Section F, Block 66, Lot 4.

Lingham, Harriette Marie Collins, M.D. (1873 – 1960)

Harriette graduated from Boston University School of Medicine in 1897. She moved west to Cripple Creek, Colorado, following her graduation. By 1902, she had joined a medical practice in Montrose, becoming the town's first female physician. Most of her medical calls were made by horse and buggy. Through the years, she became a respected and trusted doctor. She was responsible for the first x-ray machine in the county.

She is buried beside her husband William, whom she married in Montrose in 1906. Their graves are located in Section F, Block 71, Lots 6 & 7.

Peters, Phillip (1842 – 1912)

A Civil War veteran of the Third Kentucky Cavalry, known as "The Bloody Third," Phillip Peters served as first sergeant. He received a bullet in the heart during the War, and was told he would die, thereby receiving his discharge papers.

By 1882, he had settled in Montrose, running the Mears Hotel. Eventually, he owned a ranch, and raised livestock successfully for some twenty years.

He lived a long successful life, with the bullet in his heart, dying of very natural causes in 1912. He is buried with his wife Christine, in Section K, Block 31, Lots 7 & 8.

Chipeta (1843 – 1924)

The gravesite of Chipeta, the famous Indian wife of Chief Ouray, is located two miles south of Montrose, off Highway 550. There is a sign on the highway marking the exit to the Ute Indian Museum.[33]

"The laughing maiden of the Utes," Chipeta was the second wife of Chief Ouray of the Uncompahgre Utes. She was his constant companion for forty-five years, supporting her husband's peace negotiations with the white man.

Following the Meeker Massacre the Utes were moved to the Reservation on Bitter Creek, in Utah.[34] Chipeta was among those forced to leave her home in Colorado. She lived an exiled, lonely life, and blinded by cataracts. She died at Bitter Creek, Utah in 1924. She was buried at that location.

Denver Public Library
Chipeta, wife of Ute Chief Ouray.

Authorities sanctioned to have her body laid to rest next to Ouray, but citizens of Montrose had her body interred on the old Ouray farm.

On March 25, 1925, Chipeta was reburied at Ouray Memorial Park, the site of the couple's farm, two and one-half miles south of Montrose, on Highway 550.

An eleven-foot oblong cement tomb of Salida granite, marks the burial of Chipeta. To the left of her grave is a tall natural rock monument to her great husband Ouray, Chief of the Utes.[35] It seems an appropriate spot for a memorial to a great man and his wife; a site given to them, then taken away and finally memorialized.

John McCook, the brother of Chipeta, is buried to the right of her at this spot. His grave is marked by the traditional white wooden cross.

DELTA

DELTA CITY CEMETERY

FROM HIGHWAY 50 IN THE TOWN OF DELTA, TAKE 3RD STREET EAST, UP THE HILL TO THE CEMETERY ON THE LEFT.

The cemetery, overlooking the town, is well laid out and landscaped. Many graves are the result of the influenza epidemic of 1918. The veteran's section includes many graves carved by stone mason, "Cap" Smith.[36]

Blachly, Andrew T. (1847 – 1893)

A bank employee shot to death by Fred McCarty when the McCarty Gang robbed the Farmers and Merchants Bank of Delta. During the shootout, gang members Bill and Fred were also killed. Blachly left behind a pregnant wife and eight children. Dellie Blachly's child was born dead, a result of the shock of her husband's murder.

Blachly's grave is marked with a small monument in Block 1, Lot 11.

Fairlamb, Millard (1870 – 1947)

Fairlamb was instrumental in the founding of the town of Delta, incorporated in 1881. He was the first lawyer in the community and responsible for rebuilding the capital of the First National Bank, following the Silver Panic of 1893.

He is buried in Block 3, Lot 148. There is a marker.

Hammond, Henry (1855 – 1940)

Henry Hammond filed on the first homestead in the Delta area. One of the town founders, he cleared an area of trees and sage and the town of Delta was thus laid out. He opened a livery stable and saddle shop in the new town. On the side, he provided entertainment at his ranch with a horse race track.

He expanded his business to include a biweekly stage stop on the road to to North Fork. The stage soon became the only daily transportation for the heavy fruit produce of the area.

During the bank robbery by the McCarty gang, Fred McCarty was shot in Hammond's livery yard.

Hammond is buried in Block 1, Lot 55. There is a marker.

Lowe, Benjamin (1868 – 1917)

He owned a cattle ranch near the town of Delta, and trained race horses. A feud between Lowe and ex-lawman Cash Sampson escalated to a shoot out in Escalante Canyon. Both men died.

Lowe left a wife and five children. He is buried in Block 5, Lot 325. There is a marker.

McCarty, Bill (? – 1893)
McCarty, Fred (? – 1893)

Bill was a one-time member of Butch Cassidy's Wild Bunch. He and his brother Tom, along with Bill's son Fred, attempted to hold up the bank at Delta in 1893. Tom got away, while Bill and son Fred were shot to death. Customary of the time, the two were buried immediately, and unceremoniously. They were later exhumed for official identification; original reports stated the McCarty's had escaped. Identified as Bill and Fred McCarty, the bodies were reburied. Later, the bodies were re-exhumed, propped up against a wall, photographed, and reburied for the third and final time.

Bill and Fred are buried in the Delta Cemetery, in the Potters Field, just north of Block 2. Their graves are unmarked.

Sampson, Cassius (1871 – 1917)

Sampson made his career as a lawman in various ways. He was a brand inspector, deputy United States marshal, and sheriff of Delta County.

A long time feud between Sampson and cattle rancher Ben Lowe led to a shoot out in Escalante Canyon, north of Delta. Both men were shot to death.

A large marker in the Delta City Cemetery indicates Sampson's grave in Block 2, Lot 173.

— — —

Highway 160 West

FORT GARLAND MILITARY POST
LOCATED APPROXIMATELY ONE MILE SOUTHWEST OF FORT GARLAND, ON COUNTY ROAD 159.

Tobin, Thomas Tate (1826 – 1894)

Tom Tobin was an important figure in several famous incidents of Colorado's early history. Considered one of the last of the famous mountain men who blazed the trail for permanent settlement, Tobin kept company with the likes of Kit Carson, Jim Bridger, the Bent brothers, Ceran St. Vrain and Dick Wootton.

Born in St. Louis, Missouri, Tobin came west in the late 1830s with his half-brother, Charles Autobees.[37] He spent several years trapping and scouting for the Bent brothers on the Arkansas River in Southern Colorado. During this period of time, Tobin became an expert tracker and earned a reputation as a dead shot with a rifle or pistol.

Following the war between Mexico and the United States, in 1846, Tobin lived and scouted near Taos, New Mexico. By 1852, he had moved north to serve as a scout near Fort Massachusetts in Southern Colorado.[38]

Territory Governor John Evans, and Colonel Sam Tappen, commander of Fort Garland, called upon Tobin to help in the apprehension of the Espinosa gang of outlaws. Tobin was offered a reward of $2,500 to track down the murderous gang. He was given a full militia unit, but insisted on tracking the vicious killers alone, taking only three military men as backup.

The Espinosas had murdered twenty-eight men from Leadville to Canon City in the summer of 1863, by the time Tobin took over the search.

Tobin followed their trail for three days from the site of the twenty-eighth victim, leading into the Sangre de Cristo Mountains. He ambushed the trio in a meadow and methodically shot them one by one. The leader, Vivian Espinosa was not dead, so Tobin slit his throat, decapitating him. Tobin then cut off the head of Espinosa's nephew, and placed both heads in a gunny sack. Tobin brought the heads to Governor Evans in Denver, as proof to collect his reward. He never received the reward, but was given a fine rifle at an honorary dinner.

Tom Tobin is buried in a small cemetery on land where his ranch, Blanca Trinchera once stood. A granite stone marks the graves of Tobin and his wife, Maria. The cemetery is now on private land owned by the Malcolm Forbes estate. Permission must be obtained at the gate entrance. There is a marker to both Tom and Maria, however, Maria's is broken in half.

ALAMOSA

ALAMOSA CEMETERY

LOCATED SOUTH OF TOWN, AT 220 STATE STREET, JUST NORTH OF THE AIRPORT.

This serene park setting was established in September 1881. Many early burials exist, including transfers from Alamosa's prior cemeteries, all abandoned in the name of progress. Remnants of the first cemetery can be seen at the northern edge of the cemetery. The second abandoned cemetery lies east of town, between the railroad tracks and Highway 160. The other cemeteries, both at the site of Adams State College, were covered during construction. The original plat included four sections, each 310 feet square. Sections for the Elks, Knights of Columbus and VFW fraternal organizations were added later. Potter's Field is located in the northeast corner and contains 117 graves.

The cemetery has paved driveways, under towering trees and among a beautiful green landscape. It is enclosed by fencing graced with an iron archway.

Some of the unmarked graves are undoubtedly the victims of the many hangings in Alamosa's early years. A large cottonwood tree by the river was used for hangings, legal and otherwise. A cattle rustler dangled for an entire day in 1880, a not so subtle warning.

Adams, William (1861 – 1954)

A native of Wisconsin, Adams came west in 1871 on the advice of his doctor. Prone to tuberculosis, Colorado's dry climate seemed to help him regain his health. Locating in Alamosa, he and his older brother Alva, hauled railroad ties for the Denver & Rio Grande Railroad. Later they operated a large hardware and lumber store. The brothers soon expanded their business to a chain of hardware stores across the San Juan region.

Independently wealthy, "Billy" Adams turned to local politics about the time his brother, Alva entered the race for governor of Colorado. The Adams family has figured in the political history of Colorado since the state was admitted to the union.

Billy was first elected county commissioner, and later served Alamosa as mayor for two terms, all before age twenty-five. He became governor of Colorado in 1927, serving three terms. He pressured the General Assembly to appropriate funds for a new college in his home district. The Adams State Normal School, now Adams State College, was built in his honor in 1924.

He is buried in Section 3, Block 3, with a handsome memorial. His second wife, Hattie, is also buried here.[39]

Sabine, William (1840 – 1906)

An early pioneer of Alamosa, William Sabine built one of Alamosa's first frame homes in 1879. He became the director of the newly-formed First National Bank. Involved in city policy and instrumental in the growth of the town, he served on several town boards.

He is buried in Section 2, Block 3. There is a marker.

PAGOSA SPRINGS

PIONEER CEMETERY

LOCATED SOUTHWEST OF TOWN. FOLLOW 10TH STREET TO THE SOUTHWEST EDGE OF TOWN. THE CEMETERY IS LOCATED JUST PAST THE BEND IN THE DIRT ROAD.

This is the oldest cemetery in Archuleta County. Established in 1878, it is also known as Boot Hill Cemetery. The oldest marked burial is dated 1889, however, there are many unmarked burials.

Many of the bodies were removed to the new Hill Top Cemetery, at the opposite end of town, around the turn of the century. Today, the cemetery lies in near ruin, unkept and nearly forgotten. Cemetery records are incomplete, further lending to the forlorn spirit of this sacred ground.

One of the few graves remaining is that of James H. Voorhees. He was a miner and merchant, arriving in Pagosa Springs with his wife, Margaret in 1878. Active in community affairs, he served as the first county judge following the creation of Archuleta County.

His tombstone sits in the overgrown, sadly neglected cemetery, surrounded by a once handsome wrought iron fence.

HILL TOP CEMETERY

LOCATED NORTHEAST OF DOWNTOWN PAGOSA SPRINGS. TAKE FIFTH STREET NORTH TO THE TOP OF THE HILL. AT THE CEMETERY SIGN, TURN LEFT, FOLLOWING THE ROAD TO THE CEMETERY.

While the oldest marked burial is dated 1889, the cemetery was officially established in 1903. Many burials were moved here from the Boot Hill Cemetery at the south end of town. The name Archuleta is dotted across the cemetery. However, Antonio D. Archuleta, the Senator responsible for the creation of the county, died in Mexico.

The cemetery is laid out in sections, including the religious and Masonic orders. The American Legion Memorial graces the edge of the cemetery. Wide gravel roads, with street names add to the organization, dominated by the stone arched gateway entrance.

Boone, Albert Gallatin (1845 – 1916)

Born in Westport, Missouri, Albert Gallatin is the great-grandson of the famous Daniel Boone. He married Susie Fasdick at Boone, Colorado in 1876. They homesteaded in Archuleta County in 1886. Their ranch was located in Coyote Park, where they raised their six children. He served several terms as county commissioner and organized the Boone School District.

There is a dark granite memorial including the name of his son Jesse M. (1890 – 1918).[40]

Boone, Charles R. (1858 – 1943)

The son of Van D. and Mary A. Boone, the brother of Albert, he too was the great-grandson of Daniel Boone of Kentucky. Charles and his wife Ella settled on a ranch near Pagosa Springs in 1886, where they lived and worked until their death.

They are buried together. There is a Salida granite stone, marking the burial.

Born, Henry "Dutch" (1849 – 1921)

A native of Manitawoc, Wisconsin, Henry Born came west at an early age. He is known to have been in and out of Colorado Territory as early as 1859. He spent the first half of the 1860s hunting buffalo and fighting Indians. In the south and particularly in Arkansas, he was an outlaw and horse thief. By the 1870s he was scouting for the Army, and saw action at Adobe Walls in the Texas Panhandle, in 1874.

In Colorado, he mined in the Summitville and Creede districts, before arriving in Pagosa Springs. He married Ida Dillabaugh in 1900 and had four children. His homestead near Pagosa Springs, become known as Born's Lake, where he became a respectable member of the community.

He is buried beside his wife Ida, two sons, George, and Henry who died in World War II. The Born family plot is in Block 11, Lot 5.

Catchpole, Frederick H. (1874 – 1946)

Fred Catchpole was born and raised in Sterling, Nebraska, where he married Miss Mabel Strong. He engaged in the livestock business and eventually banking, where he was quite successful.

He brought his family to Pagosa Springs in 1908, where he organized the Citizens Bank. Catchpole being the outsider, he immediately got involved with the growing town and business affairs. He and his family lived in the rear of the bank building for the first few years. The bank became a community landmark, surviving fire and progress for many years. One of the oldest businesses in the town, it remained a family enterprise for generations.

Fred Catchpole served the community for sixteen years as county commissioner, and four years as county treasurer. He worked for road improvements throughout Archuleta County and was appointed by the governor to the advisory board of the Colorado State Highway Department during the construction of Wolf Creek Pass in 1916.

He is buried with his wife Mabel (1875 – 1969). There is a granite monument.

Martinez, Jose Benedito (1853 – 1944)

Born near Rancho de Taos, New Mexico, Jose Martinez was one of the earliest settlers in the Animas area, settling on land near Hermosa in 1874. At age seventeen, he married eleven-year-old Maria Liberta Valdez.

By 1879, the couple had homesteaded northeast of Pagosa Springs. The Martinez Ranch was known throughout the county. Martinez became the largest landholder in Archuleta County, with a total of seven ranches. He served as county commissioner during the 1880's, becoming instrumental in county politics.

He is buried next to his wife Maria, who proceeded him in death in 1930.

Voorhees, Margaret J. (? – 1920)

One of the legendary pioneers of Colorado, much of her early past is shaded in mystery. Of English decent, Margaret Voorhees came to America at an early age. She is among the first women on the American frontier. An aristocrat by heritage, she had a commanding presence.

In Colorado, she drifted from one mining camp to another, stacking her riches as she moved on. An independent woman, she is known to have traded husbands four times. She had a daughter by her first husband, a man named Hopkins. The daughter, Lillian, died very young. Margaret next married a Lieutenant Deland.

At Loma, Colorado, she married James H. Voorhees. Together, they ran a stock trade at various mining camps. They settled in Pagosa Springs in 1878, where they opened a general store. James died at Amargo.[41]

Margaret continued operation of the general store at Pagosa Springs, following the death of Voorhees. She later married William Ewell and divorced him twenty-five years later. She kept her home above the general store until shortly before her death.

Walker, Etheral Thomas (1844 – 1916)

A native of Virginia, E. T. Walker served in the Confederate Army during the Civil War. He moved west following the war, eventually settling in Pagosa Springs in 1890.

He is remembered for introducing the first sawmills to Pagosa Springs. His sawmill ran successfully for several years. He was a Populist, heavily involved in the politics of the area.

There is a granite monument to his memory.

DURANGO

ANIMAS CITY CEMETERY

LOCATED NORTHEAST OF DOWNTOWN DURANGO. TAKE 3RD AVENUE NORTH TO FLORIDA ROAD. FOLLOW FLORIDA ROAD A LITTLE OVER A MILE TO THE NEW LOG CHURCH ON THE RIGHT. THERE IS A DIRT ROAD DIRECTLY BEHIND THE CHURCH LEADING NORTH. FROM THIS POINT, IT IS ABOUT A QUARTER-MILE WALK UP THE HILL TO THE CEMETERY.

This tiny neglected pioneer cemetery sits on a knoll overlooking new track housing developments on Durango's north side. It is hoped that this small piece of sacred land, set aside for the loved ones of the early community of Animas City, does not succumb to the land developers in the name of progress.

Early Animas City records are incomplete prior to incorporation with the town of Durango. Cemetery records are sketchy, at best.[42] A fire in 1985 turned out to be a blessing in disguise, as much of the overgrowth from years of neglect was cleared away. The cemetery has no semblance of order. Stone markers dot the small resting spot in all directions and formation.

Under the sod and the dew
Waiting the Judgment Day
Love & tears for the Blue
Tears and love for the Gray

Animas City Cemetery epitaph

Folsom, William H. C. (1857 – 1945)

The first resident dentist, Folsom arrived in Durango in 1881, on a stage driven by Henry Moorman. By the end of his first week in town, he witnessed the murder of J. K. Pringle and the immediate lynching of Moorman.

Folsom's dental office was located across the road from the hanging site. A crude office, the equipment included a kitchen chair fashioned on top of a crate for height, and a spittoon for mouth rinsing purposes.

Dr. Folsom died in 1945, being one of the last official burials at the Animas City Cemetery.[43]

Moorman, Henry R. (? – 1881)

A stage driver and gambler, Henry Moorman shot James K. Pringle at the Coliseum gambling house in Durango. The shooting was apparently cold-blooded murder, as the parties did not know each other prior to the incident. Moorman was immediately apprehended and jailed.

Some 300 Durango citizens, members of the Committee of Safety, stormed the jailhouse, grabbed Moorman and led him to the large pine tree in front of the new post office.

The lynching of Moorman took place that evening, April 11, 1881. The committee posted a guard at the spot of the dangling body with a warning against anyone who attempted to remove the body before daylight would be dealt with by the committee. At daylight, the curious crowds formed to view the dangling corpse. The *Durango Herald* newspaper supported the lynching, taking a stand against the lawless and murder.

Moorman was buried quietly in the Animas City Cemetery. There is no marker.

Stockton, Isaac T. (1852 – 1881)

His reputation as a gunfighter added to the climate of fear, as his desire to control the ranch land of Durango climaxed in open warfare. Isaac Stockton and his brother Porter, arrived in the newly-founded community of Animas City, from Farmington, New Mexico, where

Author's collection   *La Plata County Historical Society*

Sheriff William Thompson is buried in Animas Cemetery, but his tombstone is in
Durango's Greenmount Cemetery, where his wife is buried.

they were known outlaws. Despite his reputation, Porter Stockton
was once the town marshal of Animas City.

Posing as cattlemen, the brothers were actually cattle rustlers.
Their reign of terror over homesteaders and ranchers not only includ-
ed threats and harassment, but shooting, cattle theft and accusations
of murder. The citizens of Durango formed a vigilante committee.
Somewhat effective, Porter Stockton returned to Farmington, New
Mexico, where he was later killed.

Stockton continued his terrorist ways, primarily staging drunken
shootouts. In the fall of 1881, Stockton staged his last shooting spree.
On Durango's main street, he was confronted by Colorado lawmen on
charges of murder in New Mexico. Resisting arrest, he opened fire and
was killed.

He was buried in the Animas City Cemetery with a very uncere-
monious service. The stone marker is no longer there.

Thompson, William J. (1857 – 1906)

A pioneer cowboy, a major stockman and peace officer with a reputation, Thompson was known as a fast gun and one of Colorado's most
outstanding lawmen.

Born in Bethny, Missouri, he came to La Plata County in 1882. He
and his brother George, operated a large cattle company near Fort
Lewis, a prime customer for their butchered beef. In 1890, Bill became

town marshal of Durango, later under sheriff and finally sheriff in 1898.

He faced death more than once. On one occasion, Tom Mance, a drunken relative of Thompson's, came at him with a knife, opening Thompson's stomach. He recovered and family members paid Mance to leave town. Thompson was considered a feared lawman, but a fair one.

On the night of January 8, 1906, Sheriff Thompson, on a routine street investigation, entered the El Moro Saloon, ordering the owner to shut down all gambling, a violation of the city ordinance. A verbal confrontation ensued, bringing in town marshal, Jesse Stansel. Thus the stage for Durango's famous duel was set.

There was animosity between Thompson and Stansel when Stansel lost the sheriff election to Thompson. Thompson upheld the city ordinance against gambling, while Stansel opposed it. The two argued that January night, carrying the fight outside the saloon. *The Durango Weekly Democrat* reported "It was the gamest duel ever put in Durango."

The two emptied their guns at each other and then struck each other over the head with their guns. Thompson fell dead. He suffered five shots, the fatal shot in the back. Stansel shot all his rounds, while Thompson fired two. One of Stansel's bullets hit bystander John Acord, who later died. Stansel was arrested, tried and acquitted.

Thompson was buried in the Animas City Cemetery. There is no marker.[44]

Turner, John Charles (1831 – 1902)

Charles Turner was born in Connecticut, the son of a Pinkerton detective. He went west, following the deaths of his parents. In Colorado, he was a member of the Baker Party, the famous 1860 exploration group of southwest Colorado. When the Civil War broke out, Turner left the Western Slope for Denver, where he enlisted with the First Colorado Cavalry under Colonel John M. Chivington.

Following the Civil War, he married Emma Stephens, the daughter of an employee of the wealthy Lucien Maxwell of New Mexico. In New Mexico, he became sheriff of Colfax County, where he dealt with the the likes of Billy the Kid and Clay Allison.

He returned with his family to Colorado, filing a homestead following the opening of the Ute Land Strip, near the area of Animas City. With the arrival of the railroad, the Turner family relocated to the new town of Durango, where John built an elegant seven-room house.

One of the founding fathers of Durango, he served the community as county commissioner and eventually returned to his earlier work as sheriff, in 1893. Descendants of John Turner remain prominent citizens of Durango.

He is buried in the Turner family plot, next to his wife Emma, who died in 1894. There is a stone marker.

Will, Francis J. (1827 – 1910)

Born in Germany, the son of a brewer, Francis Will left for America at age twenty-one, in 1848. He changed his name from Franz to Francis upon his arrival in New York. He married Anna Maria Mittenbuhler in 1850. The couple brought their children by railroad to St. Joseph, Missouri, the end of the line. At the start of the Civil War, the Will family moved west, arriving in Colorado Territory in 1862.

One of the earliest pioneer families of Animas City, Will homesteaded in 1877. He also purchased town lots. He opened a store on the main street and built a house on the corner of River and Fourth streets. He had a cattle ranch and later relocated his family to the new town of Durango. He operated his cattle ranch until his death in 1910.

He is buried beside his wife, Anna Marie. There is a tombstone. Mrs. Will's stone says Maria A. Their son, Herrman W. (1873-1878) was one of the first burials in the cemetery. He was killed in a horse wagon accident.

* * *

The first legal hanging in La Plata County occurred in the young town of Durango in June 1882. A public execution, the entire town turned out to witness the morbid event.

A bizarre love triangle resulting in murder, led to the hanging of George N. Woods. Woods and M.G. Buchanan both courted the recently-widowed Mrs. Ike Stockton. The two quarreled on several occasions. Ironically, widow Stanton married a man names Estes. Yet the quarrel between Woods and Buchanan continued.

In a Durango saloon, Woods shot Buchanan to death. He later gave himself up to the authorities. His trial was immediate. Found guilty of murder, his sentence was death by hanging.

The gallows were built immediately. Sheriff Watson escorted Woods up the steps to his fate. Within seconds, Woods was "jerked to Jesus" as one local resource reported.

The Animas City Cemetery seems to be the logical place of burial, as Durango did not yet have a cemetery. While the body of Woods was

removed from the state by family members, it is possible Buchanan
was buried at Animas.[45]

GREENMOUNT CEMETERY

LOCATED AT THE SOUTHWESTERN EDGE OF DURANGO. TAKE 9TH STREET
WEST ACROSS THE RAILROAD TRACKS. THERE IS A SIGN THAT LEADS YOU
AROUND THE HILL TO THE CEMETERY.

The cemetery, established in 1887, is one of the most beautiful in
all of southern Colorado. Laid out in the river valley with the mountains to the west, there are gracious hills bathed in groomed grass and
mountain sunshine. Tall shade trees grace the area and add a guarded atmosphere. The blocks are clearly marked with wide roads winding throughout the grounds. There are several sections in the cemetery, including the religious, fraternal orders, ethnic areas, and two
city sections.

Camp, Alfred P. (1850 – 1925)
Camp, Estelle M. (1857 – 1948)

A native of Cincinnati, Ohio, Alfred arrived in Colorado in 1875. He
was cashier of the bank of Del Norte in 1876. In 1879, he opened a
branch of the bank in the San Juan Valley, called the Bank of San
Juan in Animas City, the first bank in the San Juan region. Within six
months Camp moved to the new railroad town of Durango. Camp's
bank was the beginning of a dynasty, providing a fortune to the Camp
family well into the 1950s.

Heavily involved in the founding of Durango, he was instrumental
in the development, serving on several boards and active in the politics of the young town, serving as town treasurer in 1883 and 1884,
and on the school board. By the end of the 1880s, his bank had become
the strongest in the region and the only national bank in the San
Juan area. He was the dean of Colorado's bank presidents.

In the summer of 1877, Estelle McNeil, a student at Cornell
University, traveled from New England to Del Norte, to visit her
brother. Here, she met Alfred P. Camp. Romance led to marriage in
1883. Joining Camp in Durango, she found the rough railroad town
far different than her sophisticated New England heritage.

As the years passed, Estelle became the soul of Durango society.
The center of social and charity affairs, she contributed to the
Presbyterian Church and the Library Association. She was among
those who led the crusade to create the Mesa Verde National Park.

No one did more to shape the Durango of today, than A. P. Camp
and his wife Estelle. Their home on the Boulevard, (3rd Avenue,)
served many social functions and became the epitome of Durango

society. True pioneers and developers of their community, they are highly regarded to this day.

Alfred and Estelle Camp are buried together in Block 3, Lot 11.

Crawford, Bobbie (1883 – 1954)

Very little is known of her life in Durango. The granddaughter of Civil War General Robert E. Lee, Mrs. Crawford is buried beside her husband Lin, in Block 3, Lot 20 of the north City Section. Her small tombstone notes her relationship to Lee.

Day, Victoria G. (1849 – 1941)

Born in Maryland, Victoria was the daughter of a rich plantation owner. Her mother died when she was quite young. During the Civil War, she and her sister helped run the plantation by plowing the fields, planting the crops and picking the meager harvest. In 1865, the Union Army took part of the family livestock. Renegades from the Confederate Army stole the remainder.

In 1870, she married David F. Day, a Northerner, which caused much anguish in her family. Five children were born before Day left for the West in 1878. Mrs. Day and the children traveled by train to Ouray in 1881. David Day started his famous paper, *The Solid Muldoon* in 1879. One of the most powerful newspapers in Colorado, it was the voice of David Day.

Victoria was happy in Ouray, but very unhappy when Day moved his paper to Durango in 1882. In her memoirs, she tells of moving to Denver in 1885, on the auspices of providing her children better schooling. She relates her return to Durango and leaving for a third time in 1906, when she bought a ranch at Trimble Springs.[46] A son Guy, ran the ranch and later, Victoria's nieces and nephews joined her.

Following the death of David Day in 1914, she sold their holdings and bought a ranch at Bondad.[47] She lived and worked the ranch until her death in 1941.

She is buried in Block 27, Lot 51. There is a marker.

Dempsey, Stella (1885 – 1910)

The sad and lonely existence of Stella Dempsey ended with suicide in 1910. In Durango, she worked as a prostitute at the Strater Hotel. She was the sister of famed prize fighter Jack Dempsey. Following her death, Jack Dempsey arrived in Durango in a black limousine. He picked out the small granite tombstone which marks Stella's grave, located in Block 26, Lot 67, of the south city section.

Fiorini, John (1877 – 1939)

Born in Piedmont, Torino, in northern Italy, John Fiorini followed the family trade of stonecutting. His father and his grandfather cut the native Italian marble, the same used by Michelangelo, to build many of the landmarks around Milano, Italy.

Following the family tradition, John was taken to Marseilles at the age of five, where he was educated and apprenticed in the stonecarving trade.

He came to America in 1906, settling first in Silverton, Colorado. His expert hand-carved stone is evident in the City Hall building he built in 1908. In Silverton, he married Genevieve Valiton. He later moved his family to Marble, Colorado, the heart of the Yule Marble Mine. With his hand tools, he sculpted and formed much of the marble used in our nation's monuments, including the Washington and Lincoln Memorials.

Upon his move to Durango in 1917, he established the Durango Monument Works, carving many of the beautiful and unique tombstones found all over the four corners area. Using native sandstone and granite blocks, his hand carving techniques are monuments to the builder and the artist.

In keeping with the family tradition, the craft was taught to John's son, Noel. The monument business continues today, still operated by the Fiorini family.

John and his wife Genevieve are buried together in Block 14, Lot 6. There is a marker.

Salmhofer, Valiton, Ferney, Marie Catherine (1832 – 1910)

Born in France, Marie immigrated alone to America in 1850, where she lived with a brother and sister in New York. Moving west, again alone, she settled and married in Dubuque, Iowa. She and her husband, Louis F. Valiton arrived in Denver in 1861 by covered wagon. Mr. Valiton operated a mercantile and drug store in Fairplay until the business was lost in a fire in 1873. He later died in Fairplay.

In 1876, Marie and a daughter moved to Fort Garland and later Taos, New Mexico. By 1879, she had returned to Colorado, settling in Animas City. In 1880, she built the first frame house in the new town of Durango, located near the future site of the railroad depot. She married Matt Salmhofer in 1889.

Marie gave of her time and resources to the community of Durango. She was active in the Catholic church and helped the needy and sick in many ways.

She is buried next to Matt, who proceeded her in death by six months. She is buried in Block 16, Lot 2.

Denver Public Library
"Doc Suzie" Anderson at her cabin with her father and brother.

Thompson, William J. (1857 – 1906)
Thompson, Sarah (1854 – 1924)
Thompson, an early sheriff of Durango, was shot on Main Street by Jesse Stansel, while the sheriff was trying to stop an illegal gambling ring. The confrontation was the culmination of a feud between city and county factions.

There is a dark granite marker to his wife's, memory in Block 30, Lot 11. The stone also lists William. Greenmount Cemetery records show the burial of his wife, Sarah, in 1924. However, there is no record of Sheriff Thompson being moved here from the Animas City Cemetery.

— — —

North / South Highways
I–70 Northern Boundary
Highway 67 South

CRIPPLE CREEK

MOUNT PISGAH CEMETERY
FOLLOW BENNETT AVENUE WEST THROUGH TOWN. THERE IS A SIGN LEADING TO A DIRT ROAD AT THE FOOT OF MOUNT PISGAH.

Mount Pisgah Cemetery lies just west of town, on a hill overlooking the revived town of Cripple Creek. Old and rustic, as most mining cemeteries are, there is a certain charm about this place. Overgrown with weeds and thistle, perhaps it is as forlorn and forgotten as those buried there. The first known burial occurred in 1891. Emma Rickett was stricken with blood poisoning, dying before the doctor arrived from Florissant. She was buried hastily on the hill that would become Mount Pisgah Cemetery.

Anderson, Susan M.D. (1870 – 1960)

Susan's father came to Cripple Creek in 1892, starting his own business running a mining stock trading company. The following year, he put Susan through medical school in the East. While earning her medical degree, Susan contracted tuberculosis. Knowing cool mountain air was the best chance for a cure, she returned to Cripple Creek with her degree in hand. Her first medical practice was not much of a success. Medical services were very competitive; there were some fifty-five doctors in Cripple Creek in 1897. The fact that she was the only female practitioner in the area was not an advantage in a mining town.

"Doc Suzie," as she came to be called, left Cripple Creek following the death of her brother and a rumored broken engagement, in 1900. She eventually settled in Fraser, Colorado. Her medical services were warmly received and much needed in that remote mountain town.

She was a coroner for a time, and became a crusader for the town's interests, including being an instrumental part of the Moffat Tunnel operation for the Fraser Valley.

While she came to love and call Fraser home, her dying wish was to be buried at Cripple Creek's Mount Pisgah Cemetery, next to her brother John. When Doc Suzie died in 1960, the cemetery had fallen in disrepair and John's grave could not be located.[48]

Doctor Susan Anderson was buried in a newer section of the cemetery, in an unmarked grave. Astonished Fraser friends of Doc Suzie's, later placed a respectable stone etched with the serpent entwined staff, the symbol of her medical profession.

Barbee, Johnson R. (1843 – 1905)

While most of the pioneers settling in Colorado came from the East, John Barbee came from the West. Originally from Kentucky, he was prospecting in Utah when he heard of the rich gold camp at Cripple Creek.

He and his family arrived in 1892.[49] The town was so crowded that the Barbee's first home was a tent. Prospecting in the district, he managed a living, but never found his own mother lode.

He is buried next to his wife. There is a marker.

DeVere, Pearl (? – 1897)

The thirty-one-year-old beauty moved to Cripple Creek from Denver in 1893. Pearl DeVere set up her business on Myers Avenue, the Red Light District. The most prosperous of all madams in the district, she immediately rebounded from the great fire of 1896. She built the grandest brick parlor house in Cripple Creek, today a museum.

Her business catered to the highest clientele by appointment only. By Cripple Creek standards, she was a very wealthy woman.

In 1897, following a lavish party, Pearl was found dead of an overdose of morphine. She was buried on a cold, cloudy June day. A parade of carriages led to the cemetery on the hill. She was laid to rest in the lavish pink chiffon gown she had died in.

Pearl was buried in a corner of the cemetery with a wooden marker. Years later this marker was replaced with a white granite heart-shaped stone. Her grave was topped with stones from the district's mines and enclosed by an iron fence.

— — —

Highway 285

COMO

COMO CEMETERY

LOCATED NORTHWEST OF TOWN. FROM COMO, TAKE THE BOREAS PASS ROAD ONE-QUARTER-MILE NORTH TO COUNTY ROAD 33 WEST (THE FIRST DIRT ROAD LEADING WEST.) THE CEMETERY IS ON THE LEFT.

The town of Como became the division point of the Denver & South Park Railway in 1880. The railroad was organized in 1872 by John Evans, David Moffat, Walter Cheeseman, and East Coast millionaire, Jay Gould. The roundhouse, located at the edge of town, is one of the finest in the state.

Established in 1870, this cemetery replaced the Old Como Cemetery located southwest of town. Notice was given by the city marshal to remove all burials to the new cemetery by November 1870. Located on land owned by the Pacific Coal Company, the company retained ownership of the land. Cemetery lots were not for sale. Quit claim deeds were issued to the next of kin. Because of this unusual arrangement, early cemetery records were not complete. Block and plot information is scarce. Fencing was later provided by the local I.O.O.F. Lodge. The old wooden building with tin siding may have been a maintenance shed at one time.

Among the many burials are the Como pioneer families of Delaney, Peabody, and Duffy. George Montag is buried here. A general merchandiser, he arrived in 1880. He became mayor of Como in 1885, operated a ranch, and ran a freighting service to Leadville. Montag is buried in Block 6, Lot 34.

The cemetery extends back into the large grove of aspen trees, gently whistling in the wind as they stand guard over the solemn tombstones.

Near the east gate entrance is the white marble tombstone of Frank P. Volz. He was the infant son of South Park pioneer Charles Volz. Charles, a native of Ohio, came to Colorado to work for the railroad. He later joined the Denver & South Park Railway. He married Sylvia Cook, an Indian woman, in 1883. Following the death of their infant son, Charles and Sylvia relocated to Jefferson, Colorado.

Kelly, Josephine J. (1839 – 1919)

Josephine Kelly operated a two-story brick rooming house at Seventh and Rowe Streets. An inspiring violinist, she provided the entertainment at the town hall socials.

Josephine Kelly was buried with her violin in Block 4, Lot 8.

Link, James M. (1817 – 1899)

James Morrison Link, a native of Adair County, Kentucky, (Abraham Lincoln's birthplace,) brought his family west, settling in South Park in the early 1870s. Link engaged in several business adventures, including mining, livestock and the hotel business. Elizabeth Link, James' daughter-in-law, owned several real estate properties in the area.

The Link family plot is located in Lot 45 of the west section. There is a dark granite stone at the grave of James.

McLaughlin, Daniel (1822 – 1873)

South Park pioneer, Daniel McLaughlin ran a stage between Hamilton and the future site of Como.[50] A portion of the McLaughlin land later became the site of Como.

On the morning of July 26, 1864, the infamous Reynolds gang surprised McLaughlin at his stage stop, tying him to a wall. The outlaws stole a strong box containing the payroll from the local mine, which was to be transported later that day. The gang left McLaughlin's stage stop and continued a series of robberies throughout the South Park area.[51]

Daniel McLaughlin is buried in the south end of the cemetery in Lot 14. There is a marker.

Schattinger, Peter (1853 – 1935)

One of the earliest pioneers in the area, Peter Schattinger became one of the most respected ranchers near Como. He raised livestock, and sold hay to neighboring ranchers. Peter's wife Elizabeth, died in childbirth in 1890.

There is a pink marble tombstone to their memory.

Turner Family Plot

Patriarch Hiram P. Turner, a native of Maine, brought his family west for a better life. An original 59er, he settled in South Park, where he applied his stone mason trade in constructing many early buildings. Turner spent time mining in Central City and Breckenridge.

William E. Turner, son of Hiram, took up ranching near Jefferson. He died in 1895.

His white marble obelisk is quite prominent in the eastern section of the cemetery.

William's widow, Clara, married Oswald "Buddy" Schwartz, a railroad engineer. Schwartz died in a train wreck on Boreas Pass in 1909. His tombstone is next to the Turner plot.

Alfred S. Turner, son of Hiram, born in 1849, made the journey west with his father, as a boy. Alfred helped his father on the ranch and worked in the mines as a supervisor. He later owned and operated mining properties at Garo. Alfred's wife Mary, ran the store in the mining community.

Alfred and Mary are buried together in the Turner plot.

Their son Fred P., was born in 1888, died in 1918, and is buried nearby. His tombstone reads: "His life for his country."

The Turner family plot is located in the east block of the cemetery.

FAIRPLAY

OLD FAIRPLAY CEMETERY

LOCATED WEST OF THE TOWN OF FAIRPLAY. FOLLOW MAIN STREET WEST, THE CEMETERY TURNOFF IS JUST NORTH OF THE ENTRANCE TO THE SOUTH PARK MUSEUM. FOLLOW THE DIRT ROAD UP THE HILL ABOUT A QUARTER OF A MILE.

The first cemetery established for the young town of Fairplay, the oldest grave dates to 1863. The last burial occurred in 1872. According to Park County records, there are seven graves. The cemetery is perched at the incline of a hill, west of town. There is a residential area to the west. Enclosed with large wooden posts and rails, there are only three markers in the cemetery. Among the tall pine trees and thick brush can be found evidence of many other graves, some of which are distinguished by rock piles.

At the end of the cemetery is the gray granite marker of Abram Nelson Shoup. The dates 1834 – 1863 are inscribed on the monument, along with his military service.

Shoup, the brother of Colonel George L. Shoup, was a prominent resident of the South Park area and a member of the Colorado Volunteers.

Abram Shoup was a victim of the Espinosa gang's bloody rampage in the South Park area. His butchered body was found in the nearby Red Hills. His brother, Colonel Shoup, organized a posse to apprehend the gang. The Espinosas were eventually hunted down by Tom Tobin.

The tombstone of Louisa L. McLaughlin stands at the west end of the cemetery. The stone is inscribed "D 1868 77 yrs 3 months 16 days."

Louisa was the wife of Matthew McLaughlin. A Fairplay pioneer, Matthew operated one of the stage lines running from Denver to Fairplay, and from Fairplay to Leadville over Weston Pass. His livery stable at Fairplay was the largest, due to the heavy traffic in those early years. Prominent in business, McLaughlin was one of the three original officers of what would become the town of Fairplay.

Unfortunately, history, as is so often the case, records very little of the life of Louisa McLaughlin, better known as Mrs. Matthew McLaughlin.

The third stone is that of Mime McLaughlin. The inscription reads: "D 1872 22 yrs 11 months 21 days." Her relationship is unknown.

FAIRPLAY CEMETERY

LOCATED ONE-HALF-MILE NORTH OF FAIRPLAY ON HIGHWAY 285. THE CEMETERY IS ON THE EAST SIDE OF THE HIGHWAY. TAKE THE DIRT ROAD EAST OF THE HIGHWAY, TO THE CEMETERY ENTRANCE.

This picturesque cemetery lies in the heart of South Park. The entrance is graced with a white iron gate. Beautiful aspen trees whisper in the soft mountain breeze. Wildflowers and mountain sage are the only landscaping. Wide roads provide easy access.

The cemetery is divided into three sections. The city of Fairplay, the Odd Fellows, and the Masons each own a third. The land was donated by the I.O.O.F. Lodge #10, still in existence. The cemetery is well laid out in several rows. The oldest known burial is dated 1863. There are several unmarked graves in the west section, across the dirt road.

Carmody, Thomas (? – 1880)

Irish by birth, Thomas Carmody worked in the mines and smelters of the Fairplay area. He was known as a hard worker, and quiet by nature.

On a frigid March evening, Carmody enjoyed a few drinks at the local saloon. Among the crowd was William J. Porter, silently watching Carmody. When Carmody left the saloon, he encountered Porter on the street. Porter made a few derogatory remarks to Carmody, and without warning, pulled his weapon and shot Carmody. Carmody ran to a hotel, where he later died.

His grave is unmarked.

Guiraud, Adolph (1822 – 1875)
Guiraud, Marie (1830 – 1909)

A native of France, Adolph Guiraud came to America in 1850, first settling in New Orleans, where he operated a wine importing business. He moved west to Colorado in 1862.

The first to file a homestead in the South Park region, Guiraud chose his land in 1863. He homesteaded on the South Fork of the South Platte. He acquired the most valuable water rights in the area and established the most prominent ranch in the park.

In 1865 he opened a meat market in Fairplay; his ranch being the only supplier. Highly regarded by all who knew him, his friends included Fairplay's "Snowshoe Itinerate," Father Dyer.[52] Other acquaintances included Jim Reynolds, the leader of the notorious Reynolds gang.

Following the death of Adolph in 1875, his wife, Marie expanded the ranch to some 5,000 acres. She ran the largest sheep herd in the area, and raised top quality hay. On one occasion, it is said, the railroad killed all her sheep and refused to compensate her for the loss. Shortly thereafter, the railroad could no longer get up the hill on her ranch. The wheels of the engines had no traction. Eventually, the railroad gave in and paid her for her lost sheep. In turn, Mrs. Guiraud stopped greasing the tracks with mutton tallow. The ranch remained in the Guiraud family until 1941. The original home still stands, although drastically altered.

Adolph and Marie Guiraud are buried together in the wrought iron fenced plot of the Guiraud family. There is a dark granite hand carved obelisk in their memory.

Hoffmann, Johannes (1825 – 1882)

A German immigrant, Hoffmann worked for one of the mines on Mt. Cameron. He died of food poisoning. A member of the Knights of Pythias, he was buried with full honors, with the lodge officiating the services. There is a marker, carved in German.

Hoover, Louisa (? – 1878)

She was the infant daughter of J. J. Hoover, who killed Thomas Bennett in 1880.

Mayer, Frank H. (1850 – 1954)

Born in New Orleans, Frank Mayer came west to hunt buffalo. One of the most talented hunters of the nineteenth century, he was renowned for his celebrity hunting exhibitions. He made his home in Fairplay.

He died at the age of 103. A pink marble stone marks his burial plot.

— — —

The Fairplay Courthouse, built in 1874, is the oldest operating courthouse in Colorado. It holds another distinction as well; "The Hanging Court." A bit of a misnomer, for Judge Bowen pronounced very few hangings, a habit the folks of Fairplay rectified in short order.

When a drunken J. J. Hoover killed his hired ditch man, Thomas A Bennett, in 1880, Judge Bowen sentenced Hoover to eight years in prison. Hoover was a prominent citizen of Fairplay. The outraged citizens promptly broke into the jail and hanged Hoover out of the second floor window.

Accused killer, Cicero Simms was to be tried for murder the next day. The noose used on Hoover was placed on Judge Bowen's desk, a message in the strongest terms. Judge Bowen left the area without a trace, never hearing the case against Simms.

In the same year, William J. Porter, a drunk, threatened to kill the first man he saw on the streets of Alma.[53] When he killed Thomas Carmody, he was arrested and taken to the Fairplay jail. A group of citizens nailed a beam outside of the jail, threw a noose over it and proceeded to hang Porter. His last words were reportedly "pull."

A duel occurred in 1860, resulting in the death of a man named Sanford. He and a man named Pemley were childhood friends from Texas. Years later, in Park County, Sanford won the affections of Pemley's sister, having his way and deserting her. Pemley swore revenge and followed Sanford from Park County to New Zealand and back to Fairplay. Working at a gravel pit, Sanford was confronted by Pemley. A duel ensued, both fired simultaneously. Sanford was killed, while Pemley suffered a scalp wound. Pemley was acquitted of murder.

Records have not confirmed the burials of these individuals. It is possible they are among the many unmarked graves at the Fairplay Cemetery.

Rupert Sherwood and his burro, Prunes

A monument on Front Street pays tribute to a miner and his faithful burro named Prunes. Rupert M. Sherwood, a jack of all trades, and his favorite companion jack, Prunes, were loved by all of Fairplay. For over thirty years, the pair worked the mines and roamed the streets. When Prunes died in 1929, the town collected money for a monument to the legendary burro. Within a year, "Rupe" Sherwood died, some say from loneliness. His ashes were buried with his friend, Prunes the burro.

NATHROP

NATHROP CEMETERY

LOCATED ONE-QUARTER-MILE WEST OF HIGHWAY 285, ON COUNTY ROAD 162, AT THE TOP OF THE HILL.

Also known as Nachtrieb Cemetery, the site overlooks the valley where the original Nachtrieb ranch still stands. The first burial was in 1875–that of a baby Nachtrieb. There are no records of burials, however, the cemetery is still used by members of the Nachtrieb family.

Anderson, Horace Greeley M.D. (1858 – 1905)

Horace was the first born to the union of Harrison and Margaret Tull Anderson. His mother later married Charles H. Nachtrieb.

He was a physician in Chaffee County. He died at the age of forty-six, of Bright's disease. There is a marker.

Nachtrieb, Charles H. 1st (1833 – 1881)

Born in Germany, Charles Nachtrieb came to the United States with his parents, settling in Baltimore. By 1860, he was selling merchandise at California Gulch. He moved south to the Chalk Creek area, where he started a ranch. In 1868, he built the first grist and sawmills, both run by water power.

The mills were one of the several sites used as the headquarters of the "Committee of Safety" regulators. They were better known locally as the vigilantes during the Lake County War. Nachtrieb was reportedly the leader of the vigilantes, who waged war against landowners refusing to give in to their demands, such as land, water and subordination. Several men were tortured and hanged at Nachtrieb's mills.

Nachtrieb was murdered a few years after the Lake County War, at his store. His wife Margaret found the body. The murderer, Bert Remington, left the county and was never apprehended.

Nachtrieb's tall white obelisk is the only stone in Chaffee County marked with the words "Murdered."

Nachtrieb, Margaret Tull Anderson (1840 – 1910)

Born in Iowa, Margaret married Harrison Anderson, at age eighteen. The two had four children. By 1870, she was divorced and married Charles H. Nachtrieb, I. To this marriage six children were born.

Margaret helped run the ranch, tended to the farm, operated the mill, managed the finances, as well as raising the ten children.

She continued the family operation following the murder of her husband. She died in 1910. There is a marker.

Parks, Finley R. (1850 – 1909)
Parks, Alice Carrie (1864 – 1936)

Parks was a railroad man on the Denver & Rio Grande. He and his wife Alice made their home in Salida.

A rare Colorado native, Alice was born in Malta, Colorado, the daughter of Harrison and Margaret Tull Anderson. As a girl, she carried the toll money from the Poncha Pass Road to her family home at the Nachtrieb ranch. She married Finley Parks in Nathrop in 1883.

The two are buried together, there is a marker.

OFF THE BEATEN PATH:
ST. ELMO

IRON CITY CEMETERY

FROM HIGHWAY 285, TAKE COUNTY ROAD 162 WEST TO THE TOWN OF ST. ELMO. THE ROAD LEADING TO TIN CUP PASS WILL HAVE A SIGN TO THE CEMETERY. (SPELLED INCORRECTLY.)

A SECOND ROUTE IS AT THE JUNCTION OF HIGHWAYS 24 AND 306, IN THE TOWN OF BUENA VISTA. THE ROAD PASSES MT. OLIVET CEMETERY, AND FOLLOWS THE EAST SIDE OF MT. PRINCETON TO ST. ELMO, OVER COTTONWOOD PASS.

This peaceful mountain cemetery, located at the base of Sugar Loaf Mountain, was established in 1881. The original Forest City-St. Elmo cemetery, located closer to town, was soon in the way of progress for the booming mining town. The new cemetery provided a more peaceful and open resting spot. While the original cemetery still exists at the north end of town, most of the bodies were removed to the Iron City Cemetery.

Many of the graves are of infants. Sarah and Gertrude Mullins died of diphtheria. The sisters were one year apart in age and died within a day of each other in 1891.[54] The Hurley brothers both died of typhoid fever within seven years. The first boy died in 1889, the other died in 1896.

The cemetery is maintained by volunteers from the St. Elmo community. Wooden markers painted white, were recently placed on all known graves that were unmarked. Cemetery records are not complete. There are many unknown graves lost to history.

Clark–Schubert Family Plot[55]
Clark, Daniel (1842 – 1927)
Clark, Amelia H. Schubert (1850 – 1941)

Born in Michigan, Daniel Clark worked as a miner when he first arrived in the St. Elmo area in 1879. He later owned the Iron Chest Mine. In 1886, he was elected county commissioner. He later served as justice of the peace, town trustee, clerk and mayor.

His wife Amelia H. Schubert, a German immigrant, arrived with her parents in America, in 1868. The couple had eight children.

There is a stone marker. Nearby are the graves of Herman and Charlotte Schubert, the parents of Amelia Schubert Clark.

Gilbertson, Iver (? – 1884)

A miner at the Decorah Mine, Gilbertson was thawing dynamite sticks near a fire, when the sticks exploded. The nearby shop was reduced to kindling and two men nearby were thrown over the nearby dump site. Gilbertson was found with his right hand blown off and his arm shattered. He died the next day.

Lowe, Joseph H. (1864 – 1907)

Joseph Lowe was a mining engineer and held the office of St. Elmo trustee, resigning in January 1905. In 1904, he was charged with incest, involving his twenty–four-year-old niece. He was arrested in Pitkin. The niece, Mellie or Millie Frasher was originally scheduled to testify at the trial, but was released by District Attorney Augustus Pease, due to her age.

Joseph was found guilty and sentenced to the state penitentiary at Canon City on January 27, 1905. He was to serve no less than three years before being eligible for parole, and no more than five years. Evidently, he was released from prison before serving the three-year minimum sentence, as he died in St. Elmo in 1907.

Mary Murphy Mine Accident (1889)

One of the most successful mines in the St. Elmo area, the owners experienced their first major accident in May 1889.

Shoring timbers collapsed between the second and third levels, caving in on miners who were crushed to death.

T. L. Stormes was the first person
buried in the Tin Cup Cemetery.

Among the dead were John
O'Hagen, Tom Rupp and an
unidentified miner.[56]

Tom Rupp was recently from
Virginia City, Nevada and lies in
the Iron City Cemetery at St.
Elmo. The unidentified victim
was buried near the mine.[57]

Pushor, C. W. (1850 – 1889)

Pushor was a miner in the area
and owned some land. He com-
mitted suicide according to the
May 9, 1889 edition of the *Buena
Vista Democrat* and the *Salida
Daily News.*

Curiously, Mrs. C. W. Pushor is listed in the obituaries of the same
Buena Vista Democrat, but she was still alive.

Weston, Maude (1872 – 1895)

Maude Weston died of heart disease at the age of twenty-three.
She was the daughter of John Weston, a long time resident of St.
Elmo, who also died of heart disease in 1897.[58] Her mother, Abbie, the
first wife of John, died in 1888, and is buried in the Tin Cup Cemetery.

TIN CUP

TIN CUP CEMETERY

*FROM ST. ELMO, THE DIRT ROAD LEADS TO THE TOP OF TIN CUP PASS.
FROM THERE, WILLOW CREEK ROAD GOES WEST TO THE TINY TOWN OF TIN
CUP. IT IS ALSO ACCESSIBLE FOLLOWING COTTONWOOD PASS, SOUTHWEST
OF BUENA VISTA, (THIRTY-THREE MILES), OR NORTH OF HIGHWAY 50, OVER
CUMBERLAND PASS, (THIRTY-FIVE MILES), OR FOLLOWING THE ALMONT AND
TAYLOR RIVER ROAD NORTHEAST OF GUNNISON, (FORTY-SEVEN MILES.)*

The Tin Cup Cemetery is located half a mile north of town on
Service Road 765, also known as the Cemetery Road. There is a sign
pointing the direction, note the misspelling. At one time there was a
wagon road to each of the four knolls. The road stops at the Jewish
Knoll, which is lower than the other knolls. The walk to the cemetery
is a short one.

Also known as The Cemetery of Four Knolls, each knoll represents
a separate section. The Protestant knoll lies to the north. The Catholic
knoll, the largest, is in the center. The third knoll is the Jewish knoll.
The east knoll, the highest, represents no particular religious group,

but was undoubtedly the most active. Known as Boot Hill, the undesirables of Tin Cup rest here. There are several unmarked graves in
this section. Historians have speculated on the burial of a dance hall
girl at Boot Hill. Research by area historians June Shaputis and
Eleanor Harrington revealed the grave of a woman called "Pass Out."
The name came about because a few sips of liquor caused her to pass
out! Records reveal she was buried on Boot Hill, although there is no
marker.

The first recorded burial in this remote mountain resting place
occurred in 1879–that of T. L. Stormes. Because of the high altitude of
Tin Cup, many winter burials were either delayed or moved to Buena
Vista. The toll over Cottonwood Pass to Buena Vista was free, if the
body was in transport. The mourners were required to pay the toll on
the return trip.

Tin Cup did not have good luck with their lawmen. The first few
were controlled by the underworld "mob" element. Marshal Willis was
actually told who *not* to arrest. Many marshals were murdered directly or indirectly, by the mob.

Duncan, George E. (1855 – 1907)

A pioneer in the area, George Duncan was a preacher at the only
church in the mining community. His six sons attended the small
school of Tin Cup. Duncan Flats, just south of Tin Cup was named in
his honor.

He is buried in the Protestant knoll.

Emerson, Frank (? – 1882)

Frank Emerson was the first town marshal when Tin Cup was
known as Virginia City. He was part owner of the Pacific Hotel, which
was run by Maggie C. Laughrey. The two were married and made
their home there.

Emerson had a long standing feud of unknown origin, with ex-mar-
shal Thomas J. Leahy. After a few drinks at Frenchy's Place, Emerson
walked toward the Pacific Hotel. Along the way, he encountered
Leahy and the two exchanged words. Emerson turned to leave and
Leahy fired two shots from his pistol. Emerson fell dead. Leahy was
sentenced to twelve years in the Colorado State Penitentiary.

Emerson is buried in the Boot Hill knoll.

Englebright, Lowery (1865 – 1965)

On the Protestant knoll is a large tablet marker halfway up the
hill. It is the memorial to Lowery Englebright, a prominent Tin Cup
pioneer. A native of Iowa, he attended Colorado College at Colorado

Springs. He arrived in Tin Cup in 1893, working as an underground timber man for the mines in the area.

Following retirement, he took on many duties to help the community. For many summers, he hand-painted the names and dates on the wooden markers at the cemetery. Today, the markers that remain, are unreadable. He died two months short of his one hundredth birthday.

In June 1965, a memorial service was held at the town hall. It was still winter at the time of his death, delaying his funeral. The residents paid their respects, and the procession moved past the brown house on Grand Avenue, south of the bridge, where Lowery spent his final years. He was laid to rest on Protestant knoll. A silent moment was observed, flowers were placed and the crowd sadly departed.

Fisher, Kate (1832 – 1902)

Kate Fisher and her husband were slaves in Virginia. The two were sold to different slave owners. When she was freed, Kate made her way west, living for a time in both Leadville and Buena Vista, before moving to Tin Cup, where she remained until her death.

Kate arrived in Tin Cup sometime in 1879 or 1880. She was the only black woman who ran her own business, (quite successfully) in the mining town. She first operated a boardinghouse at the corner of Grande Avenue and Main Street. When word of her good cooking got around, it was necessary for the business to find larger quarters. Her hotel and restaurant on the south side of Washington Avenue, was a big attraction during Tin Cup's boom days. Somehow, she managed to keep live geraniums in the windows during the freezing winter months.

Kate's unmarked grave is in the Protestant knoll, approximately five graves south of Englebright's white marker in the west row.

Gollagher, Samuel P. (1853 – 1906)

A native of Ireland, Samuel Gollagher arrived in America at age eighteen. He made his way west by way of New York and arrived in Colorado in 1885. An early pioneer of Tin Cup, he prospected for a time before working for Carl Freeman in his general store. By 1895, he had purchased the store and married Anne Clickener, the niece of Charles Latourette. The couple had seven children.

He was somewhat of a banker for the Tin Cup miners. The miners trusted him to keep part of their pay on their behalf. He also handled the payroll for a few of mines and was once robbed. Following the robbery, he kept all the money in a strong box in the potato cellar of the store. A month after Gollagher's death, a fire destroyed the mercantile store, caused by arson, according to some accounts. However, the strong box was recovered and all depositors received their money.

His stone marker, enclosed by an iron fence, is at the north end of the east row, in the Protestant knoll.

Jameson, Andrew (1856 – 1883)

Andrew Jameson arrived in Tin Cup in 1882. He was employed as a painter before becoming Tin Cup town marshal in 1882, replacing slain Marshal Harry Rivers. The rough mining town enjoyed five months of no crime under Jameson's rule.

That ended in May 1883 with Jameson's death. A saloon fight broke out at the St. James Hotel, involving Jameson, William Taylor and a man named Bliss. Taylor fired his revolver, killing Jameson instantly. Taylor was convicted and sentenced to four years in the Colorado State Penitentiary. He said in a statement that he had no cause to shoot Jameson.

Jameson is buried in the Boot Hill knoll.

Parent, Mary B. (1869 – 1901)

Mary lived in the communities of Pitkin and Gunnison, before arriving in Tin Cup. She was the widow of J. S. Wiley and the mother of a young boy. To make a living, she operated a store from her home in Tin Cup.

In 1901, she married Alex Parent, who drove a stage and carried mail on the Tin Cup–St. Elmo route. The marriage was happy, but short.

Mary fell ill four months after the marriage and died a few weeks later. She was thirty-one.

Alex raised her son and eventually left Tin Cup, dying in Gunnison in 1930. His wish was to buried in Tin Cup beside Mary, however, the winter conditions prevented the journey.[59]

Mary Parent is buried in the Protestant knoll.

Rivers, Harry (? – 1882)

Harry Rivers was the town marshal when he was shot to death by Charles Latourette, a saloon keeper. In a true western showdown, Rivers, while patrolling the streets, was called out by Latourette. Both men drew their weapons. Latourette's bullet went through River's head, killing him instantly. The murder concluded a long feud between two who had once been friends. The courts found Latourette innocent by an act of self-defense, a controversial decision according to some Tin Cup residents.

Rivers is buried in the center of the Boot Hill knoll.

Wolfe, Oscar (? – 1916)

An interesting graveyard story, is that Oscar dug the grave that he would ultimately be buried in. The grave was dug for Billy Prior who accidentally shot himself. Billy's family changed burial plans after the grave was dug, and Billy was buried elsewhere.

Oscar died a year later and was buried in the grave he had dug for Billy. His body was found in his remote cabin. He and his brother owned the Wolfe Placer.

He is buried in the Boot Hill knoll.

CENTERVILLE

CENTERVILLE CEMETERY

LOCATED FOUR AND ONE-HALF MILES SOUTH OF THE NATHROP CEMETERY, ON THE EAST SIDE OF HIGHWAY 285. TAKE COUNTY ROAD 263 UP THE HILL TO THE CEMETERY. THERE IS A GATE WITH A CHAIN. PLEASE SECURE UPON DEPARTURE.

High on a hill overlooking the valley, this wind-swept cemetery seems lonely and deserted. Yet recently-placed mementos say otherwise. Also known as Brown's Canyon Cemetery, it is the oldest cemetery in Chaffee County. The first known burial is that of a child, William Sprague, in 1864.

Fred Bertschy donated the land to Lake County (now Chaffee County), for a graveyard, because the soft soil made for easy digging. There is much history in this small cemetery, although there are no official cemetery records.

This area was the center of the infamous Lake County War of 1874. Several of the victims, as well as the perpetrators of this event are buried at the Centerville Cemetery.

Austin Family Plot

David Edward Charles Austin was born in 1867 in Ohio. He discovered gold near Turret in 1884, and located the Independence Mine in 1897. Austin Camp is named for him, later changed to Turret. He was postmaster for several years and superintendent of the Standard Copper Corporation and Wellington Mine. His only marker is a metal funeral home plate.

Ella May Austin was the infant daughter of David E. C. and Mary Austin. She died in 1890 at age five months.

Ernest C. Austin, son of David E. C. and Mary Austin, was born in 1892 at Centerville. He was a miner and supervisor at Turret. He died in 1938, after a long illness.

Lizzie "Louisa" Austin, the daughter of David E. C. and Mary Austin, died at age three years, nine months, in 1897. Her death was the result of a horrible accident. Her brother Ernest, dropped a pick that embedded in Lizzie's head, exposing her brain.

Harrington, George (1839 – 1874)

Born in England, George Harrington was a rancher and farmer in early Lake County (now Chaffee County). His ranch, located just below Land's Hill, west of Highway 285, included 160 acres, complete with a grocery and dry goods store.

One of the more prominent landowners in the area, Harrington was the first casualty of the Lake County War in June 1874. His smokehouse was set afire by an arsonist. While fighting the blaze, shots were fired, hitting Harrington twice. The shot through the head killed him instantly. His neighbor, Elijah Gibbs, known to have threatened Harrington in the past, was arrested, tried and acquitted. The Lake County War continued for over a year.

Harrington's tombstone lays broken on the ground. It once read "Sacred to the memory of Geo. Harrington–was murdered 17 July 1874–aged 74 years."[60] The stone is located a few feet east of the F.A. and Helen Land marker.[61]

Mear, John Sr. (1839 – 1904)

John Mear came to the United States from England with his parents as a child. He was ranching in the county by 1870 and married Mary Bell Nash at Granite, in 1871.

He was a deputy sheriff of Lake County when the county seat was changed from Granite to Buena Vista. A feud erupted over the change, resulting in men from Buena Vista, stealing the county records back from Granite. Mear and his wife were held by force during the heist. Mear retained his position as sheriff, serving the newly-created Chaffee County.

He is buried in the Mear family plot next to his wife.

Morgan, Margaret E. Bassham (1856 – 1925)

One of Colorado's first natives, Margaret was born in 1856. She married Thomas Morgan in 1871. The couple owned a farm and ranch in Chaffee County and raised seven children. Three other children died in infancy.

Margaret sustained an eye injury while sweeping the farmhouse floors. The broom handle hit her in the left eye, causing the eye to pop out of the socket. She would never allow her picture to be taken full face. In her elder years, the pain became intolerable. She died on the operating table, due to cancer of the eye.

There is a marker in her memory.

Sprague, Galatia M. (1823 – 1904)

Born in Ohio, Galatia Sprague came to Colorado by covered wagon with his wife Caroline. One of the earliest pioneer families, they settled at Brown's Creek in 1865.

Galatia was a farmer and a rancher. He also practiced law, taught school and became a judge. By 1880, he owned a large amount of land in Chaffee County. He also had property in Leadville. He contributed to the community by providing the brick used it to build the Salida Poor House.

He died in Poncha Springs of Bright's Disease. There is a stone monument.

Steel, Smith (1845 – ?)

An Illinois native, and a veteran of the Civil War, Steel settled in Lake County (Chaffee County.) He owned a ranch three miles south of Nathrop. He refused to be intimidated by the Vigilante Committee of Safety, which pressured land owners into releasing certain property rights.

Smith Steel disappeared in 1903. In February of 1924, a skull and bones were found in a gulch a mile from Turett, hidden by large boulders. The remains were identified as those of Steel. Clues included the rifle found near the remains. It was identified as a .40 caliber, made in 1869. However, his famous silver watch was missing. The *Salida Daily Mail* stated he may have died from a blow to the left side of the skull.

His grave is unmarked.[62]

OFF THE BEATEN PATH:

FROM THE TOWN OF VILLA GROVE, THE GHOST TOWN OF BONANZA LIES WEST ON COUNTY ROAD LL56, WHICH FOLLOWS KERBER CREEK.

A booming mining town, boasting thirty–two businesses in the 1880s, Bonanza fizzled out almost as quickly as it sprang up. The gold proved to be low grade, and not worth refining. Within a decade, the town had nearly died. Mines reopened in the early 1900s, producing lead, zinc, and copper, and Bonanza struggled to survive.

The Bonanza Cemetery lies just southeast of the old town. There are many unmarked graves, and a few family plots. John O'Hara was shot on the streets of Bonanza by a musician named Forbush. The nature of the quarrel is unknown.

The Irish element of the mining camp set out to apprehend and lynch Forbush. Forbush was caught, but lived to stand trial, was acquitted, and left town. O'Hara was buried in the cemetery at Bonanza.

Among the burials in this forlorn mountain cemetery is Colorado author Anne Ellis. Anne came to Bonanza as a child, living through the mining boom. She went on to write several booklets on Colorado history. When she died in Denver, her last wish was granted: to be buried among the pines and scrub oak of her beloved Bonanza.

SAGUACHE

SAGUACHE CEMETERY

LOCATED SOUTHEAST OF SAGUACHE. FROM FIRST STREET, TAKE THE CEMETERY ROAD SOUTH OF TOWN. THE CEMETERY IS ONE MILE DOWN THE WELL PAVED ROAD, ON THE EAST SIDE.

The Saguache Cemetery land was deeded to the city in 1915, after forty years of operation. The oldest known tombstone is that of an infant, who died at birth on November 25, 1868. The cemetery is laid against a natural up slope to the hill at the east end. Landscaping includes a beautiful row of Aspen trees lining the west end, planted in the mid 1980s. There are several areas where the only monuments are simple rocks, with no inscriptions. New additions include the gateway at the entrance of the cemetery, sponsored by the Hayes family in 1996.[63]

Clark, Franklin (1834 – 1901)

In 1885, Clark established his Rockcliff Ranch, some sixteen miles west of Saguache. One of the largest ranches in the area, it had some nine miles of creek bottom. In its heyday, the ranch ran over 1,800 head of cattle.

Frank Clark's burial is not recorded, however, his tall tombstone is high on the hill, toward the east end of the cemetery.

Downer, James P. (1818 – 1898)

An early pioneer of Saguache County, Major James Downer settled there in 1868. He was born in Uniontown, Pennsylvania and completed his education, including some college, before joining the army in 1846.

Major Downer served in the Mexican War and saw action when American troops stormed Cerro Gordo and defeated Santa Ana and his army. Following the war, Downing returned to Pennsylvania, where he was elected to the state Legislature.

In 1856, Downer joined the freight team of Majors, Russell, & Waddell, of Pony Express fame. With the onset of the Civil War, Downer organized Company B of the Kansas regiment. He was with General Lyon when he was killed at the Battle of Wilson Creek.[64]

Following the war, Downer came west with Colonel Isaac Eaton. He settled in Saguache, where he established a ranch. Downer soon saw the need for military protection for the settlers against the Ute Indians. He formed the Downer Guard, which later became the Colorado First Regular Infantry of the State Militia. The Downer Guard was instrumental in maintaining peace in Saguache County.

Major Downer is buried near the center of the cemetery. Originally buried in an unmarked grave, his traditional white marble military issue stone gives his birth and death date, as well as his service during the Mexican and Civil wars.[65]

Lawrence, John (1835 – 1908)

John Lawrence is known in history as the founder of Saguache. He arrived in the area in 1867, homesteaded near the river and raised cattle. By 1877 he had a cattle enterprise stretching for miles. He was instrumental in plotting the township that would become Saguache, and writing the city bylaws for incorporation. He was a member of the Territorial Legislature, as well as a county judge. In 1898, he was elected to the Colorado House of Representatives.

There is a simple granite marker to his memory, which says:

Founder of Saguache.

Following his death, there was no funeral service, at Lawrence's request. His will said, "I am a non Christian believer, called an Infidel."

He is buried in Block J, Lot 93.

O'Neil, Johnnie (1852 – 1927)

The redheaded Irish saloon keeper is known in history as Saguache's jockey in the famous horse race of August 21, 1880. O'Neil rode the town's beloved racehorse "Red Buck."

The opponent was a thoroughbred named "Little Casino," raced in Iowa, Kansas, and Leadville, Colorado. Money was placed on Saguache's "Red Buck" to win, but he lost. It was the opinion of many, including John Lawrence, that O'Neil threw the race.

Tribute was eventually given to O'Neil, although posthumously. His tombstone reads: "Red Buck's Rider."

He is buried in Block N, Lot 57.

Russell, Nathan (1831 – 1895)

The first post office in Saguache County was established on April 1, 1867. Known as Russell, it was located on Nathan Russell's homestead. Russell was an established rancher who came to the area some fifteen years before Saguache was founded. The area of postal service ran from Conejos through Del Norte, to the Saguache route. This was the north branch of the Old Spanish Trail.

Nathan Russell was involved with the Territory Legislature, and worked in local politics.

He is buried in Block M, Lot 20.

— — —

Highway 9 South

BRECKENRIDGE

VALLEY BROOK CEMETERY

LOCATED APPROXIMATELY ONE-HALF-MILE NORTH OF TOWN, JUST OFF HIGHWAY 9. TURN WEST OFF HIGHWAY 9 ONTO VALLEY BROOK ROAD. THE IRON GATE TO THE CEMETERY CAN BE SEEN FROM THIS POINT.

The first cemetery in this historic town was located at the south end of Main Street. By 1882, the graves had been moved to the new Valley Brook Cemetery, save one–the grave of Baby Eberlein. Several burials from the towns of Robinson and Kokomo were also reinterred here.

The cemetery is divided in sections. The Catholic Section is to the west. The various lodge sections are above Cucumber Creek, the oldest part of the cemetery. Many veteran's graves are also located near the flagpole. As with all mining communities, several graves are unmarked and names are unknown. Evidence of sunken graves can be seen, a result of mining efforts, before the land was donated as a cemetery, by William McAdoo.

While the headstones are common to Colorado's cemeteries, the fences surrounding various plots have a historic nostalgia all their own. From simple wood to decorative iron, there are delicate baby wire, chains, and filigree throughout.

The mountain cemetery has the beautiful wildflowers and spruce trees, common to the area. It is especially attractive, due to the flowing creek meandering at the edge.

Carter, Edwin (1830 – 1900)[66]

Carter's first known presence in Colorado was at California Gulch (near Leadville). He settled in Breckenridge in 1868 as a taxidermist. Early in his career, he began collecting his mounted specimens.[67] Over the years, several of Carter's preserved specimens became endangered or extinct.

Upon his death in 1900, after years of negotiation, the Carter collection was sold by his estate to the city of Denver. The collection became the center attraction of the new Museum of Natural History, opening in 1908. Today, it is regarded as one of the best collections in the world.

Edwin Carter's body laid in state at the Capitol Building in Denver for public viewing, the first private citizen accorded such an honor. Services were held by the Masonic Lodge in Breckenridge.

Carter's grave is marked by a large granite monument, one of the more prominent in the cemetery. It is located along the road at the southern edge of the cemetery, in the Masonic Section.

Fulton, H. J. (? – 1899)

An Ohio native, Fulton served in the 18th Ohio Infantry during the Civil War. He arrived by train, in Breckenridge for a visit, in the summer of 1899. His son Carlton, owned one of the mines and a mill at the camp, high above timberline.

Because of the elevation, winter mining was difficult. On October 22, 1899, with the sun shining, H. J. Fulton said good-bye to his son, and hiked across the mountain to Montezuma, some seven miles. A blizzard caught him by surprise. His body was not found until the following June 1900.

He is buried in the family plot next to his son. There is a military monument.

Wintermute, Thomas S. (1863 – 1888)
Wintermute, Clara Remine (1863 – 1886)

In the southeast corner of the cemetery, is a small monument with a cross on the pedestal. It is a testament to two lives lost because of love, tragedy, and despair.

Clara Remine was born in Central City. She moved to Breckenridge with her family when she was a small girl in the mid 1860s. Her parents were wealthy and Clara enjoyed a lavish childhood. She was very popular and played major roles in the Breckenridge Opera House performances.

In 1885, she married Thomas S. Wintermute, a young enthusiastic businessman. He had opened a bank a few years earlier on Main Street, and became highly respected throughout the town. The wedding was a joyous event for all of Breckenridge.

By June 1886, Clara was awaiting the birth of their first child, when she took ill. A few weeks after giving birth to a daughter, Clara died, she was twenty-three.

The grieving husband never recovered from his tragic loss. On a warm June morning in 1888, Thomas Wintermute attempted to take his own life. Drinking heavily, he walked to the cemetery, where he visited the grave of his wife. Then he put a pistol in his mouth. Nearby, a funeral was underway, attended by Marshal Reeder. Witnessing Wintermute's actions, the marshal pleaded for the young man to reconsider. Wintermute returned to town, where he took a dose of morphine and fell unconscious. He died a few days later.

His funeral was conducted by officers of the I.O.O.R.M. He was laid to rest next to his wife.

ALMA

ALMA CEMETERY

LOCATED APPROXIMATELY TWO AND ONE-HALF MILES WEST OF ALMA. FROM HIGHWAY 9 AT THE TOWN OF, FOLLOW THE BUCKSKIN GULCH ROAD TWO MILES, THEN EAST ONE-HALF-MILE TO THE CEMETERY.

Also known as Buckskin Joe Cemetery, it served one of the oldest placer mining camps in the Colorado Rockies, established in 1860. The cemetery was founded the same year, largely due to a smallpox epidemic. It remains as one of the oldest preserved cemeteries in Colorado.

Like many of the early placer gold camps, Buckskin Joe's gold played out and the town was deserted by 1864. In 1872, another strike was made two miles away.

The mining camp of Alma was built around rich silver strikes in the area. Buckskin Joe and Alma share a unique distinction. The two share the same cemetery. Alma buried its dead in the Buckskin Joe Cemetery. Years later, the land was deeded to the city of Alma by a grant signed by President Theodore Roosevelt. The cemetery is all that remains of the once booming mining towns.

The cemetery is partially fenced on the west side, near the entrance. Records are not listed by block and plot. One of the more interesting tombstones is that of Colonel Frank Mayer. He lived to be a 103 years old. He was a drummer boy in the Civil War, and went on to fight in the Middle East.

Foley, Thomas (1853 – 1888)

A miner, he was caught in a blinding snowstorm while in route to his mine. His body was not found until the following June.

His monument tells the sad story.

Gumaer, Franklin P. (1863 – 1906)

A prominent citizen of Alma, Frank Gumaer was a designer and inventor. He was the owner of several patents on telegraph equipment. It is said he was the original inventor of the Yale Lock.

He is buried with his wife Ida Snell Gumaer. There is a marker.

Mulock, Joshua (1835 – 1916)
Mulock, Clara (1834 – 1899)

One of the more beautiful stones in the cemetery. Joshua operated the first trading post at Alma.

He is buried next to his wife, Clara.

Snell, George Wilkin (1850 – 1912)

A Civil War veteran, George Snell once served under General George Armstrong Custer. In the Alma District, he prospected and worked for the mines. In later years, he and his nephew hauled ore for the mines. He owned a "jack" train–a team of mules that hauled the supplies to the mines and returned the gold ore to the mill or smelter. He owned the famous mule "Prunes" until 1917.[68]

There is a marker.

Shaw, Frederick (? – 1901)

A professional gambler, Shaw had been in the Alma district for about four months in the fall of 1901. He frequented the Kimball Saloon often, where he was not well-liked. Edward Kimball, the proprietor, and marshal of Alma, was known to have argued with Shaw.

According to a special report relayed to *The Denver Times* of September 6, 1901, Shaw and Kimball had a heated argument over money due Shaw. All seemed well, until the following morning. Shaw entered the saloon at around eight o'clock a.m. With his cane, he broke several glasses and possibly struck Kimball. Kimball drew his gun and shot at Shaw, inflicting a fatal injury.

Frederick Shaw is buried in an unmarked grave.

OFF THE BEATEN PATH:

PARK CITY CEMETERY

THE CEMETERY IS LOCATED SOUTHWEST OF ALMA, APPROXIMATELY THREE MILES ON COUNTY ROAD 10, NEAR THE SITE OF THE REMAINS OF PARK CITY, ON THE NORTH SIDE OF BUCKSKIN CREEK.

Tucked away at the base of Colorado's silver producing mountains, a forgotten cemetery lays in quiet solitude. According to Park County records, the cemetery contains ninety-six graves, all unmarked except one.

The lonely white marble tombstone stands erect among the wild mountain sage. The history of this tombstone is easier to trace than that of the young child it memorializes. The epitaph reads:

> Leola M.
> Dau. of
> Francis &
> Mary E. Noel
> Born March 30, 1882
> Died April 18, 1883
> Our Darling Sleeps

Park County records show no record of Leola's birth or death. Area newspapers, including the *Fairplay Flume*, reveal nothing of her parents. Where they a transient mining family? Or perhaps travelers who lost their child along the journey? Yet that would not explain the ornately carved stone, an expensive piece in 1883.

The tombstone itself has an equally mysterious history. During the late 1950s, thieves stole all the tombstones in the Park City Cemetery, save one; little Leola's. Why was one stone spared?

Over the past century, this one tombstone in memory of a mysterious baby girl has survived theft, weather, and progress.[69] Perhaps the true monument to our pioneers.

— — —

Highway 149 South

LAKE CITY

CITY CEMETERY

LOCATED ONE-HALF-MILE NORTH OF LAKE CITY, ON THE EAST SIDE OF HIGHWAY 149, ON CEMETERY HILL.

The small cemetery, established in 1876, is simply known as "City Cemetery." Lake City residents took pride in the health of their citizens, claiming the clean air and pure water prevented disease that plagued other mining towns. Until 1876, there had not been a need for a cemetery in the infant town. The City Cemetery or "Lower" Cemetery, sits on land owned by several different private landowners, and was never recorded. Laid out at random and with very little organization, the cemetery is confusing, with crooked rows of graves.

The tombstones consist largely of crude granite and decayed wooden markers. The oldest tombstone is that of Benjamin House, dated 1876. A unique feature are the wooden fences, weathered with time, surrounding some of the plots. A row known as the pauper section, oddly enough, runs along the front of the cemetery, on either side of the gate. Records indicate a separate section was designated for the "undesirables." Recorded as Section A, it is believed it contains the graves of outlaws Betts and Browning. (The cemetery map does not indicate location).

Within a year, a new cemetery was built, leaving City Cemetery for the poor and unknown.

Bardwell, George D. (1866 – 1908)

Born in Massachusetts, George Bardwell came to Colorado in 1883. He was admitted to the Colorado Bar Association in 1893. Establishing his law practice in Lake City in 1894, he became one of the first attorneys in the mining town. He later served as county attorney.

At the time of his death, he was suspected of murder. One Peter T. Baird had recently died of cyanide poisoning. Bardwell and Baird were known enemies. Although heart failure is listed as the cause of Bardwell's death, it was widely assumed by the community that he committed suicide.

He is buried in Section D. His marble marker is in the fenced plot.

Betts, George (1846 – 1882)

George Betts owned the San Juan Central, a brothel and dance hall on Bluff Street. In 1882, Betts and James Browning were caught in a bungled burglary attempt, by Sheriff E. N. Campbell. The sheriff was killed by a single shot from Betts' pistol, in the escape attempt. Apprehended and brought to the jail at Lake City, he was lynched along with Browning, by angry townspeople.

He is buried in Section A. The original wooden marker was stolen in 1977.

Browning, James (1855 – 1882)

Browning was with Betts in the burglary attempt of a nearby ranch, when caught by Sheriff E. N. Campbell, in 1882, which ended in the death of Sheriff Campbell. Apprehended and brought to the jail at Lake City, Browning and Betts were lynched by angry townspeople from the Ocean Wave Bridge.

Buried in Section A with Betts, the graves are unmarked. The original wooden markers were stolen in 1977. The graves are near that of Benjamin House.

Estep, Louis (1874 – 1896)

Possibly the worst scandal Lake City had to bear. Louis Estep was considered a fine, upright member of the community of Lake City. Estep's fiancee, Jessie Landers, a dance hall girl, came out of her room at the Crystal Palace brothel one night and shot Estep, hitting him behind the ear. He died instantly. Ms. Landers spent five years at the state penitentiary at Canon City. She never revealed why she killed her betrothed.

Louis Estep is buried in the cemetery, although there is no marker.

Gardner, George F. (1844 – 1914)

Born in New York, George Gardner worked on Mississippi riverboats in his youth. He arrived in Lake City in 1876, operating a saloon and mining on the side. He became Colorado Adjutant General in 1901, Hinsdale County Sheriff from 1885 to 1892, and was town marshal during the trial of Alfred Packer.

He is buried with his wife Josephine, in Section B. There is a stone marker.

House, Benjamin (? – 1876)

A native of California, Benjamin House arrived in Lake City in the spring of 1876. He served with the 8th US Cavalry during the Civil War, at age 17. Known in town as a drifter, he dealt faro at the Lake City gambling houses. He died at the San Juan Central Saloon, of lung consumption in October 1876.

His simple granite marker leans against a tree, near his gravesite. This is the oldest remaining marker in the cemetery.

He is buried in Section A.

Richart, Henry (1840 –1912)

Henry Richart freighted at Black Hawk for several years before arriving in Lake City in 1875. One of the first pioneers in the area, he started a livery stable in Lake City and owned a ranch. He was prominent in the foundations of the town and helped to lay out the townsite. When his stable burned down in 1901, he retired his business. He never married.

He is buried in Section A. His stone marker is near the entrance gate.

I.O.O.F. CEMETERY

THE CEMETERY IS LOCATED THREE-QUARTERS OF A MILE NORTH OF LAKE CITY ON HIGHWAY 149, THEN WEST ON CRYSTAL LAKE TRAIL ROAD ONE-HALF-MILE.

The local International Order of Odd Fellows Lodge established the cemetery in 1877, replacing City Cemetery. This cemetery too, was never recorded and later was determined to be on land owned by the Bureau of Land Management. After a lengthy government battle in the 1960s, Lake City was allowed to purchase the land from the government. It was the first government transaction of this nature in the United States. Originally intended for IOOF members, burials were opened to the public in 1900.

The cemetery extends toward the hill, and is long and narrow. The rows are laid out and marked by signs. Pine trees, mountain sage and thorn bushes make up the natural landscape.

Avery, Henry A. (1847 – 1923)

A native of Ohio, Henry Avery was one of Lake City's pioneers, arriving in 1877. He was postmaster of Lake City, mayor in 1882, district court clerk, and county judge.

He is buried with his wife Mary Evelyn in the Avery fenced plot in Block 15, Lot 2. There is a stone marker.

Barnes, Elizabeth C. Kincaid (1864 – 1880)

Elizabeth Barnes was one of the early pioneers, coming from Iowa, by covered wagon. She arrived in Lake City in 1876. Following her death in 1880, several of her possessions were given to the Hinsdale County Museum, including dolls, and toys.

She is buried in Block 10, Lot 4. There is a stone marker.

Blair, William C. (1869 – 1948)

A native of Ontario Canada, William Blair immigrated to the United States in 1885. By 1895, he was mining in the Lake City area. Active in local politics, Blair held several local and state offices. He served the Republican Party in the Chicago convention of 1912. He was mayor of Lake City for one term in 1928. In 1890, he gained a controlling interest in the *Lake City Times,* changing the name to the *Silver World*.

He died in San Diego in 1948. His ashes were brought back to Lake City for burial. There is a marker in the Meurer-Blair family plot, located in Block 14, Lot 2.

Campbell, Edward N. (1843 – 1882)

A native of Ohio and a veteran of the Civil War, Edward Campbell and his wife arrived in Lake City in 1876. He was elected sheriff in 1880. In 1882, Campbell tried to arrest two thieves, George Betts, and James Browning. Betts shot and killed Campbell, in an attempted escape. Campbell was the first Colorado sheriff killed in the line of duty.

His military marker is located in Block 7, Lot 1.

Green, William F. (1866 – 1950)

Long time town promoter, William Green was elected county treasurer in 1918. For eighteen years, he struggled to turn around the county finances, following the disastrous decline of mining at the close of the nineteenth century. He owned two electric light plants. His interest in photography left a large collection of photos on display at the Hinsdale County Museum.

The family marker is located in Block 1, Lot 3.

Hopkins, Andrew (1856 – 1877)

Very little is known of the short life of Andrew Hopkins. He became ill en route to Lake City and contracted typhoid pneumonia. He died in 1877, at age twenty-one.

Author's collection
Peter Kennedy grave.

The first burial in this cemetery, his tall white marble stone is halfway up the hill, on the right side. It is located in Block 17, Lot 4. It is the oldest marked tombstone in the cemetery.

Hough, John Simpson (1833 – 1919)

Born in Philadelphia, John Hough was the first cousin of Civil War General and United States President Ulysses S. Grant.[70] He arrived in Colorado at age eighteen.

He operated a general store on the Santa Fe Trail near Fort Lyon, where he married the sister of John Prowers. He traded with the Indians and became a close friend to Kit Carson.[71]

By 1876, he and his wife Mary, made Lake City their home, purchasing several mining interests. He was involved in banking, and founded the Lake City J. S. Hough Fire Company. He served the town as mayor, county treasurer, and county judge. There is a memorial window to Mr. and Mrs. Hough in the Baptist Church at Lake City.

He is buried with his wife Mary, in Block 21, Lot 3. There is a flat tablet marker.

Kennedy, Peter P. (1834 – 1932)

One of Lake City's earliest businessmen, Peter Kennedy opened a shoe store in 1876. Eventually, he owned controlling interest in the Golden Fleece Mine at Lake San Cristobal. He and his wife Mildred were prominent in the Baptist church. A memorial window is dedicated to them at the church.

He is buried with his second wife Mildred in Block 21, Lot 4.[72]

Youman, Harry (1848 – 1932)

A native of New York, Harry Youman was the earliest pioneer of Lake City, arriving in 1874. He owned the sawmill in the early days, as well as a ranch, and was active in town politics. He served two terms as Hinsdale county sheriff.

He is buried with his wife Helen in Block 3, Lot 1.

Packer victims gravesite (1874)

THE SITE IS LOCATED APPROXIMATELY TWO AND ONE-HALF MILES SOUTH OF LAKE CITY, JUST OFF HIGHWAY 149. THERE IS A SIGN.

The incomplete remains of Isreal Swan, George Noon, Frank Miller, James Humphries and Shannon Bell are buried above Lake City. The infamous cannibal Alfred Packer was found guilty of murder and eating parts of his victim's flesh.[73] Their remains were discovered by county officials and buried on site, in 1874. This spot contains the oldest recorded burials in Hinsdale County.

A bronze plaque commemorates the grisly ordeal of the five Packer victims. The graves are enclosed by a post-lined fence, overlooking the Lake Fork River at the base of Slumgullion Pass.

CREEDE

SUNNYSIDE CEMETERY

FROM THE WEST END OF TOWN, THE DIRT ROAD LEADS TO THE CEMETERY AND THE GHOST TOWN OF BACHELOR. THERE IS A SIGN DIRECTING YOU TO THE CEMETERY.

Sunnyside Cemetery, established in 1890, lies high on the mesa, just west of Creede. Mountain sage, wildflowers and a few pine trees are the only landscaping.

Cemetery records are not recorded by block and plot numbers. There is no distinct pattern of the burials, although all face east. Several plots are unmarked, yet are still obvious. Walking through the cemetery today, it is worth noting several markers donated by the Women Woodcraft affiliation. Among the memorials is the limestone tree trunk honoring Richard Daugherty. Embellished with the

Woodman coat of arms, it reads "Dum Tacet Clamet" (When Silent he Speaks).

Just below the cemetery sits an old, lonely church. It was the town's original white Mission Church of the Immaculate Conception. Built in 1897, the historic church was moved to the cemetery site in 1973 to make way for a modern replacement in town.

Originally there were two cemeteries in Creede–one for respectable citizens, and another for gunslingers, criminals, unknowns, and women of the night. This area, known as Boot Hill, is located in the northern section, near the fence. Time and weather have made the sections indistinguishable.[74]

Creede Lilly (? – 1892)

Gambler Creede Lilly ruled the early mining camp until her death on the banks of Willow Creek. Creede's underworld gambling establishment paid for her burial. How she died is unknown. Her grave is unmarked.

Dooley, Andrew (1863 – 1914)
Dooley, Bridget (1865 – 1914)

The Dooley family arrived from Pennsylvania in 1903. A miner, Andrew worked at several area mines, including the Amethyst. He died of miner's consumption in 1914.

Shortly after his death, Bridget died of a medication overdose. They had four children, two of whom were adopted.

Their graves are just below the little church. Andrew's marker is of makeshift wood, while Bridget's is a marble stone.

Ford, Robert N. (1861 – 1892)

Ford's place in history is that he was the killer of Jesse James in Missouri, where he later took the name Thomas Howard. Missourians regarded him as a traitor and he was forced to flee the state. Roaming the West, he eventually came to Creede in 1892. He ran a tent saloon in Creede's first years and soon thought of himself as the "ruler" of the camp's underworld.[75] The townsfolk kept their distance from the assassin. When famed con-man, Soapy Smith arrived in town a few months later, Ford's self-proclaimed dominion came to an end.

Ford never lost his notoriety and was gunned down on the afternoon of June 8, 1892, possibly in retaliation for James' death. The killer was Ed O. Kelly, gunman and one-time marshal at nearby Bachelor City.[76]

Following a confrontation in Ford's saloon, Kelly's shotgun roared, hitting Ford's collar bone. He died instantly.

Ford was buried in a solemn service, attended by his wife, area miners and a few townsfolk. Frank James arrived the morning of the funeral. He attended the 2 p.m. service at the cemetery. James stated he was in town for a few days on business. Possibly on behalf of his late brother, Jesse? Following the service, Creede's saloons were opened and drinks were poured. Three months later, after the conviction of Kelly, Mrs. Ford had her husband's body removed to Missouri.

Bob Ford's original burial site is at the north end of the cemetery near the fence. The wooden sign shows the approximate site of the grave.

McCann, Reddie (? – 1892)

Gunplay was common in the streets of lawless Creede. Reddie McCann has the dubious honor of being Creede's first casualty from such activities.

Late on the afternoon of April 1, 1892, McCann was drinking at the bar in Murphy's Exchange. Confronted by Marshal Light, (one of Soapy Smith's cronies), the two verbally assaulted each other. Light slapped McCann and the two went for their guns. Shots were fired and McCann fell to the floor, dead.

Reddie McCann had been in Creede for six months. No one remembered where he came from. He was buried solemnly and unceremoniously.

His grave is not marked.

McKibbin Baby (?)

A very weather-worn white marble headstone marks the burial of Dr. and Mrs. S. McKibben's infant child. The McKibbens came to Creede from Canada in 1900, where the doctor set up his practice. Dr. McKibbin continued his service to the small mining community for thirty-five years.

Upon retirement, Dr. McKibbin left Creede. However, his home still stands on 4th Avenue.

Russell, Nellie (? – 1892)

A native of St. Joseph, Missouri, young Nellie arrived in Creede in June 1892. She was hired by Bob Ford to join his "ladies of the evening." A day later, she was found dead, the result of alcohol poisoning and morphine overdose. Bob Ford paid for her burial, signing the note with this epitaph: "Charity covereth a multitude of sins."

A profound epitaph with double meaning, for minutes after Ford signed for Miss Russell's funeral expenses, he was murdered by Ed O. Kelly.

Nellie Russell is buried at the east end of the cemetery, under a very small marker.

Simmons, Joe (? – 1892)

Joe Simmons and Jefferson Randolph Smith, known as "Soapy," were childhood friends in Texas. When Soapy started his infamous gambling empire in the silver camp of Creede, in early 1892, Joe Simmons was his right-hand man.

Within months of his arrival, Simmons caught pneumonia. On his deathbed, he told his friend Soapy: "No preachin' at my send off." Then Joe Simmons died.

A blinding snowstorm greeted the funeral procession as it approached Cemetery Hill. During the journey, the casket slid from the wagon, tumbling to the bottom of the hill. After a few hours of tedious work, the body was laid to rest at Sunnyside.

True to the end, Soapy Smith said a few words at the burial, then popped corks of Pomeroy champagne, and gave a toast to his friend in the hereafter. Hands were joined, songs were sung and the group danced right there at the grave!

The story of Joe Simmons' burial still lives in Creede, however the location of his grave is lost to history.

Wetherhill, Clayton (1868 – 1921)
Wetherhill, Eugenia (1885 – 1962)

The Wetherhill family homesteaded 160 acres some fourteen miles north of Creede, just west of the river. It was one of the largest cattle ranches in the county. Five generations of the family have occupied the homestead, still in existence today.

The family plot is at the top of the hill toward the center, under a large pine tree.

WASON

WASON LIES TWO MILES SOUTH OF CREEDE, A RANCH RESORT TODAY. ACROSS HIGHWAY 149, TO THE EAST OF THE WASON JUNCTION, IS THE WASON CEMETERY.

H. D. Wason owned a large cattle ranch on this land before the silver boom that would create Creede in 1892. Seeing the opportunity of a quick fortune, Wason platted his land for a town after the big silver strikes. He petitioned for the new town of Wason to become the county seat of the newly-created Mineral County. Creede officials won the contest and promptly removed the files to their town, under cover of night. However, Wason's town grew for a time and Wason himself became quite prosperous.

There are no records for the tiny cemetery at Wason. Two of the graves are believed to be those of H. D. Wason and his wife. The caves around the site are known to contain several graves of Wason pioneers, but were covered by glass fronts in the 1930s.

WAGON WHEEL GAP

JUST NORTHWEST OF THE OLD DEPOT, AND PAST THE MAIL BOXES, ONCE CALLED MAIL ROCK AT THE TURN OF THE CENTURY, IS THE WAGON WHEEL GAP CEMETERY.

There are three graves that are distinguishable. The area is known to have been the site of a bloody Indian battle. The victims were reportedly stretched by rope between the cliffs and scalped.

— — —

Highway 550 South
"The Million Dollar Highway"

OURAY

CEDARHILL CEMETERY

LOCATED FIVE MILES NORTH OF OURAY, ON THE EAST SIDE OF HIGHWAY 550.

This beautiful mountain cemetery sits in serene company with the San Juan Mountains hovering above. The soothing rush of the Cutler Creek running at the west end adds to the beauty of the area. One of the better laid out cemeteries, it retains the characteristics of all mountain resting spots. While many graves are located up the hill toward the mountain, they are not scattered. The fine landscape and gravel roadways indicate a sense of pride in the organization and layout. The majority of the cemetery is marked by blocks.

Cedarhill Cemetery was established in 1877 and deeded to the city of Ouray in 1895. A portion of the H. S. Holaday Ranch later became part of the cemetery, containing the graves of Michael and Maggie Cuddigan, who were lynched in 1884.

At the entrance of the cemetery is a plot dedicated to the Veterans of Foreign Wars. A large flagpole pays tribute to our military heroes.

Clear evidence of the hardships of a mountain life are found in Block 25. This section contains rows of babies and young children. Small stones, adorned with lambs and sad epitaphs abound.

Rathmell, William (1862 – 1954)
Rathmell, Minnie Holaday (1862 – 1943)
William Rathmell arrived in Ouray in 1880, where he taught in the rural schools north of town. He was elected county judge in 1896, a

position he held for two terms. He went into the insurance business in 1902. He became the sole owner of the Ouray County Abstracting Company, a business he operated until his death.

In 1902, he married Miss Minnie Holaday, the smart and articulate superintendent of Ouray schools. Minnie arrived in Ouray in 1876 by covered wagon. She taught her first class in Ouray at age seventeen. A son, Henry, was born to this union.

Active in community affairs, Judge Rathmell served as county assessor and county food administrator during World War I. Minnie Rathmell remained involved in school activities.

They dark gray granite stone is enclosed with a concrete border. It is located in Block 28.

Rice, John (1853 – 1924)

John Rice came to Ouray in 1883, with his wife Grace and two children. He became postmaster of Ouray in 1889, a position he held until the silver panic of 1893. With the drop in the mining economy, he was able to purchase the bankrupt San Juan Coal, Lumber and Supply Company. Incorporated in 1910, it became known as the John F. Rice Lumber Company.

He ran the lumber company until his death in 1924. His wife Grace died ten days later. They are buried together. There is a marker.

Vanoli Family Plot

The Vanoli brothers, Dominick (born 1844), and John (born 1848), were natives of Italy. It is uncertain when they arrived in Ouray, however, records show they purchased half interest in property at the west end of town in 1884.

The brothers built their famous 220 Dance House and Roma Saloon on the site. The upstairs of the 220 Dance House contained the rooms of hired girls practicing their trade. The Vanoli business was such a success in Ouray, the brothers opened another dance hall in Telluride, managed by Dominck's son, Tony.

On March 1, 1888, John Vanoli shot and killed Sam Best in the Roma Saloon. After his trial and sentence to the Colorado State Penitentiary, the citizens of Ouray petitioned for his release. Evidently, Sam Best had made quite a nuisance of himself and the town felt the killing was justified.

Eventually John Vanoli was pardoned by the governor, only to kill another man. He was never prosecuted. John died of natural causes at the age of forty-seven, in 1895.

Dominick continued the family business, along with his son Tony. Dominick's wife, Mary, was stricken with typhoid and died in 1902. Dominick died in 1910, with Tony following in 1928.

The Vanoli family plot is located in in Block 28, next to the Rathmell's. Dark granite stone mark the family plots.

SILVERTON

HILLSIDE CEMETERY

LOCATED ONE-HALF-MILE NORTH OF TOWN. FOLLOW GREENE STREET, (THE MAIN STREET) EAST THROUGH TOWN. AT THE JUNCTION OF HIGHWAY 110, FOLLOW THE DIRT ROAD TO THE LEFT. A SIGN DIRECTS YOU TO THE CEMETERY, JUST TO THE RIGHT OF THE WATER TOWER.

This historic cemetery lies against the mountainside northwest of town, and is one of the more tranquil mountain cemeteries in the state. Officially formed in 1884, there are several burials with earlier dates. The first recorded burial was in 1875. The cemetery served several mining communities, including Silverton, Eureka, and Animas Forks. As was typical of the mining life, death occurred often from the dangerous, harsh winters, and disease such as cholera, diphtheria, smallpox and typhoid. The flu epidemic of 1918 claimed a third of Silverton's residents, including the only coroner. A memorial is located in Sector Plat 1, commemorating those lost during the flu epidemic. The Hillside Cemetery is a tribute to the hardships of our early mining pioneers.

Nature claims the landscape. Aspen, spruce and pine trees abound with wild mountain flowers of red, yellow and purple, blooming in the spring and summer. The only sounds heard as one walks the hilly terrain, are those of the wind and the rushing Cement Creek to the west.

Breen, Michael (1836 – 1894)

A native of Limerick Ireland, Michael Breen arrived in America in 1856. He attained the rank of colonel during his service under General Canby during the Civil War. He first settled in the Colorado Territory at Fort Garland, where he married the eldest daughter of famed scout man Tom Tobin, in 1866.[77]

He brought his family to Silverton in 1877, where he opened a mercantile business. He became the leading supplier to the mining communities of the San Juan. Breen later served on the staff of Governor Eaton.

He is buried in Sector Plat 20.

Briggs, James L. (? – 1878)

An early pioneer of the Silverton area, Briggs built one of the first hotels known originally as Briggs House, in 1875. It was later named the Silverton House. Briggs was also owner of the Briggs Tunnel on Hazelton Mountain.

On the morning of February 15, 1878, Briggs left the tunnel enroute to Silverton. He was caught in a blinding snowstorm. A snow slide caught Briggs, carrying him some two thousand feet down the mountain to the gulch below.

His body was found late that evening, buried head down in the solid snow and ice. Officially, he died of suffocation.

He is buried in Sector Plat 17, near the entrance. His marker is a large boulder etched with the name "Briggs."

Cole, William (1851 – 1932)

Born in Ireland, William Cole arrived in America at age twenty-three, spending time in New York and San Francisco. His first trip to the San Juan area was in 1879. In 1880 he married Hannah Kenny in Conejos, Colorado.

By 1883, he had settled in Silverton, operating the City and Silverton restaurants. He opened a boardinghouse on Reese and 14th Street, followed by a men's clothing store, which he operated until his death. His clothing business was known throughout southern Colorado. He was instrumental in building the St. Patrick Catholic Church.

Following the death of his wife, Hannah, in 1891, "Billy," as he was known, took on the added responsibility of raising his five children. Another family death occurred in 1918, when his youngest son James, died in the flu epidemic.

It was shortly after this sad loss, that Billy took it upon himself to maintain the somewhat rundown Hillside Cemetery. He took pride in obtaining the family history of the loved ones buried in the cemetery. He personally took charge on Decoration Day each year.

He was laid to rest in his beloved cemetery in the lavish family vault he had erected, bearing the Cole name. He was eighty years old. The vault, with a tall cross, is located in Sector Plat 4.

Cotton, John F. (1823 – 1906)
Cotton, Amanda L. (1833 – 1920)

Born in England, John came to America with his parents at age five. Raised in Michigan, he married Amanda Reed in 1852. The couple had three children, all three dying in infancy.

The couple moved to Kansas and eventually settled in Silverton in 1874. It is believed Mrs. Cotton was one of the first white women in the San Juan country. As early pioneers, they operated hotels in Silverton and Ophir. With his savings, John bought and rented out several business properties, earning a handsome income.

The couple also gave their time and efforts to the social events of the community. They provided the music and entertainment at dances and other functions. Amanda Cotton acquired the first piano shipped to Silverton.

There were many outbreaks of sickness in the mining camp. Amanda nursed the community through hardship and tragedies.

John died in Durango in 1906, followed by Amanda in 1920. They are buried together in the family plot in Sector Plat 17.

Furrow, Rachel E. (? – 1875)[78]

Little Rachel was the first burial of record at Hillside Cemetery. Her father, Mason Furrow, was a farmer from Kansas who settled in Silverton in 1874, where he built a small cabin for his family. All seemed well when Mrs. Furrow gave birth to a second daughter, until little Rachel came down with pneumonia. She suffered little and died suddenly.

Rachel's father buried his daughter on the hill north of town, creating the cemetery. Rachel is known to be buried in the southeast corner. There is no marker.

Reed, Ruby (1868 – 1897)

Ruby Reed made her living on Silverton's notorious Blair Street, the "Red Light District." She was known among her kind to be honest and generous. Perhaps due to the loneliness of her occupation, she put a gun to her head early on the morning of October 11, 1897.

Mining communities typically buried their "lower class" unceremoniously. Not so with Ruby. She was given a church funeral and many flowers graced her casket.

Buried at Hillside Cemetery, in Sector Plat 22, a gray stone marker was erected in her memory.

Reese, Dempsey (1835 – 1890)

Born in Indiana, Dempsey Reese grew up in Minnesota. During the Civil War years, he traveled west to seek his fortune in mining. Prospecting in California, Nevada, New Mexico, and Utah, he came to the San Juan Mountains in 1869.

In less than a year, he and two partners had discovered a rich silver lode in Arastra Gulch. By 1872, the mining district had produced

$15,000 worth of silver. Incredibly, $12,000 came out of Reese's "Little Giant" mine.

Reese settled in the area that would become Silverton. One of the founding fathers of the town, he served as the first county commissioner. He was the first mayor, when he helped incorporate the town in 1876.

A life-long bachelor, he died of pneumonia in 1890, at the age of fifty-five. The funeral procession, led by Jack Sinclair's famous Cowboy Band, made its way through town, down Reese Street (named for the deceased), and slowly up the hill to the cemetery.[79] The cold and snow on that November day added to the solemn procession. The grave had been dug by Ben Hardwood, fulfilling a twenty-year-old promise.

He is buried in Sector Plat 20. There is a marker.

Roberts, Robert W. (1855 – 1886)

Robert Roberts came to America with his wife and children from Wales in 1885, settling with family members already established in Silverton.

On April 18, 1886, snow fell in the San Jauns. Within forty-eight hours, five feet of snow had fallen at Silverton. In an effort to clear the road into town, a party of five men began the clean up, moving toward Red Mountain on the Continental Divide. Among the men was Robert W. Roberts, Silverton's mail carrier. The snow was deep and still falling when an avalanche crashed down the mountain.

Roberts was crushed along with sixteen pack animals owned by Otto Mears. Robert's body was found under three feet of frozen ice and snow. The marks on his chest indicated he died from suffocation.

The funeral was held at the family home. He is buried in Sector Plat 18 with family members. There is a marker inscribed in the Welsh language.

Robin, George E. (1849 – 1907)

George Robin and his brother James, settled in Silverton in 1875, where George had several businesses, including real estate, insurance, mining interests, and a brick yard with his brother James.

For reasons unknown, George committed suicide in April 1907, by tying his wrists together and jumped into the Animas River, where he drowned. His body was found near the area where his brother James had committed suicide in 1903. A note was found addressed to his other brother, Charles E. Robin. In Latin, it read "Dying, I salute you."

He is buried in Sector Plat 24.

Robin, James H. (1851 – 1903)

James Robin came to America from Isle of Guernsey, in 1873, working many trades as he made his way west. He ran freight wagons from Walsenburg to Alamosa, and was associated with W. S. Stratton at Cripple Creek. He settled in Silverton in 1875, establishing a brick yard with his brother, George.

Prominent in early Silverton, Jim became town treasurer and trustee in 1879. His brick company expanded to include lumber. He bought mining claims, and helped build the young community of Silverton.

He married Amelia Mary Roberts in New York in 1881. Their first child, Maud Isabel, died of cholera in 1883. She was six months old.[80]

In 1891, Jim was appointed cashier of the newly-formed Bank of Silverton. By 1899, he was president of the bank and his wife Amelia, was vice president. Unfortunately, bad business investments caused financial ruin for the bank and Jim personally.

A sign on the door of the bank greeted customers New Year's Day, 1903. It read; "As Mr. J. H. Robin is missing, this bank is closed."

The townspeople searched for Jim all that day, to no avail. The following day the crew from the Durango freight train discovered his body three miles from town, near the water tank, along the rail line. He had a gunshot wound to the head. The coroner concluded suicide.

His business partners and friends attended his service at the Congregational Church. He was buried at Hillside Cemetery in Sector Plat 24.

Stanley, Horace M. (1866 – 1883)
Stanley, Patrick "Cap" (1824 – 1899)

Horace, the only son of Patrick Stanley, was born in Des Moines, Iowa. His mother was of Spanish descent, yet remains a mystery. She did not accompany Horace and his father when they came to Silverton in 1874.

An exceptional youth, he worked for Breen and McNichols Wholesale for five years, while attending school and helping his father. Determined to further his education, he attended Kansas State Institute at Lawrence, Kansas, and spent two years at the Colorado Institute in Boulder.

Horace was at the college in Boulder, when he became seriously ill with typhoid. His father was notified, but pneumonia had set in before Patrick could leave for Boulder. Horace died on November 30, 1883, he was seventeen years old.

His body was sent by train to Silverton. The entire town closed its doors for the funeral. The service was held at the Congregational Church.

His body was laid to rest near the top of the cemetery, in Sector Plat 18.

— — —

Patrick Stanley was born near Charleston, South Carolina in 1824. A veteran of the Mexican War, he received the Hope Medal for bravery. Although a Southerner by birth, he served with the New York Volunteer Infantry during the Civil War, where he held the rank of captain during his four years of service.

A successful building contractor, he left the war-ravaged East, to make a new beginning in the West. He was one of the earliest pioneers in the Silverton area, when he arrived in 1874. He advertised his building skills as the new town grew, acquiring contracts to build some of Silverton's finest buildings, which still stand. He invested in real estate and mining, becoming one of the more successful pioneers in town.

Following the death of his only son, Horace, in 1883, "Cap," as he was known, focused on his mining ventures. Well into his senior years, he rode horseback thirty miles daily to his properties on Red Mountain.

He is buried in Sector Plat 18, next to his son. The markers are enclosed with a fenced plot.

Staples, Mrs. Samuel (1869 – 1897)

Her obituary in one of the local papers, tells of the great sadness and loss an entire community felt as one of their own passed in such a sorrowful way:

"The entire population of Silverton extend to Sam Staples sincere condolences. The loss of a wife robs him of a home and robs this community of one of the best characters of womanhood. No woman was more respected, more beloved by those who knew her than was Mrs. Staples. Death resulted from childbirth, and though the mother has departed the father can get some consolation from the spark she left as proof of her existence. It was a life given for a life. Mrs. Staples had given birth to four children in previous years but they all died. It seems it was not her lot to have a home well won and children by her side. The deceased was twenty-eight years of age . . . It is too bad, Sam, but be brave and remember that while from a sigh,

> *God's plans go on as best for you and me;*
> *How, when we called, He heeded the cry,*

Because His wisdom to the end could see.[81]

Born in Missouri, Mrs. Staples settled in Silverton in 1887. She married Sam Staples in Durango, in 1888. The couple made their home in Silverton, where she gave birth to twins in 1896. Both babies died shortly after birth. A year later, a child was stillborn. She gave generously to community projects, while keeping her home the pride of her husband. Within a year, she was pregnant again. The joy turned to sorrow when she died in childbirth.

She is believed to be buried beside the graves of her baby twins, in Sector Plat 1. There is no marker.

— — —

Highway 145 South

TELLURIDE

LONETREE CEMETERY

LOCATED ON THE DIRT ROAD JUST EAST OF THE TOWN, WHICH CLIMBS A SLIGHT HILL TO THE GRAVEYARD OVERLOOKING TELLURIDE.

Over the years, several mud slides have washed away many of the graves, and snow slides have left their mark, as well. One such mud slide occurred a few years after the cemetery was established, washing away any trace of existing graves. New burials continued on top of the old burials.[82]

Snow slides are a common occurrence at Telluride. Several mass graves enclosed by rock curbing, indicate the sudden deaths caused by nature. While most are no longer marked, one such mass grave bears a stone which reads:

All Killed in Snow Slide of 1896.

Rescuers attempting to save victims of one such avalanche were caught in a second barrage of snow. All died. They were buried in one grave, the exact location unknown.

Barthel, John (1874 – 1901)

John Barthel was a young worker at the Smuggler Mine, caught in the crossfire of the miners' strike of 1901.

The large ornate marble marker lists his age as twenty-seven.

Clark, James (Jim Cummings) (1841 – 1895)

An outlaw in his youth, James Clark, alias Jim Cummings, joined William Quantrill, becoming a trusted lieutenant of the nortorious

Southern raider and outlaw, at the outbreak of the Civil War. Following the war, he headed west staying for awhile in Leadville.

By 1887 William made Telluride his home, eventually becoming city marshal. Rumors circulated of his criminal activity. One rumor involved Butch Cassidy. Cassidy made Telluride the target of his first bank robbery in 1889, when he robbed the San Miguel Valley Bank of $20,000. Talk around town was that Clark was in on the robbery. He is reported to have stated he would receive a take of the loot, if he was conveniently absent from town during the holdup. Nothing was proven, but Clark was relieved of his duties. He was ambushed on the streets of Telluride shortly thereafter.

He is buried in the Lone Tree Cemetery east of town, under a marble stone.

Parker, Arthur (1869 – 1890)

Arthur Parker was the brother of famed outlaw Butch Cassidy (Robert Leroy Parker). He lived in Telluride, working at one of the mines. He died July 5, 1890, following a fall from a horse he was racing during the Fourth of July celebration. He is buried in an unmarked grave, according to his sister, Lula Parker Betensen, in her memoirs.[83]

Remine, Lindley (? – 1928)
Remine, William (? – 1916)

Brothers who were once very close, they were in opposition during the Civil War. Lindley fought for the Confederacy, while William fought for the Union. Following the war, the two never a spoke a word to each other.

Upon William's death in 1916, Lindley made arrangements to be buried beside his brother. He got his wish in 1928.

The military white marble slabs mark their graves.

Off The Beaten Path:
Ophir

Located south of Telluride on Highway 145. Take the exit east to the town. The cemetery is located northeast of the town.

This beautiful mountain cemetery is located in the vicinity of Old Ophir, once a busy mining town. The oldest tombstone is dated 1881, however there are several unmarked graves. Golden aspens and mountain wild flowers grace the cemetery, below towering mountain peaks.

Among the many graves are several graced with wrought iron fencing, including the unmarked grave of Sven Nilson. Nilson was a conscientious mailman who carted the mail to Ophir from Silverton during all types of weather. During a blizzard on December 23, 1883, Nilson set out to deliver the Christmas mail. Advised against the journey, he was determined to see his job through.

Sven Nilson never reached his destination of Ophir. Search parties were sent out to look for him, to no avail. His body was found some two years later at the bottom of a ravine below the trail. The mail was still strapped to his back and still intact.

Sven Nilson was buried in the Old Ophir Cemetery with full honors, however a proper tombstone was never placed.

IGNACIO

OURAY MEMORIAL CEMETERY

THE TOWN OF IGNACIO, SOUTHEAST OF DURANGO, IS LOCATED ON COLORADO HIGHWAY 172 SOUTH.

The first road south of the Sky Ute Casino going east, leads to the Ute Memorial Park. Many historians have listed this area as Chief Ouray's burial site. It is actually a memorial park set on the original grounds of the Southern Ute Indian Agency. The memorial was the idea of the agency trader, L. M. Wayt, with the blessing of Chief Buckskin Charlie, in 1939. The tall native stone monument, eighteen feet high, dominates the park. It is marked on four sides with bronze busts memorializing four Ute leaders, including Severno, chief of the Capote Utes, Ignacio, the great Ute chief, Buckskin "Charley," chief of the Moache Band of Utes, and Chief Ouray, the man with a vision.[84]

To the east of the monument is a small white-washed stone marking the approximate site of Chief Ouray's death.

— — —

Following the road east from the park over the bridge, is the Ouray Memorial Cemetery.[85] The cemetery is a large one, enclosed with white fencing. Simple in landscape, it is lined with graves marked by small white wooden crosses, an Indian custom.

Just inside the the large archway entrance, is the grave of Chief Ouray. Two tall rock monuments memorialize Ouray and Buckskin Charlie.

Ouray's remains were reinterred here in an elaborate four-day ceremony in May 1925. The Indian service was followed by a controversial Christian service. A fence dividing the Protestant and Catholic sections was removed and Ouray was reburied so that he lay on both sides of the Christian portions.

Raised as an Apache near Taos, New Mexico, Ouray was fluent in many languages, including Spanish and English. His intellect impressed officials in Washington D.C. as well as his own people. In 1859, he married for the second time, a Tabequache Ute woman named Chipeta.

By 1860, Ouray, a young man not yet thirty years old, became the honorary chief of the Uncompahgre Utes in western Colorado. He understood the differences between the Indians and whites, and dedicated his life to working for peace. Considered a great leader and admired by the white people, he was often

Colorado Historical Society
Chief Ouray

ridiculed and denounced by the Indian tribes. Through his efforts, few Indian wars occurred, yet the Utes were forced onto reservations.

In August 1880, Ouray, along with Chipeta, her brother John McCook, and several Utes had gathered at the Ute agency in Ignacio. Ouray was gravely ill and apparently had been for quite some time. It was determined he was suffering from a kidney ailment, known as Brights disease.

On Tuesday, August 24, 1880, Ouray died. Within the hour his body, wrapped in blankets and placed on an Indian pony, was escorted to a secret burial location. Those who buried Ouray included Chipeta, Buckskin Charlie, Colorow, Naneese, and John McCook, among others.

Following the death of Chipeta in 1924, Buckskin Charlie revealed the secret burial site of Ouray. Ouray's bones were removed from a cave and verified in sworn affidavits by some of the Utes present at the original burial, including Naneese, Buckskin Charlie, and John McCook.

The ceremonies at the Ignacio Cemetery site lasted four days, and included the largest group of whites and Indians ever assembled at the Ute agency. Efforts were made to bury Chipeta beside her husband, but were unsuccessful.[86]

Colorado later honored Chief Ouray with a town, a park, a county, and a stained glass portrait in the Capitol dome in Denver.

* * *

The second tall stone marker memorializes Chief Buckskin Charlie. The chief of the Moache Utes, he became the leader of the Ute people, following the death of Ouray.

Like Ouray, he was of mixed Indian heritage, part Ute and part Apache. Although many years younger that Ouray, he was respected by all his people and hand-picked by Ouray to lead the tribe. He was with Ouray when he died. He made an oath to justify the faith the great leader had in him. He kept his people together, continued the work for peace and never fought the whites. In 1905, he led the Utes in the inauguration parade for President Theodore Roosevelt, in Washington D.C. The two had become great friends in the West. To his death, Buckskin Charlie believed the two races could live together in peace and learn from each other.

He died at his ranch near Ignacio in May 1936, and was buried with a full southern Ute ceremony.

— —

Just behind the two white monuments stands one of the few granite stones in the cemetery. It is that of Antonio Buck, Sr. The son of Buckskin Charlie, he was the first elected tribal chairman. (A term coined by the white man, following the institution of the reservation.) At the time of his death, he became the last chief of the Southern Utes. (A highly regarded position among the Indians, despite the effort of the white man.)

His brown granite stone reads:

Antonio Buck Sr.
1870 – 1961
Last Chief of the Southern Utes

— — —

Ghost Notes, Mysteries, & Other Related Findings

The ghost town of Rosita stands, silent, lonely and neglected. The once bustling mining supply town reached its peak in the late 1870s.

Memories of Rosita's past and several of her residents are buried in the cemetery five miles south of town, on Highway 96. There are several unmarked graves in this silent city of the dead.

Four of the graves are known to belong to a couple of rough cowboys and their victims. The drunken pair showed up at an Odd

Fellows dance and proceeded to shoot up the place, killing two of the doorkeepers. The next day, members of the town grabbed the two hung-over troublemakers and lynched them.

A real old-fashioned gun battle, ala OK Corral, took place on Rosita's Main Street. Eastern corporate "suits" tried to take over the largest mine, The Pocahontas. To protect the property, the corporate boys hired thugs, led by Major Graham. Graham was no major at all, in fact, he was an escaped convict.

The citizens of Rosita and miners at the Pocahontas rose up in arms against the takeover. The confrontation on Main Street turned into a gun battle, with Major Graham being killed. It is not known if he is buried in one of the many unmarked graves of Rosita's cemetery. Some say his body was tossed down a mine shaft.

* * *

"Commodore" Stephen Decatur drifted into Rosita during its boom, in an attempt to gain back his lost fortune.[87] He didn't. He spent his last years living in poverty and died penniless.

His weathered tombstone has long since lost any description. To the casual visitor, it seems just another grave, but history reveals he was one of many men who came west to lose his previous identity.

A Southern colonel without military experience, he somehow received the title of "Commodore." Believed by many to be a shirttail relative of Stephen Decatur, the naval hero of the War of 1812, it is also thought his real name was Bross, a brother of the then governor of Illinois. A learned schoolteacher in New York, Decatur suddenly disappeared in the 1840s, leaving a wife and two children. He settled in the Midwest for a time, where he married, and again deserted his family. He fought in the Mexican War, fought the Indians, and finally came to Colorado, in 1859. The old mountain ghost town of Decatur is named for him. Decatur arrived in Clear Creek County and helped name the boomtown of Silver Plume in 1870. Later locating in Georgetown, he became the town's favorite speaker, and frequently preached from the pulpit, delivered eulogies at the funerals, and spoke in favor of town promotion.

In 1876, the year Colorado was admitted to the Union, and the celebration of the country's Centennial, Decatur was appointed to represent Colorado at the Centennial Exposition in Philadelphia. State funds were meager, so Decatur funded the Colorado exhibit himself.

He moved to Rosita late in 1879. When he died in 1887, the town gave him the best funeral possible.

* * *

Carl Wulsten made Rosita his final home and resting spot. Organizing the German Colonization Society, he led over 300 people west from Chicago in 1870. The colony settled west of Pueblo, in the heart of Sangre de Cristo mountain range. The colony struggled through a year of bitter cold temperatures, and lack of food.

When the group disbanded, Wulsten went to work as a mining engineer at Rosita. It is said that when Wulsten first arrived in the area, he came across an Indian family mourning over the body of their dead son. The young man had been attacked by a bear. Wulsten made a splint out of aspen trees and set the father's arm, which had been broken during the struggle. Then Wulsten buried the boy.

Carl Wulsten helped many members of the Rosita area before he died in 1915.

* * *

The cemetery of Red Cliff, known as the Greenwood Cemetery is located in the heart of the old mining town. Established in 1880, the first grave was dug for a miner killed by a bear. The first funeral was held later that year. A man was crushed by a falling tree. He was buried with the finest service possible in the remote camp. With no lumber in the camp, his coffin was made from an old wagon. Every man in camp attended the funeral, dressed in their finest "duds."

A few weeks later, two miners shot it out, killing each other. Their bodies were brought to Red Cliff for burial. However, the miners refused to desecrate their cemetery with murderers. The two were eventually buried beside the Battle Mountain Road.

* * *

Otto Mears, "Pathfinder of the San Juans," did more to promote and build the San Juan region than any other pioneer. Born in 1841, he immigrated to America with his parents, in 1854. During the Civil War, he enlisted with the 1st Regiment California Volunteers. Following the war, Mears settled Conejos, where he operated a store and wheat farm. To get his produce across the mountains to the booming Arkansas Valley, he built a toll road over Poncha Pass. A second road was built from Saguache to Lake City, in 1871. A network of roads was built by Mears in 1870s and 1880s, many of which are today's highways. Mears opened Colorado's Western Slope, connecting the high mountain mining camps to the outside world and ensuring the prosperity of the San Juan region.

Mears remained a friend to the Indians, including Chief Ouray. He became a peacemaker, thereby quite instrumental in several negotiations and peace treaties.

Otto Mears died in Pasadena, California, in 1931. His memorial service was held in Silverton. His ashes were then scattered over his old toll road just south of Ouray, today's Million Dollar Highway.

The highways of the San Juan country are a tribute to Mears, a man with a vision and a keen sight into the future.

* * *

At the museum of the Colorado Territorial Prison at Canon City, is the coffin used to transport unclaimed bodies to Denver where they were used for medical research. The coffin was used over and over for several years. The medical research of inmates ended several years ago.

* * *

The ashes of famed author and astrologer, Linda Goodman were scattered in the Mt. Pisgah Cemetery, at Cripple Creek, following her death in November 1995. The author of five books, including the widely known *Linda Goodman's Sun Signs*, she moved to Cripple Creek in 1968. Close friends say she wanted the mountain solitude, with no threat from fans and outsiders. Those who knew her in Cripple Creek, say she was eccentric, and recall her strange behavior. On one occasion, she was seen stumbling along Myers Avenue, mumbling something to the effect of being in a time warp, and relating to a prostitute. In her home, she built a lavish chapel setting, where she practiced a self-designed religion of cosmic forces. She died of heart failure, related to her diabetes.

* * *

The restless spirit of J. Dawson still haunts the cemetery of Buckskin Joe. He brought his wife to Fairplay, where he mined for gold in the 1860s. Dawson met with tragedy in the summer of 1865. His body was found at the bottom of Mount Boss, where he had fallen while prospecting. His funeral was followed by burial at the Buckskin Joe Cemetery. Shortly thereafter, Dawson's bones were found in the possession of a dance hall girl at Alma. Shrugging the incident off as a weird prank, the townsfolk reinterred the bones in the cemetery. Time and time again, the bones would "turn up" in the possession of a female.

By 1872, talk of the mysterious bones made its way across the state. The people of Alma actually dumped the bones in an outhouse to be rid them. The truth and actual happenstance remain a mystery, however the stories of Dawson's reappearing bones remain.

* * *

The following narrative was uncovered in the Creede archives:

A minister in the town of Bachelor, two miles above Creede, tried to reform the wild mining camp. One winter evening in 1893, he was forced to leave his ill daughter to go on one more reform mission. Hours later, the minister returned to his cabin and daughter. In the midnight shadows, the minister saw a man in the cabin and shot him.

In the aftermath, the minister's daughter identified the stranger as the doctor. By morning she was dead. In remorse, the minister shot himself.

The three bodies were buried at Sunnyside Cemetery, in a single grave, as the frozen ground was too difficult to dig.

The grave is lost in the cemetery records.

* * *

As frontiersmen go, "Old Bill" Williams was the most stubborn, cantankerous and colorful of all, setting him apart from the serious and rigid scouts such as Fremont and Carson.

Williams was hired as a scout in 1852, by the government for a survey party building a road from Missouri to Santa Fe. Completing his duties, Old Bill spent his wages on Taos Lightening, as was his custom.

When John C. Fremont set out on an expedition from Bent's Fort in the fall of 1848, no seasoned mountain man would accept the scouting position due to the late start. At Fort Pueblo, Fremont ran into Old Bill and hired him as scout. He led the party through the trail to the Wet Mountain Valley, over Mosea Pass and into the San Luis Valley, where they were caught in a blizzard. Eleven men perished before Fremont sent four men for help.

The group was eventually rescued and blame was placed on Old Bill. However, most agree the expedition so late in the year was due to Fremont's miscalculation.

The following spring, Old Bill was sent to recover the abandoned supplies and equipment. While he was camped near the summit of Cumbres Pass, a band of Indians killed Old Bill.

The Utes later reported they had not recognized their old friend and brother by marriage, and mourned his death.

His body was never recovered.

* * *

The Cattlemen-Sheepmen War of Archuleta County climaxed in 1892, with the murder of County Commissioner William Howe. According to newspaper accounts of the time, the county seemed equally split on the emotional issue of open ranch land for cattle or fencing the range because of the sheep herds.

The Montoya family, prominent sheepherders in the area, were herding 20,000 of sheep near the Howe ranch on the San Juan River, fourteen miles above Pagosa Springs. When the Howe brothers, Abe and William refused to allow the sheep to cross their land, gunfire erupted. As the smoke cleared, William Howe was dead. The autopsy report revealed he had been hit by several bullets, including one from the rear, indicating an attempt to retreat.

A native of Missouri, William had only lived in Archuleta County three years. He was elected county commissioner. Just the previous year, he had married Miss Jennie Jellison, who had only recently died in childbirth. The infant son had died a few days before his father's murder. The child's body was still in the house.

Within a five-month period, the entire William Howe family was laid to rest. The father and infant son were interred in the same grave next to the fresh grave of Jennie. The location of the tiny rural cemetery has been lost to history.

* * *

William Bruce is believed to be the first victim of the Espinosa gang's murder spree in southern Colorado. He was killed at his sawmill on Hardscrabble Creek in 1863. His body was found mutilated in an isolated gulch, since known as "Deadman's Canyon." The family brought his body to Canon City for burial and stayed for protection. His exact burial location has intrigued family members and historians for years.

* * *

The Reynolds gang terrorized the South Park area in 1864. The leader, Jim Reynolds, stopped by the ranch of his old friend Adolph Guiraud, in July of that year. In passing conversation, he learned the time and route of the McClelland stage from the mining town of Buckskin Joe.

The following morning, July 26, 1864, the Reynolds gang held up the stage. Over $3,000 in cash and a large amount of gold was seized by the gang. They fled the scene, robbing various ranch houses in the area. Jim Reynolds and his gang again stopped at the Guiraud Ranch, although the house was deserted.

Following the death of Mrs. Guiraud, in 1909, some $80,000 in gold was found in the fruit cellar. A family stash, or a deposit, courtesy of the Reynolds gang?

— — —

Additional Cemeteries Listed by County

Alamosa County

Cemetery	1st Burial
Garnett–Speiser Cemetery	1892
Medina Memorial Gardens	1882
Stanley Cemetery	1886

Archuleta County

Cemetery	1st Burial
Arboles Cemetery	1920
Old Arboles Cemetery	? – burials moved with build ing of Navajo Res. in 1958.
Archuleta Cemetery	1885
Candelaria Cemetery	? – under north end of Navajo Res.
Carracas Cemetery	?
Chromo Cemetery	1890
Edith Cemetery	1893 – Abandoned
Espanosa Cemetery	1925 – Abandoned
Frances Cemetery #1	1918 – Abandoned
Frances Cemetery #2	1909
Horner Cemetery	1908 – under Navajo Res.
Juanita Cemetery	1920
Lone Tree Cemetery	1932 – Abandoned
Minium Cemetery	? – Abandoned
Pagosa Junction Cemetery	1911
Spiler Canyon Cemetery	1895
Talamante Cemetery	1890
Trujillo Cemetery	1918

Chaffee County

Cemetery	1st Burial
Alpine Cemetery	1879
Americus Cemetery	1898
Arbourville Cemetery	1883 – Abandoned. Highway 50 paved over cemetery.
Cleora Cemetery	1882
Droney Pasture Cemetery	1870 – Abandoned
Garfield Cemetery	1879
Giebfried Cemetery	1923
Harvard Cemetery	1876 – Abandoned
Mayol/Riverside Cemetery	1879 – Abandoned
Maysville Cemetery	1880
Monarch Cemetery	1880 – Abandoned
Monarch Park Cemetery	? – Abandoned
Turret Cemetery	1897 – Abandoned
Vicksburg Cemetery	1884 – Abandoned
Winfield Cemetery	1885 – Abandoned

Conejos County

Cemetery	1st Burial
Antonito Presbyterian Cemetery	?
Capulin Cemetery	?
Capulin Cemetery #2	?
Capulin Church Cemetery	?
Conejos Cemetery	?
De la Luz Cemetery	?
Espinosa Cemetery	?
Fox Creek Cemetery	1890
Jack Cemetery	?
La Jara Cemetery	?
Presbyterian Cemetery	?
Las Mesitas Catholic Cemetery	?
Lasauses Catholic Cemetery	?
Lasauses Protestant Cemetery	?
Lobatos Cemetery	?
Los Cerritos Cemetery	?
Manassa New Cemetery	1927
Manassa Old Cemetery	1879
Mancos Crossing Cemetery	?
Mogote Cemetery	?
Nance Cemetery	?
Ortiz Cemetery	?
Pike's Stockade Cemetery	?
Platoro Cemetery	?
San Antonio Cemetery	?
Sanford Cemetery	?
Seventh Day Adventist Cemetery	?
Soward Cemetery	?
St. Joseph Cemetery	?
Woodlawn Cemetery	?

Costilla County

Cemetery	1st Burial
Blanca Cemetery	1910
Chama Old Catholic Cemetery	1906
Eastdale Cemetery	1890
Fort Garland Cemetery	?
Fort Garland Soldier's Cemetery	?
Presbyterian Cemetery	?
Garcia Presbyterian Cemetery	1906
Garland City Cemetery	1877

Hillside Cemetery	1875
Mountain View Cemetery	1914
Mesita Cemetery	1916
Placer Cemetery	1869
San Acacio New Cemetery	1906
San Acacio Old Cemetery	?
San Francisco Cemetery	?
San Luis Old Cemetery	1869
San Luis Original Cemetery	?
San Pablo Cemetery	? – Abandoned
Shumate Indian Burial	? – Abandoned
Tobin Ranch Cemetery	? – Abandoned

Custer County

Cemetery	1st Burial
Abbott Ranch Cemetery	?
Armstrong Ranch Cemetery	?
Bull Domingo Cemetery	?
Catholic Cemetery	?
Custer City Cemetery	?
Hope Cemetery	?
AKA Colfax Cemetery	1870
Querida Cemetery	?
San Isabel Cemetery	?
Silver Cliff Cemetery	?
The Pines Cemetery	1880
Ula Cemetery	?
Wetmore Cemetery	?

Delta County

Cemetery	1st Burial
Bethleham Cemetery	?
Cedar Hill Cemetery	?
Cedaridge Cemetery	?
Cory Cemetery	?
Crawford Cemetery	?
Crim Cemetery	?
Eckert Cemetery	?
Head Cemetery	?
Hill Cemetery	?
Hotchkiss Cemetery	
AKA Riverside	?
Olsen Cemetery	?

Paonia Cemetery   ?

Delores County

Cemetery	1st Burial
Cahone Cemetery	?
Dove Creek Cemetery	?
Dunton Cemetery	?
Lavender Cemetery	1891
Nash Cemetery	1887
Peel Cemetery	?
Rico Cemetery	?
Valley Rico Large Cemetery	1883
Valley Rico Small Cemetery	1879

Fremont County

Cemetery	1st Burial
Beaver Creek Lower Cemetery	1865
Beaver Creek Middle Cemetery	1889
Beaver Creek Upper Cemetery	1883
Beaver Park Cemetery	?
Coaldale Cemetery	?
Cotopaxi Cemetery	?
Hillside Cemetery	?
Howard Cemetery	1870
Lakeside Cemetery	1877
New Hope Cemetery	1871
Odd Fellows Cemetery	1876
San Juan Bautista Cemetery	1904
Twelvemile Park Cemetery	?
Union Highland Cemetery	1886

Garfield County

Cemetery	1st Burial
Beard Cemetery	? – Abandoned
Bruce Cemetery	?
Evergreen Cemetery	?
Fairview Cemetery	?
Glenwood Springs Old Cemetery	1883 – Abandoned
Highland Cemetery	1888
Hoff/I.O.O.F. Cemetery	?
Marion/Spring Gulch Cemetery	1891 – Abandoned
Nevitt Cemetery	? – Abandoned
Rural Cemetery #2	?

near Coffee Pot Springs   ?
Spring Valley Cemetery   1891

Gunnison County

Cemetery	1st Burial
Chance Cemetery	1874
Crested Butte Cemetery	1879
Doyville Cemetery	1880
Irwin Cemetery	?
AKA Ruby Camp Cemetery	1885
Marble Cemetery	1906
Nurse-Brownlee Cemetery	1886
Ohio City Cemetery	1903
Palisade Cemetery	1882
Parlin Cemetery	1901
Pitkin Cemetery	1880
Powderhorn Cemetery	1881
Sapinero Old Cemetery	1889 – At bottom of Blue Mesa Res.
Somerset Cemetery	1905
Tomichi Cemetery	1883
Vulcan Cemetery	1890
White Pine Cemetery[87]	?

Hinsdale Co

Cemetery	1st Burial
Capitol City Cemetery	1878

Huerfano County

Cemetery	1st Burial
Badito Cemetery	?
Baxter Cemetery	?
Bustos Cemetery	?
Butte Cemetery	?
Chama Cemetery	?
Chavez Cemetery	?
Cisneros Cemetery	?
Cuchara Cemetery	?
Evergreen Cemetery	?
Farisita Cemetery	?
La Veta Catholic Cemetery	?
La Veta Cemeteries #2,3,4,5	?
La Veta Spanish Cemetery	?

Laguna Cemetery	?
Mesa Creek Cemetery	?
Oak Creek Cemetery	?
Red Wing Cemetery	?
Speed Cemetery	
AKA Old Huerfano Cemetery	?
Tombstone Hill Cemetery	?
Turner Mine Cemetery	?
Vigil Cemetery	?

Jefferson County

Cemetery	1st Burial
Conifer Cemetery	1889
Creswell Cemetery	1888
Evergreen Cemetery	1871
Foxton Cemetery	1879
Morrison Cemetery	1875
Mount Vernon Canyon Cemetery	1860
Pine Grove Cemetery	?
Pleasant Park Cemetery	1875

Lake County

Cemetery	1st Burial
Everett Cemetery	?
Malta Cemetery	1861
Remine Cemetery	?
St. Joseph's Cemetery	1888
Twin Lakes Cemetery #1	1881
Twin Lakes Cemetery #2	1915

La Plata County

Cemetery	1st Burial
Allison-Tiffany Cemetery	?
Bayfield Cemetery	1885
Cedar Grove Cemetery	?
Elco Cemetery	?
Florida Cemetery	?
AKA Hood Cemetery	?
Gold King Cemetery	?
Hay Gulch Cemetery	?
Hermosa Cemetery	?

Hesperus Cemetery	?
Kline Cemetery	?
La Boca Cemetery	?
Parrot Cemetery	1876
Shreck Cemetery	?
Thompson Park Cemetery	1896

Mesa County

Cemetery	1st Burial
Cedar Crest Cemetery	1885
Clover Cemetery	1892
Crown Point Cemetery	1888
DeBeque Cemetery	1890
Eagalite Cemetery	1886
Elmwood Cemetery	1891
Gateway Cemetery	1900
Hope Cemetery	1883 – Abandoned
Molina Cemetery	1894
Palisade Cemetery	1900
Pentecostal Cemetery	?
Sacred Heart/Calvary Cemetery	1887
Whitewater Cemetery	1880

Mineral County

Cemetery	1st Burial
Bachelor Cemetery	?
McCoy Cemetery	?
Montoya Cemetery	?

Montezuma County

Cemetery	1st Burial
Arriola Cemetery	1900
Cedar Grove Cemetery	?
Cortez Cemetery	1890
Dobbins Cemetery	?
Mesa Verde National Park	? – Over 450 burials through out the park
Yellow Jacket Cemetery	?
Grange Hall Cemetery	?
Hefferman Cemetery	?
McPhee Cemetery	?
Mitchell Cemetery	?
Morez Cemetery	?

Shiloh Cemetery ?
Towac Cemetery ?
Ute Mountain Tribal Cemetery ?

Montrose County

Cemetery	1st Burial
Button Cemetery	1902
Cedar Creek Cemetery	1886
Cimmarron Cemetery	1880
Nucla Cemetery	1905
Oak Grove Cemetery	1887
Olathe Cemetery	?
Paradox Cemetery	1901
Pea Green Cemetery	1887
Pinon Cemetery	1898

Ouray County

Cemetery	1st Burial
Camp Bird Cemetery	?
Dallas Old Cemetery	1880
Dallas Park Cemetery	1883
Grandview Cemetery	1876
Ironton Cemetery	1897
Portland Cemetery	1875
Red Mountain Cemetery	1888
Sneffles Cemetery	1870

Park County

Cemetery	1st Burial
Bailey Cemetery	1871 – Abandoned – Residential area built over.
Old Como Cemetery	1868
Dudley Cemetery	1875
Falls Hills Cemetery	?
Hall Valley Cemetery	1873
Hanging Tree Cemetery	?
Horn Cemetery	1887
Horseshoe Cemetery AKA East Leadville Cemetery	1879
Lake George Cemetery	1872
Montgomery Cemetery	1859
Weston Cemetery	1879

Pitkin County

Cemetery	1st Burial
Ashcroft Cemetery	1879 – Abandoned
Collins Cemetery	1879
Red Stone Cemetery	1901
Thomasville Cemetery	1890 – Abandoned
Tourtelotte Cemetery	1880 – Abandoned[88]
Wheatley Cemetery	1888

Rio Grande County County

Cemetery	1st Burial
Agua Ramon Cemetery	1917
Bowen Cemetery	1888
Del Norte No. 1 Cemetery	1883
Del Norte Old Cemetery	1874
Freeman Cemetery	?
Graveyard Hill	?
Homelake Cemetery	1898
Monte Vista Cemetery	1898
Monte Vista Spanish Cemetery	?
Rock Creek Cemetery	1874
Sevenmile Cemetery	1889

Saguache County

Cemetery	1st Burial
Alder Old Cemetery	1870
Bidell Cemetery	?
Bonanza Cemetery	1881
Camaro Cemetery	?
Campo Santo Cemetery	?
Chicago Cemetery	1860
Exchequer Cemetery	1880
Hillside Cemetery	1860
Iris Cemetery	?
Mirage Cemetery	?
Mirage Spanish Cemetery	?
North Park Cemetery	?
Rito Alto Cemetery	1888
Sargents Cemetery	?
Sedgwick Cemetery	1881
Teton Cemetery	1890
Tracy Canyon Cemetery	?
Villa Grove Cemetery	1870

San Juan County

Cemetery	1st Burial
Chattanooga Cemetery	1881 – Abandoned
Howardsville Cemetery	1891 – Abandoned

San Miguel County

Cemetery	1st Burial
Ames Cemetery	1880 – Abandoned
Norwood Cemetery	1893
Placerville Cemetery	1899
Poverty Flat Cemetery	?
San Miguel City Cemetery	1877 – Abandoned[89]
Westcott Cemetery	1897 – Abandoned
Wilson Mesa Cemetery	1897

Summit County

Cemetery	1st Burial
Argentine Cemetery	1884
Chihuahua Cemetery	1879
Frisco Cemetery	1882
Grandview Cemetery	1900
Kansas Colony Cemetery	?
Kokomo Cemetery	1878 – Abandoned
Lincoln Cemetery	1860 – Abandoned
Montezuma Cemetery	1881
Parkville Cemetery	1859
Robinson Cemetery	1880
Swan City Cemetery	1883

Teller County

Cemetery	1st Burial
Beaver Creek Cemetery	1892
Divide Cemetery	1891
Florissant Cemetery	1877
Fourmile Cemetery	1875
G.A.R. Cemetery	1892
Gillett Cemetery	1894
Indian Burial Ground	?
Midland Cemetery	1892
Pioneer Cemetery	1891
Spring Creek Cemetery	1893
Sunnyside Cemetery	1892
Woodland Park Cemetery	1891

— — —

Sources

Aspen Historical Society
Chaffee County Museum
Colorado Historical Society
Creede Historical Society
Creede Museum
Cripple Creek Museum
Denver Public Library Western History
Fisher, Cara–Canon City Public Library
Fremont County Historical Society
Gunnison County Cemetery Records
Gunnison Pioneer Museum
La Plata County Historical Society
Lake City Historical Society
Lake City Museum
Lake County Courthouse
Miller's Funeral Home – Gunnison
Pitkin County Library
Saguache Museum
San Juan County Museum – Silverton
Smith, Duane A. – History Professor, Fort Lewis College
Summit County Historical Society
Swan, Stephanie–Basalt Town Hall
Winkler, Jean–Basalt Regional Library

Newspapers

Alamosa Independent
Aspen Daily Times
Aspen Times
Buena Vista Democrat
Buena Vista Herald
Canon City Daily Record
Canon City Times
Chaffee County Republican
Colorado City Iris
Colorado Republican
Colorado Springs Gazette
Creede Candle
Creede Chronicle
Denver Republican

Denver Tribune
Durango Daily Herald
Durango News
Durango Weekly Democrat
Fairplay Flume
Ignacio Chieftain
La Plata Miner
Leadville Herald
Leadville Daily Herald
Leadville Herald Democrat
Park County Republican
Pagosa Springs News
Pagosa Springs Sun
Rocky Mountain News
Rocky Mountain Sun
Salida Daily Mail
Salida Daily News
San Juan Herald
Silverton Democrat
Silverton Weekly Miner
Silverton Standard
Summit County Journal
The Aspen Times
The Denver Times

Interviews

Fiorini, Duane – Family Craft Memorials, Durango
Hall, Cecil – Saguache
Johnson, Edward – Creede
McDaniel, Robert – Director, Animas Museum, Durango
Phillips, Tim – Sexton, Crystal Valley Cemetery, Manitou Springs
Shaputis, June – Chaffee County
Swanson, Erik – Cripple Creek, Alma, Fairplay

— — —

Chapter Six Notes

[1] Old Colorado City is now considered a part of West Side Colorado Springs, and is not to be confused with Colorado City.

[2] See Palmer, William J. Evergreen Cemetery, Colorado Springs.

[3] See Meeker Massacre, Chapter 3.

[4] See Crown Hill Cemetery, Chapter 2.

[5] Cemetery historian, June Shaputis has headed a community project to place markers at the children's graves.

[6] There is one grave on the grounds of the Colorado State Reformatory. George W. Conway, an inmate, was shot in an attempt to escape during a riot in 1895.

[7] Grace Episcopal Church records list DOD as 1923.

[8] Wyoming Census of 1880.

[9] Records reveal she used the names Condrell, Wiable, Milsom and Hewitt.

[10] The equipment for this organization was donated H.A.W. Tabor, and is on display at the Buena Vista Heritage Museum.

[11] Tax records reveal her name as Elizabeth Marshall, later changed to Elizabeth Enderlin.

[12] See Centerville.

[13] Now a legal holiday, known as "Memorial Day."

[14] Courtesy, Lake County Library.

[15] See Cody, William Frederick.

[16] Newspaper accounts give DOB as 1842.

[17] This cemetery is not organized by block and plot.

[18] Cemetery records do not list block and plot.

[19] Date reported in the Aspen Daily Times. Cemetery records list DOD as 1887.

[20] The Davis grave is located near the Confederate Veteran Section. It is the original location.

[21] The death penalty has since been reinstated in Colorado. Gary Davies was executed in 1997.

[22] Mary Humphreys is buried in this section. A black woman, she owned a bordello on West Front Street. Mary died in 1949. There is no marker.

[23] Her marker incorrectly gives the spelling as Evens.

[24] One of the original brass checks is in the possession of June Shaputis, Chaffee County historian.

[25] Records at Salida differ, giving date of birth as 1841, 1843, and 1844.

[26] Cy Warman died in Chicago, in 1919.

[27] Salida Mail article 1977, and records of June Shaputis.

[28] See Alfred Packer in Chapter 3.

[29] Now a part of the impressive Gunnison Museum.

[30] Mary Parent is buried in the Tin Cup Cemetery.

[31] See Clark, Jim and Horn, Thomas.

[32] See Packer, Alfred.

[33] The Ute Museum, located on the property, gives great insight to the Ute Indians and the life of Chipeta.

[34] See Meeker Massacre.

[35] The remains of Ouray are buried at the Ouray Memorial Cemetery in Ignacio.

[36] "Cap" Smith, a Civil War Veteran, built a cabin of masonry walls in Escalante Canyon, where he is buried.

[37] See Autobees, Charles Chapter 4.

[38] The fort was later moved and renamed Fort Garland.

[39] Billy Adams divorced his first wife, a granddaughter of Colonel Chivington.

[40] The monument mistakenly lists the middle initial of Albert as "C."

[41] See Pagosa Springs Pioneer Cemetery.

[42] Several sources of information, including a 1996 updated cemetery inventory may be seen at the Animas Museum in Durango and the Durango Library.

[43] A few burials did occur intermittently up to the 1960s. Ironically, the last in 1960 was Rev. William Folsom, son of William Folsom.

[44] Hood Mortuary records the burial at the Animas Cemetery and gives a date of birth of 2/29/1857. There was no February 29 in 1857. There is a tombstone at Greenmount Cemetery, Durango, listing William J. Thompson and his wife, Sarah. See the Greenmount Cemetery listings.

[45] According to historian Duane Smith, the body of George Woods was removed from the state.

[46] Sarah Decker Chapter of the D.A.R. papers of Victoria Day, including recounts of son George Vest Day.

[47] David Day is buried Denver's Fairmount Cemetery.

[48] Several years later, the Anderson plot was discovered. The gray marble pillar bears the names of Susan's brother, grandfather, and other family members.

[49] Barbee's daughter is the author of Cripple Creek Days and Return to Cripple Creek.

[50] Daniel is not to be confused with Matthew McLaughlin, who ran a stage operation from Fairplay.

[51] See Ghost Notes.

[52] See Dyer, John L.

[53] Historians have listed Porter's first name as Sam. Newspaper accounts list him as William J.

[54] The original wooden marker was stolen some time ago. The white granite stone was placed in the fall of 1994.

[55] Two of the Clark sons, Herman D. and Frank E. are also buried in the family plot.

[56] O'Hagen may be buried in Salida.

[57] Source–A History of Chaffee County, Shaputis.

[58] John Weston died in Denver.

[59] See Parent, Alex.

[60] Chaffee County Burials, June Shaputis.

[61] Harrington's wife Helen, later married F.A. Land.

[62] Records of Steel's burial reveal he may have been buried in Salida. Due to the condition of his remains, this is unlikely.

[63] Area historian, Cecil Hall was instrumental in the project.

[64] Fort Lyon is named in the general's honor.

[65] The American Legion ordered a gravestone for the major placed in 1996.

[66] The marker incorrectly gives date of birth as 1828.

[67] His cottage on North Ridge Street stands as a museum.

[68] See Fairplay.

[69] Tom Jenkins of Littleton has since located descendants of Francis and Mary Noel in California.

[70] Hinsdale County Historical Society.

71 Some of the gifts given by Carson are at the Lake City Museum, in possession of the Hinsdale Historical Society.

72 Kennedy left his 3rd wife, Laura Biggs, a widow.

73 See Packer, Alfred Chapter 2.

74 Because cemetery records do not list burials by block and plot, there is no distinction as to who is buried where. Therefore I have treated both sites as one.

75 A large stone in the center of downtown Creede marks the site of Ford's saloon.

76 Ford's killer is sometimes referred to as Ed O'Kelly.

77 See Off The Beaten Path, Highway 160 West.

78 While obituary notices differ, listing date of birth as 1868 and 1870, Hillside cemetery records list the burial date as 1875.

79 Sinclair formed his band in Silverton in the 1880s. They performed at events such as Colorado Governor Routt's inauguration, the Cattlemen's Association at Kansas City, and in Washington D.C. for the inauguration of President Harrison.

80 Little Maud is buried in the Hillside Cemetery. There is no marker.

81 The Silverton Weekly Miner, July 9, 1897. Records do not reveal her given name.

82 There are no cemetery records. The town's museum has received a grant for cemetery research, yet not in progress at this writing.

83 Butch Cassidy, My Brother, Betensen, Lula Parker.

84 There are many misspelled words on the bronze plaques, including Buckskin "Charley."

85 Originally known as the Ute Cemetery, or the Ignacio Ute Cemetery, the sign reads: "The Ouray Memorial Cemetery."

86 See Montrose and Chipeta.

87 This is not the same Stephen Decatur of journalistic fame, who spoke the famous words "My county right or wrong."

88 Now under the Tourtelotte Ski Run at Aspen.

89 Remains removed to the Lone Tree Cemetery at Telluride.

Unusual, Clever
and Humorous Epitaphs

Many a tombstone inscription is a grave error.
-Laurence Peter

Despite this cynic tone, epitaphs and inscriptions are a fine source of fun and information. In the eighteenth and nineteenth centuries there were informal libraries of verse and short statements available in clergy archives, in catalogs from monument makers, and in funeral parlors. The most common source of inscriptions was the Bible, where relevant verses could be taken with relation to the feelings of the dearly departed.

The selection of an epitaph gives the survivors an opportunity to express their emotions, display their faith, and publicly declare a special and permanent relationship with the deceased.

Formal relationships produced dutiful sentiments, while love relationships often poured out passionate compositions. The death of a child produced painful and sad prose. The passing of an older relative who had lived a long, good life, generated philosophical reflection.

Within these generalizations, lie the unusual and exceptional epitaph. Many can be found in the cemeteries of Colorado. The following is only a sampling:

Musician on Tour
Epitaph of Jimmy Lamb
Sunnyside Cemetery, Creede

———

Peace be to his dust
Tombstone of G.H. Stunce
Cedar Hill Cemetery, Ouray

———

*My good people, as you pass
by,
As you are now, so once was
I.
As I am now, you soon must
be,*

John Houser photo
Tombstone of Pearl Stubbings in the Littleton Cemetery.

Prepare yourselves to follow
me.

This epitaph, found on a lonely tombstone, is in Crested Butte. Irwin Cemetery, also known as Ruby Camp Cemetery, at the Summit of Kebler Pass.

Variations on the same theme can be found in other Colorado cemeteries, and across the nation, such as the following:

Remember friends as you pass by
As you are now so once was I
As I am now so you must be
Prepare for death and follow me
Epitaph in the Caribou Cemetery

— — —

In eastern Weld County, on a private ranch near Stoneham, is a lone grave with the inscription:

Here lies the man who forgot to close the gate.

— — —

Here lies a man named Zeke.
Second fasted draw in Cripple Creek.
Tombstone in Victor

— — —

He was young
He was fair
But the Injuns
Raised his hair

— — —

An engraved advertisement on the granite tombstone of seven-year-old Elizabeth Jane Himan reads:

courtesy G.P. Higman sculptor
Franktown Cemetery

— — —

I Am Ready
Epitaph of Elizabeth Downer
Rosita Cemetery
— — —
The End of the Trail
J.L. Sanderson Monument, Columbia Cemetery, Boulder
Sanderson was a stagecoach driver.
— — —
He called
Bill Smith
A Liar
Mount Pisgah Cemetery, Cripple Creek
— — —
Step softly, a dream lies here.
Lester Owens Epitaph, Breckenridge Cemetery
— — —
Walter Xerxes Yansai Zabriskie (1879 -1945)
His Pagosa Springs Tombstone initials read:
W.X.Y.Z.
— — —
Here lie the remains of D.C. Oakes,
Who was the starter of this damned hoax.

The story of D. C. Oakes' published guide book, leading to a great gold rush in Colorado, is known throughout Colorado history primarily as a hoax. Hundreds of discouraged gold seekers, returning to the East, buried Mr. Oaks in effigy. A small mound of dirt marked with buffalo bones and the epitaph inscribed with charcoal and axle grease, was seen by thousands of travelers, including D.C. Oakes himself![1]

[1] See Oakes, D.C. Chapter 1.

Epilogue

What man proposes, God disposes.

Cemeteries remain the last untapped institution of culture and history. Increased interest in ancestry as well as historic preservation has brought the historical source of the cemetery to the forefront. Additionally, cemeteries are a reflection of life.

It is with that idea that this book was written. By walking through the rows of tombstones, reading the inscriptions, the history of Colorado comes alive. Our cemeteries should be honored for the history, as well as respected for those who lie there.

While every attempt has been made to secure historic facts on our pioneer cemeteries, and those buried within, it was not always possible. In some cases, recorded history simply did not exist. Therefore the appendix of historic cemeteries was created.

The earliest "garden" cemeteries were visited and enjoyed for perhaps one or two generations before Coloradans decided that constant contact with death did not suit their adamant optimistic nature. The cemetery was a place for family gatherings, picnics were held and children played. This practice ceased with the urgency and complexity of settling a new frontier. The westward movement made looking back an impractical thought. Most twentieth-century Coloradans do not consider the cemetery a part of their daily lives. The invention of "memorial parks," with manicured lawns and flat "tablet" markers, for lawn mowing ease, are a part of the modern conveniences.

But there is evidence of a renewed interest in historical and artistic burial grounds, and that interest may eventually help to save the "modern" cemetery from the same mentality that gave us postwar urban renewal.

Let us remember and protect the memory of our Colorado Pioneers by preserving and restoring their final resting place. Let this be our contribution to the founders of this great state.

God grant the century we face
Compare in honor to the last,
May generations yet to be
Revere the builders of the past.

O, grant their legacy of faith
Be ours in meeting future years;
Give us their vision bright and clean
The strong, the gallant pioneers.
Elin Fredstrom

– – –

A Cemetery is a place of Rest, a place of Peace, and
a place of Beauty.

Walk through the lanes, enjoy the peace and quiet,
and the natural gracefulness.

Leave the cemetery untouched, taking only memo-
ries and photographs.

Linda R. Wommack

Bibliography

Bates, Margaret – *A Quick History of Lake City*

Beshoar, Michael, M.D. – *All About Trinidad*

Betz, Ava – *A Prowers County History*

Black, Robert C. – *Island In The Rockies*

Cairns, Mary Lyon – *Grand Lake: The Pioneers*

Cheyenne County – *Cemetery Records and Tombstones*

Daniels and McConnel, *The Springs of Manitou*

Dyer, Mary – *Echos of Como*

East Morgan County Historical Society – *Morgan County History*

Eberhart, Perry – *Guide to Ghost Towns and Mining Camps*

Feitz, Leland – *Quick History of Creede*

Feitz, Leland – *Soapy Smith's Creede*

Florin, Lambert – *Tales the Western Tombstones Tell*

Fiester, Mark – *Blasted, Beloved Breckenridge*

Fort Morgan Heritage Foundation – *One Hundred And Eleven Trees*

Fort Sedgwick County Historical Society – *History of Sedgwick County, Colorado*

Hall, Frank – *History Of The State Of Colorado* Volumes 1 through 4

Harrison, Louise C. – *Empire and The Berthoud Pass*

Hawthorne, Roger – *Lest They Be Forgotten*

Hopkins, Walter S. & Millikin, Virginia Greene – *The Bible and the Gold Rush*

Howe, Hazel M. – *The Story of Silver Plume*

Humbeutel, Lacy – *Nuggets From Chalk Creek*

Idaho Springs Historical Society – *History of Clear Creek County*

Lamm, Richard and Smith, Duane – *Pioneers and Politicians*

Lecompte, Janet – *Pueblo Hardscrabble Greenhorn*

McQuery, Lela O. – *Colorado Cemetery Inscriptions*

Marr, Josephine L. – *Douglas County History*

Mumie, Nolan – *Auntie Stone's Cabin*

Noel, Thomas – *Colorado Catholicism*

O.L. Baskin & Company – *History of the Arkansas Valley*

O.L. Baskin & Company – *History of the Clear Creek and Boulder Valleys*

Pauly, Nell – *Ghosts of The Shootin'*

Perry, Eleanor – *I Remember Tin Cup*

Petten, Silvia – *Boulder, Evolution of a City*

Phillips County – *History of Phillips County* Volumes I & II

Rockwell, Wilson – *Memoirs Of A Lawman*

Sarah Platt Decker Chapter, DAR – *Pioneers of the San Juan Country*

Schader, Conrad F. – *Colorado's Alluring Tin Cup*
Saint Vrain Valley Historical Society – *They Came To Stay*
Shaputis, June – *Chaffee County Burials* 1987
Shikes, Robert H. M.D. – *Rocky Mountain Medicine*
Smiley, Jerome – *History of Denver*
Smith, Duane A. – *Durango Diary*
Smith, Duane A. – *Rocky Mountain Boom Town: A History of Durango*
Simmons, Virginia McConnell – *Bayou Salado*
Vandenbusche, Duane – *The Gunnison Country*
Watrous, Ansel – *History of Larimer County*
Wells, Dale – *The Logan County Ledger*
Wolfe, Muriel – *Stampede to Timberline*
Wolfe, Muriel – *Timberline Tailings*

Index

The Author

Linda Wommack

Linda Wommack is a Colorado native who has enjoyed Colorado history since childhood. She is a distant relative of Bob Womack, the man who discovered gold at Cripple Creek.

Linda has published several books dealing with the history of the state, including *Colorado Gambling: A History of the Early Days*, *Cripple Creek Tailings* and *Colorado History for Kids*. The latter book was recommended by the National Teachers Association, two years in a row, as the history book of choice for the state of Colorado.

Linda's articles have appeared in *The Casino Player*, *The Tombstone Epitaph*, *The American Epitaph*, *True West Magazine*, *The Gold Prospector*, *The Colorado Gambler* and *Solitude in Stone*. She also has written a monthly history column for *The Rocky Mountain News*.

Linda is a member of the National Mining Association, Colorado Historical Society, National Historic Preservation Committee, Colorado Independent Publishers Association, Western Writers of America, Colorado Cemetery Association, National Association for Cemetery Preservation and the Colorado Genealogical Society.

The Colorado Collection
From CAXTON PRESS

Pioneers of the Colorado Parks
by Richard Barth
ISBN 0-87004-381-1 paper 276 pages $17.95

Colorado Ghost Towns Past and Present
by Robert L. Brown
ISBN 0-87004-218-1 paper 322 pages $14.95

Central City and Gilpin County: Then and Now
by Robert L. Brown
ISBN 0-87004-363-3 paper 200 pages $8.95

Jeep Trails to Colorado Ghost Towns
by Robert L. Brown
ISBN 0-87004-021-9 paper 245 pages $10.95

Colorado on Foot
by Robert L. Brown
ISBN 0-87004-336-6 paper 309 pages $10.95

Ghost Towns of the Colorado Rockies
by Robert L. Brown
ISBN 0-87004-342-0 paper 320 pages $14.95

Uphill Both Ways: Hiking Colorado's High Country
by Robert L. Brown
ISBN 0-87004-249-1 paper 232 pages $7.95

Telluride: From Pick to Powder
by Richard L. and Suzanne Fetter
ISBN 0-87004-265-3 paper 196 pages $9.95

For a free catalog of Caxton books write to:

CAXTON PRESS
312 Main Street
Caldwell, ID 83605-3299

or

Visit our Internet Website:

www.caxtonprinters.com

Caxton Press is a division of The CAXTON PRINTERS, Ltd.

WC